Child Development and Social Policy

Theory and Applications

McGraw-Hill Series in Developmental Psychology

Consulting Editor: Ross A. Thompson

1) Carole Beal: *Boys and Girls: The Development of Gender Roles*
2) Fredda Blanchard-Fields and Thomas Hess: *Perspectives on Cognitive Change in Adulthood and Aging*
3) Sandra L. Calvert: *Children's Journeys Through the Information Age*
4) Virginia Colin: *Human Attachment*
5) Celia Fisher and Richard Lerner: *Applied Developmental Psychology*
6) Matthew Merrens and Gary Brannigan: *The Developmental Psychologists: Research Adventures Across the Life Span*
7) Rolf E. Muuss: *Theories of Adolescence, 6/e.*

Child Development and Social Policy

Theory and Applications

Edward F. Zigler
Yale University

Nancy W. Hall
Yale University

Boston   Burr Ridge, IL   Dubuque, IA   Madison, WI   New York   San Francisco
St Louis   Bangkok   Bogotá   Caracas   Lisbon   London   Madrid   Mexico City
Milan   New Delhi   Seoul   Singapore   Sydney   Taipei   Toronto

McGraw-Hill Higher Education

A Division of The **McGraw-Hill** *Companies*

CHILD DEVELOPMENT AND SOCIAL POLICY: THEORY AND APPLICATIONS

This book is printed on acid-free paper.

1 2 3 4 5 6 7 8 9 0 DOC/DOC 0 9 8 7 6 5 4 3 2 1 0

ISBN 0–07–072724–4

Editorial director: *Jane E. Vaicunas*
Executive editor: *Mickey Cox*
Editorial coordinator: *Sarah C. Thomas*
Senior marketing manager: *James Rozsa*
Senior project manager: *Jayne Klein*
Production supervisor: *Sandy Ludovissy*
Coordinator of freelance design: *Rick Noel*
Compositor: *Carlisle Communications, Ltd.*
Typeface: *10/12 Palatino*
Printer: *R. R. Donnelley & Sons Company/Crawfordsville, IN*

Cover designer: *Sean M. Sullivan*
Photo: © *CORBIS IMAGES/Hulton-Deutsch Collection-Children Holding Hands*

Library of Congress Cataloging-in-Publication Data

Zigler, Edward, 1930–
    Child development and social policy : theory and applications / Edward F. Zigler, Nancy W. Hall.—1st ed.
      p.   cm.
    Includes bibliographical references and index.
    ISBN 0–07–072724–4
    1. Children—Government policy—United States.   2. Child development.   3. United States—Social policy—1993—   I. Hall, Nancy Wilson.   II. Title.
HQ792.U5Z54   2000
305.23'0973—DC21   99–15843
                                                                 CIP

www.mhhe.com

About the Authors

EDWARD ZIGLER is Sterling Professor of Psychology, head of the psychology section of the Child Study Center, and Director of the Bush Center in Child Development and Social Policy at Yale University. He is the founder of the School of the 21st Century, which has been adopted by more than 600 schools nationwide, and cofounder of the COZI model, which is a combination of Dr. James P. Comer's School Development Program and Zigler's 21st Century Schools. Zigler regularly testifies as an expert witness before congressional committees and has served as a consultant to a number of cabinet-rank officers. He was one of the planners of Project Head Start and Project Follow Through. President Carter later named him chair of the 15th anniversary of the project. Zigler was the first director of the U.S. Office of Child Development (now the Administration on Children, Youth, and Families) and Chief of the U.S. Children's Bureau. Recently he was a member of the Advisory Committee on Head Start Quality and Expansion of the planning committee for the Early Head Start program for families and children ages 0 to 3.

NANCY W. HALL is a consultant to the Yale University Bush Center in Child Development and Social Policy in New Haven, Connecticut, and a contributing editor at *Parents* magazine. A graduate fellow of the National Center for Clinical Infant Programs (now Zero to Three), her research focuses broadly on the social development of infants and young children and more specifically on parent support, early intervention, and such policy issues as child care, early childhood education, drug abuse, and work/life issues.

This Book is Dedicated to Two Outstanding Individuals of Differing Political Parties, Senator Edward Kennedy and Eliot Richardson, in Recognition of Their Lifelong Work in Behalf of All of America's Children.

Brief Contents

Contents

Foreword

Children are sometimes called the "silent citizens" of society. They cannot vote or exercise political influence, advocate effectively on their own behalf, or create compelling public demonstrations of their needs. Yet hardly a week goes by without our attention being drawn to some issue of child development and social policy. A report is released by a government agency with new statistics concerning child poverty. A political candidate criticizes the crisis in the schools and promises reform. A young child is discovered badly beaten by parents who had previously been reported for suspected abuse. The White House convenes a conference on early brain development and early education. The current rate of infant mortality in the United States is compared with rates in other industrialized nations. A national columnist criticizes the quality of day care, and urges mothers to stay home with their young children. Continued funding for Head Start is again debated by Congress. Parents ponder whether the new Roth IRA offers a good way to save for a college education for their offspring. And so on.

Our appreciation of the importance of social policy for children reflects a new understanding of children and their development. In traditional times, offspring were regarded as parental property and had little place in an adult world until they were grown. In the contemporary world, by contrast, children are more often viewed as a community asset and a collective responsibility: "It takes a village to raise a child." In traditional times, the child's world rarely extended beyond the family and immediate neighborhood. In the contemporary world, by contrast, we recognize how broader forces in the economy, public health, government, and education shape children's lives within and outside of the family. In traditional times, moral value and worth were not inherent in human life, but were progressive achievements of growing maturity. In the contemporary world, by contrast, the recognition that even the youngest child has fundamental human rights motivates concerted efforts to protect and defend their interests. These basic rights have most recently been articulated in the United Nations Convention on the Rights of the Child, which has been signed by the large majority of member states (except the United States). In traditional times, policies meant to assist children usually resulted from outrage at the harms and deprivation that children were discovered to suffer. While this remains so in the contemporary world, social policies for children are also motivated by the desire to strengthen and optimize the inborn potential that exists in every newborn infant.

Our contemporary understanding of children and their development compels, therefore, attention to public policy. As child development is shaped by a complex social ecology, policies for children guide the conditions in which children grow.

In *Child Development and Social Policy: Theory and Applications,* Edward Zigler and Nancy Hall advance this view in a remarkable text that acquaints readers with the needs of children, the efforts of advocates, the relevance of research, and the policy-making process. Both authors have a long history of commitment to children and to public policy. Professor Zigler was the first director of the Office of Child Development, which was created in the early 1970s to coordinate child and family policy initiatives for the federal government. Throughout a long and distinguished career, he has contributed to a better understanding of the needs of children and families, and has advanced proposals concerning child care, parental leave, Head Start, early intervention, family support, and many other issues to better address those needs. He has also contributed to raising the awareness of developmental scientists concerning the importance of policy-relevant research, founding the Bush Center in Child Development and Social Policy at Yale University, where Nancy Hall also works. Together, these authors offer a thoughtful, insightful, and current look at the policy landscape that affects the lives of children and their families, and the new directions in which policy reform for the future should proceed.

The range of topics discussed in this book provides a bracing realization of how profoundly children of all ages are affected by public policy. From the moment of conception, public health programs, medical insurance policies, and medicaid coverage influence the quality of prenatal care that mothers receive, and postnatal care that children are provided, especially if they are from disadvantaged backgrounds. A child's early experience is significantly shaped by the care received at home (influenced by parental leave and other "family friendly" policies) and outside the home, where the quality, cost, and regulation of child care are influential. If the family is shattered by divorce, domestic violence, or child maltreatment, public policies concerning child support and child custody, family preservation, and foster care will shape the future of family life. When children enter public education, policies concerning educational goals and their attainment provide the framework for everyday learning in the classroom. If the child has special needs associated with a disability, is a member of an ethnically underrepresented group, or comes from a socioeconomically disadvantaged background, special programs designed to provide assistance offer opportunities for affirmation and support that might otherwise be lacking. In profiling these and many other areas of child and family policy, Zigler and Hall remind us of how interconnected are the development of children and the social policies meant to help them.

Child Development and Social Policy: Theory and Applications also informs about the policy-making process. Throughout these chapters, the reader observes how programs for children and families are shaped by the discoveries of developmental scientists, the concerted efforts of advocacy groups, the give-and-take of politics, the opportunities presented by moments of public attention and concern, the capabilities (and limitations) of government agencies, and the evolving values and priorities of our culture. At times, a comparison of family policies in the United States with those of other countries provides a jarring realization of how the unquestioned assumptions guiding our view of the relationship among children, families, and government are unshared by those living in other cultures. Quite often, the problems facing children and their families seem daunting and intractable, unchanging even in the face of concerted government activity, and inspiring hopelessness and even cynicism about the possibility for real advance. But Zigler and Hall guard against despair with their reminders of the good ideas that arise from developmental research, the advances in children's well-being that have occurred historically, and the enduring goodwill toward our youngest citizens that is part of our society.

This volume is part of the *McGraw-Hill Series in Developmental Psychology*. This series has been designed to enrich and expand our common knowledge of human development by providing a forum for theorists, researchers, and practitioners to present their insights to a broad audience. As a rapidly expanding scientific field, developmental psychology has important applications to parents, educators, students, clinicians, policy makers, and others who are concerned with promoting human welfare throughout the life course. Although the fruits of scholarly research into human development can be found on the pages of research journals, and students can become acquainted with this exciting field in introductory textbooks, this series of specialized, topical books is intended to provide insightful, indepth examinations of selected issues in the field from which undergraduates, graduate students, and academic colleagues can each benefit. As forums for highlighting important new ideas, research insights, theoretical syntheses, and applications of knowledge to practical problems, I hope that these volumes will find many uses: as one of several specialized texts for advanced coursework, as tutorials for scholars interested in learning about current knowledge on a topic of interest, and as sourcebooks for practitioners who wish to traverse the gap between knowledge and application. The authors who contribute to this series are committed to providing a state-of-the-art, accurate, and readable interpretation of current knowledge that will be interesting and accessible to a broad audience with many different goals and interests. I hope, too, that these volumes will inspire the efforts to improve the lives of children, adolescents, and adults through research and practice that are much needed in our world.

As one who has taught undergraduate and graduate seminars in child and family policy, I have longed for a book like this one. As the complexion of public policy concerning children continues to evolve, perhaps we can hope that *Child Development and Social Policy: Theory and Applications* not only foreshadows but also is a catalyst for the growth of much-needed new initiatives to support children's development in the future.

Ross A. Thompson
Series Editor

Introduction: The Evolving Focus of Child Study

The chief importance of child study when it first arose as a budding discipline was that it was meant to teach us much about our adult selves to come. This "child is father to the man" approach inspired Charles Darwin to keep a detailed biography of his infant son. Less than half a century later, Sigmund Freud's studies of children promoted the idea that early childhood is a period during which the adult to come is formed in all his or her vicissitudes.

Today this approach is still valid. In recent decades it has been complemented by the empirically derived knowledge that the influences we bring to bear during childhood, particularly early childhood, have profound implications for the course of development and the ways in which we can enhance an individual's physical and mental health. Throughout this century, however, and particularly in the latter part of the century, we have as a culture placed a growing emphasis on childhood for childhood's sake. As the baby-boomers have matured and become parents and even grandparents, our focus on our children has intensified. No longer are children viewed—as they were to a great extent up through much of the nineteenth century—as miniature adults with few different needs of their own. Instead, especially within the past 30 years, and especially in the United States, we have developed a culture of childhood. Within the past 10 years, this phenomenon has grown even stronger: children and the events that shape their lives are increasingly a focus of media attention, of social concern, of political action. Whole industries have grown up around the needs, or perceived needs, of children: consumer products, educational services, child care, parent education, health care services and products are all targeted at making children's lives rich and fulfilling—not just for the benefit of improving their later lives, but also to make their everyday lives rich, safe, and happy.

At the same time, however, a sort of cultural disjunction has arisen. If we are committed to doing everything we can to improve the lives of children and families, to make them happy today, productive tomorrow, and healthy and safe throughout their lives, actions must be taken on their behalf that are beyond the purview of parents. Many of the systems affecting children today can only be manipulated, for better or worse, by taking social action on a larger scale. Certainly parents can play an important role here, but to achieve the goals we have implicitly set for our children, we must widen the arena and expand the number of players willing to act on their behalf.

Thus there arose, beginning formally in the 1960s (though its roots go further back) a movement combining the study of children, their growth, development, and needs, with efforts to conceive and implement social policies to keep the nation strong and healthy. That these two concerns should be rolled into one field of study and action might still seem peculiar to some, but to others this is a logical marriage of compassion and pragmatism. If we are going to mount programs for and spend money on children, and if these programs are to be the most efficacious and cost-effective, they should be based on what we actually know about children and how social concerns and events interact with the most fundamental phenomena of child development to affect their lives.

This brings us to a third wave of child study, the wave to which this book pertains. Not only are we concerned with how early events and conditions in a child's life affect that life as it is ongoing. Not only are we concerned with how these events and conditions affect the adult the child will become. We are also concerned with children as social capital—children whose lives and circumstances affect the strength of the nation as a whole. This volume, then, is dedicated to giving you, the reader, an introduction to the ways in which child development study and social policy issues intersect. In short, this book asks three questions:

- How does our knowledge base about how children grow and develop inform the policy process?
- What happens to children and families when this knowledge base is ignored or neglected during the development of social policy?
- What are the implications—both now and in the future—for our communities, cities, states, and the nation as a whole when we give short shrift to the needs of children and families?

We assume that you, the reader, have some basic knowledge of human development, that you have perhaps taken one or more courses on child development or general psychology courses in which early development was discussed. We would also urge you to supplement this basic understanding, as you read through this book, with a continuing awareness of the policy issues facing children and families. Supplementing your reading and class discussions with attention to local, state, and national news items about children's concerns will make the principles and conditions described in this book come alive, and provide you with current and relevant examples of the problems with which child and family policy scholars are concerned.

Throughout the writing of this book we have been reminded constantly of the Red Queen's line from Lewis Carroll's *Through the Looking Glass:* "It takes all the running I can do just to stay in one place!" Characterizing the legislative climate surrounding any one children's issue—never mind a dozen or more related issues—has been a difficult task. We have watched, along with the rest of the world, as the late 1990s brought debate, proposals, more debate, and controversy from every corner to bear on topics ranging from welfare to education to child care to health care to juvenile crime. Bills came and went, were acted on, were killed, were passed and vetoed, were passed and enacted into law, as we struggled with how best to record these fleeting changes and to define their implications for children and families in the United States.

From the beginning we determined that the best way to deal with this issue would be to rely on you, the reader, to be an active partner in this process. What we have tried to do is supply you with a stable framework in which to interpret the changing menu of concerns, the changing cast of characters, and the changing array of legislative proposals, advocates' contributions, media reactions, and the implications for children themselves, that will be current when you study child development and social policy.

Ironically, it is somewhat in our favor that so many of the issues covered herein are perennial. We can predict with some certainty that whether you are reading about child-care standards or immigration, immunization programs or subsidized housing, the same questions will frame the debate: Who should be responsible for implementing and funding the services in question? Who should receive them? How can the effects of these interventions be measured, and how can we use these outcomes to help us shape the next step in the evolution of these issues?

We have developed the themes within this volume along a model that reflects issues in child and family development that have been of public concern for decades, if not centuries. We feel certain that they will continue to be of concern. In each chapter we have tried to outline a problem, to describe—in a snapshot of current events that will more or less resemble the situation facing children as you face these issues—the status of children and their families vis-à-vis a given issue. We have gone on to describe the basic principles of child development, well established through empirical research, that pertain to this issue. Most of all, we have tried to sketch out the policy picture that derives from the intersection of these conditions and these principles. What will happen if policy solutions are implemented when a problem is identified? What will happen if they are not?

In the chapters to come, the major problems and issues facing children and their families in the United States today will be explored in depth. Each chapter will highlight the social policy issues of concern in each area and bring to bear on their analysis empirical data on child development and family functioning relevant to each topic. We have arranged these in what we believe is a logical order, but it helps to have a sense of the whole picture of child life in America in order to make sense of each individual concern. Herewith, we offer a very brief snapshot of the status of children in our country today, along with a set of principles that we believe will guide the interested student to find an answer to our most basic question: How should we apply what we know about children to what we should do for children?

ACKNOWLEDGMENTS

We are grateful to Marilyn Barry and Arlene Kindilien, whose considerable efforts and continual patience were essential to this effort. In addition, the expertise and contributions of Elizabeth Gilman, Sally Styfco, and Carmen Arroyo were invaluable. Carol Ripple's timely and indefatigable assistance with the production of figures and tables was a blessing. Marianne Gerschel of the Spunk Fund and Vivien Stewart of the Carnegie Corporation of New York supported us at critical stages of our writing—we thank you. Thanks also to the following reviewers of this text: Barney Rankhorn, *University of Texas, Tyler;* Joanne Faraver, *University of South California;* Carol Hodes, *Pennsylvania State University;* James Garbarino, *Cornell University;* and Dana Bukatko, *College of the Holy Cross.*

At McGraw-Hill, Sarah Thomas's keen eye, critical acumen, and considerable patience were helpful throughout the many phases of writing this book; Beth Kaufman and Jane Vaicunas were also instrumental in helping us through this process. We are particularly grateful for Ross Thompson's keen eye and support as he read several versions of the manuscript.

Finally, we want to thank Bernice Zigler, David Wilson, and Margaret Howell. Without your patience and support through long hours and late nights, this book would never have gotten off the ground.

Edward F. Zigler
Nancy W. Hall
New Haven, Connecticut
1999

CHAPTER 1

Issues in Child Development and Social Policy

THE STATE OF CHILDREN IN THE UNITED STATES

Much is made today of the changes in the culture of American children. Developmental psychologists generally agree that although the family has undergone radical changes during the past several decades, it remains the most important institution in influencing child growth and development. Many researchers emphasize, however, the need to acknowledge and study the multiple forms that families take. Only a small percentage of all families in the United States have the form of the traditional nuclear family, with the father as breadwinner, the mother as homemaker, and two or more children living at home.

Some of the forms that families now take are dual-earner families, single-parent families, children being raised by grandparents or other relatives, unrelated persons living together, and **"blended families"** created by the divorce and subsequent remarriage of one or both parents (Hamburg, 1992; Weissbourd, 1996). Tension exists between those who feel that good families can come in a variety of configurations. Other analysts decry the widespread acceptance of nontraditional families (Popenoe, 1996). Both sides, however, pay attention to evidence regarding the needs of children; although their social and political perspectives might diverge, their recommendations for actions that would enhance the lives of children in America often have much in common.

Perhaps, though, the fundamental nature of child and family life has not changed as much as we believe. Many authors challenge the idealized and sentimental notions of perfect, invariably functional families as being both of recent origin and politically driven (Coontz, 1993, 1997; Skolnick, 1991). Gillis (1996), for instance, notes:

> Looking back from the 1990s, and preoccupied with rising divorce and illegitimacy rates, we perceive the 1950s as a rock of stability. But that was a decade gripped by anxiety about family life, and especially about the threat posed by the new youth cultures. The 1950s version of the traditional family was an idealized image of the Depression family, which was imagined as holding on by holding tightly to one another. But those who lived through the 1920s and 1930s would not have recognized themselves in the myths that later generations made of them, for these were the same people who saw themselves to be in the midst of a sexual revolution. (p. 5)

Even the Victorians, Gillis notes, were consumed with anxiety over the rise of urbanization and the loss of community and a secure sense of family life.

Popenoe (1996) refers to the years between 1800 and 1950 as a golden age for child rearing, and sets those years in sharp contrast to the late twentieth century. Many other analysts, however, would probably disagree with such a statement. As unacceptably high as infant mortality rates are today, they are low compared with those of the early twentieth century, when, in some areas, close to half of all deaths were of children under 5 years of age. Child abuse was widespread, universal public education was not firmly established until early in this century, life-saving medications and procedures we take for granted today were still undreamed of, and most children had to labor in either factories or farms

(Hall, 1991). As students of child development and policy, we must guard carefully against romanticizing childhood's past.

The temper of our times—a changeable economy, tense political and social conditions, changes in family **demographics,** and taxpayer resistance to the growing costs of government programs—means that we must carefully examine the effects these issues have on our youngest citizens. The crises facing children and families in America are manifested in a number of disturbing national statistics. America, the richest and most technologically advanced country in the world, ranks first among nations in military technology, first in gross domestic product, and first in health technology. Why, then, do we rank eighteenth in infant mortality, and dead last in protecting our children against gun violence (Children's Defense Fund, 1998g)? Why do 45 percent of American children live in or near poverty (National Center for Children in Poverty, 1997)? Why are almost half a million U.S. children homeless (U.S. Conference of Mayors, 1994)? Why is the United States the only industrialized nation on earth that does not provide universal health care to children (Carnegie Corporation, 1994) and one of only three industrialized nations in the world without paid infant-care leave (Kamerman & Kahn, 1995)? At least 70 countries provide paid infant-care leave of at least 12 weeks; the United States is not one of them. Some members of Congress are in favor of paid leave—notably Congresswoman Lynn Woolsey, who is spearheading such an effort—but there was considerable resistance to even the unpaid leave that was signed into law. And do figures like these tell the whole story?

Statistics like these *have* led to the charge that America is not a child-oriented society. Children's problems have been identified at least since the nation's first White House Conference on Children, held in 1909 (Beck, 1973; Zigler & Finn, 1981). At that conference Jane Addams, among others, asked why more was not being done on behalf of children. The same question has surfaced at the beginning of each decade ever since (even though the White House Children's Conferences themselves were discontinued in 1980 by President Reagan) and looms large at the turn of this new century. Thousands of dedicated people and organizations in the field of child development have been working for decades to improve the lives of children and families in America. As a nation, however, we have been unable to translate the concerns of individuals or interest groups into a sense of responsibility for *all* of the nation's children.

CHANGES IN FAMILY LIFE

Changes in family structure have been prominent in recent decades, of course, but these in themselves might not necessarily be stressful to children (Scott, 1993). Instead, various factors often associated with these changes might be stressors. For example, there might not be stress associated with living in a single-parent family per se. The negative effects might be due to the fact that a significant number of such families are poor and subject to a variety of environmental stresses, and the children of these families are at risk for experiencing consequences commonly associated with living in poverty, including health and nutrition deficits, attenuated school performance and attainment, and poor employment outcomes later in life (Children's Defense Fund, 1998j; Garfinkle & McLanahan, 1986; Huston, 1991; McLanahan, Astone, & Marks, 1991).

Of children born in 1997, half will spend at least a part of their childhood in a single-parent family. In the vast majority of cases, "single-parent family" is merely a euphemism for "mother-headed family"—only about 10 percent of children in single-parent families are living with their fathers. Because women's incomes tend to be lower than men's, these children are at far greater risk for exposure to poverty (Ermisch, 1991). Single-parent families are by no means homogeneous, but generally they are characterized by female heads of household, poverty, and the presence of young children (U.S. Bureau of the Census, 1997).

Most single-parent families are the result of divorce. In 1900, 6 marriages per 1,000 ended in divorce (Popenoe, 1996). Although the divorce rate has stabilized somewhat in recent years, approximately half of all marriages today end in divorce (Wallerstein & Blakeslee, 1996). Nearly as many children, however, are brought up by one parent, typically their mother, because of the increase in children born to unmarried women. In the early 1950s, only 17 percent of children grew up apart from their biological fathers; today that figure is closer to 36 percent and is expected to rise to nearly 50 percent by the early part of the twenty-first century (Popenoe, 1996). The increase in the proportion of births to unmarried mothers, from 5 percent in 1960 to nearly one in three in 1991, also contributes to this phenomenon (Popenoe, 1996; U.S. Department of Health and Human Services [USDHHS], 1993). As this book goes to press, 25 percent of all American children are being raised in single-parent homes; for Black children, this figure is over 60 percent (CDF, 1998g).

Living in a single-parent family increases a child's risk of living in poverty by almost 500 percent (National Center for Children in Poverty, 1993), but many two-parent families also need social support. Many are isolated from extended family members and community support networks. Greater mobility due to job hunting and job-related moves exacerbates these problems (Packard, 1972). Access to a support system is important because it can mediate the negative consequences of stress for children and families (Garmezy, 1985; Gore, 1980).

Parental Employment and Child Care

Since World War II, American women have entered the out-of-home labor force in greater and greater numbers. Nearly two-thirds of the women in this country with young children work outside the home, largely out of economic necessity. Many parents—mothers and fathers alike—are spending longer hours than ever in the workplace, drastically reducing the time they have available to spend with their children. A survey conducted by the Families and Work Institute (1998b) indicates that American men currently average 48.8 hours of work a week and women average 41.7 hours a week. Relatively few parents take advantage of policies implemented by some employers to improve workplace flexibility. Even when parental leave following the birth or adoption of a child is an option, very few parents can afford to take it (Hochschild, 1997a, 1997b).

Even before the recent changes in welfare legislation, approximately 7,750,000 children were being cared for, at least part of the time, by someone other than a parent (Children's Defense Fund, 1997c). The shrinking welfare safety net is expected to increase by almost 4 million the number of women whose children need at least part-time supplemental child care by 2000 (Dodson, Joshi, & McDonald, 1998; Dodson & Rayman, 1998). The American child-care system is already in chaos (Gilman & Zigler, 1996; Hofferth & Phillips, 1997). A rich body of research advises us that the lack of availability of high-quality, accessible, affordable child care is taking its toll on the well-being of this nation. What we know about the outcomes of poor-quality care enables us to postulate that a large proportion of our nation's children are at risk of suboptimal development; what we still do not know about the effects of such care should raise flags of alarm in those who are concerned about children. There is ongoing debate over the implications of decades of substandard child care, what the outcomes are likely to be, and who should be responsible for monitoring and improving this situation.

American Education   *resources spread unequal to minorities*

As critics argue that the American education system has failed, new waves of reform are sweeping the field. Federal implementation of "Goals 2000," an attempt to unify and strengthen schools nationwide, has led to controversy over virtually every facet of the educational system. Critics of the educational system point to statistics indicating that 1 student out of every 8 fails to graduate from high school, that students' math and science scores lag behind those of other nations, and that only 25 percent of American students receive a college degree (Children's Defense Fund, 1997c). Supporters, on the other hand, argue that the United States has one of the strongest systems of free, universal public education in the world. Troubling to both groups, however, is the disparity between white and minority group students in scores and achievement. Here again the resources being afforded one group are not adequately reaching others.

Child Health

American children are not receiving the health care one might expect for the youngest citizens in one of the richest nations on earth. Most American children are in good health, but there is a growing gap between the health of upper- and middle-class children and the health of children who live in or near poverty. Over 10 million children lack health insurance coverage. More than $27 billion will be cut from the food stamp program over the next six years, much of it by terminating or drastically reducing assistance to low-income families with children (Children's Defense Fund, 1997b). Chronic poverty is also associated with higher incidence of acute and chronic health conditions (Huston, 1991). There is also a powerful (if indirect) link between poverty and disorders of mental health (Albee, 1986; Knitzer, 1996; Rutter, 1979). Lack of prenatal care, low birthweight, poor housing, and exposure to environmental hazards like lead poisoning all place children at risk for developmental problems. Of course, poverty is not synonymous with problems like these. Many poor children are well supported by their parents and other caring adults. But many other poor children face the worst problems and have the lowest level of access to social supports and other buffers (Carnegie Corporation, 1994; Hamburg, 1992; National Commission on Children, 1991; Weissbourd, 1996).

The Changing Face of the American Child

Throughout this book we note the changes evident during the last few decades in the demographic makeup of American children. Increasing racial and ethnic diversity has become a fact of life in this country, at once enriching the experience of children and raising difficult policy questions (Allen & Grobman, 1996; Miller, 1994). The nearly 23 million Hispanics/Latinos in the United States, for instance, are a heterogeneous group with many differences in country of origin, language, history, and religious practices. This group is growing three times faster than the non-Hispanic U.S. population, and also has the youngest median age (25) of any ethnic minority group (Miller, 1994). Even so, there has been relatively little research on the special needs and strengths of this group. Health and developmental indicators for this and other ethnic minority groups lag behind those of whites. Traditional models of service provision and intervention do not typically take into account the unique strengths and needs of ethnic cultures within the United States.

With the increasing perception among U.S. citizens that economic and social resources are scarce, racial and ethnic intolerance has grown. In particular, immigrant populations have become a target for hostility, to the extent that even legal immigrants and their children, and even the U.S.-born children of foreign nationals, have been increasingly threatened with being cut off from the most basic social services. Racial tensions that might seem more characteristic of the 1950s have resurfaced (Allen & Grobman, 1996; Lambert, 1981) and have become a prominent feature of the policy landscape. Although the legal complexities of such issues are beyond the scope of this book, the areas at which knowledge of child development and policy development intersect to speak to these issues will be an important feature in the developing field of child and family policy.

ECONOMIC CHANGES: POVERTY, WELFARE, AND WELFARE REFORM

One of the most significant social changes in the past decade has been the increase in the number of American children who live in poverty (Children's Defense Fund, 1998c, 1998g). Young children are the fastest-growing group of poor Americans. Currently one child in four in the United States lives in poverty (National Center for Children in Poverty, 1997). For African American and Hispanic American children the situation is even worse: approximately 40 percent of these

[handwritten margin note: increased ethnic diversity — lack of research on special needs & strengths — net w/ hostility bc of "lack of resources"]

[handwritten note at bottom: 1 in 4 children live in poverty]

children are poor (Children's Defense Fund, 1997c). In the past two decades, the median real income (adjusted for inflation) of families with young children has dropped by one-third (Children's Defense Fund, 1997c). These economic problems are even worse for the growing number of single-parent families.

Of the 15 percent of families in America who are considered to be poor, approximately 60 percent receive some form of public assistance (Albelda, Folbre, & Center for Popular Economics, 1996). Most receive only about 60 percent of what is needed to bring their family income above the poverty level. The average family on welfare consists of a mother and two children. Fifty-five percent of women on welfare do not have a high school diploma, but most have spent some time in the paid labor force. Over two-thirds use welfare to get through a specific period of economic crisis, and remain on the welfare rolls for fewer than two years, though half of these reapply at some later point. The average total time spent on welfare is six years. Only 1 percent of welfare recipients are teenage mothers (Withorn, 1996).

What Does Poverty Mean?

Most of us are shocked when we hear that approximately one out of every four children in the United States lives in poverty. But what *is* poverty? The ways in which poverty is defined by scholars, by legislators, and by social welfare programs all have an impact on children's lives, the way we understand them, and the way we work to improve them.

The most widely used index of poverty is the "poverty level" established by the federal government. Based on the idea that approximately one-third of a family's budget is spent on food every month, federal officials set the poverty level at three times the current "economy food budget." Adjustments are then made for factors like family size and the number of children under 18. Annual adjustments are made to account for increases in the cost of living. As of this writing, the poverty level for a family of four with two children under 18 is $15,771 per year (Kilborn, 1996).

Critics on both the left and the right have argued about the accuracy of this way of defining poverty. Economic conservatives feel this overestimates poverty because "in-kind" awards like food stamps and Medicaid are not counted as income. Research indicates, however, that even when only cash income is considered, fewer than one-quarter of the children under 18 who make up the poverty group under the traditional definition are excluded (Danziger, Haveman, & Plotnik, 1986; Huston, 1991).

Others argue that poverty ought to be defined in comparison to the average standard of living in a given area. Families whose incomes are less than 50 percent of the median for an area, for instance, might be considered "deprived" by such a standard (Hernandez, 1989). Still others point out that many children who, in essence, have no incomes at all—children who are homeless or are shuttling through the foster care system, for instance—make up a significant but statistically invisible proportion of poor children, leading us to underestimate the scope of this problem (Huston, 1991).

Who Is Poor?

Most of the stories we read in the news or see on television about children living in poverty depict young black children, typically living in single-parent families in large urban areas. In reality, however, poverty has a much more diverse
profile. Between 1975 and 1994, the young-child poverty rate grew twice as fast
in the suburbs as in urban areas, and twice as fast for white children as for
blacks. Recent demographics indicate that rural women are far more likely than
urban women to live in poverty. Lower levels of education, poor employment
rates, and job opportunities concentrated largely in the service sector contribute
to this phenomenon (Gorman & Haynie, 1998).

One-third of poor children in the United States live in the South; one-half of
those live in extreme poverty, with family incomes less than half of the poverty
line (Children's Defense Fund, 1998c, 1998e). Of the 100 poorest counties for
children, 84 are in the South. Among poor southern families, more than 7 out of
10—a higher proportion than in any other area—have a family member who
works. Nationwide, children living in two-parent families in which at least one
parent is employed were 2½ times as likely to be poor as children from single-
parent families. Almost two-thirds of poor young children have at least one
parent who works full- or part-time (Children's Defense Fund, 1998f, 1998g; National Center for Children in Poverty, 1996). Low wages and lack of educational
and job-training opportunities are serious obstacles that prevent these families
from climbing out of poverty (Dodson, Joshi, & McDonald, 1998). Rural poverty
is as pervasive as urban poverty, but it is less visible to the public and to policy
analysts. Rural poor families are also more likely to be two-parent families, making them ineligible for government support (Jensen, 1988).

As currently conceived, the poverty level provides little more than a snapshot image of how many children are living in poverty at any given point in
time. Analysis of the economic circumstances of U.S. children and their families
shows that poverty is not a static phenomenon, but a fluid, dynamic phenomenon affected by many factors. Some analysts argue that it is more accurate to acknowledge the transitory nature of poverty as both families and the economy
change. Such analysts distinguish between persistent and transitory poverty
(Bane & Ellwood, 1996). Both kinds of poverty can have lasting negative effects
on children, because poverty of any sort can result in reduced opportunities for
children, greater transience, and greater exposure to emotional and material
stress (Emery, Hetherington, & DiLalla, 1984).

Transitory poverty is most likely to result from a sudden economic crisis—
a job layoff for a parent, for instance, that causes a family to go through a limited period of economic hardship, or a divorce that leads to a relatively brief economic decline. One-third of American children experience poverty for at least
one year (Duncan, 1991).

Others, among them the children of teen parents and the children of poorly
educated parents, are more likely to live in persistent poverty (Duncan, 1991;
Furstenberg, Brooks-Gunn, & Morgan, 1987). Only about 1 child out of 20 lives
in poverty for more than a decade, but an additional 7 percent of children were

poor for 5 to 7 years (Duncan, 1991). Here again, racial differences are striking—among black children, fewer than 1 in 7 lived comfortably for the 15 years encompassed by one longitudinal study of family income, and more than 25 percent were poor for at least 10 of the 15 years (Duncan, 1991).

The Consequences of Childhood Poverty *eliminates opportunities*

To what extent does persistent poverty reduce opportunities later in life? Students of social science will understand that causal connections are rarely direct and straightforward. Being poor does not in and of itself account for diminished success and well-being later in life. Living in poverty *can*, however, take a tremendous toll on a child's future by eliminating opportunities that facilitate success: Educational opportunities for children living in economically deprived areas are likely to be substandard (Kozol, 1991), and health problems associated with poverty both challenge healthy development itself and interfere with academic performance. In addition, environments in which suboptimal housing, homelessness, and chronic family and community violence are pervasive contribute to a persistent climate of failure and hopelessness. It is little wonder that children reared in such environments are at elevated risk of social, educational, and physical difficulties.

Greater State Responsibility

Welfare reform, historically supported by conservative Republicans, is today being championed by many Democrats as well. Arguing that welfare makes it more difficult to address the federal budget deficit, and that it "undermines the work ethic" (Withorn, 1996), promotes sexual promiscuity and out-of-wedlock births, and contributes to the breakup of families, in the 1990s many policy makers on both sides of the political fence came to believe in the need to eliminate "welfare as we know it" in the United States. As supports to low-income families became less and less popular with the American public at the end of the twentieth century, there was a decrease in the amount of public money allocated for services to the poor. Since 1981, restrictions in available funding and eligibility criteria left many former recipients of programs like Medicaid, Aid to Families with Dependent Children (AFDC), and (after 1996) Temporary Assistance for Needy Families (TANF) with attenuated benefits or no benefits at all. Even those families eligible for the Earned Income Tax Credit, a federal wage supplement for low-income families, find the credit inadequate to meet their minimum needs. Overall, the total income of poor families has decreased significantly over the past thirty years.

Even as many policy analysts called for major changes in the welfare system, others expressed concern about the shrinkage of the safety net that is supposed to protect low-income families from poverty, hunger, and homelessness. This group argued against hasty or arbitrary changes in the delivery of public assistance. Against the advice of many policy analysts and child and family advocates who believed the welfare system might be changed more gradually, and

The New Homeless

Families with children are the fastest-growing segment of the population experiencing homelessness in America, making up nearly 40 percent of those with no homes (U.S. Conference of Mayors, 1994). In New York City alone, in 1981 there were fewer than a thousand homeless families; by 1995, there were nearly six times as many (U.S. Department of Housing and Urban Development, 1994).

During the Reagan administration, the number of new poor families receiving federal housing assistance was cut from 400,000 per year to 40,000 a year; legislation enacted under President Clinton reduced this number to zero. Of the 15 million households that qualify for federal housing assistance, fewer than 5 million actually receive it (DeParle, 1996b). More than 400,000 families are homeless in America; another 2.5 million live transient and stressful lives doubled and tripled up with relatives and friends.

Several factors help account for this still-growing crisis. A decline in real income among American families, inflationary rises in rents, and a lack of affordable rental properties mean that a majority of low-income families spend over 40 percent of their income on housing (Children's Defense Fund, 1998g). No new federal funds for low-income housing were provided in 1996, 1997, or 1998, and public housing facilities are declining in number as age and poor upkeep—more fallout from the federal funding crunch—render older units uninhabitable. Existing units in reasonable condition are increasingly likely to be offered to families living above the poverty level

as federal housing subsidies for poorer families have been withdrawn. Welfare reform efforts are only intensifying these problems.

Homeless children face even greater hardship than other poor children. The problems involved in trying to attend school regularly, receive regular and appropriate health care, and maintain any sense of stability are nearly insurmountable in the face of chronic or severe poverty (Wood et al., 1990). When frequent moves, unsafe and unstable housing, or outright homelessness are added to these burdens, regular school attendance becomes virtually impossible. A recent report on school attendance among children living in shelters indicates that virtually none of the young homeless children eligible for preschool in their respective communities actually attend these programs (National Law Center on Homelessness and Poverty, 1997). Homeless children are much less likely to complete school on time than are poor children who have more reliable housing (Children's Defense Fund, 1998f, 1998g).

Some efforts have been made at the federal level to extend housing subsidies set to expire at the end of the 1990s. State and local governments increasingly bear the responsibility for making provisions for homeless families (Weinreb & Buckner, 1993). Foundations and private groups like the Neighborhood Reinvestment Corporation and Habitat for Humanity also help take up the slack left by the withdrawal of so much federal support, but the inadequacy of policy responses to the needs of homeless families continues to grow.

[Handwritten marginal notes:]

more families living in poverty because

problems homeless kids face...

[handwritten annotation at top: Clinton signed in TANF which eliminated standards for gov. aid, shortened time period for parents to find jobs after receiving help, and caps eligibility for aid at 5 yrs. RESULT → 20% savings of welfare expenses. AKA the "Devolution Revolution"]

with more thoughtful provision for a successful transition from reliance on public subsidy to self-sufficiency (Ellwood, 1988; DeParle, 1996a; Horn, 1996; National Center for Children in Poverty, 1995a), President Clinton signed into law in 1996 a welfare bill that fundamentally changed the nature of assistance to poor children and their families.

The new law replaced AFDC with a program called Temporary Assistance for Needy Families (TANF). TANF differs from AFDC in a number of fundamental ways. The most important of these is the elimination of virtually all federal standards dictating how TANF funds will be disbursed. States now have almost complete discretion about how to spend the block grants from which TANF funds are taken. AFDC dictated that states had to help all needy families with children; TANF makes no such guarantee. TANF enables states to shorten to two years or less the time period within which parents must find work after first receiving public assistance, and it caps lifetime eligibility at five years or less. TANF guidelines result in an immediate savings of 20 percent of previous welfare expenditures, by encouraging states simply to drop people from the present rolls by modifying eligibility requirements (DeParle, 1996a). This shift in responsibility has often been referred to as the "devolution revolution" (Horn, 1996).

Further cuts in welfare expenditures are being realized through budget cuts authorized as a part of the 1997 bipartisan agreement to balance the federal budget. Approximately $50 billion in budget cuts will come from capping, curtailing, or eliminating programs intended for children and families. Almost $24 billion will be cut by eliminating Medicaid, food stamps, and Social Security Income benefits for legal immigrants. Another $23 billion will come from cuts to other food stamp recipients, largely from families with children, and a third group of cuts will be made in the area of services to disabled children (DeParle, 1996a). On the positive side, a recent federal initiative, the **Child Health Insurance Program (CHIP)**, provides funding to make health insurance available to previously uninsured U.S. children. CHIP is a voluntary program that requires participating states to provide 20 percent of the funding needed to insure the children in their jurisdiction.

[handwritten annotation in right margin: budget cuts: coming from social services]

Critics argue that the conditions placed on welfare recipients and the restrictions placed on eligibility are neither new ideas nor viable ones: By attempting to control the behavior of poor women without offering support services to make the transition off welfare easier, more successful, and more humane, proponents of the new welfare legislation ignore the lessons of past attempts to reform welfare (Withorn, 1966). In the 1960s, 1970s, and 1980s, programs like WIN (Work Incentive Program), JOBS (Job Opportunities and Basic Skills Training), and FSA (Family Support Act of 1988) failed because these welfare-to-work efforts were not supported by adequate training, employment assistance in the form of transportation subsidies, appropriate child care, and health care guarantees for those who earned too much in the program to continue to qualify for Medicaid (DeParle, 1996a; Ellwood, 1988; Horn, 1996; Piotrkowski, 1996; Vobejda & Havemann, 1997). Based on these past programs, critics argue, many families in the new programs will simply "time out" by not meeting employment criteria

[handwritten annotation in right margin: reform failed bc didn't support transition from welfare to job. previous welfare pd didn't during when welfare ended.]

A Shift in Ideology: Social Attitudes Toward Welfare

When the Social Security Act was first passed in 1935, its primary goal was to permit poor women to stay at home and raise their children (Aaronson & Hartmann, 1996; Bassuk, 1996; Jacobs & Davies, 1994; Kagan & Pritchard, 1996; Withorn, 1996). Government assistance served a family preservation function; without this "widow's benefit," many women would have been forced to put their fatherless children into orphanages. Child raising was not viewed as a leisure activity, nor were these women demonized as lazy or blamed for their own poverty. This attitude stands in sharp contrast to that implied by Temporary Assistance for Needy Families (TANF) requirements. Consider, for instance, that only thirteen states have voluntarily adapted TANF language that would exempt women with children under 1 year of age from work requirements (Children's Defense Fund, 1997c).

Within thirty years of the passage of the Social Security Act, the public attitude toward welfare and the women who receive it had shifted dramatically. At the inception of the family assistance program, 40 percent of recipients were widows, and the typical recipient was characterized as "a West Virginia mother whose husband had died in a mine accident. Honest, hard-working, God-fearing, White Protestant folk" (Patrick Moynihan, quoted in Mead, 1996). By the 1900s, 62 percent of welfare mothers were nonwhite, only 2 percent were widows, and over half had never been married at all. As Mead (1996)

notes, "As AFDC became less representative of the nation, the program became more difficult for nondependent Americans to accept" (p. 53).

The popular bias against public assistance and those who receive it has always gone hand-in-hand with a tendency to try to "improve" those recipients found less deserving, or even to deny them altogether, often on the basis of marital status or ethnicity. In the 1930s and 1940s, some states refused to award AFDC to black women in order to keep them working as domestics and farm laborers (Jencks, 1992; Withorn, 1996).

The dominant attitude toward welfare recipients today is more like the one prevalent in the nineteenth century than that of 1935; today's attitude is that public assistance has a corrupting effect on poor families (Mead, 1996). No longer is our primary goal to provide support and assistance to mothers so that they can stay at home with their children. Instead our goal is to curb government spending by bringing mothers to, or back to, the paid workforce. However, this goal is based on the misconception that the dichotomy facing families today is represented by a choice between labor or leisure; the policy "cure" (Aaronson & Hartmann, 1996, p. 584) overestimates the ability of welfare recipients to find work in a time of low unemployment—the odds against them are compounded by their lack of training and transportation, and the unavailability of high-quality, affordable child care.

within the new time limit (Aaronson & Hartmann, 1996; Danziger & Danziger, 1995; Pavetti, 1995).

Deciding whether these welfare reform efforts have been successful will depend on how we define our goals, notes Horn (1996). We must decide up front whether the purpose of welfare and its restructuring are to put mothers to work, or back to work, or whether our intention is to improve the lives of children through the judicious and fair distribution of economic subsidies. Such clarification of goals is an essential step in determining whether our policy efforts have been fruitful.

Two years after TANF was first implemented, analysts are divided over how successful the movement is likely to be in the long run. Supporters point to figures showing dramatic declines in the number of welfare cases; as of this writing, caseloads are down in 49 states, though the degree of decline varies from a 1 percent drop in Nebraska to a 77 percent drop in Idaho (USDHHS, 1998b). Nationally, the number of families receiving welfare dropped by 39 percent between 1993 and 1998—from nearly 5 million to just over 3 million (Dodson & Rayman, 1998).

Such figures, however, tell only a part of the story. Closer examination of the lives of former welfare recipients indicates that many have indeed found adequate employment. Others have not been as fortunate. Nearly three-quarters of Milwaukee, Wisconsin, residents who left the welfare rolls for paying jobs, for instance, were unemployed or underemployed a year later (Children's Defense Fund, 1998h). A large proportion of the jobs available to participants in welfare-to-work programs offer only below-poverty-level wages; for those who are new, or newly returned, to the workforce, even full-time employment is unlikely to yield more than $10,000 a year (Children's Defense Fund, 1998g). The challenge of finding job training, transportation, and child care further limits the potential success of the reform effort (Center on Hunger and Poverty, 1998; Dodson, Joshi, & McDonald, 1998; Dodson & Rayman, 1998). One report noted that New York City needed child-care slots for an additional 29,000 children in order to accommodate welfare-to-work employees, but the city planned to fund only 6,000 slots ("City Needs More Child Care Slots," 1998). Until such problems are addressed, the real success of welfare reform is unlikely to be as impressive as simple enrollment figures indicate.

A NEW FIELD COMES OF AGE

Attempts to give children and families priority in our national agenda have been, to date, only partially successful. We have learned a great deal about how children develop, how their families function, and how certain variables act to enhance or impede this functioning. We have learned a great deal about advocating for change. In spite of this, only in the relatively recent past have these two fields merged to give rise to the unified study of child development and social policy. Even today, advocates for children struggle against historical models of policy development, in which policy is based more on "prevailing

policy is focused on politics, not research + practice

political winds" than on "substantial input from research and practice" (Shore, 1993). The result has often been a patchy arrangement of ill-conceived, politically expedient efforts, more often based on meeting adults' needs than those of children.

Researchers in developmental psychology have become increasingly appreciative of the close link between basic research in child development and the application of that research. Basic research is generally defined as any research that is motivated by the desire to expand knowledge. Applied research is defined as research conducted in an effort to solve a problem or in order to provide information that can be put to some specific use. Although these two types of research are distinct by definition, they actually overlap and contribute to each other, to the benefit of both. Recently, the Society for Research in Child Development (SRCD) has recognized the potential value of applied and/or social policy research that utilizes scientific research to the benefit of children. Accordingly, its journal *Child Development* has decided to welcome researchers to submit for publication articles dealing with applied work (Zigler, 1998).

Applied research in developmental psychology encompasses a broad array of studies, as the field has practical applications and relevance for a number of areas, including pediatrics, law, social work, urban planning, and education. Increasingly, researchers recognize that some of their work should be directed toward understanding and solving contemporary problems faced by children and families (Hamburg, 1992; Kamerman & Kahn, 1995; Zigler, Kagan, & Hall, 1996; Weissbourd, 1996). This trend in the field has been precipitated by several developments, most notably the implementation during the 1960s and 1970s of federally sponsored social programs like Head Start. The proliferation of a wide range of such programs provided an opportunity for developmental psychologists to apply their knowledge and training to new areas of study, such as children's services, that had not previously received attention from the scientific community (Garwood et al., 1989).

Also contributing to the growth of this new field was the realization that children are influenced not only by the people in their immediate social settings but also by aspects of the larger and more remote social systems such as the school, the workplace, the community, the government, and the mass media. As a result of this new understanding, developmental psychologists have broadened their research to include ecological studies that examine development within a wide social context (Bronfenbrenner, 1979; Hetherington, Hagan, & Anderson, 1989).

When Does Applied Research Become Policy Research?

For developmental psychologists, the benefits of being involved in social policy issues include not only the opportunity to contribute to the well-being of children, but also an opportunity for research. The chance to study the effect of societal changes on children has the potential to contribute even more to the policy process. Outcomes related to changing workplace demographics, for instance, or to changes in access to early intervention programs, provide feedback to policy-makers, child advocates, and developmental psychologists alike (Hall, Kagan, & Zigler, 1996; Strawn, 1992).

Many argue that developmental psychologists have not only an opportunity, but a responsibility, to use their knowledge to help inform policy by sharing their information and expertise with those who are in a position to influence the lives of children—educators, legislators, and other public office holders (Hall et al., 1996; Zigler & Finn-Stevenson, 1993). In this context, developmental research is policy research, merely by virtue of having been applied during any stage of the policy formation process. Unlike policy-oriented research that measures such things as the number of Asian American voters in a given area or the per-pupil expenditures in a certain school district, most social policy research involves elements that are somewhat subjective. Because of this, developmental research has been criticized by some as inexact and unreliable.

Certainly, social scientists and those who rely on the findings of social scientists must pay heed to this concern (Kimble, 1989; Maddux, 1993). Our own biases, interests, and beliefs will inevitably inform our work (Maccoby, Kahn, & Everett, 1983; Silverstein, 1993a, 1993b), but they do not necessarily render it undependable. By being aware of our own attitudes, and by taking care to adhere to rigorous methodological principles, we can safeguard against most bias in our work. One way to do this is to employ research assistants who are blind to (that is, kept in ignorance of) a given study's hypotheses while collecting and analyzing data. Another way is to take care, in selecting study subjects or participants, to avoid potential prejudice by choosing them in ways that minimize bias.

Assumptions About Child Development and Policy

A number of constructs and theories that arise from the study of child development are so central to our discussion of child development and social policy that they bear emphasizing here. Other issues, such as the discussion of research design in chapter 2, will be discussed as they become relevant.

Developmental Sequences

One of our most basic assumptions is that development in children proceeds in universal, more or less orderly **sequences:** The child must complete the growth and development characteristic of one phase before successfully proceeding to the next. Thus, an infant must gain control over his head, neck, and back muscles before he can sit alone. A preschool or school-age child must learn that letters are symbols for sounds before she can learn to read. An adolescent must develop a sense of her own identity as a competent person separate from her parents if she is to make a successful transition to adulthood.

When we consider the nature of intervention to support children in their development, selecting the correct point at which to intervene is often critically important. We have come a long way since the 1960s and 1970s when it was felt that there might be "magical" periods at which to apply simple interventions to raise children's IQs or permanently enhance their social development. Each period of development grows naturally out of each preceding period, so that we must do our best to understand each point in the developmental continuum and promote interventions and supports that strengthen and enrich each one. Children need different things at each period, but their needs are great throughout childhood.

Workers in the field of human development believe that children have a considerable degree of plasticity—for instance, that the child's health and behavior are amenable to a certain amount of change in response to outside interventions, such as early education programs intended to enhance school readiness, supplemental maternal nutrition during pregnancy, and stimulation during the first few years of life to promote healthy brain development. Scholars and service providers concerned about children's needs must continually ask themselves at what age children could best benefit from the policy or intervention in question. At what point in life will a particular policy impart the greatest benefit to children and families? At what point would it be most cost effective?

Difference Versus Deficit Controversy

Numerous studies have found that average IQ scores for children from low-income families tend to be 10 to 15 points lower than average IQ scores for children from middle-class families. In general, the higher a family's **socioeconomic status,** the higher the IQs of both parents and children. Average educational performance, too, has tended to be lower for children from low-income areas and ethnic minority children. Statistics like these have led to what is often called the "difference versus deficit" controversy.

One hypothesis offered for years is that social class differences in intellectual performance are related to genetic differences. Because representation in a low socioeconomic class is higher among some ethnic groups, most notably blacks, Jensen (1969) contended that the lower average IQ scores of low-income black children are evidence of a genetic factor in intelligence, and that these children are, therefore, genetically inferior. However, most investigators consider the strong relationship between IQ and social class to be primarily environmental in nature (Weinberg, 1989). Factors related to cultural bias in measuring devices (like IQ tests) and lack of motivation to do well on the test (Zigler & Seitz, 1982; Zigler & Butterfield, 1986) are more likely to account for the differences.

The notion that social class differences in IQ, in educational performance, and in other aspects of behavior stem from genetic differences in intelligence is controversial because of the erroneous label it attaches to some ethnic groups and because of its many social and political implications. For instance, if we believe that intelligence is an inherited trait, then we would not strive to implement programs designed to improve the educational achievement of economically disadvantaged children. But if we believe that intelligence is affected by environmental factors, then we would contend that such programs are important.

Often the solutions proposed to address these problems are based on myths that in turn spring from one or another position on this difference–deficit continuum. Whether you believe the research supporting the notion that welfare encourages out-of-wedlock pregnancies or the studies refuting this notion, for instance, depends in large part on where you find yourself on this difference–deficit continuum. Similarly, the tendency to develop and mount "one-size-fits-all" interventions that treat all participants identically also has its origins in program developers' positions with respect to this controversy (Allen & Grobman, 1996). Bear this controversy in mind as you read through this book, and as you study problems related to children and families, and their proposed solutions, throughout your life.

Changing Models of Interaction

In the early days of child study, few researchers looked beyond the child *per se* when studying behavior and designing interventions. Children themselves were the object of study (Hall, 1991; Kessen, 1965). By the 1960s, however, a new view of children recognized that even the youngest child's behavior can best be understood *in context*. From our empirically derived understanding of the way mothers and infants interact, arose the notion that the child is an active participant in her environment, not merely being acted upon by parents but actually mediating the nature of her world by influencing those around her (Stern, 1985). Newborns, for instance, use their gazing, reaching, facial expressions, and vocalizations to signal their needs to their caregivers (Hall, 1997; Tronick & Cohn, 1989). These cues influence the behavior of the caregiver, whose own actions in turn affect the child; thus arises a cycle of interactions many psychologists refer to as a dance. In keeping with this more sophisticated understanding of parent/child interactions and child behavior, researchers adopted research paradigms that examined the child's behavior vis-à-vis other people, and the focus shifted from the child in isolation to the parent/child (often the mother/child) dyad.

The logical extension of this type of thinking was applied by developmental psychologist Urie Bronfenbrenner (1979). Bronfenbrenner's *ecological model* captures the notion that the child exists within a social and cognitive context of interacting influences and agents, and that interactions among these actors are bidirectional. Imagine the child's world to be represented by a series of concentric circles with the individual child at the center. Each circle represents a sphere of influence that affects the child's life. These spheres, which include family, child care, community, school, the media, the workplace, and government, to name but a few, are nested within one another, extended outward from the child herself.

Bronfenbrenner's model quickly became the standard view of the child and her world. Family members influence the child's development more strongly than any other agent, but family members, too, exist within a social environment that can affect the child directly or indirectly. Taking the ecological model one step further, we might employ, rather than the concentric circles, a metaphorical structure that bears a close resemblance to a hypertext web on a computer network such as the Internet. In this case, simultaneous multiple non-linear linkages express the pattern of influences on a child's development. The child is affected at once, for instance, by the quality of his interaction with his parents, by his overall health and nutritional status, by the qualities of the child care he receives, by the safety of the neighborhood in which he lives, and by hundreds, if not thousands, of other variables. In turn, each of *these* is affected by other factors. The quality of the mother/child interaction, for instance, is influenced by the baby's temperament, by the mother's feelings about motherhood and child care, by her relationship with the baby's father and with her own family, and so on. Such a model can more accurately capture the complex patterns of influence, direct and indirect, on the child.

A more complex model, such as the ecological web in which the child acts and is acted upon, also enables us to envision the nature of the interactions among those who influence the child. In a classical ecological model, for instance, government and its role in influencing children and child development falls outside the spheres represented by the child, her family, her community, and so on, yet government and other areas in which child and family policy are made are very much a part of this interactive web. As you continue to study the evolving field of child development and social policy, try to be mindful of the ways in which these multiple influences affect the child's world, and thus the child, and of how the child's behavior, in turn, interacts with these to create a fluid and dynamic environment in which development takes place.

Prevention Versus Treatment

A group of people were fishing in a stream when a small child floated past them. By acting quickly, one of the anglers was able to catch the child and save it from drowning. Soon afterwards, another child was swept downstream—this child, too, was saved through quick action. Before long, however, another child, then another and another, rushed along on the current, and the would-be rescuers had their hands full trying to catch and save them all. Suddenly, one of the fishermen turned to leave. "Hey!" called the others. "Where are you going? Aren't you going to stay here and help us save these children?" "No," he replied, "I'm going to wade upstream and stop the scoundrel who's throwing them in!" (Harris, 1992).

This parable is often related as a means of describing the difference between prevention and treatment approaches to intervening in the lives of children (Harris, 1992). The concept of primary prevention—intervening early to prevent a problem from developing later on—became especially prominent in the 1960s and 1970s as an outgrowth of President Johnson's War on Poverty. With the discovery that much of the mental retardation and school failure in the United States was linked to poverty, inadequate health care, and environmental deficits in the lives of many young children, efforts were undertaken to prevent, rather than remediate, these problems. Early intervention is often taken for granted today, but in the early days of programs like Head Start and the Carolina Abecedarian Project, such a concept was revolutionary. Its effectiveness had to be demonstrated through the mounting of pilot programs and then through assessment of short- and long-term outcomes of program participation.

Multiple Causes of Behavior

Research tells us that poverty is strongly associated with an elevated risk of school failure, truancy, and dropping out. Does being poor *make* a child a bad student? What mechanisms account for this relationship? When a research study identifies a phenomenon as a causal factor, it is tempting to think of it as the only cause for the behavior being studied. However, a child's behavior and development are not that simple. Most behaviors of interest to child development professionals have multiple causes. Even though the researcher must isolate those causes in order to study each one independently, it is generally understood that individual variables rarely function in isolation in a child's natural environment.

In the case of school-age children living in poverty, we might postulate that educational outcomes are affected by a large group of variables, including health factors, early developmental opportunities, parental experience with and attitudes toward education, teachers' and administrators' expectations, and adequacy of school facilities, to name but a few. The vast majority of issues and problems affecting children and families are easily as complex as this example. Cultivating the habit of generating such lists of potentially relevant variables, and theorizing about the relative contributions of a variety of factors in the child's and family's environment, will serve you well as you consider questions of policy in this class and in the future.

As you read through the coming chapters, it is essential to acknowledge that every issue which has an impact on children and families is multifaceted. "Doing the right thing" for children isn't always simple. Economic, demographic, social, and political issues bring complexity to the process of family policy development. And views on children and families—and who should make and implement decisions on their behalf—are informed not only by science, but by traditions ancient and modern, by religion, and by values and mores that vary with the region, the time, and the political tenor of the nation. Consider the changes in family structure that many cite as proof of the imminent extinction of the American family. Is the increasing diversity of family constellations and parental roles in the United States a strength, representing a step forward for those who do not fit the traditional model (Hite, 1994; New & David, 1984)? Or do these changes in and of themselves cause problems for children and weaken the social fabric (Popenoe, 1996)? Even if we as individuals adhere to a particular position on this question, and on others, it is rarely, if ever, possible to say that all other positions are simply wrong. We cannot perform effectively as advocates for children unless we acknowledge the positions of others who are affected by our attempts to guide policy development, and try to synthesize the best of all of these positions.

In all such cases, we believe the deciding vote should be cast on the basis of scholarship and our child development knowledge base. There are no final truths in social science, but the absence of absolutes in our understanding must not be allowed to obstruct policy construction. Some social conditions are so severe and pressing as to warrant policy construction or immediate pragmatic action even in the absence of consensus on the data. When this occurs, the efforts made need to be based on wise judgment, well informed by scholarship, with provisions for the evaluation and revision of programs as needed. We should not wait, for instance, for outcome data showing that children who have eaten at least one nutritious meal a day get higher test scores than hungry children in order to support policies that alleviate children's hunger.

As the authors of this book we cannot disguise our own beliefs that children are important social capital in this nation (Rauch, 1989) and that the quality of their early experiences will eventually affect the entire nation, for good or ill. No matter what the reader's—or the governor's or the senator's or the president's—political convictions, it is essential that we base decisions that will affect the lives of the nation's children and families, and, by extension, the strength of the nation itself, on what we know about child and family development.

SUMMARY

Within the past two decades, the field of child development and policy study has come of age. This book attempts to lead the student through a reasoned and empirically informed argument for the proposition that what we, as individuals and as a nation, do for children and their families ought to be based on what we know about their needs and how best to meet those needs.

Demographic changes affecting families in the United States have been rapid and dramatic since the close of World War II, and virtually all of these changes—in employment patterns, in child-care practices, in the nature and provision of public schooling, even in the demographic makeup of children themselves—have had a profound impact on children and families. Half of today's young children will spend some portion of their lives in single-parent families, owing to both increasing numbers of out-of-wedlock births and a divorce rate that has stabilized at near 50 percent. These changes and a steady increase since World War II in the number of women in the paid labor force have contributed to record numbers of children being cared for by someone other than their mother. Even prior to the implementation of welfare reform provisions in the late 1990s, close to 8 million young U.S. children spent some portion of every day in the care of persons other than their parents. As a nation, we have not responded to these demographic changes with supportive programs for parents. The United States remains the only industrialized nation in the world without **paid national infant-care leave.** Our child-care system is chaotic, in poor supply, and poor in quality.

Social and political response to issues like these has been polarized. Many analysts eulogize the "golden age" of family life, pointing to the 1950s or even the nineteenth century as simpler, healthier times for children and parents. Others dismiss these notions, noting that these periods were characterized by poor child health, significantly higher infant mortality rates, and the same anxieties about social change and world peace as today's parents experience.

It is difficult to determine what, if any, historical period is or was most favorable for families. Many changes, such as advances in medicine and in the technology of everyday life, have been positive; others, such as the decline in children's access to medical service, have been detrimental. Other findings are mixed or ambiguous (for instance, we still cannot say whether child care is, overall, advantageous or disadvantageous, on average, for American children). And in far too many cases, advantages available to many children are unattainable by others. Even in areas in which U.S. children are at an overall advantage compared with their peers in other nations, increasing disparities in educational outcomes, child health, child-care quality, and housing opportunities within our country are reflected in different outcomes for children of different ethnic groups and socioeconomic statuses.

The field of child development and policy study has arisen and grown to address such issues. Helping the student grasp the basic principles of child development and the best ways to apply theoretical and empirical research on children and families to policy issues is the key to uniting what we know about children to what we can—or should—do for them. All of these issues will be considered as the readings ahead give the student the tools to make informed decisions about child development and social policy, and to become an active participant in this growing field.

The Policy Process

Imagine that you are the parent of small children. As you read your daily paper or tune in a news broadcast on television or on the radio, your attention will probably be drawn by stories having to do with budget cuts in education, or with the reinstatement of a particular health care safety net, the absence of which would have had a serious negative impact on public health. You avidly read the news of changes to the boundaries of your school district, or prick up your ears when you hear a report about proposed legislation that might give you more time off from work to be with your children. If you are like most parents, other stories don't seem as pertinent. What direct impact could an "omnibus budget bill" possibly have on your child? What difference does it make to your family whether Congress passes this or that version of a tax reform plan?

As you read through the remaining chapters of this book, we hope that it will become clear that many policies in which the words *child* and *family* might not even appear can have profound implications for children. Child policy isn't limited to bills and proposals that determine how much money is to be appropriated for Head Start or how children will be affected by changes in welfare policy. Children's lives are affected, sometimes subtly, sometimes dramatically, by legislation affecting *how* things are to be done (including how money is to be spent and collected), *what* structures within government make it easier for policies beneficial to children and families to be enacted, and *who* is to be responsible for child welfare.

Before we discuss the process through which policy is developed, and the variables and factors that play a role in the growth and implementation of policies that have an impact on children and families, let us stop and consider what we mean by *policy*. Many experts who write about child and family policy are concerned strictly with legislation written and enacted at the state or federal level. We believe, however, that policy should be understood in a much broader context. How much money Congress should appropriate for Head Start programs in a given year is a policy decision, but so is whether the children at a particular elementary school should wear uniforms. Whether to implement federal standards for day-care quality is a policy issue, but so is whether a small bank will offer day-care resource and referral services to its employees.

One workable, albeit lengthy, definition of public policy was proposed by Pizzo (1983): "public policy is defined as a course of action consciously selected by publicly funded institutions (particularly government) from among several possible methods of approaching a concern brought to the attention of decision makers within these institutions" (p. 62). In keeping with our original broad focus, however, and in order to keep the spotlight on children, we would like to modify this definition slightly. We propose, therefore, that child policy is any principle, plan, or course of action that has an impact—intended or not—on the lives of children and families.

THE PURPOSE OF POLICY

What does child policy do? Child and family policies are designed to do one or more of the following.

- *Provide information.*The Children's Bureau, established by federal legislation in 1912, for instance, was founded in part to provide statistical and demographic information on children (Bremner, 1971b; USDHHS, 1987; Zigler & Muenchow, 1985). Until this time, no reliable records were kept of the births or deaths of U.S. children. During the Children's Bureau's first decades, teams of women were sent to interview thousands of mothers whose infants had died during or shortly after childbirth (Bradbury, 1956). The information thus collected helped to spur the passage of the Sheppard-Towner Act of 1921, authorizing the first federal-to-state grant-in-aid program and the establishment of almost 1,600 child health clinics (Pizzo, 1983).
- *Provide funds.* One of the main tasks assigned to Congress is the establishment of a budget for the United States and the allocation of funds in accordance with that budget. These moneys are released either directly to individual programs, or, as is often the case today, to individual states in the forms of **block grants** that state governments must then administer, allocate, and distribute to cover their own program demands. Legislation concerned with distribution of funds is one of the types of legislation that have the greatest impact on children and families.
- *Provide services that prevent or solve problems.* Early childhood immunization programs fall into this category, as does legislation that provides for remedial educational services. Note that programmatic children's policy decisions are not always made in *favor* of children—some result in the restriction or elimination of funding, or in restricted eligibility for support services.
- *Provide infrastructure that supports other policy efforts on behalf of children.* To make any significant progress, we must have a mechanism or forum in Congress in which concerns about children and families can be heard. Thus legislation that establishes bipartisan bodies like the House Select Committee on Children and Families and the Senate Children's Caucus is just as important to child and family issues as laws that fund sound health or education. Though the Republican and Democratic parties have more-or-less distinctive philosophical approaches to governing, and general legislative agendas, neither has a monopoly on commitment to what is best for our nation's children and families, and political diversity among committee members is often a strength.

 These bipartisan committees have held hearings on family stress, changing demographics, family violence, infant mortality, latchkey children, television violence, children's injuries, child care, and other topics. Such hearings focus a spotlight on these issues by generating publicity and by promoting research on which to base future policies. The existence of such forums for the coverage of children's issues promotes the formation of new coalitions to study children's problems, and sends a signal to legislators that the public wants them to pay attention to family concerns. The White House Children's Conferences, held every ten years since 1909, were discontinued by the Reagan administration, but recent years have brought a revitalization of the role of the White House as a pulpit for drawing attention to issues significant to children and families.

Child Policies and the National Interest

There is another way of looking at child and family policies, and that is in the context of how such policies affect the nation as a whole. The National Commission on Children has arrived at a list of goals to which children's policies should aspire. In recent years children's advocates like Children's Defense Fund president Marian Wright Edelman have argued that children should be viewed as "social capital," the investment of which, through support and proper treatment, will enrich and strengthen the entire country. With this as a background, the National Commission on Children (1991) suggests asking the following questions about any given children's policy proposal:

- Does it ensure economic security for the nation, or is it based more on the need to provide security for children in the form of appropriate nurturing and caregiving?
- Will it increase educational achievement?
- Will the policy help to prepare adolescents for adulthood?
- Is it likely that this policy will strengthen and support families?
- Does it create a moral climate for children?
- Will it ensure adequate health care for all children?

The State of Child and Family Policy in the United States

Although these questions and processes we have described provide admirable guidelines for the development of child and family policies, the student of these issues must understand that they are rarely, if ever, actually the central questions in determining which policies get implemented. "Decision making about children's lives," writes one policy analyst, "has evolved piecemeal and without benefit of much compelling or thoughtful analysis" (Brewer, 1983, p. 63). Children's policies tend to be proposed, passed (sometimes), and implemented under crisis conditions. They are typically stopgap measures rather than thoughtfully planned efforts formulated at leisure. They tend to propose potential ways to solve, rather than to prevent, children's problems.

THE HISTORY OF CHILD POLICY IN THE UNITED STATES

During the nation's first century, the hardest task facing children was simply surviving. The chance of living to adulthood in the colonies was only about 50 percent. The passage of another century brought little improvement; over half of all deaths in New York City in 1869 were of children under 5 years of age (Smith,

1869). Congenital problems, infectious diseases, failure to breast-feed, and unsanitary living conditions accounted for the greatest proportion of these deaths (Kopp, 1983). Consequently, among the earliest child-oriented policies were those intended simply to keep children alive: laws regarding sanitation and the provision of safe supplies of milk were some of the earliest of these (Hall, 1993).

Changes in American society following the Civil War had an inestimable impact on the lives of children. Kessen (1965) has outlined three such changes. First, the world of the workplace and the world of the home became polarized in response to increasing postwar industrialization in America. Secondly, the expectations for and societally sanctioned roles of men and women diverged markedly; women were assigned a place in the home, and men were more traditionally associated with the out-of-home workforce. Finally, the world of the young child came to be associated with that of the mother, and child rearing became increasingly the responsibility of women (Hall, 1987).

The late nineteenth century brought other changes as the idea flowered that society could best be improved through the protection and care of children. Cravens (1987) referred to the period from 1870 to 1920 as the **child welfare era.** Restrictions of child labor, the conception and later enforcement of universal education in America, the establishment of societies for the prevention of cruelty to children, the founding of reform schools, orphanages, and child study institutes, and a growing attention to the physical and medical needs of children all mark this period as a sort of renaissance for children, in theory if not always in actual practice (Bremner, 1971b; Jacobs & Davies, 1994; White, 1979).

Such advances in child welfare paved the way for child policy in the twentieth century. Concerns about these and other issues, discussed at the nation's first White House Children's Conference in 1909, prompted the establishment of the United States Children's Bureau, the first federal agency devoted solely to concerns of child health and welfare. During this same era, Congress passed the Sheppard-Towner Act. Though it was soon repealed by opponents spearheaded by the American Medical Association (who represented the interests of physicians), Sheppard-Towner established models for badly needed maternal and child health clinics.

In the next several decades, the Children's Bureau and a network of child study centers created at universities throughout the nation collected a wealth of data on children and the factors that placed them at risk for poor medical, social, and cognitive outcomes. Federal policies at the time concentrated on the children who most often were felt to be unfortunate and needy recipients of public charity—these tended to be white children living in poverty. A growing body of evidence attested to the harms accruing to children from poverty and suggested ways to ameliorate the effects of such privation.

The 1930s brought the establishment of the Society for Research in Child Development (SRCD), but although a number of government and public welfare agencies involved in the study and assistance of children also flourished in the 1930s (Anderson, 1956), decades would pass before SRCD and other child study agencies became involved in the policy process. Moreover, many efforts on behalf of children were halted or severely curtailed by the Great Depression.

Following World War II (which, ironically, had ushered in the first federally sponsored child care, enabling women to participate in the war industry) came a period of renewed prosperity for many families. Two of the effects of this period of relative national affluence went hand-in-hand: First, an alarming disparity became apparent between middle- and upper-socioeconomic-status children and children living in poverty; and second, the nation determined to devote its resources to doing something about the poverty in which too many American children lived. The Johnson administration's War on Poverty and Great Society programs responded with federal involvement in and support for programs such as Women, Infants and Children (WIC), which provided food supplements for infants and toddlers and for pregnant and nursing women; Medicaid; food stamp and school lunch initiatives; Title XX of the Social Security Act, which provided child-care subsidies; and Head Start, the most ambitious and far-reaching preschool intervention ever mounted in the United States.

By the early 1970s, funding the war in Vietnam had channeled away much of the prosperity that had made the United States as a nation so generous with its children. At the same time, scholars, acting in a new role as child advocates, were delivering mixed reports on the efficacy of the energy and money being invested in early intervention and social support programs. As we continue throughout this volume to discuss these and more recent developments in the history of child policy, we will discuss in detail the role that scholars played—and continue to play—in child policy; this period saw the birth of such efforts.

THE POLICY PROCESS

Prerequisites

Certain features are necessary and sufficient to the successful development of social policies. First, the citizenry must have a sense of the immediacy of the problem at hand. This often results from the cumulative impact of a perennial problem (substance abuse, juvenile crime) that the public perceives as worsening, but a crisis or tragedy that befalls a single family can also be a powerful policy motivator. In 1994, a 7-year-old New Jersey child named Megan Kanka was kidnapped and murdered by a neighbor with a history of convictions for sexual offenses against children. This highly visible case—and widespread public expressions of concern by citizens that their children could be vulnerable to similar attacks—led several states to enact so-called "Megan's Laws." The New Jersey Sexual Offender Registration Act of 1994 (Breig, 1996), the prototype of these laws, mandates the registration with local law enforcement officials of sex offenders released from prison, and—depending on the perceived likelihood that the perpetrator will commit new offenses—the notification of residents that a convicted sex offender has moved into the area.

Events like these generate a groundswell of public awareness and public sentiment. Thus New Jersey also met the second condition for successful development of policy: there must exist a broad-based lobby working to support the foundation of the policy. Following the news of Megan Kanka's murder and the announcement that the suspect in the killing had a history of arrests for sex offenses and had been released after serving only a few months of a ten-year sentence, the public outrage was enough to stir citizen's groups into action.

The third requirement for successful policy development is that there must be pivotal leverage points within the government to which to apply pressure in favor of passage of legislation or implementation of policy. In New Jersey, both the state congress and the governor's office were eager to comply with public demand that something be done to safeguard the state's children. (Be aware, however, that many have argued that "Megan's Laws" are both unconstitutional and ineffective at protecting children because they promote a false sense of security among parents—see Brieg, 1996, and Davis, 1996, for a full discussion of these issues).

Stages in Policy Development

Like the growth of children themselves, the evolution of child and family policy can be thought of as a developmental process. Regardless of whether a policy issue arises at the national, state, or local level, or whether a given concern is expressed within a major corporation, a small business, a local school district, or a community, policy development typically follows the same steps.

The **initiation phase** begins when a given problem is first identified. Suppose that medical researchers and practitioners begin to suspect that measles cases are on the rise again. A decline during the 1980s of the percentage of U.S. children inoculated against measles resulted in an epidemic that affected 55,000 children between 1989 and 1991. A fifth of these were hospitalized; 130 died. The recognition of this problem marks the beginning of the policy process. Evaluation of the full scope of the problem, begun informally during the initiation phase, characterizes what Brewer (1983) calls the second, or **estimation phase** of policy development. Systematic exploration of the extent of the problem can enable the responsible parties to make educated guesses about what will happen if any of several courses of action are taken, and what the consequences might be if no action is taken. In our example, agencies like the Centers for Disease Control and Prevention reviewed their epidemiological data on the incidence of measles to determine whether cases really were on the rise. Health organizations and children's advocates determined that several factors helped account for the decline in widespread protection against measles—among them the complicated scheduling of the series of vaccinations required to inoculate a young child against measles, the cost of these vaccinations, and, above all, lack of awareness among parents that the disease was still around and that it was potentially a devastating, even deadly, disease. All of these findings were factored into projections of how widespread the problem could become and what its implications might be both with and without intervention.

The search for **solutions** (Brewer, 1983; Weiss, in press) occupies the next stage, and leads to either a choice of one or more courses of action, or a decision to take a wait-and-see approach. In a typical case, a number of different, sometimes unrelated, agencies may propose solutions, one or more of which are then put into action in the **implementation stage** of this process. In our measles example, Congress decided to allocate increased funding to subsidize early childhood immunization programs while government and public health agencies at all levels mounted a public education campaign aimed at encouraging parents to have their children vaccinated against measles. Health registries helped to locate unvaccinated children, and local school boards became more vigilant about ensuring that all kindergarten students had proof that their immunizations were up to date. Private-sector parties got involved as well. For instance, Hallmark, the greeting card company, provided hundreds of thousands of immunization reminder cards to be sent to the parents of young children.

The fifth, sixth, and seventh phases of the policy process complete the loop begun with recognition of a problem. After proposed solutions have been executed, **evaluation** of the plan's effectiveness is the next appropriate step, though this can take place weeks, months, or even years after the problem has been addressed. The effectiveness of the measles-reduction program, for example, might not be fully known for years, though it looks as though the program is having an impact: by 1996 the rate of measles among young children had fallen to fewer than 1 case per 100,000 children, a drop from 44 cases per 100,000 in 1990 (Children's Defense Fund, 1997c). *Termination of ineffective or outmoded programs* (Weiss, in press) is the logical next step, along with the final stage in the process, revising or reviewing decisions about whether to end programs that have completely solved the problem in question, or whether to modify them in some way to make them more effective. Ideally, these final stages form a sort of feedback loop—again, the modified programs might be evaluated for their effectiveness and further modifications to the programs might be made.

Doing the Right Thing Is Not Enough

As we have noted, this is not the best of all possible worlds for children's policy development. The list of the stages in policy formulation we just outlined is at best a guideline for what a child-friendly model should look like. In reality, the process is complicated by the number of varying positions that vie for representation of their interests in the finished policy product, by the scope and nature of the problem itself, and by the availability of the resources necessary for its redressal.

The Players

The number and nature of the players in the policy process add another layer of complexity. Broadly speaking, the participants involved in deciding any given policy question fall into three groups: those who are affected by the issue at hand, those who have expertise in the area in question, and those who have the authority to bring about change (Aronson, 1993). One of the central topics defining the Clinton administration's focus during its first four years, for example, was whether health care coverage could be provided, equitably and affordably, for all Americans regardless of their economic, employment, or health status.

Like many overarching policy issues, the question of universal health care provision had come up before, most recently during the Nixon administration. Now, as then, many voices were heard.

The most numerous voices were those of the American populace. At the time, 12 million U.S. children were neither covered by private or employer health insurance nor eligible for Medicare or Medicaid (Carnegie Corporation, 1994). Even parents with full-time, year-round employment were more likely to be without insurance than to have coverage for their children; nonwhite families were disproportionately uninsured or underinsured (Lowe, 1993; Schroeder, 1993). The very idea of a universal health care plan, therefore, particularly in the earlier days of this controversy, was wildly popular among voters. Employers, too, had a stake in determining the outcome of this plan, and many feared that the burden of subsidizing such care would handicap large corporations and bankrupt smaller ones. Insurance companies feared that they would either be bypassed altogether, or that their programs, policies, and costs and benefits would be dictated by the federal government. And congressional leaders, under pressure from both private and public sectors, put forth a variety of proposals either describing how universal coverage could be achieved or explaining why it couldn't or even shouldn't be.

In the months following President Clinton's call for the development of a universal health care plan that would cover all Americans, the United States witnessed what seemed to many to be a free-for-all in Congress, the media, and behind the closed doors of lobbying groups and corporate coalitions. Months of debate produced mountains of paperwork detailing everything from the broadest of rationales for universal health care plans to the minutia of the mechanisms necessary for providing it. President Clinton's own plan took more than 250 pages to describe and was published as a commercially available paperback book (White House Domestic Policy Council, 1993). A fast and furious advertising campaign ensued in which such coverage was alternately depicted as a fundamental right of all citizens and an Orwellian nightmare in which Americans would lose all control over their own medical decisions, and the tone of the whole discussion changed.

Confused by the variety of information and misinformation on what the differing health care proposals would mean for the United States, public sentiment in favor of such a plan gradually waned. In the end, no compromise could be reached between President Clinton's demand for full coverage for all Americans and congressional attempts to meet the expressed needs of all of the players involved. The call for universal health coverage was ultimately dropped from the congressional agenda, although certain provisions were made to expand coverage for low-income children, and other options continued to be explored at the state level. Certainly, however, this same issue will come up again at the federal level in future years.

Social scientists were not absent from this debate. The Children's Defense Fund gathered data based on the plans that, of the several health care plans proposed in Congress, were most likely to succeed. From these numbers they were able to project the probable outcomes for children and families of each of these plans. Similarly, the National Center for Children in Poverty, the American Academy of Pediatrics, the March of Dimes, and other groups who advocate for children and families weighed in with information on what they believed would be the outcomes for children and families of any reform in health care coverage.

Social scientists today are active participants in the policy process, but this has only been the case for the past few decades. Although psychology has existed as a field for approximately 120 years, and though child development has been studied more or less systematically since before the turn of the century, many social scientists were previously reluctant to apply their talents to the Byzantine business of policy. Historically, even social scientists themselves have tended to depreciate their role in social policy formation. Lazar (in Kagan, in press) cites only the following three studies as having had a direct impact on policy decisions.

In the 1940s, Rene Spitz studied infants in institutional care. These infants, who were given only the most rudimentary custodial care, spent virtually all of their time in cribs. They were handled briefly for diaper changes and bathing, but they were seldom held, cuddled, or talked to, even at feeding time, when bottles were propped within their reach. Spitz (1945) found that these children were grossly delayed by these experiences in both their social and cognitive development, and that even their physical growth was stunted. This work revolutionized thinking about the nature of nonparental child care and led to improvements in the care of children in orphanages, hospitals, and even child-care facilities; it is still cited today when child-care quality is studied or discussed.

Research also played a small but critical role in *Brown v. Board of Education.* The significance of the 1954 Supreme Court case was twofold. First, the justices overturned the constitutionality of the "separate but equal" doctrine previously upheld in the 1896 *Plessy v. Ferguson* case. They decided unanimously in favor of the argument by the young attorney Thurgood Marshall that segregated schools are inherently unequal. Secondly, they rule that segregation makes the statement that blacks are inferior to whites. Research by Clark and Clark (1952) was presented as evidence on this point: In the Clarks' study, which involved black and white dolls, black children indicated their belief that the white dolls were superior. The presentation of the Clarks' data was a pivotal point in the argument in favor of Brown.

The third case cited by Lazar involves a group of studies. In 1983, the Consortium for Longitudinal Studies published the findings of a number of independent studies of the impact of early intervention on children at high risk for the development of social or educational deficits. By presenting empirical evidence of the effectiveness of preschool programs that targeted in some cases the child and in other cases the entire family, the Consortium paved the way for a wave of such programs and had a direct and positive impact on congressional willingness to support such efforts.

Child policy in this nation is characterized by an eleventh-hour, piecemeal approach, both to program implementation and to the funding of support efforts. We are somewhat more sanguine than Lazar, however, about the effect that social science has had on policy development. A classic survey of federal decision makers found that 91 percent were able to describe specific instances of how social sciences research had influenced their decision making (Caplan, 1975; see also chapter 3 for a discussion of how social scientists might have more effect on policy). The Society for Research in Child Development (SRCD) has also adopted an important role by welcoming into its respected journal papers on using scientific research to benefit children. Although the acceptance of research related to social policy has been slow and gradual within the field of psychology, SRCD's decision to admit into its pages articles dealing with applied work will likely do much to encourage greater social responsibility within its membership, as well as to foster more rigorous applied studies that might enjoy greater acceptance in the scientific community (Zigler, 1998).

There is no question that the role played by social scientists in policy development is sometimes controversial. Social scientists are often perceived as being, as a group, somewhat to the left of the political center. This stereotype is largely unjustified, but it is true that social science data are often offered in support of programs intended to benefit groups who are traditionally seen as being politically marginalized, such as poor families and their children. It is important to bear in mind, however, that as social scientists come to be taken for granted as legitimate players in the policy arena, groups from all segments of the political spectrum are beginning to employ social science methods and data in the service of mounting and evaluating programs. The Cato Institute and the Heritage Foundation, for instance, are conservative think tanks whose members make use of information gathered and interpreted by social scientists.

More recently, the involvement of social scientists in policy development has come to be taken for granted (though it might still be resisted in some camps). Making use of the knowledge bases available to psychologists, social workers, social science researchers, educators, medical practitioners, and others who work directly with children and families and who can speak knowledgeably about their needs strengthens the utility and long-term effectiveness of social policies.

Beyond political and ideological considerations, social scientists must combat other popular images of their profession and their potential contribution to the policy process. Input derived from social science research might also be suspect because of the complexity of the phenomena with which they deal. Unlike hard sciences, in which formulae and rules that describe the relationships among variables can be rigorously defined, psychology, psychiatry, sociology, and related fields study outcomes that are multiply determined and often difficult to operationalize. Moreover, scientists and policy makers are creatures of different worlds. As Weiss and Jacobs (1988) note, they have different norms, expectations, time pressures, resources, and influences. Policy makers do not always know how to approach and seek the input of researchers and clinicians, nor do they always know what sorts of information to ask for. They might not know whether the data they need are currently available, or whether they ought to commission new studies; when they do request new studies, they might not be sure how to instruct the investigators chosen to design them. Issues of research methodology are usually outside the sphere of the policy maker, who is apt to want results within a briefer time frame than that in which the researcher is accustomed to working, and who is unlikely to be thoroughly versed in the statistical and methodological issues underlying the interpretation of research findings.

By the same token, academicians often lack an understanding of the practical issues facing children and families, and of how their own work might be applied to such areas. Social scientists, too, are limited by the framework of their professional field—they might balk at being asked to provide data on questions not of their own defining, and be galled at policy outcomes that seem to them inconsistent with or not directly following from their findings. The complexities of the policy process, with its balance of resources, political pressures, and constituencies, can frustrate the social scientist who feels that the outcome of her research should be sufficient to prompt legislators to "do the right thing."

Knowledge derived from research can, in fact, drive policy, as the examples above illustrate. But knowledge seldom is translated directly into action. Findings from studies of what constitutes high-quality child care, for instance, might clearly define the appropriate caregiver-to-child ratios for different age groups, but individual state legislatures, hampered by dwindling funds available through block grants and increased competition among many worthy recipients of these moneys, cannot always accommodate these requirements.

In future chapters, we will explore more fully the role of social scientists in the policy process. Here it is important to describe the ways in which—and the stages at which—empirically derived and clinical data are most likely to influence the outcome of policy debates. Once a problem has been identified, social scientists are especially able to provide useful input in three ways. First, social scientists are better experienced than policy makers at formulating the questions that need to be answered in order to both understand social problems and arrive at their solutions. Second, social scientists play an indispensable role in conducting the actual research necessary to provide a database from which to identify these solutions. Identifying groups of people to study, selecting the most appropriate surveys, tests, and other measurement tools, drawing samples from the populations in question, supervising the collection of data, and performing the statistical analyses of the data as they are gathered are all appropriate roles for social scientists. Finally, social scientists are needed to help with the interpretation of research findings, and they can assist policy makers as they derive the implications for policy development (Weiss and Jacobs, 1988).

THE POLICY PRODUCT

In the United States, virtually all family policy tends to share certain characteristics. We will not go into detail about these here, but your understanding of the policies and decisions discussed throughout the book will be enhanced by your awareness of them. First, in policy development the emphasis is almost invariably on the economic bottom line (for the nation, a state, a private company, etc.) rather than on whether a given policy enhances the mental health or

 # talks

social competence of those affected by its provisions. Policies that benefit children and families are far more likely to be enacted if they serve adult and/or economic goals.

target / *poverty*

Second, child and family policy tends overwhelmingly to be targeted rather than universal. For instance, food supplements under the federal Women, Infants and Children (WIC) program are available, not to all new mothers and their children, but only to those who meet certain income and age requirements. Like WIC, most social programs for children and families are **means-tested,** available only to families living below certain income levels. Arguments based on cost containment fail to address social and economic benefits accruing from universal programs like public education.

treatment not prevention

In addition, U.S. child and family policies are overwhelmingly treatment-oriented rather than focused on **primary prevention.** And although this is changing slowly, as we will discuss later in this chapter, policy makers still only rarely consider the body of empirical research on the needs of families and children when making policy decisions that will affect their lives. Instead, the child and family policy arena is characterized by actions taken only as a last resort, and by a focus on treating problems after the fact rather than on implementing policies that would reduce or prevent the development of problems in the first place. Given this background, it is no surprise that policies are often enacted without a full appreciation of their long-term implications (Shore, 1983).

    ## *Child Legislation and the Proper Role of Government: An Ongoing Debate*

The tension between those who favor a nonintervention policy for government and those who feel that its responsibility is to care for and provide services for its citizens can be detected in virtually every policy debate having to do with legislation that would affect children and families. As a testament to the fact that this is a perennial debate, consider the following excerpt from the *Congressional Record* of the 62nd Congress. The debate concerns legislation that this same Congress signed into law in 1912:

Senator Heyburn of Idaho: I am not going to discuss the bill at length, but I am very loath to see the matter come to a vote. . . . The jurisdiction established over the children of mankind in the beginning of the human race has worked out very well. It is in accord with the rules of nature. It is based not upon duty

but upon the human instinct that establishes the principle upon which all duties rest. The mother needs no admonition to care for the child, nor does the father. . . . [W]e know from some other measures which have been introduced, some from the same source, that [this bill] contemplates the establishment of a control, through the agencies of government, over the rearing of children. There are other measures now pending in committees of this body going much further, going to the extent of interference with the control of a parent over the child. . . . This is not a proper subject for legislation. It is a police measure. . . . No one can be more sympathetic than I am with the needs, the welfare, and the comfort of the children of the country, but I am not willing to substitute any other control for that of the parent.

Congressional Record, 62nd Congress, 2nd Session (1911–1912), XLVIII, Pt. 1, 189.

Legislation affecting children and families in the United States often is passed only reluctantly, and even more often is not passed at all because of a pervasive reluctance among policy makers to "intrude" on family life. The political zeitgeist supports the notion that government intervention, in the form of service provision or the establishment of standards, interferes with parental rights. This position stands in opposition to the notion that the government's role *is* primarily one of service provision to its citizens.

These two positions came head-to-head in 1971 in a classic confrontation over the appropriate function of government, when President Nixon was given the opportunity to sign into law the nation's first comprehensive child-care bill, the Comprehensive Child Development Act. The act's becoming law appeared likely until a coalition of conservative political organizations like the John Birch Society and conservative religious groups mounted a massive grassroots campaign founded on the idea that the bill would interfere with "a family centered approach" to child rearing (Nixon, 1971; Zigler & Lang, 1991). In the end, after passage by Congress, the bill was vetoed by President Nixon. Social scientists wishing to have a positive influence on the development of child policy would do well to keep this in mind and to affirm that the primacy of parents' roles will not be undermined—and will, when possible, be strengthened—by such policy.

A fourth characteristic of U.S. policy is that it stresses treatment rather than primary prevention. Ironically, this is in spite of data from fields as diverse as medicine, education, early intervention, social work, and others that establishes beyond dispute the cost-effectiveness of primary prevention and early intervention.

In the chapters ahead, we will outline broadly defined topics of policy concern such as child health, child care, and education. These topics vary in the situations on which they comment, in the problems they pose and the opportunities they offer to children and families, and in the solutions that might exist to address these problems, but all of them can be better understood in terms of the framing principles presented in this chapter. In the future, too, whether you are a scholar, parent, concerned citizen, or policy maker yourself, these principles can serve as both guidelines and a place from which to start a more in-depth understanding of the policy issues affecting children and families in the United States.

SUMMARY

In the 1980s and 1990s, questions pertaining to the welfare of children and families became what are now apparently permanent fixtures on the nation's social agenda, but this was not always the case. As our nation grew, the goals of child policy evolved as well. Up until the early years of the twentieth century, for instance, merely maximizing children's survival rates was the most important thing that could be done for children. Today, child and family policy fulfills a number of roles, including the provision of services intended to prevent or solve problems, the establishment of administrative infrastructure related to children's issues, and the creation of bodies charged with the oversight of these and other projects. It must be emphasized that policies related to child welfare are not always pro-child; the needs of children are often perceived as conflicting with the needs of special interest groups.

Milestones in our history have been associated with changes in the way children's issues are perceived. Demographic changes and an increasing polarization between home and work life, and between the traditional roles of men and women, redefined childhood and, consequently, views on who should be held accountable for meeting children's needs. Increasing industrialization in the twentieth century and changes in the labor force following World War II brought additional changes. By the 1960s, a stable economy not yet seriously challenged by the Vietnam War, coupled with an increasing disparity between prosperous and economically disadvantaged families, prompted a call for societal responses to poverty and educational deficits. This period represented the greatest leap forward in child policy in our history. And it brought into the policy arena a diverse group of players with diverse needs and interests: representatives of judicial, legislative, and executive governments at the national, state, and local levels, and child advocates, parents, and the media. In addition, social scientists, who were not always welcomed or respected by policy makers in the past, began to play a central role in evaluating and implementing policy options.

The history of child and family policy in the United States reflects a variety of pervasive themes that still characterize the policy arena today: tension between different views of the purpose and responsibility of government for its citizens; debate over whether such responsibilities should be taken on primarily by the state or by federal government; and an adult-centered, economically oriented approach to child policy. Policy decisions affecting children and families continue largely to be crisis decisions, intended to fix rather than prevent problems, with solutions targeted to the narrowest possible group of recipients. In spite of these characteristics of the policy-making process, recent attention to children's issues and the fact that social scientists have become permanent players in this field lend hope that the situation is slowly changing in the direction of positive action for children.

CHAPTER 3

Influences and Advocates

The child advocacy movement looks both forward and backward. Proponents of policies that serve and protect the best interests of children and families must constantly assess the potential outcomes of their actions (whether successful or not). At the same time, the historical roots of the child advocacy movement continue both to shape public and private perceptions of the movement and to mediate its effectiveness. In this chapter we will explore the nature and meaning of advocacy for children in the United States, its origins, its different faces, the strategies and forces that shape it, and its accomplishments and failures.

Exactly what is child advocacy? As you begin to answer this question, consider the following scenarios:

In the nineteenth century, a national labor organization—motivated by concern for the jobs and wages of its adult constituents—lobbies its members to support passage of legislation restricting child labor.

In the 1970s, research by two pediatricians (Klaus & Kennel, 1976) suggests that a critical period for the establishment of a healthy bond between mother and child occurs immediately after birth. Although further research indicates that the development of an attachment between mothers and children is far more complex and subtle than their research indicates, this seminal work on "bonding" is to a large degree responsible for the widespread implementation of sensitive, family-oriented policies in hospital labor rooms, newborn nurseries, and maternity wards.

A large business corporation and a richly endowed philanthropic foundation both subsidize a public radio network's reporting on child and family issues.

The parents of a 7-year-old boy with multiple disabilities, unhappy over the level of services available to him in their school district, work to convince their reluctant school board that the law requires it to pay the cost of the child's tuition and transportation to a special education program in a private children's psychiatric hospital.

A small study group at Yale University meets in the mid 1980s to discuss the ways in which a U.S. national parental leave policy would affect children, families, and businesses. Eventually the recommendations of this multidisciplinary committee are considered by legislators drafting the bill that becomes the first U.S. family leave act.

A large corporation polls employees about their child-care needs and establishes an on-site child-care center.

When a mother learns that her premature newborn son, who died following cardiothoracic surgery, was given no anesthesia during his several operations, and that newborn surgery without anesthesia is routine, she tirelessly petitions lawmakers and medical associations to legislate against this practice. A wave of research on pediatric pain management is launched, and the U.S. Department of Health and Human Services issues a statement in support of reform in this area; the practice gradually changes (Hall, 1992).

Each of these situations, all of which represent real events, features an action taken on behalf of a child or children, and yet they are all very different in nature. Which of these situations involve child advocacy? What social and political conditions facilitated change in each case? What variables impeded change? What other issues are involved in these situations? In this chapter we will address issues that will help you to answer these questions.

WHAT IS CHILD ADVOCACY?

Advocates for children are those who press for reforms that will result in better lives for children, or for the maintenance of the status quo in areas in which children are being well served by existing policies and practices. As we will see later on in this chapter, advocates can be individuals or groups, and can operate on any level—federal, state, or local—at which decisions regarding policies and practices affecting children and families are made. They might work alone, or in collaboration with other advocates. They might be concerned with a single issue, or with the overall well-being of children.

Changes in the ways governments, schools, or businesses operate with respect to the needs of children and families rarely occur in the absence of advocacy. Children are seldom able to act for themselves in legislative and regulatory arenas, so the need for adults to advocate for them is obvious. If a problem exists, some person or group must see to it that the public is made aware of the issue, and press for change. When policies and practices safeguard and improve the welfare of children and families, some person or group must monitor the situation and work to sustain these efforts. Advocacy has been practiced in these ways for as long as people have cared for and protected one another (Blom, Keith, & Tomber, 1984; Imig, 1995; Zigler & Finn-Stevenson, 1993).

Advocacy from Antiquity to the Present

In chapter 2 you read about the beginnings of child policy in the United States, but in fact the roots of the advocacy movement are hundreds of years old. Child social policy was being enacted as early as the second century A.D., when a foundation to save female infants from destruction was established by the Empress Faustina (Garrison, 1965). Brephetrophia, or children's asylums, were established by the Council of Nicea in A.D. 325, and a century later the Council of Vaison similarly designated the church as being responsible for the welfare of homeless children (Zigler & Hall, 1989). Many believe that in 787 the Archbishop Datheus of Milan established the first foundling hospital (Cone, 1983), and although its success is reported to have been limited, others followed suit: Pope Innocent III ordered the building of institutions to care for the many illegitimate children left in the wake of the thirteenth-century crusades, and the Roman Empress Catherine II built similar facilities (Radbill, 1974). Erasmus and Plutarch spoke out publicly against the abuse of children. Henry II of France and England's King James both showed themselves to be child advocates by passing laws forbidding the concealment of the birth of a child. Historians of child welfare (Ariès, 1962; Boswell, 1988; Radbill, 1974) describe laws against infanticide in numerous ancient and modern civilizations.

More recent antecedents of the modern child advocacy movement can be found in the social reforms of the late nineteenth century. Increasing divisions of labor between men and women and between home and workplace redefined parenting, implicitly assigning more responsibility for daily child care to women (Kessen, 1965, 1979; Stendler, 1950; Wertsch & Youniss, 1987). The societal changes associated with the dawning of the Industrial Revolution were accompanied by further shifts in the meaning of childhood. The image of the child as a noble savage whose innate goodness might emerge as a matter of maturation if unhindered by society had already been popularized by the publication of Rousseau's *Emile* in 1792 (Kessen, 1965). This depiction was a stepping stone to the nineteenth-century image of the child as the hope for the future of the country. The seeds of these changes were sown during earlier centuries. The work of seventeenth-century philosopher John Locke had emphasized the role of experience in shaping the child, and Swiss educator Johann Pestalozzi, in 1774, described the importance of childhood as a period of learning (Cone, 1983; Kessen, 1965).

The most radical changes in our conceptions of childhood, though, were ushered in by Charles Darwin and Sigmund Freud. Darwin, through his studies of evolution and his documentation of early childhood (Darwin, 1877), "gave us the child as a legitimate source of scientific information about the nature of man" (Kessen, 1965, p. 117). Sigmund Freud revolutionized the study of childhood and our conceptions of the child through his emphasis on childhood as the

---

 ## The Founding of an Advocacy Group
The Society for the Prevention of Cruelty to Children

In the spring of 1874, a social worker in New York City discovered a young girl chained, starved, and beaten in the apartment of her adoptive parents. Eight-year-old Mary Ellen Wilson, known in media reports as "Little Mary Ellen," became the focus of a celebrated child protection case, generating tremendous media interest and arousing strong public sentiment. When the case first came to the attention of the New York City Police Department, they refused to take action, as there existed at that time no laws to require or allow them to intervene when children were abused by their parents or guardians. The case became known, however, to a Mr. Henry Berg, a prominent New York social figure and the founder of the Society for Prevention of Cruelty to Animals. Through his intervention, Mary Ellen's case was brought to trial, and her adoptive mother was found guilty of felonious assault. The case did not come under the auspices of the SPCA itself, as is sometimes held, but Berg's influence and the graphic and lengthy newspaper coverage of the trial were the main catalysts in the founding of the Society for the Prevention of Cruelty to Children in 1875.

Bremner, 1971b

most influential period of life. Although Freud is rarely credited with being a developmental thinker, many have acknowledged the debt that we do owe him: "the greatest and most beautiful effect of Freudianism is the increasing awareness of childhood as the most important single influence on human development" (Kazin, 1957, p. 59).

Increasing media attention to child labor issues (Bremner, 1971a, 1971b; Cahn & Cahn, 1972) and the need for a better and more uniformly educated populace ushered in a new period of reforms in child welfare during the late nineteenth and early twentieth centuries. Child labor restrictions and the birth and gradual growth of universal public education eventually moved thousands of children from workplaces to schools. The fifty years following the Civil War were also characterized by the proliferation of child study institutions, advances in pediatric medicine, and the establishment of reform schools and orphanages (Cravens, 1987; Jacobs & Davies, 1994; U.S. Department of Health, Education and Welfare, 1976).

Child Labor Restriction: An Illustration of the Principles of Child Advocacy

The movement that opposed child labor in the United States has been called the first national child advocacy movement (Ross, 1983). During the last two decades of the nineteenth century, political and rhetorical pressure—both formal and grassroots—were brought to bear in this area. In 1881, the American Federation of Laborers (AFL), in their first meeting, committed themselves to the abolishment of child labor practices. The first formal national advocacy group for children, the National Child Labor Committee, was formed to address this issue.

The plight of underage workers in mills and factories was terrible indeed. Children as young as 5 years old were forced to work ten to twelve hours a day, six days a week, in abusive conditions for meager wages. Many died or were permanently crippled by the ill health that resulted from backbreaking physical labor, continuous exposure to extremes of temperature, the environmental hazards in mills, mines, chimneys and factories, and malnutrition (Cahn & Cahn, 1972). It is important to note, however, that compassion and concern for these children was *not* the sole, or even the primary, motivating force behind the calls for reforms. Instead, groups like the AFL were spurred to action largely by the desire to protect and conserve these jobs for their own constituency: adult workers who were often shut out of the labor force by the steady supply of cheap child labor.

This point illustrates a basic principle of child advocacy that cannot be overemphasized: Though concern and compassion for children and families typically lies at the heart of child advocacy, successful bids for reform are more likely to be driven by economic agendas and a focus on adult and general societal welfare. The child welfare campaigns likeliest to be successful are those in which it can be demonstrated that "doing the right thing" for children has positive, measurable, and far-reaching ramifications for business, industry, or government.

The timing of child labor legislation was also propitious and illustrates another axiom of successful child advocacy. As Ross (1983) notes, by the time the National Child Labor Committee became active in 1904, children were already being phased out of many of the jobs in question as a function of the increasing complexity of many of those occupations. Thus it is essential to emphasize that the *timing* of social and political events plays a critical role in the passage of legislation or the rendering of policy decisions affecting children. Only when the convergence of ideas and events is optimal will children benefit.

The tasks assumed by the National Child Labor Committee were eventually shouldered by the U.S. Children's Bureau, founded by President Taft in 1912. This agency represented the federal government's commitment to participation in child welfare activities. Not until 1916, however, was the first federal prohibition against child labor signed into law; this law, along with a second one passed in 1918, was declared unconstitutional by the Supreme Court. The nation's first child labor law to be let stand by the Supreme Court was not implemented until 1930. Thus, another principle of child advocacy is illustrated by the history of child labor in America: Even under the best of circumstances, policy development is a long, slow process.

Advocacy in the Great Society: The 1960s and 1970s

In more recent history, the 1960s and 1970s saw a major shift—in favor of government support for children and families—in child policy making, a shift that both resulted from and bolstered the burgeoning advocacy movement. The conception of advocacy also expanded during this period to include some new players; in particular, research and scholarship assumed a pivotal function. The role of advocates as collectors of knowledge about children and as distributors of that information to policy makers assumed a new importance. At the same time, the role of academic child study as a source of this information raised new questions about whether scholars should stop at building the kind of empirical databases useful to child advocates, or whether scholars might function in an advocacy role themselves (Imig, 1995).

Throughout the 1960s and 1970s, but particularly during the Kennedy, Johnson, and Nixon administrations, the federal government contributed substantial resources to the development of social programs. State governments, too, promoted and assumed an important role in the provision of social welfare services. As these events developed, new players began to emerge and to play a variety of roles in the development of child policies and programs.

Children's advocates during this period were unlikely to be formal groups organized for the purpose of supporting social policy initiatives. Instead they were largely grassroots patrons of change: civil rights groups, unions, churches, consumer and public interest groups, and organizations of professionals in the areas of education and social welfare. Parents, too, perhaps spurred by movements promoting gender and racial equality, joined the ranks of advocates for children; as we will discuss more fully later in this chapter, their actions are uniquely effective in several ways (Pizzo, 1983, 1995; Zigler & Finn-Stevenson, 1993). These new players tended to support increased federal funding but at the same time created a new antifederal rhetoric based on their objections to "government interference" and "red tape."

A number of changes at this time stimulated researchers' interest in social policy. As state and federal governments contributed more resources and attention to the development of social programs, social scientists discovered new opportunities to participate in the policy process. The roles and tasks of social scientists in the policy process are many and varied. Some were first conceptualized during the 1960s and 1970s as opportunities arose to help design and implement programs aimed at improving children's lives. Programs like Project Head Start were natural settings in which to both serve children and learn more about their needs and their development.

It was also at this time that scholars in child development began to understand that they might use their knowledge to shape decisions made on behalf of children. Although there were significant tensions between purely academic research in this area and the applications of that research to "real-world" situations involving children and their families, scholars in greater numbers began not only to believe that they might apply their understanding to improving the quality of life for children; they also began to feel ethically compelled to do so (Stipek & McCroskey, 1989).

Finally, practical considerations prompted policy makers to seek the advice of experts in child development, education, and child health. Even when policy decisions, such as those related to the Johnson administration's War on Poverty, were motivated largely by moral and ethical concerns, the distribution of human and material resources was still driven by economics. To support and promote such actions, proof was needed that actions mandated on behalf of children were, in fact, addressing the targeted problems (e.g., educational failure, ill health) and that they were making a positive difference.

To mount programs that would effectively remediate the outcomes of poor education, health, housing, and child care in the United States, policy makers had to understand how children's environments affected their social, cognitive, and physical development. It was only natural for them to call upon developmental and clinical psychologists, pediatricians, sociologists, and educators and ask them to share their expertise, to gather **baseline data,** and to help establish programmatic goals for their efforts. Psychologists and other experts participated in government task forces, boards, and commissions. They testified before Congress. They acted as consultants for legislators and executive branch decision makers alike, all in the name of improving the lot of children and families.

The roles of scholars and experts developed as programs developed. One of their most important tasks revolved around investigating the outcomes of child and family programs. Did the programs do what they had set out to do? Were children better off for having participated in social service programs? Was program effectiveness long-lasting, and did it have any unintended consequences, either positive or negative? As the answers to these and related questions (which will be explored in coming chapters) were provided by scholars, precedents were set regarding the appropriateness of using child development scholarship to inform legislative and programmatic decisions. Though these precedents are not always honored, the argument for giving scholarship an important role in policy making was firmly established at this time.

Childhood Social Indicators

As program development and the surrounding research efforts grew, a body of knowledge was assembled in response to questions about the status of children and families in the United States (Zill, Sigal, & Brim, 1983). Information gathering, one of advocacy's most important tools, is not new. Julia Lathrop, first director of the U.S. Children's Bureau, began her job by collecting statistics and other information on childhood mortality. The role played by data like these grew as experts on children became more involved in the policy process. Today there are many child advocacy groups whose primary function is the collection and dissemination of information about the health and well-being of American children. The Washington, D.C., based Children's Defense Fund, for instance, while it performs many tasks in the service of children and families, performs an invaluable service by educating the public in general, and legislators in particular, about the often-unmet needs of children and families (Children's Defense Fund, 1998g).

Similarly, groups like the National Center for Children in Poverty, which tracks data on the economic and social consequences of poverty among families with children, serve a number of important functions by collecting and disseminating information about child welfare. The National Council for Jewish Women's Center for the Child has mounted efforts to improve family day care, encourage equitable treatment for working women, and strengthen parent involvement in children's education. A critical component of each of these efforts has been the collection and dissemination of relevant data on the problem in question.

Such data have three important functions: First, such information, which is collected on a yearly or more frequent basis, enables us to chart the status of children over a period of time, and points up areas in which we are making progress with respect to maintaining or improving child welfare, and those in which we are failing to advance or are even slipping. Second, collections of information on the status of children and families serve as a resource for those who design policy, as well as for those in both academia and the media: Reporters on issues of child development, scholars, and educators all rely heavily on such statistics to convey their messages about the effectiveness of child policy in the United States. Finally, the general public, by being made more aware of the issues children and families face today, are able to be more informed parents and more active participants in the policy-making process. Advocates who gather information on childhood social indicators play an especially important role during election years.

Even so, childhood social indicators still do not play as important a role in policy-making decisions as do, for instance, economic indicators like the Dow Jones Industrial Average, the New York Stock Exchange Composite Index, or the Consumer Price Index. Miringoff and his colleagues (Miringoff, 1995; Miringoff, Miringoff, & Opdycke, 1996) point out that the available data on the nation's financial health are gathered on a frequent and regular basis (daily, weekly, monthly, quarterly, and annually). Indices that measure and catalog child health and welfare, such as the infant mortality rate or the incidence of child abuse, are typically reported only once a year, and even then often involve a time lag, so that data being reported in a given year might reflect the status of events a year or more previously.

This problem has been noted before. One of the U.S. Children's Bureau's earliest tasks was the compilation in one volume, the *Handbook of Federal Statistics on Children* (U.S. Children's Bureau, 1913), of a more comprehensive picture of the status of children than that presented by data that were isolated in individual official documents. Although legislators since then (most notably Senator Walter Mondale) have called for a similar reporting forum, only the short-lived and irregularly published *Social Indicators* (U.S. Bureau of the Census, 1974, 1977, 1981), which was ultimately discontinued by President Reagan, came close to meeting this goal. Happily, social scientists have felt keenly the need for reliable and wideranging data on the status of children today, and a recent volume on indicators of child well-being presents the findings of researchers in areas such as economic security, family structure, health, and education (Hauser, Brown, & Prosser, 1998).

In the absence of an official and inclusive federal document on child welfare, private advocacy agencies have sought to fill the void. Perhaps the most successful and comprehensive of these efforts is the *Index of Social Health*, released annually by the Fordham Institute for Innovation in Social Policy (1995) at Fordham University in New York. Researchers at the Institute have developed an index of social health for children by combining national statistics for each of six social problems: infant mortality, child abuse, number of children in poverty, teen suicide, drug and alcohol abuse, and school dropout rates. The higher the incidence of these problems, the lower the index. The most recent of these indices is depicted in figure 3.1.

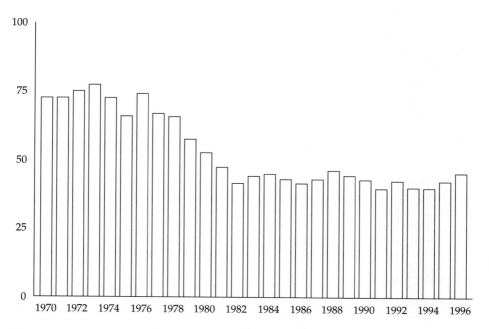

FIGURE 3.1. Index of Social Health, United States, 1970-1996.
Source: 1998 Index of Social Health: Monitoring the Social Well-Being of the Nation. Fordham Institute for Innovation in Social Policy. © Marc L. Miringuff, 1998.

CHILD ADVOCACY TODAY

Without benefit of advocacy, there can be no changes in the ways that governments, businesses, or educational institutions operate. Whenever a challenge or problem has an impact on children's lives, some individual or group must see to it that the institutional representatives responsible for policy making become aware of that problem and press for solutions. Advocacy has been defined as a combination of acting in behalf of one's own interests, pleading the cause of others, and defending or maintaining a cause (Zigler, 1984; Blom, Keith, & Tomber, 1984). Essentially, child advocates monitor the conditions of children's lives to ensure that needed improvements are made.

To bring about changes in practices or laws, policy makers and the public must first be made aware that there is a problem. Pressure must then be brought to bear, by advocates or by the general public, on those who are in a position of power over the situation in question. Finally, there must be receptive decision makers in Congress (or on the appropriate level, if the issue is a state or local one) willing to effect the required change. This usually occurs only if the solution to the problem in question is consistent with the legislator's personal and political agenda, or if the legislator's constituents are able to convince her that helping to implement a solution would be politically expedient for her.

The goals of child advocates might be pursued through single-issue campaigns (e.g., the elimination of corporal punishment in schools, adoption reforms, or anti-drunk-driving crusades), or they might be more general goals having to do with overall child welfare (the scope of the issues addressed by the Children's Defense Fund is a good example of the latter).

In addition to working with or targeting legislators and other decision makers in their efforts to promote positive changes for children and parents, advocates must also reach the general public. By bringing to the public a sense of the immediacy of children's needs, advocates generate further power on behalf of children. By mobilizing voters, and by prompting individual citizens to express to these same policy makers their own interests in having solutions to children's problems found, advocates broaden the power base of children and families and of those committed to addressing their needs.

As responsibility for children and their programs is increasingly shifting away from the federal government and onto the shoulders of state and local officials, advocates must adjust their focus to work with these policy makers. Later in this chapter we will examine the skills and strategies advocates must develop in order to do this effectively.

Advocacy at Work

Child advocates have focused on numerous important issues, such as child abuse and neglect, physical punishment, health care, and the special needs of poor children and children with disabilities. In their attempts to better children's lives, advocates direct their efforts at Congress and to local, state and federal governments, as well as at the courts, public schools, and various social service agencies.

A number of child advocacy groups, for instance, work on child-care issues. The New York–based group Child Care Action Campaign (CCAC) has been a particularly effective advocate for children and families in this area. Through diligent and skillful work with media representatives, CCAC has successfully generated public awareness of and interest in child-care issues and the problems that characterize much of the child care in the United States. Similarly, the Families and Work Institute (1998a, 1998b)—which was founded in 1989 by Dana Friedman and Ellen Galinsky, who are pioneers in the study of work life—consults and supports research on areas in which work life and family life intersect. The National Association for the Education of Young Children has also been especially diligent at increasing the availability of high-quality child-care slots through its child-care accreditation program.

Representatives of such groups inform policy makers of various issues that can result in poor-quality child care, such as staff turnover, low staff wages, and lack of training. Working in conjunction with child development researchers, and working through both professional publications and the

 ## Action for Children's Television

One advocacy group that officially is defunct but continues to affect the lives of children is Action for Children's Television (ACT). Established in 1963 by Peggy Charren, ACT struggled for more than thirty years with the television industry and with the federal groups with the power to regulate programming, scheduling, and the kinds of advertising viewed by children. ACT effectively promoted limits on the number and types of commercials that can be shown during children's programs and compelled networks to devote a certain percentage of children's programming time to educational programs. (That some networks have defined programs like "The Jetsons" and "The Flintstones" as educational, however, indicates that there is still plenty of work to do in this area—see Andrews, 1992.) Regulation of violent and indecent content in children's programming is another area in which ACT's groundbreaking efforts continue to inform the ongoing debate.

Decision making in this area is not a straightforward process. The television industry has powerful advocates of its own and a lot more money than child advocates can bring to bear. Advertisers have a large stake in programming decisions; the dollars they bring to the television industry represent considerable power. First Amendment issues are also raised by many—even those who oppose violent or overly commercial programming—whenever increased government regulatory power of the media is proposed (Wilcox & Kunkel, 1996).

In 1993, Peggy Charren retired and ACT ended its long run as a powerful children's advocacy group. Its many successes are reflected in the fact that children's programming is no worse than it is. Its greatest success is clearly in having fostered public awareness of and concern for issues in children's programming. With the departure of ACT from the advocacy arena, however, new groups must step in to shoulder responsibility in these areas.

mainstream media, these groups disseminate the results of research about the effects of child care. Advocates challenge federal and state policy makers and business executives to work together to build a child-care system in America that can meet the diverse needs of working families and their children.

Other Groups, Other Interests

Obviously, children's advocates are not the only ones involved in policy making. Other groups and individuals affect the outcome of policy decisions affecting children and families. To maximize their effectiveness, advocates for children need to be aware of these groups and their strategies. In many cases, children's advocates can learn a great deal from these other players and can advance child welfare by working alongside them.

Lobbies and Lobbyists

The difference between lobbyists and advocates is somewhat difficult to pinpoint. In general, the term *lobbying* connotes work for hire on behalf of a commercial interest, whereas the term *advocacy* is more often applied to noncommercial or social welfare interests. Advocacy is also a more general pursuit: lobbyists often target specific pieces of legislation, but lobbying is just one thing that advocates might do while defending a particular cause or issue (Congressional Quarterly, 1988). The nomenclature, however, gets muddled from time to time. It would not be incorrect to say, for instance, that the American Academy of Pediatrics lobbies for health care reform benefiting children, nor to say that the tobacco industry employs lobbyists to advocate for them with members of Congress.

Lobbyists speak of their goal as being "advocacy of a person's views or interests" (Andrews, 1995), and define themselves as "educators facilitating First Amendment rights to 'petition the government for a redress of grievances' " (Pitman, 1995). Lobbyists themselves constitute a large lobby interested in protecting their access to members of Congress: the number of registered special interest groups has grown 400 percent since 1955 (Cigler & Loomis, 1995). There is even a national organization of professional federal lobbies, the American League of Lobbyists.

Although they work largely behind the scenes, lobbyists play a powerful role in policy-making decisions in the United States. Many view them in a negative light (Greider, 1992; Frontline, 1996; Samuels, 1996), complaining that in a country where political power is supposed to accrue to the people on a "one person, one vote" basis, the strength of lobbies who have direct access to members of Congress is based on the number of members and the amount of money they have, factors that are far from uniform among such groups. Lobbyists tend to be political insiders—former members of Congress or attorneys with political ties—and many work full-time in Washington, D.C., or in state capitals. They represent the interests of trade unions, farmers, business and industry, minorities, women, senior citizens, veterans, environmental groups, gun owners, educators, and hundreds of other special interests.

One of the main functions of lobbyists is to insulate supporters of and contributors to political candidates from direct contact with the politicians they are supporting. For example, business representatives, whose interest in the outcome of specific pieces of legislation often outweighs partisan concerns, might make generous contributions to the campaigns of candidates in both parties, while wishing not to be publicly identified with either (Frontline, 1996). On behalf of their clients, lobbyists petition legislators to vote for or against specific legislation, provide research and technical assistance to individual members of Congress or Congressional committees, help to draft legislation, and monitor the progress of legislation for their clients. They might sponsor dinners, parties, and other fund-raisers, or vacations for legislators.

Lobbyists also work directly with the public, mounting telephone or letter-writing campaigns (often providing the letters for constituents' signatures) aimed at convincing legislators to vote a particular way. Finally, lobbyists work to protect their own interests, resisting regulation and restriction of their activities by Congress, arguing (an argument which many support) that their activities are protected by the First Amendment to the Constitution, which defines the right of the people to "petition the government for a redress of grievances" (Congressional Quarterly, 1988; Congressional Quarterly Online, 1995; Pitman, 1995).

Legislation governing the size of contributions to political candidates is strict, but not without loopholes. A $1,000 limit is put on the amount an individual may give to any candidate, but there is no limit on the number of such contributions that may come from a single family or company as long as no *individual* member of either contributes more than $1,000. Moreover, although direct contributions to campaigns are regulated in this manner, much of a candidate's support from lobbyists might come in the form of "soft money." Donations of services—the use of a private company's airplane to transport a candidate to a speaking engagement, or the free use of a banquet facility for a party fund-raiser, for example—are not always covered by lobbying legislation (Frontline, 1996).

Children are affected every day by the actions of lobbyists. The push for health care reform that occupied Congress for much of 1994, for instance, was quelled largely by the actions of lobbyists promoting the interests of the health care and insurance industries. Lobbies for conservative causes were directly responsible for mounting the letter-writing campaign that convinced President Nixon to veto the Comprehensive Child Development Act in 1971, legislation that would have established a national network of child-care centers. And lobbies for businesses and industry supported President Bush's veto of the two family and medical leave acts that were passed by Congress during his administration, in spite of widespread public support for this legislation.

Political Action Committees

Like lobbyists, political action committees (PACs) represent the interests of specific commercial or ideological groups to members of Congress. PACs differ from lobbyists in that they have one specific role: to raise and distribute campaign contributions to candidates for public office (Congressional Quarterly, 1988). PACs are prohibited by law from lobbying, that is, from working for or against specific pieces of legislation. Like advocates, some PACs are connected with specific economic interests, whereas others are formed to support a certain political or ideological position or to promote a single issue. PACs tend to favor incumbent candidates. KIDSPAC, for instance, was formed in 1981 to support the election and reelection of congressional candidates who have demonstrated their support for children and families. This political action committee focuses on a wide range of issues that affect children, and has raised over $2 million to support both incumbent and challenging candidates for the House and Senate.

The rise of PACs as a power in the legislative process occurred in response to campaign finance reforms during the early 1970s that put strict limits on the amounts that corporations, unions, and other interests could contribute directly to political campaigns. PAC contributions to any given candidate during any given election are also limited, but PACs may legally spend an unlimited amount to help elect a candidate. For instance, they can mount independent advertising campaigns on a candidate's behalf. Candidates may also receive unlimited PAC money as long as no *one* PAC contributes more than $5,000.

Even with restrictions on their activities, PACs contribute substantially to political activity. In 1994, for instance, 46 percent of campaign receipts to incumbent candidates for Congress came from PACs (Donovan & Moore, 1994). Senatorial candidates get an average of 30 percent of their campaign funds from PACs; candidates for the House of Representatives get 44 percent of theirs from PACs (Donovan, Thomas, & Vernon, 1993). Many, however, are critical of the inequality of influence inherent in the activities of PACs; some members of Congress will no longer accept direct contributions from PACs (Congressional Quarterly, 1988).

The Role of Business and Industry

Although the role of the government in facilitating family life is clear, there are limitations on the extent to which government can provide for the nation's children. There is only so much money to go around. Obviously, then, support for children and families must also come from the private sector. For example, the private sector can help children and families in those areas in which work and family life overlap. With over 68 percent of the mothers of children under age thirteen in the workforce (Children's Defense Fund, 1998g), and with the increase in the number of single-parent families, the impact of the workplace on family life has become a relevant issue. According to several recent studies, work and family life are interdependent (Families and Work Institute, 1998a, 1998b; Levitan & Conway, 1990). The interplay between these two worlds and its effects on the child concern developmental psychologists.

Life for dual-career and single-parent families can be stressful. These families need to make child-care arrangements for infants and preschoolers and to find after-school programs for older children. School vacations and days when children are ill require other solutions. Because family stability and other family concerns affect worker satisfaction and productivity (Families and Work Institute, 1998a; Zinsser, 1992), it is in the best interests of the private sector to offer services and benefits that can help their employees' families.

Although the private sector's role has been slow in developing, several attempts have been made to accommodate family needs, including changes in the work structure to allow flexible work arrangements and part-time job opportunities (Bureau of National Affairs, 1988; Child Care Action Campaign, 1989). Some firms even enable parents to take considerably more time off following the birth or adoption of a child than is guaranteed by the Family and Medical Leave Act, and many do so at partial or full pay.

Other companies, both large and small, offer an array of family-friendly benefits to employed parents. Some U.S. companies have on-site child-care centers or subsidize the cost of child care. Company-based child-care centers have been successful for such corporations as Stride-Rite in Massachusetts and Bayer Pharmaceuticals in Connecticut. Not all corporations can afford to operate such facilities, of course; as alternatives some companies offer child-care subsidies, pretax child-care spending accounts, and resource and referral services for families looking for such care. To cut expenses in this area, some companies are forming coalitions that enable them both to pool their family-support resources and save money. The American Business Collaboration for Quality Dependent Care, for instance, has spent more than $27 million to improve child-care and elder-care services provided by businesses (Moskowitz & Townsend, 1995).

Support Services Offered by a Growing Number of U.S. Companies

Working Mother magazine annually lists the "100 Best Companies for Working Mothers." This list, besides being useful for parents, has gained a certain cachet among businesses, many of which now strive to be included on it. As competition for skilled workers increases, so does the list of services offered. In addition to traditional employee benefits like health insurance and savings plans, many companies now offer a growing range of family-friendly services. Here are a few typical examples:

Resource and referral services for child care

Resource and referral services for elder care

Pretax set-asides for dependent care (children or elders)

Sick-child leave in excess of that granted by the Family and Medical Leave Act (FMLA)

Childbirth or adoption leave in excess of that granted by the FMLA

Adoption assistance

Flex-time arrangements for parents

Phase-back arrangements for new parents

Telecommuting

Job sharing

Compressed work weeks

On-site child care

Sick child day care

Prenatal care incentives, such as free infant car seats

Tuition assistance for employees' children

On-site services such as dry cleaning, diaper services, and take-out meals

After-school, vacation, and holiday child care

Monetary baby bonus

Several cities use zoning regulations to ensure that businesses help with child care. In San Francisco, an ordinance requires developers to either provide space for child care or contribute to a child-care fund. In Seattle, zoning rules for building projects require new buildings to include space for child care (Kyle, 1987).

Industry can help facilitate family life in many other ways (Child Care Action Campaign, 1989). Often child development researchers help business and industry executives plan and implement these projects. Moreover, some researchers are investigating whether changes implemented in the workplace really benefit children. Do parents who take advantage of flexible working arrangements actually spend more time with their children? Do such changes in work schedules reduce stress for parents? Given the option of infant care leaves, do parents use them? Meanwhile, it is clear that offering family-friendly benefits is good for companies. Patagonia, a California-based manufacturer of outdoor wear, for instance, saved nearly $229,000 in reduced turnover and tax breaks in 1994 because of its generous child-care program (Moskowitz & Townsend, 1995).

The Media

In 1980, one of the country's leading media specialists wrote, "An examination of the Vanderbilt Television News Archives for 8 years showed little attention of any kind paid to children and youth. An average of 63 stories a year mention children and youth on the network evening news" (Gerbner, 1980, p. 239). Today such a count would likely be far different. As Muenchow (1996) notes, stories about children and families, the problems they face and the solutions they seek, are no longer relegated to women's magazines and the back pages of the features sections of newspapers. Media attention to children's issues, which was on the rise throughout the 1980s, increased even further during the 1990s as welfare, health care, child care, and education reforms dominated state and federal legislative agenda, and as media attention focused on perceived crises related to drug use, youth violence, and other family-oriented issues.

The media—newspapers, magazines, radio and television, the film industry, and the Internet—are ostensibly in a neutral role, but in actuality they have a real and profound effect on how the public in general and lawmakers themselves view the issues families face. Even if we were to assent to the idea that most representatives of the media are ideologically neutral—and certainly this is not the case—coverage of issues and events would still be a powerful shaper of attitudes and behaviors. Merely because time and space are limited in print and on the airwaves, relative to the amount of material that might receive coverage, the editors and news anchors who select which stories will run, and in what context, wield enormous power. The media's lack of space and time contributes pivotally to what the public does—and does not—get to see (Graber, 1989).

Moreover, the traditional model of presenting news stories almost invariably emphasizes certain details over others, relies heavily on a crisis-oriented approach to reporting, and tends to confirm, rather than challenge, the public's perception of the status quo. Reporting on drug abuse is a case in point. Although research indicates that drug use among Americans is actually declining, stories on the dangers of and threats posed by drug use persistently confirm what most people believe—that drug use is on the rise. Reporting on crime reflects a similar distortion of what statistics actually show (Hall, 1998; Horgan, 1993; Zigler & Hall, 1997).

The power of the media to reach millions of people at once, however, makes them an invaluable tool for child advocates—just as they are an invaluable tool for those who lobby against actions that would improve the lives of children and families. A "Headline News" report on CNN or a heartrending family story on Oprah has the power to affect the outcome of legislative debate, the choices parents make for their families, or even a national election. At times just the threat of media coverage has been enough to spur policy makers to act (Graber, 1989).

How can child advocates make the best use of media coverage? First, by providing media representatives at the right level (local, state, or national) with facts about the status of children and families in a format that is easy to use (Join Together, 1994). Many advocacy groups provide news briefs and press releases highlighting pertinent statistics and events, often tying them to proposed legislation. Second, by taking every opportunity to analyze and explain how larger issues in the news would really affect children (Bloch, 1992). Tax cuts proposed by the Republican leadership in the 104th Congress, for instance, are often cited as a measure that will help children in the long run by lowering the national debt and keeping interest rates down. Advocates can help reporters to explain how such abstractions would affect real people by noting that such cuts would, among other outcomes, deny Title I educational assistance to over 1 million children, raise college costs for 5 million students, and exclude almost 200,000 eligible children from attending Head Start (White House, 1995). Finally, advocates can sponsor events that spotlight and provide current information on child and family issues, and include representatives of the media to help promote public awareness of these.

Foundations and Commissions

Foundations and commissions can also advance the causes important to children and families in a variety of ways. They also can have much in common with the media, especially when promoting messages derived from research or task forces studying particular topics of importance in children's lives. Foundations tend to be privately supported—the Robert Wood Johnson Foundation and the Carnegie Corporation are two examples of philanthropic organizations that devote time and private money to the promotion of child welfare.

Commissions might be private, or they might be government sponsored, though they are authorized to act independently of government bodies and are, at least in theory, free to reach their own conclusions based on the evidence they gather. The National Commission to Prevent Infant Mortality is such a group. Such bodies, might, however, find their work to be of limited usefulness if the governing official to whom they report downplays their findings for political reasons. For example, research showing high U.S. infant mortality rates can embarrass a president; a commission's recommendation that marijuana be decriminalized might be out of keeping with a president's personal values or commitments with respect to fighting drug use. In such cases, these reports might be embargoed—that is, not released to the public or the media—or they might simply be disavowed or buried under conflicting reports from other sources.

During the 1980s and early 1990s, however, a number of important reports released by foundations and commissions did receive substantial media coverage and have had a significant impact on the public's awareness of child and family issues. The report by the American Bar Association (1993) on the unmet needs of children and families, the *Starting Points* report from the Carnegie Corporation (1994) on the nature and importance of the first three years of life, the report *Five Million Children* by the National Center for Children in Poverty (1990), and the National Commission on Children's final report *Beyond Rhetoric* (1991) are all examples of rigorously researched reports on the status of children and the actions that must be taken to fulfill their needs. Each of these succeeded in raising public awareness of these issues and putting pressure on policy makers to take action.

Parents

Parents themselves often play a valuable role in the process of policy making. Among the first and most effective children's advocates, parents of children with special needs in the 1960s and 1970s modeled their campaigns for appropriate educational and other options on the successful actions of the civil rights movement and the women's movement (Pizzo, 1995). Parents bring to child advocacy a sense of urgency driven by their concern for their own children, along with an intimate and immediate understanding of what it is like to live day to day with the issues that face children and families.

Parents are a busy, beleaguered constituency, but they are a powerful one and are beginning to make their elected officials—as well as challengers for elected office—aware of their needs. During the 1988 presidential campaign, parents presented President Bush with results of a survey showing that 75 percent of respondents believed that the federal government should take responsibility for developing policies to make high-quality child care affordable and accessible (Zinsser, 1989). In addition, Bernice Weissbourd and pediatrician T. Berry Brazelton are helping parents to join together in a coalition called Parent Action. Parent Action's statement of purpose calls for societal and governmental support to promote goals including, but not limited to, family-friendly workplace policies, improved infant-care leaves, improved public education, and preventive health care. In later chapters we will explore in more depth the specific roles played by parents.

Other Players

This is not an exhaustive list of the groups involved in the policy-making process. Policy making is often accomplished by the courts, as when the U.S. Supreme Court engineered a paradigm shift in American education by striking down so-called "separate but equal" educational arrangements and calling for the speedy desegregation of schools in its 1954 ruling in *Brown v. Board of Education of Topeka*. Governments themselves can promote children's policies. The

Parents of children who have been injured or have died traumatically can strongly influence national policy and opinion. Sometimes parents who have lost their children to similar tragedies band together, as with Mothers Against Drunk Driving (MADD). Since its inception in 1980, MADD has lobbied to strengthen existing laws and adopt new ones on issues such as license suspension for repeat offenders and the age-21 drinking age, and to increase public awareness about impaired driving.

Another group, the National Organization of Parents of Murdered Children, was founded in the early 1970s by Charlotte and Bob Hullinger of Cincinnati after their daughter, Lisa, was murdered. This organization hosts a number of programs aimed at supporting those who have lost loved ones to violence, protesting the paroling of convicted murderers, and raising public awareness of how the media use murder as entertainment.

Occasionally a single family's anguish is directed toward reforming national policy. On July 29, 1994, 7-year-old Megan Kanka went across the street to her neighbor's home to see his new puppy. The neighbor, Jesse Timmendequas, beat, raped, and murdered Megan. The horror of the event was exacerbated by the discovery that Timmendequas, unbeknownst to anyone in the community, was a twice-convicted sex offender and child molester. Megan's parents, Richard and Maureen Kanka, channeled their grief into campaigning relentlessly for legislation that would protect children from known sex offenders. They lobbied successfully for the rapid passage of a New Jersey statute, known as "Megan's Law," that requires that local communities be notified when convicted sex offenders settle in the area. Following the New Jersey ruling, Megan's parents pushed for national legislation. "We need uniformity across this country

to successfully protect our children from pedophiles," said Maureen Kanka. In their quest, they gained the support of many politicians and influential organizations, including the National Center for Missing and Exploited Children. Their efforts succeeded when, in 1996, President Clinton signed "Megan's Law" into federal law (PL 104-145), requiring some form of community notification.

The 47 states that have versions of Megan's Law have a variety of notification requirements. Alaska's includes posting information on the Internet regarding all paroled sex offenders in the state. Connecticut releases the names and addresses of offenders to anyone who calls to request the information. New Jersey, on the other hand, has tight controls and releases information only to a few select individuals. Since the federal legislation was signed, however, its constitutionality has been called into question. As of 1997, the law had been upheld by several state supreme courts in cases brought by offenders who feared that exposure of their past crimes to the community could cost them their jobs and ruin their lives. Indeed, before New Jersey made its notification policies more restrictive, early townwide notification had resulted in some incidences of harassment and vigilantism. In early 1998, the U.S. Supreme Court refused to hear challenges to Megan's Law, a move that finally ended three years of contention surrounding the New Jersey legislation. Maureen Kanka, who had traveled about 50,000 miles since Megan's murder, advocating for laws designed to protect children from sex offenders, said she had always been convinced that the law was fair and just. She and her husband Richard were rewarded with the satisfaction of seeing their lobbying efforts affirmed in a way that had a chance of sparing other families from experiencing anguish like their own.

Administration for Children and Families, the by-now only vestigial Children's Bureau, and the White House Children's Conferences, which drew attention to children's issues throughout the twentieth century until they were discontinued during the Reagan administration, have all improved the welfare of children and families. Such groups, however, must answer to two masters—the children whose well-being they promote, and the governmental bodies within whose jurisdiction they operate. Children are rarely the winners when the competing demands of government come into conflict with (sometimes expensive) policies that would serve families.

STRATEGIES THAT SHAPE CHILD AND FAMILY POLICY

Unlike the advocates representing business and governmental concerns, child advocates are often poorly organized. A survey of state legislative leaders regarding their perceptions of the efficacy of child advocates and their impact on the legislative process reveals that child and family advocates have a great deal to learn from the strategies employed by the other players in the legislative arena (State Legislative Leaders Foundation, 1995). Although the survey findings indicate that state legislators generally consider child and family issues to be important, child advocates do not appear to be playing as powerful a role as they might in framing the social policy picture. Legislators voiced a number of specific concerns about the child policy field and the role played by child advocates:

- Legislators' perception of and understanding of children's issues is impeded by the fragmentation in much of this field. Instead of being presented with a clearly defined children's agenda, legislators receive a number of messages from individuals and organizations representing a variety of children's interests; these groups are often competing for limited resources.
- Children's advocates are often seen by legislators as being tied to liberal and Democratic groups and causes. In an era in which much of the legislative leadership is conservative and Republican, children's advocates would be more effective if they were seen as bipartisan with respect to children's issues.
- State legislators do not feel they are well informed on children's issues, or on the status of children and children's programs within their districts.
- Legislators rarely hear from individual constituents or grassroots children's advocacy groups voicing concerns about children's issues.
- Legislative leaders do not understand what advocacy groups do, or how they differ from lobbyists. As the report indicates, legislators "perceive advocates as 'elitists' who view the legislative process and state legislators themselves with disdain or skepticism" (State Legislative Leaders Foundation, 1995, p. vii).
- Children's advocates are rarely trained in the strategies needed to successfully promote children's legislative agendas. Moreover, they are usually underfunded, particularly compared to professional lobbyists backed by clients' dollars.

A number of these strategies are critical for children's advocates who hope to enact positive changes. Strategies used by successful lobbyists and advocates for business and industry include the following:

- *Be willing to learn new skills.* For example, few child development scholars are experts in economics, but a knowledge of the budget process and the tax system enables advocates to understand and cope with the implications for children of changes in these areas. Knowing the legislative process is essential.
- *Become an effective communicator.* Knowing how to disseminate pertinent information at different levels and for different target audiences is crucial. Writing a press release to be sent to local newspapers and television studios is no less important than, but is very different from, helping a senator's staff to draft child-care legislation or providing state legislators with statistics on child health care coverage.
- *Build coalitions.* Too often, children's advocacy groups find themselves *competing* with each other for attention, funding, and political favors. Working together toward a common goal—even though this typically involves difficult compromise—can enable diverse groups to achieve more than if they worked individually with fewer resources and less political clout.
- *Learn to work with the press.* Good relationships with representatives of the media can be used to promote understanding of children's issues.

LOOKING TOWARD THE FUTURE

Will there ever be a powerful children's lobby? Perhaps not. But parents, educators, physicians, economists, and, above all, voters who have children's interests at heart will continue to work toward safeguarding and increasing benefits for children. It is clear that children's advocates cannot hope to achieve beneficial changes for children simply because promoting child welfare is "doing the right thing." If that were the case, research about the needs of children would be transformed instantly into positive action and there would be no need for a book like this one. Instead, advocates must work together with other similarly focused individuals and groups, they must coexist and compromise with others competing for the same political or economic resources, and they must recognize and respect the power of all the players in this arena.

SUMMARY

Child advocates are groups or individuals who press for improvements in conditions that affect children and families, or promote the maintenance of circumstances that benefit children. Advocacy, the roots of which reach far back into history, has many different faces today; children's causes are espoused and promoted by parents, scholars, foundations, commissions, religious organizations, the courts, and the media. Not all of these groups promote solutions to children's problems out of a sense of altruism; family-friendly policies often are implemented because they also have a more general social and economic benefit. In addition, implementation of children's policy is often a matter of timing and other circumstances.

The roots of child advocacy reach back at least as far as the second century A.D., but modern advocacy in the United States began following the Civil War, when charitable groups, often associated with religious institutions, began to take responsibility for families living in poverty. Interest in what might be done for those perceived as socially and economically disadvantaged flourished, eventually extending to government institutions. By 1909, the White House held its first conference on children's needs and interests. Such conferences continued to be held every decade until they were discontinued by the Reagan administration during the 1980s. In the first half of the century, child advocates focused largely on issues of physical health and mortality. In addition, many brought children's interests to the attention of academic institutions and philanthropists who founded child study institutes at many of the country's leading universities.

During the Johnson administration in the 1960s, advocates both promoted the establishment of intervention programs for disadvantaged children and guided the implementation of such efforts. Government bodies eager to find the most effective ways to spend their funds sought the expertise of scholars familiar with child health and development. These academicians and researchers, in turn, studied the outcomes of intervention programs, and many became advocates themselves, appealing to local, state, and federal governments to expand and continue the most effective programs. From their studies of child and family programs and the needs of children and families, scholars derived "childhood social indicators," data that paint a picture of the conditions of children. However, policy continues to be driven more powerfully by national economic indicators than by the needs of children.

The 1980s and 1990s brought a shift in the national ethos regarding the role of government in the lives of children and families. The balance of power has shifted as advocates who were successful as grassroots organizations in the 1960s and 1970s have evolved into well-organized and well-funded national advocacy groups. Conservative groups like the Heritage Foundation and the American Enterprise Institute exemplify organizations that started small and became powerful and influential political forces. In response, however, child advocacy organizations like the Children's Defense Fund and the National Center for Children in Poverty gained new adherents; the balance of power between these two contingents continues in a state of flux.

Lobbyists and political action committees are special groups that have an impact, not always positive, on children's issues. By bringing political, economic, and constituency pressures to bear on politicians and candidates for political office, lobbyists and PACs are often able to influence a candidate's awareness and understanding of an issue, and even to influence the way candidates will vote on specific pieces of legislation. By emulating many of the strategies employed by lobbyists and PACs, children's advocates can be more effective in working to achieve their goals.

Starting Strong and Staying Strong

For a large proportion of our nation's children, the experience of growing up in the United States is not like it used to be. Families today are struggling to cope with rapid and startling social change. U.S. demographics have changed profoundly during the last three decades, resulting in shifts in the economy, in the labor force, and in child-rearing patterns. Such changes have had a marked influence on the lives of U.S. citizens in general, and on U.S. infants in particular. Moreover, there is a growing discrepancy between the image of the United States as a family-oriented nation and the harsh reality of the failure of U.S. social policies to keep pace with the new realities of family life. Critical needs of infants and families are going unmet. Although the full impact of this situation cannot yet be assessed, it is clear that our youngest citizens are already suffering the most serious repercussions. They are not alone, however: by extension, today's parents, their employers, and their communities are all experiencing the impact of the tension between the needs of children and the lack of policies to address them.

The most striking change stems from an increase in the percentage of women in the out-of-home workforce—a change attributable in part to the economic need for two incomes in most families, and in part to the rise of single-parent households, the vast majority of which are headed by women. Experts in child development disagree as to how children are affected by placement in full-time, nonparental care during the first year of life. With roughly two-thirds of all mothers of infants in the paid labor force, such placements are now routine, and many are made as early as two weeks after birth.

Other changes, too, have had an impact on the way children in this nation are growing up today. The increase in the number of families in varying stages of dissolution has resulted in a kaleidoscopic variety of new definitions for "family." In the last 50 years, the percentage of children living with two parents, both in the paid labor force, has increased from 5 percent to 38 percent. The percentage of children living in one-parent families with an employed parent has risen from 2 percent to 13 percent (Hernandez, 1995). Child-care costs for these families have risen without an appreciable increase in child-care options. Although the divorce rate has stabilized after an increase in the second half of this century, approximately 50 percent of married couples still divorce. As a group, the children of these couples experience an array of family types and care arrangements. Children and families are beset by problems related to poverty, unstable employment, crime, drugs, and child abuse and neglect. In many cases, family functioning becomes so fragile that children must be removed from the home of their biological parents and placed elsewhere.

In this chapter we will take a look at large-scale national programs designed to get families with newborn or newly adopted children off to the best start possible. One of the programs is already in place, the other is a reality for families in other nations but still a dream for U.S. children and their parents. Later in this chapter we'll explore the program and policy issues most integral to an altogether different sort of program (but still one calculated to support families on a large scale)—foster care and family preservation.

PARENTAL CARE LEAVE

Patterns of employment for women in the United States increasingly resemble those of men. Most American women participate in the labor force; whether they are single or married, they enter the out-of-home workforce for the same reasons that men do—to support themselves and their families. Almost three-fourths of women who received maternity leave returned to work within six months of childbirth. In 1960, fewer than 1 woman in 5 returned to work once she had children (Kamerman & Kahn, 1995; Zigler, Hopper, & Hall, 1993).

In spite of these figures, the United States was the third-to-last industrialized nation in the world to establish a national parental leave policy; only New Zealand and Australia still lack such a plan. Ours is still unusual in that it covers only a small percentage of workers and provides no wage replacement. Seventy-five other nations pay such a benefit, which includes, on the average, a four- to five-month leave with replacement of 60 to 90 percent of a woman's wages. Only about 50 percent of U.S. workers are eligible to take the leave; far fewer can afford to do so (Cordes, 1997; Frank & Zigler, 1996).

Research findings on how children are affected by placement in full-time, nonparental care during the first year of life are mixed (Belsky, 1986, 1987; Bierly, 1996; Gilman & Zigler, 1996). Some researchers have found a decline in the quality of the infant's attachment to its parents associated with early nonmaternal care, whereas others find no ill effects (Kamerman & Kahn, 1995). Infants, even very young ones, are being placed in supplemental child care in larger numbers than ever before and at increasingly early ages. It is no longer unusual for children to be placed in out-of-home care as early as two weeks after birth ("Human Services Reauthorization Act," 1990). Fewer than half of U.S. children under age 6 have a nonemployed parent who can provide full-time child care (U.S. Department of Labor, Bureau of Labor Statistics, 1994a).

The Developmental Rationale for Parental Leave

There is growing concern that placing a child in substitute care during the first three years of life could be detrimental to both child and parents. An infant's first weeks of life are a **sensitive period** for the development of reciprocal relationships (Bronfenbrenner, 1988; Hopper & Zigler, 1988). The child's development of a sense that the world is a stable, predicable place depends largely on the sense of continuity and responsiveness provided by the child's caregiver. We cannot as yet predict with certainty what the effect of multiple caregivers on children so young will be (Frank & Zigler, 1996; Gilman & Zigler, 1996; Zigler, Hopper, & Hall, 1993).

The transition to parenthood, no matter how joyful, is one of the most stressful experiences in a person's life (Belsky, Spanier, & Rovine, 1983). It takes time for a mutually satisfying parent-infant relationship to emerge, and adequate social supports are essential for the development of this relationship (Crockenberg, 1981; Crnic et al., 1983). But instead of finding supports commensurate with the stresses of this important period, parents are forced to select from a severely limited range of less than optimal alternatives: One parent, usually the mother, must stay home, often at the risk of the family's economic stability; or parents must place their infant in substitute care long before they feel ready to do so. Women who must return to employment outside the home before they feel ready report feeling stressed, guilty, and cheated out of a time filled with important experiences (Farber, Alejandro-Wright, & Muenchow, 1988).

Though parents typically cherish their infants from birth, it takes time to develop the emotions and familiarity that ensure a strong sense of attachment. Parents and infants need thousands of opportunities for interaction on a regular basis to establish a pattern of interaction that will enable them to recognize and respond to each other's social signals and cues. Research shows that even during the earliest weeks of infancy, parent-infant interactions are bidirectional and reciprocal—infants influence the nature of these interactions and are not passive objects of parental behaviors. This attunement to each others' rhythms—which has been compared to an intricate and intimate dance in which the partners learn to synchronize their behaviors—provides an important foundation in the infant's developing sense of self. Through their interaction with their parents, infants come to realize that they can influence and affect their environment. Infants then begin to build a sense of security and trust within the family relationship and environment (Brazelton, 1986, 1988; Brazelton, Koslowski, & Main, 1974; Lieberman, 1993; Stern, 1974). Because this stability is essential if the infant is to feel comfortable enough to begin to explore and experience the world (Bretherton, 1985; Parke, 1981), the ramifications for both social and cognitive development are profound.

Research on the family system also supports the need for granting leaves. The period immediately following birth has been described as significant for redefining family roles (Belsky, 1985; Goldberg & Easterbrooks, 1984; Minuchin, 1985). Following the birth or introduction of a new child, all family members—mothers, fathers, and siblings—need time to adjust and negotiate their family relationships and roles. Each member of the family feels disruption at the arrival of a new baby. Time is necessary to allow for a comfortable transition and to regain family equilibrium. Although these relationships are dynamic and do continue to change, the period following the introduction of a newborn into the family is one of the most important transitional periods in a family's life.

Balancing the demands of pregnancy and parenting with those of labor force participation must also be considered as critical variables when determining how best to meet the needs of parents and children. Employers' needs, too, must figure into such an equation; although concerned with profitability, businesses also have to meet certain employee needs in order to optimize productivity and to attract and keep good workers. A survey of over 2,000 female wage and salaried workers from a variety of types of employment indicates that employer accommodations to the needs of pregnant employees and those with infants under 1 year of age result in fewer days missed because of pregnancy-related complaints, and a far higher percentage of employees who work into the third trimester of pregnancy. Greater employer flexibility also resulted in lower levels of stress being reported to women in the workplace with infants at home (Families and Work Institute, 1997a, 1997b; Matthiessen, 1997; National Council of Jewish Women, 1993).

The Legislative History of the Family and Medical Leave Act

The drive to enact and enforce family leave legislation—usually called maternity leave in its earlier guises—has a long history. The original laws relating to the employment of women during their childbearing years in this country were exclusionary in nature, intentionally designed to protect men's jobs by discouraging the employment of women. The discriminatory nature of such laws made them a target for legal challenges in the 1960s and 1970s. By 1978, the Pregnancy Discrimination Act of Title VIII of the Civil Rights Act specifically mentioned pregnancy in its definition of sex discrimination practices (Zigler & Lang, 1993). The focus of this law was not on maternal and child health, however, but on attempts to reduce or eliminate discrimination related to the provision of employment benefits (Kamerman & Kahn, 1995). Enforcement of the act was difficult because discrimination was often hard to prove. Women continued to lose their jobs—and the incomes they needed to raise a child—as a result of becoming pregnant.

In the 1980s and 1990s, perspectives on employed women and their children shifted as family demographics changed. With more women in the workforce to stay, conservative forces expressed concerns about the numbers of children in nonmaternal care and the decline in the amount of time parents had available to spend with their children. In the late 1960s, parents spent about 30 hours a week with their children; within 25 years this figure was only about 17 hours (Hernandez, 1995; Kamerman & Kahn, 1995). At the same time, forces stressing equal rights for women and the government's role as a provider of social services urged Congress to pass leave legislation similar to that in European and other nations. For a comparison of family and medical leave in various countries, see table 4.1.

These two political camps, though taking different paths, arrived at the same conclusion: parents and children ought to be able to spend an extended period of time together following childbirth or adoption. Agreeing on the means to achieve this end, however, was difficult. Opponents of government intervention in the lives of families decried congressional actions that might be interpreted as telling parents how to raise their children. Business lobbies also opposed passage of such an act, on the grounds that it would be prohibitively costly for small businesses. Liberal forces sought even longer and more widely applicable leave legislation than that proposed on several occasions.

Parental leave legislation came before Congress in 1985. Versions of this bill came before Congress again in 1987 and again in 1989 before finally being passed by both houses in 1990. President Bush vetoed the legislation. This veto came in the face of mounting evidence that parents not only wanted such an option but felt it was the proper role of the federal government to provide it, in

TABLE 4.1 Family and Medical Leave: An International Comparison

Country	Duration	Percentage of Wage	Who Is Eligible?	Additional Leave Available
Austria	16 weeks	100	Mother	Extended: 3 years (variable pay)
Canada	15 weeks	55	Mother	Extended: 24 weeks for either parent (unpaid)
Denmark	28 weeks	100	Mother/father	Routine illness: 1 day/year Chronic illness: 1 year
France	16 (6 months for 3+ children)	84	Mother	Extended: 2 years Routine illness: 10 days/year
Germany	14 weeks	100	Mother/father	Extended: 2 years
Sweden	12 months	80	Mother/father	Extended: 6 months Routine illness: 60 days/year
United Kingdom	14 weeks	100	Mother	Extended: 28 weeks
United States	12 weeks	0	Mother/father	None

Sources: International Labour Office, The costs of social security (Geneva, Switzerland: Author, 1997), and S. B. Kamerman & A. J. Kahn, *Starting right: How America Neglects Its Youngest Children and What We Can Do About It* (New York: Oxford University Press, 1995).

much the same way that the governments of other nations did (Kaitin, 1994; Kamerman & Kahn, 1995; Zinsser, 1989). When family leave again made it through Congress in 1992, however, President Bush vetoed it again. In April of 1993, the bill was passed for the third time. This time President Clinton, newly inaugurated, enacted into law the Family and Medical Leave Act (FMLA). As the first non-disability-based parental leave law in U.S. history, the FMLA was a revolutionary piece of legislation. In signing the FMLA into law, President Clinton noted his recognition of the fact that families had a right and a responsibility to be with their new child in the weeks and months following childbirth or adoption. Equally important was his acknowledgment of the government's role in making such a leave possible.

The impact of the FMLA has been more theoretical than practical, largely owing to its built-in limitations on eligibility and affordability (Cordes, 1997). Specifically, the FMLA provisions include the following: 12 weeks of unpaid leave every 12 months to care for a newborn, newly adopted, or seriously ill child, parent, or spouse; job protection; and a certain amount of flexibility in the use of leave time—leave may be taken on a part-time basis, for instance, if medically necessary. Employers are granted the right to require 30 days' notice, except in unusual circumstances; to require that employees use accrued vacation and sick time as a part of their leave; and to compress leaves to 12 weeks per family when both spouses work for the same company (Blair et al., 1995; Chira, 1993; Shellenbarger, 1993b).

What the FMLA does not do is just as significant. A serious drawback to the legislation is that it does not cover everyone (Frank & Zigler, 1996). Coverage is excluded for employees who work for companies employing fewer than 50 workers, whose jobs are in the upper echelons in large corporations, and who work part-time or who have worked less than a full year. Moreover, even those who are covered by the provisions of FMLA are seldom able to take the leaves offered, because the leaves are unpaid. In essence, the act provides (unpaid) family leave for the employees of only about 5 percent of our nation's employees.

A multidisciplinary panel of nationally recognized experts in child development, pediatrics, economics, public health, social policy, law, and business was convened in 1983 at the Yale Bush Center in Child Development and Social Policy to recommend a design for family leave legislation. This panel concluded that new parents should be offered a 6-month minimum leave—3 months with partial wage replacement, and 3 months unpaid (Zigler & Frank, 1988; Frank & Zigler, 1996). Medical science acknowledges that 6 to 8 weeks is the bare minimum essential for physical recovery following childbirth; complicated births, cesarean sections, and premature deliveries require even more time (Eisenberg, Murkoff, & Hathaway, 1989; Pritchard, MacDonald, & Gant, 1985).

Two years after the enactment of the FMLA, a bipartisan commission established to study the use and effects of the act have concluded that "the impact has been minimal" ("All Things Considered," 1995). By 1997, only about 4 percent of the eligible workers have taken family leave under the provisions of this act; the most significant impediment to greater reliance on such leaves has been the lack of income replacement. Of those taking the leave, nearly half are men. Most of these take the leave to attend to their own health emergencies, but there is a slow increase in the number of men taking child-care-related leaves.

This commission also concluded that fears about the costs to businesses of granting family leaves have been unfounded. Over 92 percent of businesses complying with FMLA have reported no increase in administrative costs or turnovers or any decline in productivity (Cordes, 1997). Policy analysts have made several suggestions for making the FMLA more responsive to the needs of the families it was designed to serve and protect: Expanding the employers covered by the act to include those with 15 or more employees, inclusion of part-time workers, expanding the parental leave allowed to at least 4 to 6 months, and providing at least partial wage replacement for part of the leave, possibly through Temporary Disability Insurance or unemployment compensation programs, would have a profound positive impact on the number of families able to benefit from family leave legislation.

CHILD ALLOWANCE AND FAMILY ALLOWANCES

Good-quality infant care is the most difficult and expensive to obtain, costing as much as $12,000 per year in some cities (Children's Defense Fund, 1998g). Again, parents are faced with a range of poor choices: They must sacrifice necessary income to stay at home and care for the new baby; add the precariously high cost of good-quality infant care to the family budget-balancing act; or compromise quality (and possibly the child's development) by settling for a less costly, and perhaps also less appropriate, care setting. In the end, having such a poor range of choices is often tantamount to having no choice at all. Parents are forced to raise their infants and toddlers according to the limitations of their pocketbooks rather than the dictates of their own ideals and aspirations.

Parents in virtually all other industrialized nations and even in many developing countries have another alternative. These nations provide a **family allowance,** or **child allowance,** directly to families for each child in the home. This is typically a flat amount for each child, although in some countries the allowance varies with age, birth order, and the number of children in the families (Kamerman, 1996). Based on the idea that children benefit the nation and not just the family, these governments invest in their upbringing to improve the odds that—through stable and caring child rearing—they will become useful, productive citizens later in life (Children's Defense Fund, 1998g; Rauch, 1989). No country's child allowance is generous enough to obviate the need for parental employment, but many provide enough income supplement to allow parents either to extend a parental leave or, should they elect to return to the workplace earlier, to pay for higher-quality child care. Most European-style child allowances do not end after infancy, either, but continue through the school years; some extend to the age of majority or beyond (Kamerman & Kahn, 1995).

How Child Allowances Work

Funding mechanisms for such an allowance vary from country to country. In France, where the policy was originally implemented as part of a pro-natalist effort, the government pays no benefit for the first child; a larger allowance is paid for third (and subsequent) children than for a second child. This non-means-tested child allowance is available for nine months, beginning in the fifth month of pregnancy. Eighty percent of French families meet financial eligibility criteria for an additional allowance that continues until the child's third birthday (Kamerman & Kahn, 1995).

Similar arrangements are made in other nations. The Canadian government provides a modest allowance for all children under 18, though this stipend is taxed as income. The Austrian government provides an allowance for each child equaling 15 percent of the average female wage, and a plan implemented in West Germany in 1986 provides for a universal allowance from birth to 6 months, followed by a stipend available according to financial need. Sweden gives a tax-free allowance for each child under 18 and a paid parental leave, among other family support benefits.

In some nations (Israel, for instance), a tax credit for families with children replaces the child allowance. The U.S.'s Earned Income Tax Credit (EITC) serves a similar purpose, but is available only to people who work but do not have sufficient income. The EITC helps offset increases in living expenses and social security taxes. As of 1999, this tax credit was worth up to $2,312 to families with one qualifying child, and $3,816 to families with two or more children. The credit is applied regardless of a family's income tax liability, increasing the likelihood of their receiving more than they paid to the Internal Revenue Service. The EITC is not available to parents with no earned income or those who in 1999 earn more than $26,928 (one child) or $30,500 (two or more children). (The maximum credit is obtained by those earning roughly half of these amounts.) If the credit were applied to families with too little income to obtain much tax relief under the present plan, the funds could be used to replace income, as well as to finance good-quality child care for those who work outside the home.

A U.S. Proposal

Proposals have been put forth that such an allowance be made available in the United States by expanding the Social Security system to provide an annual stipend of approximately $5,000 to families for a child's first year (Zigler & Lang, 1990). At present, when two parents are working, 7.65 percent of a family's income goes into the Social Security fund for use at some future date. Through the child allowance, some of these funds would be made available when they are needed for the transition to parenthood.

Such a plan would be consonant with increasing federal child and family program funding levels through a Social Security add-on. In the child allowance trust-fund plan proposed by Zigler and Lang (1990), funds would be released on a yearly basis directly to parents, to be used at their discretion. The plan is thus consistent with an emphasis on choice in family support planning: A parent can elect either to care for a child at home or to purchase infant care. These funds could be realized either through a flat tax or a graduated Social Security tax increase.

The ideological basis for the child allowance is conservative and family-oriented. Moreover, the proposed funding mechanism is entirely consistent with the original goal of the Social Security system—to relieve families of the economic burdens of caring for family members. The goal of such a plan is to give families a real choice by offering a wider range of realistic child-care alternatives.

A CRISIS IN FAMILY LIFE: CHILDREN OF SHATTERED FAMILIES

Growing up in circumstances of social deprivation, instability, or poverty can have long-term social and cognitive consequences for children. Research indicates that these problems are often present for children whose parents divorce (Hetherington & Clingempeel, 1992; Horner & Guyer, 1993; Maccoby, 1984). In a long-term study of the consequences of divorce, for instance, Wallerstein discovered that the emotional effects of divorce can linger for years (Wallerstein & Blakeslee, 1996; Wallerstein & Kelly, 1996). Wallerstein and her colleagues concluded that the anxiety, depression, and emotional instability that result from divorce for many children outstrip the damage children sustain from living with unhappily married parents. Moreover, recent evidence suggests that remarriage brings disruptive effects to children's lives that are equal to or greater than those of divorce (Hetherington & Clingempeel, 1992).

Some studies conclude that, as one researcher put it, "a good divorce is better than a bad marriage" (Applewhite, 1997). Many psychologists today argue that divorce is preferable if it removes children from a context of pervasive tension, parental fighting, or domestic violence (Applewhite, 1997; Gilman, 1998). If one parent or both can maintain a close relationship with the child following divorce, and can foster for the child a sense of security, continuity, and consistency in discipline and daily life, the child might actually reap some benefit from the parents' divorce.

However, if the divorce process and aftermath are characterized by tension or open conflict between ex-spouses, by drastic or unpredictable changes in the child's daily life, by economic hardship, by custody battles, or by contests between the parents for the child's affections, the child is likely to manifest poor emotional or behavioral outcomes (American Academy of Child and Adolescent Psychiatry, 1997; Applewhite, 1997; DeBord, 1997; Maccoby & Mnookin, 1992).

In addition to suffering the virtual loss of a parent and a familiar way of life, children are frequently used as pawns in divorce proceedings and might be called upon to take sides by warring spouses who force children to shoulder inappropriately weighty emotional burdens. Also devastating to children's mental health can be the loss of community, activities, and schoolmates if the custodial parent decides to move to another area. These harms are compounded by situations where the parents engage in protracted court battles, especially if the young child is called upon to testify. The lack of psychologically sound and uniform guidelines for these procedures across jurisdictions is strikingly arbitrary and unenlightened in terms of what is age-appropriate for and considerate of the child's interests and psychological well-being.

In addition to the potential emotional harms of divorce, many children suffer economic hardship as well, particularly those who are abandoned economically by noncustodial parents who refuse or are unable to pay child support. The decline in income for female-headed families after divorce is well-known. For these children and women, income drops by about 40 percent between the years just before and just after divorce, and living standards fall to about two-thirds of their former levels (Duncan, 1991; Ohio State University, 1998), forcing many of these children into poverty that can either be transitory or chronic (Lang, 1994; Huston, 1991b). McLanahan, Astone, and Marks (1991) note, for instance, that 50 percent of mother-headed families live in poverty, as compared with 12 percent of married-parent families. This change in economic status exposes the child to all the major developmental risks associated with poverty. A child who falls into poverty after divorce might be moved to an unfamiliar neighborhood where she or he encounters not only the dangers of malnourishment, poor schools, and poor housing, but also violence, substance abuse, and crime.

How well children cope with divorce depends upon several factors. Preschool children tend to be more susceptible than older children to emotional and behavioral problems following divorce. Only children appear to experience greater stress than children with siblings. Boys exhibit behavior problems for a longer period of time and have more difficulty interacting with others after parental divorce than girls do. When the divorced parents treat each other civilly and respect each other as parents, children are less likely to experience stress related to feeling torn between them (DeBord, 1997; Wallerstein & Blakeslee, 1996; Wallerstein & Kelly, 1996).

The largest issue typically raised for a child by parental divorce is custody. Research on whether single-parent custody or joint custody is more beneficial for the child is mixed. Some argue that joint custody confuses and stresses children and prolongs their exposure to the same parental interactions that led to the divorce (National Organization for Women, 1998). Others support joint custody, which is now the more prevalent practice, arguing that joint custody is more likely to reduce conflict, protect the rights of both parents, give the child the benefits of continuing regular contact with both a mother and a father, and reduce the likelihood that the noncustodial parent will neglect either the child or the child's financial support (Bender, 1994; Children's Rights Council of Maryland, 1998; Luepnitz, 1982). Again, parental attitudes and behavior appear to be a more critical factor for the child's outcome than the actual nature of the custody arrangement (Wallerstein & Blakeslee, 1996).

Foster Care

Interventions for orphaned or abandoned children have a long history. For instance, in medieval Europe, institutions were created to care for the large numbers of illegitimate children born during the Crusades. These were similar in spirit and practice to the orphanages that sprang up in the mid to late 1800s to accommodate the large numbers of European immigrant youth and the children of deceased soldiers following the U.S. Civil War (Davidson, 1994; Jacobs & Davies, 1994). Prior to this time, indigent families were typically housed together in almshouses subsidized by individual municipal governments; Davidson (1994) ironically refers to this system, with its emphasis on housing families together in this way, as "another form of family preservation" (p. 68).

The end of the nineteenth century saw significant demographic shifts, among them a growing trend away from an agrarian economy and toward town-based commercialism, and a widening gap between the poor and the middle class. The latter change, in turn, soon resulted in a change in the national zeitgeist whereby poor families came to be vilified rather than pitied. At the same time, public sentiment was aroused by a growing number of reports of the Dickensian conditions in far too many almshouses. The abuse, disease, malnutrition, and premature death common in these institutions played a part in their closure or the removal of the children confined in them. In the 1850s, 17,000 children were housed in almshouses; by 1910 this figure was less than 3,700 (Downs & Sherraden, 1983).

As was the case with almshouses, funding and oversight responsibility for orphanages and foster care originally fell to individual states. Between the end of the Civil War and the start of the twentieth century, a number of states established boards of charities, whose chief responsibility was the transfer of children from almshouses to orphanages or foster homes (Davidson, 1994). By 1900, close to 100,000 children had been placed in orphanages (Bremner, 1971b).

Before long, however, orphanages were plagued by the same ills that had characterized almshouses—overcrowding, disease, and poor care. Foster care arose in the late nineteenth century as an alternative to institutional care. The earliest foster care arrangements often revolved around indentureships, in which a child worked in exchange for keep, but there were "free" arrangements as well, in which the foster child was regarded as a member of the family. The shift from orphanages to foster care was gradual; not until the 1940s did the number of children in foster care exceed the number housed in orphanages (Davidson, 1994). As the number of children in such care increased, so did the complexity of the bureaucracy designed to oversee foster care arrangements. State boards of charities were charged with both regulating the quality of the care received by foster children and with supervising the children placed in foster homes (Costin & Rapp, 1984).

Davidson (1994) describes the pendulum swings in public opinion and policy initiatives related to the care of dependent children. In the early twentieth century, a number of states enacted statutes requiring mothers to retain custody of their children during early infancy; this trend broke precedent with earlier practice, which had used the absence of a father as grounds for the removal of children from maternal care (Bremner, 1971b; Costin & Rapp, 1984). The establishment of Mothers' Pension Laws, later enacted at the federal level as the Social Security Act of 1935 (Aid to Dependent Children), further strengthened efforts to keep indigent children with their families of origin.

Boarder Babies

The abandonment of babies in hospitals by their mothers immediately after birth has become a major social concern. With the rise in homelessness, AIDS, and drug addiction, these newborn "**boarder babies**" began appearing in hospital wards in ever higher numbers. The Department of Health and Human Services (USDHHS) reported that in 1991, 22,000 babies were deserted in 851 hospitals nationwide (USDHHS, 1992). Of these, 75 percent tested positive for drugs at birth. These children might be unclaimed, without family, and destined to enter the foster care system without ever knowing a home of their own. Some are boarders because hospital staff believe the mother to be unfit and child welfare agencies have taken protective custody, sometimes despite parental objections.

Hospital stays for these children cost as much a $1,500 a day. The length of stay can be very long, sometimes as much as six months, even though the children are physically able to leave the hospital. About two-thirds of the babies have some contact with their mothers, and only about 2.5 percent are eventually freed for adoption (Jetter, 1995). Many spend substantial amounts of time in foster care.

In some communities, early intervention services have been implemented to reunite and assist these babies and their mothers. Five federally funded projects now provide educational and supportive services. One of these, the New Jersey Project BABIES, involves mothers in counseling and in parenting skills classes; half of the mothers in the project have kept their babies and brought them home (Jetter, 1995). Similar projects in other major urban settings have also experienced success. For example, the D.C. General Maternal and Child Health Project in Washington, D.C., engages future parents at an early stage, before such problems as abandonment take place. This hospital runs a 10-week support program for pregnant patients from its drug-abuse and prenatal wards. The women meet weekly and receive skills training and outreach services. Each is assigned a support worker to help the future mother get to her medical appointments and stay drug-free. Programs like these have been established in other cities, including Atlanta, Chicago, and New York; all have shown a dramatic decrease in the number of abandoned babies as a result (Van Biema, 1994). The Chicago program, which even provides housing for homeless clients, has been known to offer its patients follow-up services for as long as three years. As these programs show, carefully designed prevention services are clearly an effective remedy for the problem of boarder babies. Unfortunately, the risks to children growing up in many of these households do not end once the child goes home from the hospital; many of the families require long-term support. Supportive services offered to the family during the baby's first year or more of life could have long-term beneficial effects.

In spite of such supports, children continue today to be placed in foster care when circumstances of their upbringing were deemed deleterious enough to outweigh whatever benefits might accrue from remaining with their families. Poverty, parental drug abuse, violence, mental illness, and criminality have all resulted in an unprecedented number of children being placed in foster care due to abandonment, child abuse, or neglect. Approximately 65 percent of the 3 million cases of reported child abuse in 1992 involved neglect (Children's Defense Fund, 1998g; Sedlak & Broadhurst, 1996). Crack cocaine use by mothers has also contributed to a large jump in the reports of abandoned or neglected infants (Children's Defense Fund, 1994a). Over 22,000 babies nationwide have also become "boarders" in hospitals, kept in newborn nurseries or special boarder units for weeks or even months after they are medically fit to be discharged, typically because their mothers are homeless or otherwise too incapacitated by poverty, drug use, or mental illness to provide them with a home (Jetter, 1995).

Until recently, it has been difficult to obtain state-by-state data from child welfare agencies, because there was no uniform reporting method. The situation has been alleviated somewhat by the creation of the Multistate Foster Care Data Archive, a joint project of the U.S. Department of Health and Human Services (USDHHS) and the University of Chicago's Chapin Hall Center for Children. In 1997, the archive released its most recent report, covering the states of California, Michigan, Missouri, Illinois, New York, and Texas (Children's Defense Fund, 1998g). In these states, which together account for nearly half of all the U.S. children in foster care, the rates of foster placement more than doubled between 1983 and 1994, with most of the increase in urban areas (Wulczyn, Harden, & George, 1997).

Data from the same study also indicate that most of the infants and young children in the foster care system during the years surveyed were returned to their homes within two years, though 20 percent reentered foster care within five years. One child out of six was eventually adopted, and another one-sixth remained in public care for six years or more. Infants and young children remained in foster care much longer than did those entering the system as older children (USDHHS, 1997a, 1997b; Wulczyn, Harden, & George, 1997).

Twenty percent of the children entering foster care during this period were younger than 1 year (Children's Defense Fund, 1994b). The duration of an infant's stay in foster care varies considerably, ranging from a median of 11.7 months in Texas to 43.4 months in New York (Chapin Hall Center for Children, 1993). Duration also varies by age: In New York, children 1 to 5 years old had a median foster placement of 30.1 months. The median length of placement for 12- to 17-year-olds was 12.3 months.

Many children in foster care today have been damaged by circumstances far worse than those that were typical in the 1980s (Dugger, 1993). Family destruction brought about by homelessness, parental use of crack cocaine, and now the impact of AIDS are all swelling the numbers of foster children, many of whom have suffered extraordinary emotional blows and deprivations (Dugger, 1993). The number of children expected to lose a mother to AIDS-related disorders by the year 2000 is estimated at 80,000 to 125,000 (Children's Defense Fund, 1994b).

Many of the children now in foster care have sustained multiple traumas that have impaired their development, and many of these children have serious emotional problems, which renders their placement in stable foster homes or in appropriate treatment facilities highly unlikely. Foster parents typically do not have the economic resources or specialized training to cope with a deeply disturbed child. Economically pressed state agencies also lack the costly treatment resources needed to help these children.

The already overburdened child welfare system is struggling to treat a growing number of children with serious psychological problems (Children's Defense Fund, 1998g). The number of children under age 13 in New York's state psychiatric hospitals doubled in the years from 1985 to 1992 (Dugger, 1993). A study of a sample of these children determined that 70 percent previously had been in foster care. A third had not received any psychiatric treatment prior to hospitalization. Much of the reported rise in serious disorders among foster children has been attributed to the inability of the welfare system's overwhelmed and undertrained staff to perceive that a child is in difficulty before serious illness has taken hold. However, it is not entirely clear whether all such hospitalized children actually require residential treatment; as Knitzer (1996) has pointed out, some are in a residential psychiatric setting because no other placement or treatment is available.

A significant part of the problem is the low availability and quality of family foster homes throughout the country. The sheer number of foster homes appears to be decreasing: between 1987 and 1990 alone, the number of available foster homes decreased by approximately one-third (Chamberlain et al., 1992; McDonald et al., 1997). Several factors contribute to the decline in numbers of foster homes: the higher percentage of women now in the out-of-home workforce, the low compensation paid to foster care homes, and the increasingly challenging, multiproblem children who are now seen in foster care (Children's Defense Fund, 1998g). Many foster care parents are inadequately paid, are minimally screened by licensing agencies, have little or no training, and are largely unmonitored in their care of children. Under these circumstances, it is not surprising to learn that foster children can suffer harm through the neglect or outright abuse of a foster parent. Even when a dedicated, loving foster parent is located to care for a child with special problems, supplementary resources are rarely available to help the foster parent cope with a child who has, say, a serious psychiatric problem or attention deficit disorder. If we are to have a better-functioning system of foster care, we will need to assess individual children's needs more effectively; select, train, and monitor foster parents more carefully; compensate foster parents more fairly for their efforts; and provide outreach and support networks for these often isolated foster parents.

The Family Preservation Argument

The history of the care of dependent children is characterized by swings between efforts to place children in environments more appropriate (at least in theory) than poor or abusive homes, and attempts to help the families in question to maintain custody of their children. Family preservation movements, in one form or another, have been in vogue off and on at least since the heyday of the almshouse.

Today, advocates of **family preservation** promote keeping the child out of foster care by providing supportive services to the family of origin in the home setting. Some programs focus on helping children to stay with their biological parents instead of being removed to foster care; others work at reuniting children and parents already separated by drug use, family violence, neglect, mental illness, or extreme poverty. It is far better, argue the adherents of family preservation, to help parents function more effectively as parents than to transfer children from their own homes into foster care. To this end, resources are devoted to interventions such as drug counseling for the parents, parent skills training, job counseling, and better housing for the family, in order to shore up the family's resources and encourage better parenting. Programs vary from state to state, but both voluntary and court-ordered participation are common (Administration for Children and Families, 1996).

The family preservation argument has found supporters in government: The use of such placement prevention services received legislative mandate in the form of the 1980 Public Law 96-272 (Adoption Assistance and Child Welfare Act), as well as in the enactment of the Family Preservation and Support Services Program as part of the Budget Reconciliation Act of 1993. Through this Family Preservation Act, states are to receive about $900 million over five years to reshape child welfare programs and to develop family support and family preservation services (USDHHS, 1996). Although this legislation takes a laudably preventive stance toward child welfare, a controversy has developed as to whether family preservation services are demonstrably effective or should even be attempted in all circumstances.

The family preservation movement is based loosely on several assumptions: that the parent-child bond is always present, strong, and positive in nature, that most families have the capacity to provide nonabusive, "good enough" parenting, and that many placements of children are inappropriate. Some of the assumptions inherent in the family preservation argument, however, have little or no research support (Rossi, 1991). There is no clear evidence that a strong parent-child bond exists in all cases, despite anecdotal and clinical data. Similarly, there is inadequate evidence on the issue of appropriateness of foster placement; given that the goal of placement is to err on the side of protecting children from danger, a certain amount of inappropriate or overly conservative placement is inevitable. Moreover, appropriateness is hard to define, because it depends on what might be equally ambiguous definitions of abuse and neglect.

Research on the efficacy of family preservation services is also difficult to conduct and to evaluate. A large-scale review of current and past family preservation programs is being carried out by the Chapin Hall Center for Children at the University of Chicago along with a carefully controlled empirical evaluation of outcomes for some 2,000 children at risk for foster care placement. This study uses a randomized design in which a computer program assigns cases to experimental and control categories. About 600 of the cases are to be followed for at least a year beyond treatment (Schuerman & Rossi, 1998).

Several problems plague even this study, however. One difficulty is determining which children are "at imminent risk" for placement. To gain enough subjects for the study, Chapin Hall researchers have had to broaden their case criterion to "at some risk," a change that significantly alters the population under study. Clearly many of these children would not face placement anyway, regardless of what services are provided to the family. One could argue that any child is at some risk of placement. Thus an additional problem for researchers is selecting the indicator of success: should "reduction of placement" be the measure, or is "better family functioning" the goal of these programs? Either of these potential criteria can be hard to express in concrete terms (Rossi, 1991).

A thorough review of the literature on family preservation programs reveals flawed studies and inconclusive, but not altogether promising, results. Some continue to champion these programs as being inherently better than foster care. Some experts adhere to the idea that such programs are more humane and less expensive than foster care (Fong, 1996; Goldstein et al., 1996; Wexler, 1995). Research results tend not to support this position, however. Marked success in preventing placement has not been found either in programs offering intensive services or in those specializing in crisis intervention. Although methodological problems make it difficult to assess the true effectiveness of most programs (Littell & Schuerman, 1995; Magura, 1981), a large enough body of research exists in this area to permit some stable conclusions to be drawn regarding the effectiveness of the family preservation approach. Few studies show significant differences in placement rates between families offered support services and comparison group families not provided such care; numerous programs actually reveal higher rates of foster care placement among children offered family preservation programs (Littell & Schuerman, 1995).

We also know that many children suffer serious harms and deprivations in their own homes. Public attention has been drawn to the controversy surrounding family preservation programs by the dramatic failures in a few such programs that resulted in the deaths of children reunited with abusive parents. The case of 6-year-old Elisa Izquierdo, who was beaten to death by her crack-addicted mother after months of severe abuse, aroused the interest and the ire of many citizens nationwide who had never heard of family preservation programs. A promising and appealing child who had been born addicted to crack but who had blossomed in the custody of her father, Elisa had been thriving and performing well in her Montessori school. When Elisa's father died of cancer, however, she had been returned to the custody of her mother.

The warning signs that Elisa was in trouble were immediately apparent. Neighbors repeatedly reported to the New York City Welfare Administration (CWA) that they heard Elisa screaming and begging for mercy. Two other children had already been removed from Elisa's mother's home. Officials at the public school to which her mother had Elisa transferred reported her injuries to CWA. Elisa's mother herself begged caseworkers to remove Elisa from the home; they responded that they were "too busy" to investigate. Two months before Elisa's seventh birthday, her mother killed her by throwing her against a concrete wall. A police officer reported that there was no part of her body that had not been cut or bruised. He called it the worst case of child abuse he had ever seen (Van Biema, 1995).

Elisa Izquierdo's story is not unique. In 1989, Los Angeles county paid $18 million to settle lawsuits brought on behalf of children who were abused while in the county's custody (Hornblower, 1995). Twelve hundred children are killed each year by their parents or caretakers (Beck, 1996). One of these was 15-month-old David, abused and finally smothered to death by his mother. His parents had already lost custody of his older sister because they had severely abused her, and caseworkers had received reports that the parents were abusing David. Child abuse expert Richard Gelles (1996) blames casework loads and the philosophy of family preservation, which emphasizes the rights of biological parents.

The variables that contribute to incidents like these are not difficult to identify. Budget cuts have trimmed personnel and material resources from child protection programs. As of this writing, Congress is considering a bill that would cut almost $3 billion more from child protection programs across the nation (Smolowe, 1995). At the same time, between 4 and 10 million children are scheduled to be cut from welfare rolls as a part of congressional attempts to balance the national budget. Such cuts are likely to result in additional child abuse cases as poverty levels and family stress increase.

Even now, social services caseworkers are overburdened and undertrained (Beck, 1996; Brandwein, 1995; Dina, 1995; Gelles, 1996; Van Biema, 1995). Required to make life-and-death decisions on a daily basis, caseworkers feel unappreciated when their actions do protect children, and guilty when they do not. A 1995 survey of former child protection caseworkers in Arizona revealed that two-thirds of them left their jobs because of pressure and stress (Smolowe, 1995).

In child protection cases, especially when the child is suffering grievous physical or emotional harm, the welfare of the child should be the foremost concern (Goldstein et al., 1996). There are certainly many families that can improve their functioning with the addition of supportive services to ease them through rocky times, but strong evidence indicates that not all such families will be able to provide optimal or even adequate care for their children with the limited supports available. Concentration of our resources on helping a few physically abused and neglected children to remain safely at home might deflect us from the larger task of improving the lives of countless desperately deprived children whose level of physical danger would never result in out-of-home placements (Magura, 1981).

Family support programs like Head Start and the Yale Child Welfare Research Program (Provence & Naylor, 1983; Seitz, 1985), predicated on the belief that parents raising children in impoverished or high-risk environments can develop their skills and become better caregivers and socializers of their children, have been shown to be effective at enhancing parenting so that parents in turn can support their children. Such programs, in which families are provided with a broad range of child care, parent education, pediatric screenings and care, and referrals for other community-based services, have been shown to have a positive impact on children's health, safety, and educational status, as well as on family economics, parental education, and the spacing of subsequent births (Seitz, 1996).

Adoption

With the growing conviction that the foster care system in the United States is a failure has come a call for the reform of policies governing how adoptions are handled (Forbes, 1995; Jacobs, 1994; Sheehan, 1993). Of the half a million foster children in this country, only about 50,000 are available for adoption. In spite of the fact that 2 million couples and individuals are eagerly seeking children to adopt, most of these children will wait for years before being placed permanently with a loving family, if indeed they are ever adopted (Children's Defense Fund, 1998g; Craig, 1995; Forbes, 1995; Glazer, 1993).

One of the more positive aspects of the family preservation program is its acknowledgment that sometimes "permanency planning" for children means not resettling a child with her biological family, but clearing a path for permanent adoption. Foster care was never meant to be a long-term solution, but only a brief stop along a road that was to lead ultimately to the child's return to a stabilized family system or entry into a permanent place with a loving, adoptive family. Of 5,000 children whose placement plans made them immediately available for adoption in the early 1990s, fewer than 600 were adopted, and those adoptions took an average of 4 years (Children's Defense Fund, 1998g). Almost half of all foster children remain in foster care at least 2 years; many remain in

---

 Kinship Care

One attempt to help resolve the problems facing the nation's troubled foster care system is an increasing reliance on what is known as **"kinship care"**—informal arrangements in which an at-risk child is placed with a relative other than a parent (Crumbley & Little, 1997; Heger & Scannapieco, 1998). A 1997 survey revealed that over 10 percent of grandparents have custody of one or more grandchildren for six months or more (Children's Defense Fund, 1998g). The 1996 census indicates that 2.14 million children in the United States live with a relative other than a parent; two-thirds of these relatives are grandparents.

Welfare reform might pose a threat to kinship care arrangements. Many recipients of Temporary Assistance to Needy Families (TANF) who are caring for a relative's child on an informal basis might be forced to place the child in foster care in order to fulfill TANF work requirements. A few states are offering such caregivers a monthly allowance in order to prevent foster care placement of the children in their charge; other states are gradually making arrangements to achieve the same goal.

the system for more than 6 years. It is not unusual for foster children to be in and out of foster care for years, alternately being placed with foster families and being returned to their biological parents, some repeatedly.

Approximately 15,000 children each year "age out" of foster care, having become too old to be adoptable. An amendment to the Adoption Assistance and Welfare Act provides for programs to prepare older foster children to live independently after leaving the system, but many of these young adults go straight from the foster care system to welfare dependency and/or homelessness (Craig, 1995; Piliponis, 1996; Soto-Maldonado, 1996).

Proponents of stronger adoption laws tend to equate stronger laws with those that emphasize the rights of the child over those of the biological parent or parents. Several well-publicized adoption cases in the early 1990s drew attention to the tensions that develop when the best interests of the child and of the biological parent come into conflict. In the 1993 DeBoer case, Roberta and Jan DeBoer lost custody of their adopted daughter Jessica after her birth parents were able to overturn an initial relinquishing of parental rights. Televised images of Jessica, by then a toddler who had always considered the DeBoers to be her mother and father, screaming as she was handed over to a biological mother and father she had never known, galvanized public sentiment in favor of child-oriented rulings but did little to change judicial practice in such cases.

Similarly, the adoptive parents of "Baby Richard," who were the only parents the child had ever known, lost custody of Richard when the biological father successfully challenged the adoption on the grounds that he could not have relinquished parental rights because he was led to believe that his girlfriend's pregnancy had resulted in a stillbirth. Despite the fact that the biological father, by then married to the birth mother, had never met the child, the Illinois Supreme Court upheld a 1994 lower court ruling that custody of 3 1/2-year-old Richard be given to the birth parents.

Unfortunately, where children's rights exist only after all adults' rights have been considered, dramatic scenes of adopted children taken from their homes to be placed with a previously unknown biological parent will continue. Many children lack a permanent home because their biological parents, who might be incapable of caring for them for years, nevertheless refuse to relinquish them for adoption. A related issue is the plight of a child whose chances for adoption are diminished because no adoptive parents of the child's ethnic or racial background have come forward to give him a home. Should policy err on the side of seeing that child placed in a loving home, even when that home might contain parents of a different race? (See "The Battle Over Transracial Adoption.")

The 1997 passage by the Clinton administration of the Adoption and Safe Families Act was meant to promote adoption and other permanency options by putting the child's safety above the rights of the parents, by requiring criminal record checks of all potential foster parents, and by establishing adoption incentives for individual states (Children's Defense Fund, 1997a).

In a case that received much publicity but that has had minimal impact on policy, a California mother addicted to drugs gave up her daughter at birth. The daughter was immediately taken home by a family who intended to adopt the

The Battle over Transracial Adoption

The number of children placed in out-of-home care due to abuse or neglect has been steadily growing; if the present trend continues, there could be as many as 900,000 children in such care by the year 2000 (McRoy, 1995). Many of today's foster children are waiting for adoption, and an estimated one-half of these are minority children (Bartholet, 1994). Minority children wait twice as long as white children to be adopted, an average of 2 years versus 1 year; moreover, they are less likely than white children to be permanently placed (Westat, 1986). Why is this so?

One of the reasons has been child welfare policy, usually unwritten, that disfavored transracial adoption and often required minority children to wait until a suitable family of the same race could be found. In 1972, the National Association of Black Social Workers (NABSW) began speaking out against transracial adoption, claiming that allowing whites to adopt black children was comparable to cultural genocide, and that only black parents should be permitted to raise black children unless all efforts to reunite the family of origin or to find a same-race adoptive home have been exhausted (NABSW, 1988; Kennedy, 1995).

At one time, many black families were disqualified from adopting by economic and other adoption criteria, some of which have been altered to permit more minority families to become adoptive parents. A 1986 study determined that 50 percent of all minority adoptive families had incomes below $20,000 per year, and 20 percent had incomes below $10,000 per year (Westat, 1986). In contrast, 14 percent of nonminority families had incomes below $20,000, and only 2 percent had incomes below $10,000. Despite an apparent desire to adopt among

black families, and some relaxing of the requirements, there still appear to be insufficient numbers of black adoptive families. Several factors, including low agency recruitment of black families, along with a suspicion of public agencies among blacks, and a possible anxiety that they are unlikely to meet agency criteria, have combined to reduce the number of prospective African American adoptive parents (Simon & Altstein, 1992).

Today, under the Adoption Assistance and Child Welfare Act of 1980, federally funded agencies offer subsidies to minority families who wish to adopt; these forms of assistance are not available to white families. However, other, noneconomic screening criteria for prospective adoptive parents have not been abandoned. Candidate families are still ranked in terms of parental suitability. Yet, to expand the pool of black families, some adoption agencies have loosened their requirements (such as those regarding home size, marital status, and employment history) to include as prospective adoptive parents black families who would have been excluded had they been white candidates (Bartholet, 1994). Despite such measures, minority children have still been forced to wait longer for permanent homes, making both liberal and conservative policy makers, including large numbers of disappointed white prospective parents, question the wisdom of insisting on a racial match before a child may be adopted (Forbes, 1995).

A similar storm has arisen with regard to Native American children, who have been adopted transracially in large numbers. For example, Native American children made up 7 percent of the South Dakota population in 1968 but 70 percent of the adoptions. In Wisconsin, the likelihood of a Native American child being removed from home was 1,600 percent greater than it was for a non-Native child. In 1978, Minnesota reported that 90 percent of the state's nonrelative adoptions of Native American children were transracial (North American Council on Adoptable Children, 1978). Finally in 1978, this situation was addressed by the enactment of a federal statute. The Indian Child Welfare Act (P.L. 95-608), which was drafted to prevent the breakdown of Indian families and tribes, provided that child custody cases involving a Native American child would be transferred to tribal jurisdiction. The legislation also provided funding to establish Indian child and family service programs on or near reservations to help prevent the breakup of Indian families (Simon & Altstein, 1992).

In 1994, Senator Howard Metzenbaum of Ohio introduced the Multiethnic Placement Act (MPA), which became law in 1994. This legislation, similar to a Connecticut law passed in 1986 and other state statutes, was designed to prohibit foster care agencies from denying prospective, otherwise qualified parents the right to adopt black children solely on the basis of race. The cultural, ethnic, or racial background of a child may be considered in foster care or permanent placement decisions, but it cannot be the dispositive criterion. Subsequently another version, attempting to repeal the 1994 act, was sponsored by Representative Jim Bunning of Kentucky, a Republican. The Bunning version, which was defeated, was designed to prevent delays in child placement resulting from the wait for a qualified minority family (McRoy, 1995). Meanwhile, the U.S. Department of Health and Human Services has issued guidelines pursuant to the MPA that make it illegal for states to delay a child's adoption while agencies search for a qualified same-race family. State agencies that fail to comply will risk losing their federal funding.

Despite recurrent furor in the news media and among social work professionals, a majority of both black and white families appear to believe that the most important issue in adoption is to place a child in a permanent home as soon as possible. CBS News polls, taken in 1971 and 1991, of black and white Americans on the transracial adoption issue found that 71 percent of blacks and 70 percent of whites supported the idea of transracial adoption at least in some circumstances. Research to date seems to show that children raised in transracial adoptive homes are as content, have as much self esteem, and do not have greater adjustment difficulties than children raised by adoptive parents of the same race (Simon & Altstein, 1993; McRoy & Zurcher, 1983).

The current form of the Multiethnic Placement Act will likely prove a lightning rod for litigation as the practical import of its provisions are tested by both agencies and prospective adoptive parents. Cases involving Native American children continue to prove thorny, as jurisdiction shuttles from state court to tribal court, with ambiguous appeal rights. Attempts to repeal the MPA will doubtless continue as well. The phrase *the best interest of the child* has become ever more difficult to interpret in the case of adoptees, and achieving a just and beneficial result in every case remains a challenge for policy makers.

child they named "Caitlin." After three months, Caitlin's biological mother turned up for the first time since her birth, demanding $15,000 in cash before she would permit the adoption to be finalized. When, on the advice of their attorney, the potential adoptive parents refused, the birth mother revoked her consent for the adoption to go forward. At the age of 8 months, Caitlin was removed from the only home she had ever known. Within days, the birth mother, who was still using drugs and who had also lost custody of her two other children, was evicted from her apartment for fighting. Caitlin was removed and placed, not with the family she knew as her own, but in foster care. This decision was made to honor a request made by the birth mother, who had relinquished care of Caitlin in the first place (Jacobs, 1994).

Under what circumstances should a biological parent's parental rights be legally terminated? This question often arises when the biological mother is a substance abuser. One prominent policy analyst proposes that it be made easier to terminate the rights of parents deemed to be unfit: Besharov (1996) suggests that the criteria for termination "should be the parents' demonstrable inability to care for their children, coupled with their unwillingness to accept or respond to a reasonable offer of drug treatment. Since termination should only be pursued when there is a reasonable likelihood of adoption, the focus should be on younger children, especially abandoned infants" (p. 35). Others urge caution, noting cases in which accelerated adoptions of children in the foster care system are not always as successful as those that are allowed to take longer to complete. A Massachusetts plan to "fast-track" adoptions received widespread legislative and popular support, but ultimately resulted in the failure of many adoptions and the returning of hastily adopted children to foster care (Lakshmanan, 1995). Whether adoptions proceed slowly or parental rights are terminated more quickly to allow children earlier access to permanent homes, adequate support services are likely to be the key to success.

Whose rights are paramount in questions of custody and adoption? Under what circumstances should a biological parent's rights be terminated, and how long should this take? What role, if any, should such a parent play in the life of an adopted child? These are grave questions for policy makers, who are at least becoming more aware of the mental health consequences for children who grow up without a permanent home or who are forcibly removed from a foster or adoptive home in which they have flourished. In 1993, Congress provided funds to states to improve aspects of the current child welfare system. Among these reforms are enhanced training for child welfare staff, foster parents, and adoptive parents; matching grants for states that wish to improve their foster care and adoption data collection systems; and funds for state courts to help them remove barriers to placing children in permanent homes (Children's Defense Fund, 1994b; Forbes, 1995; Ryan, 1995). Until such reforms are enacted, however, children still have few rights under present legislative frameworks, underscoring the fact that child advocates and child development scholars alike have much work to do in informing the growing child welfare debate (Leach, 1993).

SUMMARY

A variety of large-scale programs implemented at the federal level seek to provide benefits to support children and families as they start out their lives together, or to strengthen them as they encounter child-rearing crises related to poverty, drug use, crime, and family dissolution. The 1993 Family and Medical Leave Act was the first non-disability-based parental leave to be enacted into U.S. law. Parents have long sought such a benefit, but restrictions in the FMLA limit its usefulness or render the mandated leaves completely beyond the reach of too many families. A European-style child allowance, proposed by many child advocates for U.S. families, would help bridge the gap between services provided for families and those they need by supplementing family income to extend family leaves (or make them possible in the first place) or to purchase good-quality infant care.

There is a long history of tension between foster care programs and family preservation initiatives. At present, mandated family preservation efforts seek to promote family integrity over the dissolution that often results in foster care, but to date the services available are limited in both scope and duration. As a result, family preservation programs have not shown themselves to be as useful as advocates had hoped. With the virtual failure of the foster care system and the lack of proven effectiveness of family preservation efforts, many policy makers and advocates are calling for reform of adoption regulations, which at present tend to favor the needs of biological parents, no matter how unfit, over those of children.

None of these solutions will be achieved without effort and commitment, and they cannot be achieved at all under an ideology unwilling to prepare for the future. We are optimistic, however, that they will be achieved, both because of a growing insistence by parents that the government and other groups take a large measure of responsibility for meeting the needs of families, and because the businesses and decision makers responsible for the implementation of family-supportive policies are becoming more willing to make long-term investments in human capital. Parents, especially new parents, are a busy, beleaguered constituency, but they are a powerful one. Commitment to getting our children off to a good start makes good sense in the long run, not only for individual children and families, but for the nation as a whole.

Early Intervention and Family Support

Imagine that school officials in a low-SES, rural area are concerned about the lack of school readiness of incoming kindergartners. School personnel from this district team up with developmental psychologists at a local university to mount a preschool enrichment program for a sample of children in this area. State legislators, long concerned about the high costs of remedial programs and the impact of children's low educational attainment on the community as a whole, agree to provide partial funding for a pilot for this program for three years; a local business consortium chips in as well. Flyers inviting participation are distributed through a local pediatric clinic serving mostly families on Medicaid, and 20 children are placed in the program three days a week. The first 20 children on the program's waiting list are assigned to a **comparison group.** At the end of a year, researchers from the university discover that the children who received the program now score significantly higher on developmental scales than do comparable children who did not participate in a preschool program. Legislators who championed the program declare it a success.

Funding to conduct a longitudinal evaluation of program effectiveness is built into the program's grant, and a follow-up study is conducted when the children are in first grade. This time the evaluators discover that the mean developmental scores of the two groups are no longer appreciably different. (Such a temporary increase in developmental quotients (or other measures) is sometimes referred to as a **suntan effect**—a positive benefit that appears to fade out over time following cessation of the intervention.) There is a strong negative reaction to this news in the state legislature, and a proposal to renew the program's funding for another three-year period is defeated.

The original evaluation of our imaginary program continues, however. Ten more years pass, and our evaluators visit these children, who are now 16 years old, at their homes. This time they discover that the program children, though once again scoring no higher on tests of IQ than the nonprogram children, are more likely to be in school (many of the waiting-list children have dropped out), have a higher grade point average than comparison children who are still in school, and are, on the average, receiving fewer costly remedial services in school. This **sleeper effect** (an effect that is not discernible immediately following an intervention) raises questions about the mediating variables that account for the delayed positive effects. In the case of our 40 children, for instance, family questionnaires reveal that many of the parents of program children used the hours during which their children were in preschool at the time of the original intervention to attend high school or college classes themselves and to further their own educations. Researchers hypothesize that the parents' own demonstrated commitment to education, along with their enhanced ability to obtain steady and lucrative employment, has contributed to their children's commitment to school.

This somewhat oversimplified example illustrates some of the issues involved in mounting and evaluating early intervention efforts. Later in this chapter we will discuss some of these in more detail. This case provides some information about this type of program, but it raises as many questions as it answers. Just what is meant by early intervention, what characterizes such efforts, and what policy issues shape their development and application? How are early intervention and family support programs alike, and how do they differ? Which type of program is more effective? All of these issues will be explored in this chapter.

A YOUNG FIELD

When Project Head Start was first implemented in 1965 as an experiment in improving children's lives, it was viewed by scholars and policy makers as a pilot program that might touch the lives of just a few preschoolers. Today Head Start is a fixture in the lives of hundreds of thousands of families, and is credited with enhancing the social competence, educational success, and health of children all over the nation. Hundreds of thousands of additional children receive support through programs similar to the preschool intervention described above.

Other intervention efforts improve the lives of children by providing parenting education, improved access to health care, **developmental screenings,** services for children at risk for developmental disability or delay, or high-quality day care or preschool experiences (indeed, any such child-care program is necessarily a form of early intervention). For the purposes of this chapter, the term **early intervention** will be used to designate programs that target children directly; the term **family support program** will be used to describe interventions that consist only of a parent intervention component.

The field of child and family intervention has evolved rapidly. There were a handful of early intervention programs in the early 1960s (Darlington et al., 1980; Berrueta-Clement et al., 1984; Bredekamp, 1987), but the first Head Start pilot program was considered revolutionary. Certainly it would not have occurred to many parents or professionals to call for services of this type. Even less attention would have been paid in the form of policy mandates meant to guarantee service provision. But within the past 30 years or so, a massive body of work has been developed that speaks to the efficacy of programs designed to improve the lives of children and families.

During that 30-year period the field has been characterized by controversy, theoretical excesses, pendulum swings in public attitudes toward and beliefs about what intervention might achieve, and a variety of attitudes (some not as laudable as others) held among child development professionals about the very people whose welfare we were trying to improve (Meisels & Shonkoff, 1995; Shokraii & Fagan, 1998; Zigler, 1995). The major controversy was—and, to some extent, continues to be—whether early intervention has any long-term benefits for children (Consortium for Longitudinal Studies, 1983; Darlington et al., 1980; Zigler & Berman, 1983). As a rich and reliable fund of information on the results of such programs grew, a second question gained ascendancy: Could greater and more persistent positive effects be achieved through working directly with *parents* in addition to or even instead of intervening with children alone? As we will see later in this chapter, programs that work with both parent and child to achieve lasting two-generational benefits have found considerable support. A sample of the types of programs studied and the findings that put the first of these controversies to rest once and for all, and that continue to inform the second question, will be described later in this chapter.

WHAT IS EARLY INTERVENTION?

Today we are inclined to use the phrase *early intervention* without questioning what it really means, but since the 1960s new ideas have emerged about both what it means to "intervene" in the lives of children and what constitutes "early" (Frank Porter Graham Child Development Center, 1998; Shonkoff, 1993). New evidence indicates that important opportunities for intervention have already come and gone by the time a child reaches the preschool age at which Head Start eligibility began in those earliest years (Begley, 1996). Indeed, critical efforts to optimize child health and development are now made during infancy, during the prenatal period, and, in some cases, even before conception (Carnegie Corporation, 1994; National Commission on Children, 1990; Pfannenstiel, Lambson, & Yarnell, 1991; Shonkoff, 1993). Moreover, debate over the assumptions underlying that first Head Start effort and other intervention programs has led workers in this field to examine many times over the models on which such efforts were built.

Early intervention, as it is broadly conceived today, can take any number of approaches to problem solving or prevention in any area important to the lives of children and families. Though the classical portrait of early intervention depicts the provision of education-oriented assistance to preschool-age children, other services and services delivered at other age ranges are equally entitled to wear the early intervention hat. *Early intervention* is generally taken to refer to actions taken before a child reaches school age, even as far back as the prenatal or even the preconception period. One useful definition says that early intervention is "a systematic and planned effort to promote development through a series of manipulations of environmental or experiential factors initiated during the first 5 years of life" (Guaralnick & Bennet, quoted in Bricker & Veltman, 1990; Meisels & Shonkoff, 1995).

Adequate prenatal care, screening newborns for PKU and sickle cell anemia, and administering antibiotic drops to newborns' eyes are all forms of early intervention. So are parenting education programs for pregnant adolescents, therapeutic preschool programs for children with identified developmental disabilities, and programs that help parents get in touch with community agencies that can provide them with needed services.

What sorts of outcomes can be achieved through early intervention and family support? Specific program goals typically address one or more of three areas:

- *Enhancing educational readiness.* Programs like Head Start and the Perry Preschool Program were originally intended to optimize a child's chances to do well in school by helping them develop the motivation, skills, and understanding they needed to succeed educationally.

- *Improving child health.* The Women, Infants and Children (WIC) program of the U.S. Department of Health and Human Services (see chapter 6 for a full discussion of this program) delivers nutritious food supplements to pregnant and nursing women and young children with the express goal of improving nutritional status and decreasing the risk of health problems related to low birthweight and iron-deficiency anemia.
- *Supporting parents.* Programs like the Missouri-based Parents as Teachers provide support in the form of home visits (beginning during the third trimester of pregnancy) and developmental screenings to help parents to enhance their child's development and to identify any problems that might impede their child's healthy development and later school success (Hall & Zigler, 1993; Levine, 1988). Parent support groups might, but do not necessarily, contain a child-oriented component as well.

Clearly, these goals are not wholly separable. Improvements in physical health, for instance, are important for helping children to attain their full potential at cognitive and social tasks. Parent education has been associated with higher levels of school readiness in their children, with diminished rates of child abuse and neglect (Daro, 1993; Olds, 1992), and with improvements in the social and economic welfare of entire families. Most intervention programs address more than one of these. As this chapter will demonstrate, broad-based, comprehensive early intervention programs are likely to result in a wide range of positive outcomes, attained in ways that are cost-effective as well.

In addition, program evaluators have begun to look to early intervention efforts as a means of achieving results that might not have been expected by program mounters. Longitudinal evaluations of some programs, stretching into adolescence, have found associations between program participation and lower than expected rates of truancy, arrest, and other forms of delinquency (Berreuta-Clement et al., 1984; Farrington et al., 1990; Zigler, Taussig, & Black, 1992; Graves, 1998; Hall & Zigler, 1993, Hirokazu, 1995; Yoshikawa, 1995). The extent of early intervention's capacity to ameliorate these and other social problems, such as drug abuse, adolescent pregnancy, or poverty, is still being explored (Slavin, 1998).

Basic Assumptions

Several fundamental assumptions underlie the theoretical basis for intervening in the lives of children and families. The first of these is that the early childhood period and the experiences that occur during that time have important implications for later child and adult development (Bloom, 1964; Hunt, 1961). Such a belief is well established in many fields concerned with children, including child psychology, psychiatry, education, and pediatrics (Bricker & Veltman, 1995; Meisels & Shonkoff, 1995). We have described in earlier chapters how an ecological perspective on child development focuses on the importance of the systems that influence child outcomes; a truly effective intervention program would result in the enhancement of several spheres of the child's psychosocial ecosystem.

Bringing in the Men: Getting Fathers Involved

A growing body of research provides evidence for a basic idea: that fathers are important for children. All too often, the focus has been exclusively on mothers' interactions with their children. Where are the fathers, and how does attending to them and their special contributions change our research paradigms, our clinical approach to childhood intervention and outcomes, and our policy focus? Although the majority of mothers are now working outside the home, most report feeling that their husbands are not as involved in parenting activities as they could be (Cowan & Cowan, 1992). Divorce rates, which continue to hover around 50 percent, pose a significant challenge to father involvement, as does the increasingly high rate—now over 30 percent (Popenoe, 1996)—of births to unmarried women. Violence against young black men takes many fathers out of the picture permanently; some inner-city communities appear to suffer from a virtually total absence of fathers and father figures.

The absence of an involved father, whether he is physically gone or is present but emotionally unavailable, comes at a high cost to children and families. Experts agree that children who have a close, warm relationship with their father reap benefits not available to father-absent children. Among these are a healthy sense of independence, higher IQs, and greater social competence; some even theorize that men involved early in the care of their children are less likely to engage in sexual abuse later on (Adler, 1997; Nord, Brimhall, & West, 1997). Fathers also contribute indirectly to the healthy development of the child when they provide emotional support and respite for the mother (Crockenberg, Lyons-Ruth, & Dickstein, 1993; Lieberman, 1993).

Just having a father at home is not enough to provide these benefits; he needs to be emotionally and physically available to his children. Growing up without an available father does not necessarily *cause* negative outcomes, but it has been associated with increased risk of a variety of socially incompetent behaviors. On the other hand, growing up with an involved father in the picture can optimize positive outcomes (Levine & Pittinsky, 1997).

Positive outcomes of father involvement accrue not only to children, but to the fathers and mothers as well. According to Yale Child Study Center psychiatrist Kyle Pruett (1993, p. 46), "men and children can affect each other as profoundly as any relationship that they will ever have in their life." Mothers also stand to benefit as men share in the care and education of their children (Levine, Murphy, & Wilson, 1993). Recognizing the importance of and need for increased father involvement, in 1995 President Clinton requested every agency of the federal government to review its programs and policies with the express purpose of strengthening the role of fathers in families.

One effective way to get fathers involved with their children is for early intervention programs to develop policies designed to welcome and support them. Too often, men do not feel welcome in the female-dominated world of early childhood programs, and a special effort must be made to encourage their participation. Encouraging paternal involvement might require innovative outreach techniques. In their research on ways to get men involved, Levine and his colleagues (1993) cite several components that can reach out successfully to fathers. These include using school bus drivers as program recruiters, encouraging women to encourage men, making an effort to include fathers in home visits, and reaching out to all men in a given community, not just fathers.

One program that has made a concerted effort to focus on men is Avance. Located in San Antonio, Texas, Avance's goal is to strengthen and support families through center- and community-based services. In the late 1980s, the program's director, Gloria Rodriguez, noted that while the women involved in the program were doing well, the men, many of whom had a limited education and were unemployed, were being sidelined. Recognizing the need to support fathers and thereby to support families as a whole, Avance developed a curriculum for fathers that emphasized personal and parenting skills. In weekly meetings the men gather to discuss a range of issues such as Latino family life, drug abuse, child abuse, and nutrition. By reaching out to fathers, Avance has strengthened their connection to their children and families, and has paved the way toward their continuing involvement as their children grow.

Secondly, early intervention theory is posited on the understanding that genetic and biological problems can be overcome or attenuated through efforts initiated early in the life of the organism in question—in our case, a child (Bricker & Veltman, 1995). There is also a wealth of evidence that psychosocial, behavioral, and educational problems can be remediated or prevented with the right kind of attention at the right stage of development (Darlington et al., 1980; Levine, 1988; Meisels & Shonkoff, 1995; Zigler & Berman, 1983).

A third defining assumption guiding effective intervention theory and practice is that the solutions to the problems faced by children and families today must be as diverse as the problems themselves. Educational failure, juvenile criminality, child abuse, poverty, and poor physical and mental health—to name just a few issues—are multiply determined. It stands to reason that the most effective mediation for these problems will be multifaceted and instituted in ways that affect multiple areas of family ecology at once (Shonkoff & Meisels, 1990).

Finally, it is imperative that early intervention programs, and the legislative and administrative efforts that fund and promote them, be informed by what is known about how best to support children and families. By blending science and advocacy, we can best identify the simplest pathways by which to support the complexity of human development (Shonkoff, 1993). Such an approach must take full advantage of both developmental theory and empirical data.

The History of Early Intervention

Most of the early intervention efforts with which we are familiar today have their roots in the 1950s and early 1960s, when research findings seemed to indicate that intelligence could be increased dramatically and simply, and that environmental stimulation and enrichment were the keys to achieving such a goal. This enthusiasm for intellectual improvement was spurred by research showing that animals reared under environmentally suboptimal conditions performed poorly on tasks of learning and problem solving. The findings seemed to indicate that early deprivation has the potential to create a permanent deficit in cognitive ability. The idea that early enrichment programs could counter the ill effects of **environmental deprivation** flowed logically from such results. The popularity of early enrichment was furthered by Joseph McVicker Hunt's book *Intelligence and Experience* (1961), in which the author argued that intelligence, rather than being genetically fixed, is essentially a product of environmental inputs. Hunt went on to suggest that when children are given a truly optimal set of early experiences, their IQs can be boosted as much as 70 points (Hunt, 1961). The notion of "magical" or **"critical" periods** in a child's development was also at its zenith, leading to suggestions that if these experiences were not delivered during the early period of development, their effects would be attenuated or even negated (Bloom, 1964).

Hand-in-hand with the concept of preventive inoculation against the ill effects of poverty went the idea of **"the magic period,"** that time during which intervention was believed to be almost magically effective. Nearly every age of a child's life has had its champions. Some say that the prenatal period is of paramount importance and that good prenatal care prepares a child adequately for life and safeguards a baby against developmental difficulties. Others endorse the first year of life as being the best period for intervention and have gone so far as to imply that simply hanging a mobile over a child's crib will promote sound development. Others have devoted their attention to the first three years of life (White, 1990), the two years before school (early Head Start efforts), or the first three years of school (Bereiter, 1972).

By now, of course, we realize that even the best inoculation is of little lasting value without appropriate "booster shots"—continuous helping efforts throughout childhood. Providing a child with good parenting during the first year of life, for instance, doesn't obviate that child's need for good parenting at other stages of development. We have learned to guard against the idea that there is one and only one period during which intervention efforts will have maximal, indelible effects. Every age of the child is a magic period, and we must take care not to shortchange one age group in our efforts to help another.

Widespread acceptance of the environmental mystique—that is, a belief in the idea that a small change in the environment will produce major changes in development—and the notion of magical periods led to naive and grandiose hopes for preschool programs. These hopes were buttressed by early reports of IQ gains averaging 10 points following almost any intervention program, including the first six- to eight-week session of Head Start. Many scholars and policy makers, including President Johnson himself, contributed to the naive idea that a few weeks of effort at just the right stage of development could wipe out both past and future effects of poverty.

Had such scholarly beliefs prevailed at another time in U.S. history, early intervention efforts might not have achieved the prominence they did. As it was, however, the optimism of psychologists and educators about what might be achieved for children coincided with a period of national optimism and fiscal prosperity. The early 1960s were characterized by a strong national sense of pride and optimism. A healthy economy, not yet overburdened by the costs of the war in Vietnam, contributed to the feeling that the United States had both the energy and the resources to devote to domestic problems. The successfully developing space program was a source of great pride and international acclaim, contributing to the feeling that much might be accomplished by science in the service of children and families.

At the same time, the problems of racial, social, and economic inequality came into the limelight. Estimates indicated that nearly one-fourth of Americans, half of them children, were poor. Poverty was blamed for the rising crime rate and for the increase in the number of individuals who were unable to assume productive roles in business, industry, or military service, mainly because they had little education. Professionals and politicians suddenly acknowledged what had been the case for a long time: low-SES children generally did less well in school and scored lower on IQ measures compared to children of upper- and middle-income **SES**. At the same time, the problems of poor children were blamed on what were perceived as cultural deficits, giving rise to the now-antiquated term *cultural deprivation*. The theoretical basis for the deficit model came from early studies of children's environments and of animal learning and development (Hunt, 1961). Above all, there was a grand spirit of optimism, an unflagging belief in our ability to improve the lives of troubled and troubling children by minimizing or even eradicating social class inequalities in the United States. One front of the Johnson administration's War on Poverty was the preschool intervention program, of which Head Start was the best-known example (Zigler & Muenchow, 1992).

The enthusiasm for this new approach to preventing developmental and educational problems was so great that many believed not only that early environmental enrichment would enable lower-SES children to perform on a par with their higher-SES peers, but that the effects of such interventions were indelible, even in the face of later environmental insults.

HOW AND WITH WHOM SHOULD WE INTERVENE?

Before mounting an intervention program, some decisions have to be made about the most basic nature of the services to be provided. The most important question revolves around the target of the intervention—To whom will services be provided? This question really has two types of answers. One concerns the level at which interventions are targeted. Is it more effective, for instance, to intervene directly with children, or to work with parents who will in turn pass on benefits of support and education to their children in the form of more competent parenting? Or should the program do as Head Start does, work with both parents and children? Another question involves defining the nature and degree of the risk for disability, developmental delay, school failure, or other problems the child must face before intervention can be justified. It is easy to argue that, in theory, any promising intervention should be provided to as many children and/or parents as possible, but implementation of *universal* services is costly and strategically difficult. The only truly universal service provided to children in the United States is free public education. Economic, intellectual, and material constraints on resources make it necessary to *target* specific "at risk" groups for receipt of interventions.

Risk can be classified in several ways. The most common classifications include "at risk" categories related to a diagnosed developmental disability (e.g., Down syndrome or PKU), biological vulnerability (e.g., prematurity, low birthweight, or complications of labor and delivery), or environmental vulnerability (e.g., poverty, a teen parent, child of a teen parent, abused or neglected, malnourished, or exposed to family or community chaos or violence) (Meisels & Wasik, 1995).

Targets of Intervention

The Child in a Family Context

For decades the conventional mental health approach has focused on the child in isolation. The developers of the first Head Start program were prescient enough to postulate that the most effective program would be comprehensive in nature, providing a variety of services, and would involve parents directly. The success of Head Start confirmed this hypothesis; the seminal efforts of workers like Bronfenbrenner (1979) and Belsky (1981) led to a greater recognition that children live and function as interactive members of an open system. Long after this ecological principal came to be accepted as a basic tenet of developmental psychology, however, many intervention programs continue to segregate children from their families for treatment.

Most approaches to early intervention now emphasize the importance of the family context in early socialization. In fact, one of the most effective ways to improve the lives of children is to intervene directly with parents (Seitz & Provence, 1995). This type of early intervention acknowledges the importance of the nature and quality of the parent-child relationship (Zigler, Hopper, & Hall, 1993). Where there have been interventions to optimize parenting skills and parents' understanding of child health and development, demonstrated improvements range from lowered rates of child abuse and neglect (Olds, 1992) to improvements in children's commitment to education (Hawkins & Weiss, 1983).

Parents are the most important agents of socialization during early childhood. Throughout infancy and toddlerhood, and even during the preschool years as the child is becoming increasingly independent from her parents and open to interacting with and learning from others (other relatives, peers, teachers, day-care providers, the media, etc.), the family undeniably maintains the primary position in the socialization and education of the child. Any changes in the child's social world are set against the background of the family; the quality of this relationship largely determines the extent to which the child's further social relationships and cognitive development will prove successful and rewarding (Hopper & Zigler, 1988; Zigler, Hopper, & Hall, 1993). If the child and the parents are able to establish successfully a nurturing, warm, but not overly dependent relationship, it is far more likely that the child will be eager to explore her world, to meet and interact with others, to enjoy social relationships outside the family, and to grow up to be a socially competent individual. If the parents, on the other hand, are either overprotective, domineering, and punitive, or lax and overly permissive, failing to establish their identity as authorities and caregivers, it is far less likely that the child will successfully accomplish these vital tasks (Baumrind, 1968).

In addition to nurturing the child's growing social self, the parents' role in the development of the child's sense of his own worth and identity is paramount. Long before the preschool period the child has already begun to develop a sense of the degree to which he is valued by the family; reinforcement of this sense of being unique, important, and valued by important people in his life results in the internalization of these ideas and a growing sense in the child's own mind of his value (Rubin, 1980; Corsaro, 1980). Conversely, the child who does not feel valued, or who has seldom been made to feel good about his own characteristics and sense of self, will lack such feelings. In spite of a current educational trend to try to *teach* feelings of self esteem to children, no empirical data suggest that such programs are effective long-term. It seems far more likely that the successful groundwork for feelings of genuine self-worth must be laid during the earliest years, and by the child's first teachers: the family (Zero to Three, 1992).

Finally, the family does act in just that capacity—as teachers. All learning takes place in an environmental context, especially learning during the preschool period. For the young child, the family acts as a sort of lens through which all experience is filtered. Selective reinforcement of the child's experiences and of the ideas and events she encounters takes place within the family. This foundation profoundly shapes the child's behavior, attitudes, and beliefs about what is and is not acceptable, what is and is not effective, and what is and is not rewarding, establishing patterns that will shape the child's behavior and attitudes for life.

Two-Generation Programs

Two-generation programs, another wave of intervention programs that hold promise for improving the quality of life for infants and families, focus not just on infancy, but on infants and parents (usually mothers) simultaneously. By working directly with parents as well as children, program mounters hope to facilitate positive changes in parents' lives that will further improve the lives of their children through improving parenting skills, family socioeconomic status, and parent education (Johnson & Breckenridge, 1982; Owen & Mulvihill, 1994). Avance, a Texas program serving primarily low-income families in San Antonio and other cities, exemplifies such an approach. In addition to Head Start, day care, and developmental screenings for children, a parent component provides education for parents with children under age 3, and includes medical, mental health, and nutrition services, social service and counseling referrals, substance-abuse education and treatment referrals, and access to a library and to transportation to and from programs. The Avance Basic Literacy and Advanced Education Assistance Program is a follow-up to the parent education program; one phase of Avance's services offers GED courses, English as a Second Language, and college- and job-related training.

An in-house evaluation of Avance's program after the first nine months demonstrated (through the use of pre- and posttest data) that participants were "more hopeful about their future, more willing to assume an educational role with children, less severe in their conceptions of punishment, and more willing to utilize their social support system" (Levine, 1988). Results of a more formal evaluation that included data from comparison groups indicated that Avance mothers provide more organization and more stimulation in their children's lives, are more responsive to their needs and more positive in their interactions with them, talk more to them, and spend more time engaged in teaching them. Mother-child interactions in the Avance group were characterized by greater mutual responsibility and turn-taking and enhanced enjoyment for both mother and child. A 17-year follow-up of program graduates indicated that 94 percent of children who had attended Avance programs had completed or were still attending high school or GED programs. Almost half of the children who had graduated were attending college, and almost 60 percent of mothers who had initially dropped out of high school had completed their GED; many had attended some college or training program after high school (Hall & Zigler, 1993; Levine, 1988).

In her review of the two-generation intervention model, Smith (1991) notes that early childhood intervention programs on their own will not solve the problems of poor children. Nor will job-training programs aid mothers if child care and other family-based services are unavailable. She recommends an expanded commitment to programs of this type; the establishment of an interdisciplinary research network to assess their impact; and the collaboration, support, and guidance of a variety of federal agencies.

Conditions for Growth

No matter which type or target of intervention is selected, certain conditions need to be met by programs before growth and development can be fully optimized. Broad-based programs usually try to address as many of these as possible. Experts (e.g., Barnard, 1993; Carnegie Council, 1994; Zero to Three, 1992) list the following as being among the most critical conditions for early growth:

- Timely and appropriate prenatal care
- Avoidance by mother of substance abuse
- Access to health care
- Community embeddedness
- Access to social services
- Responsive caregivers
- Caregivers with a basic understanding of child development
- Attention to biological conditions that might attenuate development
- Safe environments

By working with parents and children in a family context, two-generation programs are in a unique position to achieve these goals.

PROGRAM EVALUATION

Any responsibly mounted intervention effort should include an evaluation component. It is important not only to be able to determine whether a program has met its objectives, but also to discover whether it has resulted in other anticipated or unanticipated consequences for participants (Hauser-Cram, 1995). Research can be conducted at virtually any stage of an intervention effort (Beer & Bloomer, 1986); the two most basic forms of evaluation concern the intervention *process* and the *outcome* of the services provided. In **outcome evaluation,** researchers attempt to determine the extent to which change has occurred because of the intervention. **Process evaluations,** which can occur throughout the course of the intervention, focus on the means by which the intervention services are delivered, and deal with issues that arise during the actual provision of the program.

If scholarly concerns suggest the use of evaluations, then policy concerns virtually dictate them. Whatever the goal of a policy initiative—childhood immunization drives, school lunch programs, preschools for high-risk children, or efforts to prevent substance abuse or early pregnancy—legislators and their constituents want to be able to determine their effectiveness. In this case, effectiveness is often defined, not simply in numbers or percentages of problems ameliorated or prevented, but in terms of **"cost effectiveness."** In other words, in parlance derived from defense spending, how much bang can we get for our buck?

Government-funded programs are often expected to show an immediate positive effect. However, long-term outcomes for many intervention programs are not fully understood for many years, possibly for generations. The fact that program outcomes continue to generate and spread outward like ripples on a pond bears witness to the effectiveness of these programs; it also makes it difficult to seek funding from agencies that expect more immediate returns for their investment.

Reliance on an ecological model tells us that the child's development is influenced not only by the family system, but also by other systems far removed from the family's control. The child is influenced by the family, which in turn is influenced by the nature and effectiveness of our major social systems, such as the world of work, the school, child care, the media, and available health services. Any complete evaluation of an early intervention program would assess whether the entire ecology of the child has become more conducive for human development. In the real world, few evaluation programs achieve this sort of scope, but as the examples to come illustrate, evaluators must be open to explore possible outcomes beyond those anticipated by program mounters.

Program evaluation is meant to answer one question: Does the program succeed? As simple as this sounds, this one question implies several others: Did the program result in the change or changes expected? Did unexpected benefits accrue to participants instead of, or in addition to, the ones specified in the program's statement of goals and objectives? Does the program appear to result in unanticipated *negative* changes? Suppose, for instance, that a drug education program is administered to preschoolers with the goal of preventing substance abuse later in childhood or adolescence. If the program results in an immediate increase in children's knowledge of the dangers of drug abuse, but also alienates parents whose children learn to criticize their social use of legal drugs like alcohol and tobacco, has this program succeeded (Hall & Zigler, 1993)?

In addition, program evaluators must consider questions concerning the sample that received the intervention. Is the program's effect (or lack of effect) uniform among all participants, or did some subgroups or individuals experience more change than others? Did program benefits extend to other family members or to the community at large (McAdoo, 1994)? Evaluators of an early intervention program whose goal was the reduction of juvenile criminality, for instance, might want to look at whether rates of delinquency also declined for the siblings of program participants, and at the savings realized in a community when court and incarceration costs are minimized.

Because "early intervention" can mean many different things, no one type of evaluation can possibly enable us to determine how effective such programs are (Shonkoff, 1993). Instead it is important to note that, in a broad-based program, outcomes are many and multiply determined. Their effectiveness is also likely to vary with participant characteristics. An Infant Health and Development program aimed at optimizing development in **low-birthweight** children, for instance, was found to be more effective with children whose mothers had less formal education and less effective when the infants' birthweights were extremely low (Brooks-Gunn et al., 1992, cited in Shonkoff, 1993). Moreover, the positive outcomes sought in the mounting of a program might be joined by or replaced by others not originally anticipated.

PRINCIPLES OF EARLY INTERVENTION

Short-Term Versus Longitudinal Evaluation

Program developers, grant providers, and legislative bodies authorizing funding for treatment and research are anxious to demonstrate the effectiveness of programs they support. Therefore the effects of an early intervention program are typically evaluated soon after the administration of the intervention. The answers sought at this time are usually fairly straightforward: Were mothers who received a nutrition intervention less likely to have a low-birthweight baby? Did Head Start participants score higher than non–Head Start peers on developmental measures? Were parents who had been visited at home by social workers more knowledgeable about infant health and development?

As the preschool example at the start of this chapter shows, however, not all of the effects of an intervention program will be immediately apparent. Building a long-term, or **longitudinal research** component into an evaluation effort allows program mounters to determine which changes persist and which fade out, and whether any new benefits of the program become apparent after the termination of the intervention. Longitudinal evaluations enable researchers to study the same subjects over years, but have the disadvantages of being expensive and time consuming. The full effects of a program might not be understood for years, or, in some cases, a generation or more.

Group Assignment

Evaluation research originally evolved from physical sciences in which human subjects considerations were not at issue. For instance, as Hauser-Cram (1995) notes, no ethical conflicts or statistical confounds resulted from assigning, say, this plant seed into one experimental condition and that plant seed into another. Such questions immediately arise, however, when research involves human subjects, especially when some of those subjects are children.

Suppose researchers want to mount a program in which pregnant teens will be able to participate in free child development classes and receive weekly home visits from a social worker and a nurse-midwife. By providing such services, program mounters hope to reduce levels of child abuse among young parents by teaching appropriate parenting skills and increasing their understanding of and expectations regarding normal child development.

How should the researchers select the young women who will participate in this intervention? They could post notices in area high schools asking for volunteers, but this would introduce at least two potentially confounding variables into the research design: (1) Program mounters would reach only girls who are still in high school; girls who dropped out, either before or after becoming pregnant (arguably those for whom such an intervention could be most valuable) would not be included; and (2) asking for volunteers could result in a **selection bias,** as the girls who are most motivated to volunteer might differ in some significant way from girls who are, for a variety of reasons, less likely to sign up for such a program. Further, such a narrowly selected sample impedes researchers' ability to apply the findings of the research to pregnant adolescents in general. But if a second group of girls is recruited through clinics providing subsidized prenatal care, new variables (motivation, level of education, degree of peer support, etc.) will make it difficult for evaluators to determine what proportion of change observed can be attributed to the intervention.

Comparison Group

To determine the effectiveness of an intervention, recipients of the services in question must be compared with individuals who are similar to study subjects in important ways, but who did *not* receive the intervention. Depending upon the nature of the study, intervention participants and comparison group members might be **matched,** or paired for statistical comparison, on the basis of gender, age, socioeconomic status, labor and delivery characteristics, health status, family makeup, education, or other variables. By matching carefully, evaluators are able to hypothesize with more certainty that changes following intervention are actually attributable to the intervention and not to some extraneous variable.

Researchers must take care, however, that the very reason why comparison group members did not receive the intervention doesn't set them apart from participants in any meaningful way. For instance, program volunteers cannot be compared meaningfully with people from the same community who did *not* volunteer, without raising issues of selection bias. Random assignment of individuals to service or nonservice groups is arguably the strongest type of research design but it can raise troubling ethical and practical issues. The ethical problem of depriving comparison-group members of services is sometimes resolved in part by providing them with intervention services after outcome data are collected. Practical problems can also wreak havoc with random assignment design. In the real world of their communities, members of the comparison group might occasionally, without the knowledge of the experimenter, be receiving as many or even more intervention services than the experimental group (see Reynolds, in press).

One solution, as in our preschool example, is to ask waiting-list members to serve as a comparison group. Another is to use each intervention participant as his or her own control group by administering pre- and posttests to measure change as a function of the intervention. Such an approach has its own pitfalls, as program-oriented change might be confused with changes that result from maturation or from other events that occur concurrently with the intervention. In the real world of human subjects research, these issues are rarely resolved fully or neatly. Arriving at a workable solution tailored to each particular set of circumstances, however, is a prerequisite for mounting any evaluation effort.

Attrition

Attrition—the loss of participants from the pool of evaluation study subjects over time—can also complicate a research design. In our example about the rural preschool intervention, for instance, it is unlikely that researchers would actually have been able to locate all 40 subjects for follow-up. Study participants move away, have their telephones disconnected or their numbers changed, withdraw from studies, and even die. If a researcher on the 10-year follow-up team cannot locate 8 of the original subjects, 20 percent of the original sample has been lost. Often the missing subjects have the most stressful or chaotic lives; without evidence, however, there is no way for a research team to determine whether the presence of these subjects would have weighted the study findings in one direction or the other. It is somewhat less damaging if attrition from both intervention and comparison groups occurs at roughly the same rate, but the higher the rate of any attrition, the more the accuracy and applicability of the evaluation findings are compromised.

In the descriptions of the intervention efforts that follow, data derived from evaluation research are provided wherever they are available. But how do we justify mounting early intervention programs when information of this type cannot be supplied? The designers of programs that are intended to have an impact on areas not addressed before, for instance, must rely heavily on the available science base, carefully examining the literature on all areas that might have an impact on the question being studied. When the Robert Wood Johnson Foundation wanted to devote funding to preschool programs that would decrease the likelihood that participants would engage in substance abuse later in life, they asked developmental psychologists to define areas that had an impact on the development of drug-related behaviors. By evaluating existing programs and reviewing the developmental literature on risk, resiliency, juvenile delinquency, and substance use, psychologists were able to advise the foundation that the most promising approaches should be broad-based, multidisciplinary, family-oriented programs that stress parental behavior as much as child development (Hall & Zigler, 1997).

SOME PROMISING PROGRAMS

Head Start

Since its inception over 30 years ago, few programs for children have generated more controversy than Head Start. Championed and protected by many, decried as a "boondoggle" and a "scam" by others (Hood, 1992, 1993), and misunderstood many times over by supporters and detractors alike, Head Start has been both praised for its effectiveness and criticized—even by those who value and respect the program—for not living up to its full potential. Most of all, Head Start has been at the center of the debate over the role government should take in the lives of children and families (Zigler & Styfco, 1993).

Head Start's History

A direct outgrowth of President Johnson's War on Poverty, Head Start was a revolutionary program in many ways. By tailoring even its early programs to take advantage of family and community strengths, Head Start sidestepped many of the pitfalls inherent in the deficit model of intervention. By providing meals, dental care, and health screenings and health care, Head Start became the first large-scale broad-based program of early intervention. Perhaps most importantly, Head Start has always involved parents in program planning and implementation, making it one of the first programs to address children's needs in a family context (Bronfenbrenner, 1975, 1979).

Sargeant Shriver, who was at that time the head of the Office of Economic Opportunity and the chief strategist of the Johnson Administration's War on Poverty, in 1964 called for the development of a preschool intervention program to address educational inequalities related to poverty. Because the request was unprecedented, no guidelines were available to aid program developers as they made decisions about program content, size, and duration. A planning committee of 14 experts from a range of fields including education, health, child development, and mental health came up with a proposal for a preschool program that went well beyond merely being educational (Zigler & Muenchow, 1992; Zigler & Valentine, 1979).

The planning committee recommended the development of a pilot program that would improve physical health, enhance mental processes (particularly conceptual and verbal skills), and foster social and emotional development, self-confidence, and relationships with family and others, social responsibility, and a sense of dignity and self-worth for both the child and family ("Recommendations for a Head Start Program," 1965). Note that only one of these seven goals was specifically related to intellectual performance.

The panel Shriver convened recommended that he mount a small pilot program, but the Johnson administration was anxious to wage a larger, child-oriented battle in the War on Poverty. The first Head Start program was a series of six- to eight-week summer programs that began in 1965 and served over 500,000 children. The rapidly mounted program was implemented through individual grantee programs throughout the nation. Because the program sprang up so quickly, not all of the grantees ran high-quality programs; variation in quality has been a characteristic of Head Start Programs from the beginning (Frede, 1995). The positive side of the diversity among individual programs, however, is that each bore the stamp of its own community and was answerable to the needs and the characteristics of the population being served. This heterogeneity has long been recognized as both a strength of the program and a weakness (Hall & Zigler, 1993; "For Head Start, Two Steps Back," 1992; Zigler & Styfco, 1993; Zigler, 1992).

Today Head Start annually provides services to over 800,000 children 3 to 5 years old, most of whom attend a half-day session throughout the school year. In some areas, full-day programs and home-based interventions are available. Federal guidelines mandate that at least 90 percent of enrolled children be from families whose income falls below the poverty line; at least 10 percent of enrollees must be children with disabilities. Eighty percent of Head Start funding comes from the federal government; the remainder comes from other, usually local, sources, which can be in the form of in-kind services. Each program is required to include six components: early childhood education, health screening and referral, mental health services, nutrition education and hot meals, social services for the child and family, and parent involvement (Zigler & Styfco, 1993).

Head Start's Effectiveness

With its broad-based, two-generation approach, and its heterogeneous pool of attendees, Head Start has been a difficult program to evaluate. Eligibility for participation was defined by law, making random group assignment to intervention and comparison groups impossible. Furthermore, many of the constructs addressed by Head Start goals had never been fully defined or operationalized, and few measurement tools were available at the time to assess constructs like **"social competence"** or parental behaviors. Misunderstandings about its goals have led to further difficulties.

Because of all of these difficulties, and because the prevailing public enthusiasm was for efforts that would enhance cognitive development, virtually all of Head Start's early evaluations focused on whether the program would produce cognitive gains among its participants. Elements such as Head Start's seminal new health component were virtually ignored by early evaluators. Early findings indicated that IQ scores did, indeed, climb by about 10 points following participation in the pilot program. A near-fatal blow to Head Start, however, was struck when research conducted at Ohio University and the Westinghouse Learning Corporation revealed that the cognitive gains achieved by the children were short-lived (Cicirelli, 1966). As in our opening example, many legislators were disappointed by what appeared to be poor potential on the part of Head Start to promote academic success and spoke of withdrawing funding.

The parents whose children participate in the project eventually saved the day by lobbying for the continuation of the program. New research findings (Consortium for Longitudinal Studies, 1978, 1983) also helped to convince Congress that Head Start should be allowed to continue. Data from these studies confirmed that IQ gains following program administration do fade out, as the Westinghouse study had indicated. The Consortium studies, however, went on to examine new variables, and concluded that participants were less likely to be held back a grade in school, and that they were less likely to require placement in special education classes.

Other longitudinal evaluations of the effects of Head Start have also confirmed its success. The Head Start Synthesis Project (McKey et al., 1985), a meta-analysis of over 200 evaluations of Head Start programs, pointed to gains in the areas of overall health status, immunization rates, improved nutrition, and enhanced social competence. Families of participants, too, were strengthened through their involvement in Head Start. In being too ready to write off Head Start as a failure because it was not associated in significant and permanent gains in IQ, critics of the program missed the bottom line: Head Start does, indeed, prepare children for later success in schools by improving their health and overall social competence. Participation in Head Start can enable children to use the skills they have more fully.

In spite of Head Start's demonstrated effectiveness, criticism of the project has at times been vociferous. Many still focus on the program's failure to increase IQ scores, ignoring the wide range of positive outcomes in other areas. Others confuse the program with other types of intervention. Head Start is often confused with the Perry Preschool Program, which differed from Head Start in that it did not provide the range of services to either children or parents that Head Start did. The Perry Preschool Program has also been the subject of extensive longitudinal evaluations (Schweinhart, Barnes, & Weikart, 1993) that have published data on positive program effects on everything from academic commitment to juvenile delinquency. These findings have generally been easier for the general public to understand than the findings released on the effects of Head Start. Criticism has also been leveled at Head Start by those who note that a follow-up program enhances its effectiveness (Kantrowitz, 1992), something that Head Start promoters have said for years (Zigler & Styfco, 1993).

With its large, congressionally approved budget, Head Start has been a target for the budget axe in virtually every round of debate on the issue. Even politicians who espouse child-friendly views on early intervention, and who publicly praise what the *New York Times* has called "the motherhood and apple pie of government programs," often support budget cuts when the time comes to vote; as a result, Head Start has begun to lose some budget battles, resulting in centers that close for the summer, reduced teacher training, failure to reach more than half of the children eligible for the program, and a decline in overall program quality (Hass, 1995; Zigler, 1992, 1993).

Even those who first helped design Head Start call for program improvements to reverse the problems that result from budget cuts. The media pick up on this apparent contradiction and can cause Head Start to suffer a crisis of confidence (Zigler, 1992). For a timeline of the history of Head Start, see figure 5.1.

The Future of Head Start

Head Start was designed to be flexible and responsive to the needs of those it serves, and the data on Head Start's effectiveness continue to be overwhelmingly positive. So it is likely that Head Start will survive, though it is also likely that budget battles will continue to be a part of its future (Zigler & Styfco, 1996). Head Start remains the largest provider in the United States of health care services to poor children, delivering medical and dental screenings and referrals to every child it serves, and bringing immunizations up to date. Thousands of low-income parents have found jobs and job training through Head Start. Many find them with the program itself, as bus drivers, receptionists, classroom assistants. Some pursue further education and become teachers; 35 percent of all Head Start teachers are parents of current or former Head Start children; many have earned Child Development Associate credentials, as well as college degrees, and have entered careers in this field.

The most successful Head Start efforts will be those that continue to respond creatively to the problems faced by children and families as we head into the twenty-first century. One Head Start program in Murray, Kentucky, has forged links to public school programs, enabling it to serve twice as many children as it would have by relying on traditional forms of Head Start funding alone. A Head Start program in Cedar Rapids, Iowa, is part of a coalition of other state and community agencies, among them HUD, the United Way, the state's department of education, and local businesses. By pooling their resources and their expertise, and by taking advantage of the Community Services Block Grant and emergency housing grants, this coalition has mounted the "Inn Circle" program for homeless families, and provides day care, Head Start classes, GED classes, literacy and adult education opportunities, job training, substance-abuse counseling, and advice on reaching personal, education, and vocational goals (Replogle, 1994). As it moves into the next decade, Head Start's biggest challenges will be to provide services to a greater proportion of eligible children, and to achieve a uniformly high level of program quality while maintaining the diversity that is one of its greatest strengths. Mills (1998) has provided a good overview of the many Head Start programs throughout the nation.

Carolina Abecedarian Study

The Abecedarian study, which was begun in the early 1970s, provides some of the most important data available on the effects of early intervention. Mounted as a direct attempt to ameliorate the effects of persistent poverty, the study is

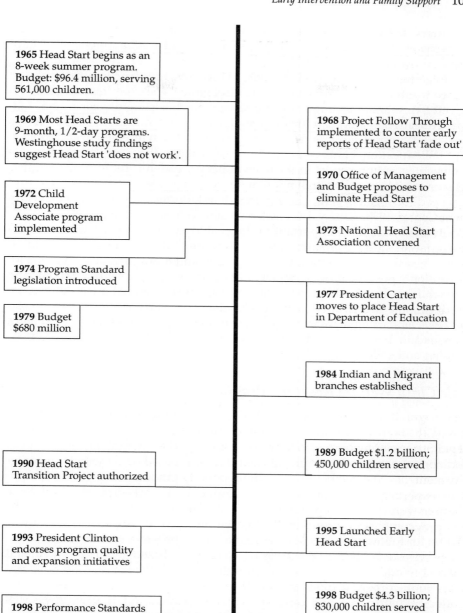

1965 Head Start begins as an 8-week summer program. Budget: $96.4 million, serving 561,000 children.

1969 Most Head Starts are 9-month, 1/2-day programs. Westinghouse study findings suggest Head Start 'does not work'.

1968 Project Follow Through implemented to counter early reports of Head Start 'fade out'

1970 Office of Management and Budget proposes to eliminate Head Start

1972 Child Development Associate program implemented

1973 National Head Start Association convened

1974 Program Standard legislation introduced

1977 President Carter moves to place Head Start in Department of Education

1979 Budget $680 million

1984 Indian and Migrant branches established

1989 Budget $1.2 billion; 450,000 children served

1990 Head Start Transition Project authorized

1995 Launched Early Head Start

1993 President Clinton endorses program quality and expansion initiatives

1998 Budget $4.3 billion; 830,000 children served

1998 Performance Standards include children younger than age 3 for the first time

FIGURE 5.1. A brief history of Head Start.

also noteworthy as a demonstration that the earliest intervention is the most effective way of achieving lasting social, cognitive, and academic benefits (Campbell et al., in press).

In a randomized controlled study, 111 infants and their families were assigned to either an experimental or a control group. The experimental group received five years of an educational intervention consisting of year-round, full-day, educational child care or preschool, along with nutritional supplements and social support services. The control group children received everything except the educational intervention. Follow-ups at age 15 reveal that the benefits of this intervention persist in the form of better academic performance, higher IQ scores, higher levels of retention in the correct grade for the child's age, and less need for social or remedial services (Frank Porter Graham Child Development Center, 1998; Ramey, 1994; Ramey, Campbell, & Blair, in press).

In one of the most important findings associated with participation in the Abecedarian study, evaluation studies indicate that the younger the children were when they entered the study, the greater and more persistent were the intervention's positive effects (Begley, 1996; Ramey & Campbell, 1992). Waiting until children begin school to start to implement educational interventions can produce some effects, but this approach will not be nearly as effective, or as cost-effective, as starting in infancy. This was the reasoning behind Early Head Start, launched in 1994 to provide comprehensive Head Start–like services to poor families and children ages 0 to 3.

Yale Child Welfare Research Program

First begun in the late 1960s, the Yale Child Welfare Research Program has followed 18 children from 17 families since birth. All children were firstborn, except for one sibling born during the course of the project. Mothers were chosen during pregnancy from hospital obstetric records based on these criteria: inner-city residence, income below the federal poverty guideline, no serious complications of pregnancy, and no mental retardation or marked psychosis. Twelve children were black, 2 were white, 2 were of mixed parentage, and 2 were Puerto Rican. A comparison group of 18 children matched for sex and ethnicity was chosen for follow-up purposes one year after the program ended.

Services provided by the program were broad-based, family oriented, and tailored to address the needs of each individual family. For slightly over two years (until program funding ended), participants received services that included pediatric care and developmental screenings; home visits (by social workers, psychologists, and a nurse) to provide budget planning, nutritional information, and help in establishing links to other community services and support agencies; and, for families desiring it, high-quality, university-based day care (Provence & Naylor, 1983).

Regular evaluations of the program have been conducted since its ending up to the present time. Immediate program effects included better health care for program children and mobilization of parents to enable them to obtain needed services. When program children were 13 and comparison group children were 11, a follow-up study revealed a number of positive effects for the children and their families. Program children were less likely to have been retained a grade or more in school and were less likely to be requiring remedial educational services. Teachers reported that program children got along better with teachers and peers and had fewer behavioral problems than comparison-group children. The behavior of program boys was rated significantly more positively overall by their teachers than that of comparison-group boys, who had higher rates of truancy and other problem behaviors, including cheating, lying, and serious disobedience. Parents, too, had more problems with comparison-group children than with program children. Mothers of comparison-group children were more likely to report that, at age 11, their children were stealing, staying away from home overnight, and fighting, and in general appeared to be engaging in or were at higher risk for involvement in juvenile delinquency (Rescorla, Provence, & Naylor, 1982).

Family effects at the 10-year follow-up also reflected positive outcomes for program participants. Families of program children had fewer children and spaced their births at greater intervals than comparison-group families. There was also a slight positive difference in the number of two-parent families (more likely in the program group) and in the number of program families who were working rather than receiving public assistance. For mothers, program participation was associated with having gone on to a higher level of educational attainment (Seitz, Rosenbaum, & Apfel, 1985). No overt drug-related variables have been reviewed to date by program evaluators, but it is clear that many of the **resiliency** factors (e.g., ties to family, commitment to education) are stronger in program families.

The Yale program has also been shown to be cost effective. Money spent on services to each family has more than been matched by money saved by the school system on grade repetitions and provision of special services. Furthermore, fewer program families were receiving AFDC or other forms of public assistance at follow-up, increasing the cost-effectiveness of program participation (Seitz, Rosenbaum, & Apfel, 1985).

Perry Preschool Project

Program developers at the High/Scope Education Research Foundation recruited 123 black, lower-SES 3- and 4-year-olds from Ypsilanti, Michigan, who were felt to be at high risk for attenuated cognitive development and consequent school failure (Berreuta-Clement et al., 1984). Through **random assignment,** roughly half of these children were placed in the control group and attended no program; the other half attended a high-quality, cognitively oriented preschool program for either one or two school years. Frequent **home visits** by teachers kept parents involved; monthly meetings of the parents of intervention children enhanced the social support networks of these parents.

Extensive evaluations carried out (albeit largely by program developers, rather than independent researchers) with all program and comparison children for 19 years reveal significant program benefits (Barnett, 1995; Berreuta-Clement et al., 1984). Intervention children manifest a number of characteristics that indicate positive program outcomes, including better attitudes toward school, lower rates of grade retention and placement in special education, and higher performance on achievement measures, school grades, and standardized tests. Sixty-seven percent of program children graduated from high school (as opposed to 49 percent of comparison children); significantly more program children went on to postsecondary education. Moreover, at age 27 (the most recent follow-up year), program participants exhibited greater overall social competence, as indicated by higher employment levels and lower use of welfare-type supports. Although arrest rates for both groups are high, program youth were arrested less often.

The Perry Preschool Project has also been praised for its cost-effectiveness. High/Scope investigators estimated the savings resulting from reduced grade retention and lower levels of involvement in the criminal justice system of program graduates. By the time program participants were 19 years old, taxpayers had saved $7 for every dollar spent on the program (Barnett, 1993). It must be noted, however, that the program was fairly expensive to mount. The annual price per child, in 1992 dollars, was estimated to be $7,600, more than twice as much as Head Start spent per child (Zigler & Styfco, 1993).

Interpretations of these outcomes emphasize the program's ability to enhance school readiness, leading ultimately to a higher commitment to education, higher success levels in school, and, ultimately, lower delinquency rates (Barnett & Escobar, 1990; Berrueta-Clement et al., 1984; Zigler, Taussig, & Black, 1992). Most programs to prevent or reduce delinquency have met with limited success. Because these problems are rooted in many different systems, it is not surprising that systemic, ecological approaches to finding their solutions have been more effective. Evaluations of such programs indicate that they work by addressing the risk factors associated with substance abuse and other forms of social incompetence. One hypothesis regarding the mechanism of this effective intervention is that successful early experiences contribute to a sort of **snowball effect**—increasing the likelihood of other successful experiences in school and other social contexts, increasing self-esteem, motivation, sociability, and physical and mental health. Furthermore, family support alters in a positive way the child-rearing environment, generating high positive parental expectations for children, improving parents' child-rearing skills, and enabling parents to support their children in their growing drive for educational attainment (Hale, Seitz, & Zigler, 1990).

Parents as Teachers

All parents in Missouri school districts who have children under 3 years of age are eligible to receive services from Parents as Teachers. This largely parent-oriented program has been in operation since 1981. State funding provides for parent education and developmental screening for some families; local school districts might provide coverage for other families to be included, and some funding comes from foundations and corporate giving. The program is now active in 47 states and six countries (Parents as Teachers, 1998; Pfannenstiel &

Seltzer, 1985). Some components of this model have been integrated into the "21st Century School" program now operating in 17 states.

The Parents as Teachers (PAT) program is based on the assumption that parents are the best teachers of their very young children. Accordingly, support in the form of home visits (beginning during the third trimester of pregnancy) and developmental screenings is provided to help the parents enhance their child's development and to identify any problems that might impede their child's healthy development and later school success (Nudd, 1989; Pfannenstiel, Lambson, & Yarnell, 1991).

Trained parent-educators provide developmental education and parenting guidance during regularly scheduled home visits. In addition, PAT sponsors and facilitates group meetings among participants to encourage the development of social support networks and a sense of comraderie among participants. Developmental screening of participating children is carried out on an informal basis at each home visit, and a formal assessment is conducted yearly. This screening includes assessments of motor, social, cognitive, and language development, and also hearing and vision tests. Referrals are made to the appropriate professionals for children who are found to have unusual problems.

Independently conducted outcome studies indicate that program effects are significant and carry over at least into elementary school. Several studies have found advances in linguistic, cognitive, and social development among participants; these gains persisted at least into the first or second grade, in spite of wide variation in preschool, child care, and kindergarten experiences; in addition to putting children on the road to school success, the program also leads to demonstrable cost savings by reducing the need for remedial and special education (Drazen & Haust, 1994; Pfannenstiel, 1995; Pfannenstiel & Seltzer, 1985). Additional outcomes are still being reported: one study of the Texas Parents as Teachers program has even indicated that program participation reduces the likelihood of violent behavior among some boys, though the same effect was not found for all groups (Graves, 1998; Mathieu, 1995). Table 5.1 compares early intervention programs.

THE FUTURE OF EARLY INTERVENTION

Just as our conceptions of early intervention itself have changed, so have the policy challenges related to its development and delivery. Shonkoff (1993) has noted that today's intervention programs must be based on goals that are well-defined and that can be quantified objectively to allow for the measurement of changes that occur as a result of program implementation. To be supported by and consistent with policy objectives, intervention programs must also reflect the values of the families and communities served. At the same time, program designers and legislative supporters must find a way to continue to provide strong programs at a time when economic resources available for early intervention are shrinking.

TABLE 5.1 Comparison of Early Intervention Programs

Program	Target Group	Components	Evaluation: Design and Findings
Abecedarian Project	Preschoolers (6 weeks to 8 years)	Full-day educational child care	Random assignment to intervention and comparison groups. Findings: Higher academic achievement, lower special education placement, and lower grade retention (see Campbell & Ramey, 1994).
Chicago Child Parent Center	Low-income 3- to 9-year-olds	1 to 2 years half-day preschool Full-day kindergarten grades 1–3	Nonintervention comparison group. Findings: Duration of intervention significantly associated with outcomes; any participation was associated with higher academic achievement (stable up to ninth grade), lower grade retention, and lower special education placement (see Reynolds, 1997).
Comprehensive Child Development Program	Low-income preschoolers (0 to 5 years) and their parents	Developmental screenings Home visits Parent training (child development, literacy, vocational training, etc.)	Random assignment study. Findings: No significant group differences on child outcomes; some data showing higher parent employment in treatment group. One of 21 sites showed better outcomes than others (St. Pierre et al., 1997).
Early Head Start	Low-income Newborns to 3-year-olds	Home visits Part- and full-day child care Parent education Comprehensive mental and physical health services	Random assignment to treatment and comparison groups. Program began in 1995; evaluation under way by Mathematica Policy Research (1995–2000).

Program	Population	Services	Findings
Head Start	Low-income preschoolers (3 to 5 years)	Half- or full-day preschool Case management Parent involvement Comprehensive mental and physical health services	Numerous studies with various designs. Findings: Positive outcomes for Head Start vs. comparison children are reported in several studies. Some studies report "fade out" of positive cognitive effects after grade 3 (see, e.g., Abelson, 1974; Lee et al., 1990; McKey et al., 1985).
High/Scope Perry Preschool	Preschoolers (3 to 5 years)	Half-day preschool for 1 to 2 years Home visits	Random assignment to treatment and comparison groups. Findings: Higher rate of high school completion, higher grades and achievement test scores for program group (see Schweinhart, Barnes, & Weikart, 1993).
Olds Prenatal/Early Infancy Project	Low-SES primiparous women	Nurse home visitation, prenatal to 2 years postpartum	Random assignment to treatment groups that vary on duration of services. Findings: Better birth outcomes, lower child abuse, fewer accidents and poisonings (see Olds, 1997). Replication study in progress.
Yale Child Welfare Program	Low-SES primiparous women	Home visitation Day care Pediatric visits Developmental exams	Time-lag control group. Findings: Better school attendance, less use of remedial services, better socialization; also, better outcomes for later-born siblings (Seitz & Apfel, 1994).

To continue to work alongside policy makers in the development and implementation of early intervention programs, child advocates will have to define their goals clearly, be realistic in their expectations regarding what any given intervention can achieve, be sensitive to the needs and strengths of families (not just children) in different settings, and be prepared to mount rigorous and timely evaluations of program outcomes (Shonkoff, 1993).

Early intervention programs in the United States have been in operation for several decades, long enough for some of the earliest programs to accumulate an impressive track record of service to families, enhancing parental commitment to and reinforcement of their children's educations, positively modifying the parenting styles and attitudes, and providing parents with the supports needed to increase the range of options available to themselves and their children. Further research in this area is essential, both in terms of continuing longitudinal follow-up contacts with the participants of programs already demonstrated to have some effectiveness, and with respect to mounting new, prospective, longitudinal studies that build on what we have learned from others. But it seems clear that early intervention represents a promising and cost effective approach to the enhancement of overall social competence.

SUMMARY

In the relatively short history of early intervention, even its definition has changed. Compared with three decades ago, children at risk for developmental, health, and educational problems are more likely to be provided with services at an earlier point in their lives, sometimes as early as the prenatal or even the preconception period. Moreover, services provided are far more likely to be broad-based, reflecting an ecological perspective on the influences on the developing child, and to focus on parents as well as or instead of the child.

The most fundamental assumption underlying the field of early intervention is that early childhood, and events that occur during this time, have long-lasting and profound consequences for later child development, health, and behavior. Furthermore, the notion that the effects of biological or genetic problems can be overcome or partially ameliorated through the provision of certain social, medical, developmental, or educational services is basic to this area.

A key intervention decision concerns identifying the most effective target of services. Most approaches to early intervention now emphasize the importance of the family context in early socialization, and thus target either the child within the family or the entire family for service delivery. Decades of research indicate that by intervening to optimize parenting skills and parents' understanding of child health and development, improvements can be made in many areas, including lowered rates of child abuse and neglect. The immediate recipient of the intervention will vary with the nature of the services provided. Whether the target is the child, the mother, the whole family, or the community, the outcome is likely to affect all of these.

Goals of early intervention include, but are not limited to, the delivery of timely, high-quality prenatal care; helping parents and children avoid substance abuse; increasing access to maternal and child health care; helping a family forge links to their community; teaching parents and child-care providers to be responsive caregivers; improving environmental safety; and enhancing children's cognitive development and educational readiness.

The question whether early intervention is effective has been answered in the affirmative by years of longitudinal research on the consequences of participation in an early intervention effort. Specialized evaluation research reveals that comprehensive intervention programs can enhance academic success, social competence, physical and mental health, and overall family functioning. It is helpful to build evaluation components into early intervention programs from the start, and to provide for rigorous, methodologically sound evaluation studies conducted by independent researchers who have no stake in the findings of such studies.

Process evaluations look at the means by which the intervention services are delivered. Outcome research looks at the changes that accrue to the targets of intervention services. Both are critical to determining whether, and how, a given intervention meets its goals. In addition to determining whether preset goals of the program were met, a thorough evaluation should also help determine whether there were any unexpected consequences, positive or negative. Further research might also examine whether program benefits (or deficits) can be found in siblings, parents, or other persons who may have been peripheral to the original intervention design.

In an era of budgetary conservatism and increased competition for available intervention dollars, supporters of early intervention must be willing to work alongside policy makers to convince them that such programs have both long-lasting and financially sound outcomes. Early intervention programs will survive and continue to be successful only by seeking creative solutions to problem solving and funding crises, and by clearly and realistically defining their goals, then demonstrating their effectiveness through ongoing process and outcome evaluation research.

The Challenge of Child Care

The very meaning of "child care" has shifted over the past four decades. In the 1950s and 1960s, the term *child care* typically referred to the activities involved in rearing one's own children. Today the term *child care* is more likely to conjure up a different image. For some, that image is of bright, sunny rooms full of children, playing happily as they are watched over by energetic, creative, devoted caregivers. For others, the term conjures up visions of tearful children clinging to equally tearful mothers who are employed for a variety of reasons, but who anguish over these daily separations. And for many others, it evokes a portrait of dull misery, with too many children being cared for by too few people with too little qualification in cheerless, even unsafe, environments. Which of these scenarios is accurate? Every one.

For several decades the United States has been in the throes of a child-care crisis, the full impact of which might not be apparent until today's small children are adults. The crisis stems from one thing: a lack of high-quality, developmentally appropriate, affordable, accessible supplemental child care. As we near the turn of the century, we can no longer ignore the necessity of providing such care to every child in this nation, nor can we underestimate the consequences of failing to do so.

In this chapter we will seek to answer a number of basic questions about supplemental child care in the United States. What types of child care are available, and how are they used? What do we know, and what remains to be learned, about the effects of such care on child development? To what extent should child care be regulated by the government—and to what extent is it? What is meant by high-quality child care, and who should be responsible for its provision? Finally, what solutions can we identify to address child-care problems in this country?

As we explore this area, we make a number of assumptions about child care and its use by American families:

- *Every mother is a working mother.* In spite of its many rewards, being a parent is the most difficult—and the most important—job on earth. Every mother (and father) who cares for a child works hard, night and day, week after month after year, with no pay and few material benefits for that work. For this reason we prefer the terms *employed mothers* or *mothers in the out-of-home labor force* to the term *working mothers.*
- *Child care is the concern of fathers as well as mothers.* Most of the literature on the use of child care and its effects on children focuses on the mother-child dyad. Though the research base is gradually expanding to include information on father-child interactions as well (Lamb, 1981; Families and Work Institute, 1998a), the bias in our own writing reflects the predominant focus on the effects of child care on mother-child relationships. Within the next few years, however, the gender balance within the workforce will have shifted to being more nearly equal (Families & Work Institute, 1998). We expect that as this occurs, a corresponding shift will take place in research, with the roles of fathers, siblings, and extended family members eventually being considered in the day-care equation.

- *Child care is not a substitute for parental care.* Many people speak of substitute child care. We believe the use of such arrangements is typically better thought of as a *supplement* to care provided by parents (Caldwell, 1987; Scarr & Eisenberg, 1993). Except under extraordinary circumstances, care by parents is still the norm, even in families in which both parents work outside the home.

CHANGING ROLES

No change has affected the day-to-day life of the American family more than the entry into the labor force of over half of all U.S. women with young children. As a consequence, over 13 million children under 5 years of age, and over half of the nation's infants, spend at least a portion of their time in the care of someone other than a parent. Three-quarters of the mothers of school-age children are in the paid workforce (Children's Defense Fund, 1998b; Bureau of the U.S. Census, 1997; Wellesley College Center for Research on Women, 1996). A generation ago, most women left the paid work force upon marriage or the birth of a child, and stayed home until all of their children were nearly grown. In 1950 the percentage of women with children under age 6 who were working outside the home was 11.9 percent. Today fewer than 7 percent of families fit the traditional, mother-at-home/father-at-work stereotype of the American family (Silverstein, 1991). The result of all of these changes is that more children are spending more time, starting at younger and younger ages, in the care of persons other than their parents. Many children are being placed in such care as early as 2 weeks after birth. Fathers, too, are spending more time in the workplace than ever before; between 1969 and 1989, time spent on the job per year rose by 158 hours. For a worker with a 40-hour work week, this is the equivalent of an extra month each year spent on the job—and away from family (Higginbotham, 1993).

The greater reliance of today's families on supplemental child care is attributable in part to most families' economic need for two incomes, and in part to the rise of single-parent households, the vast majority of which are headed by women. The median annual income for families in the United States, adjusted for inflation, has fallen steadily over the past two decades. Family income would have declined even more precipitously than it has if women had not joined the labor force to supplement family earnings. According to the New York–based Families and Work Institute (1995), 55 percent of employed women provide over half of their family's income. Women enter the paid labor force for the same reasons men do—to feed, house, and clothe themselves and their children (Louis Harris Associates, 1989; Zigler & Hall, 1988; Stolley, 1993).

Among single-parent families, the economic need for work is even more acute. Almost half of the working women with children under 3 are their family's sole breadwinner (Kamerman, Kahn, & Kingston, 1983). If the mother in these families does not work, family income is approximately $4,500; if she does work, it is only $9,000 more. Clearly, then, in both single-parent families and those in which there are two wage earners, most mothers are in the workforce primarily out of economic necessity (Hofferth & Phillips, 1987).

Given these numbers, it is essential that our nation have in place a system that provides at least adequate care for the children of these families. Determining whether we do in fact have such a system at present involves examining the nature, quality, availability, cost, and accessibility of child-care facilities currently in operation in the United States. An examination of this system starts by asking a most basic question: Where are the children?

TYPES OF CHILD CARE

One of the first decisions parents must make regarding child care is which type is most likely to meet their needs and those of their child. Child care in the United States falls into three basic categories: in-home care, family day care, and center care. Some of these can be further divided into other types, and each has distinctive characteristics that have both advantages and disadvantages (see table 6.1).

In-Home Care

In-home care, as the name implies, is provided within the child's own home, typically for only one child or for the children of only one family. The smallest category of child care, this type of care can be further divided into that which is provided by a relative (other than a parent) and that provided by a nonrelated babysitter, *au pair*, or nanny. A recent study indicates that, among the employed mothers of children under 5 years of age, 3 percent rely on nonrelative, in-home care, and 7 percent rely on relatives to care for their children in the child's own home. These figures vary with age, however; such arrangements are far more likely to be used for children age 2 and under than for older children (Families and Work Institute, 1994; Hofferth et al., 1991).

In-home care can conjure up images of Mary Poppins types in upper-class homes, but the truth is that such care is more likely to be provided by teenagers who have little experience or training in child care, by older women who have their own families to care for, or by illegal immigrants whose off-the-books wages are provided by women who make little more themselves than they pay the women they hire.

Nannies and private sitters might be well trained in child development, or they might be high school dropouts with little background to prepare them for providing high-quality care. In the worst cases, parents unwittingly hire a caregiver who is unsuited for the work, who is unreliable, or who ignores or even mistreats the children in their charge. Even when an in-home caregiver is good, and many are, frequent turnover is a problem. No statistics are available on in-home caregiver turnover, though, because such caregivers tend not to be licensed or registered, and pay arrangements are often made "under the table."

It is often supposed that care by a relative is best for children, on the grounds that a relative will love and care for them better than a nonrelative, but research shows that this is not always the case. Children are not more likely to be securely attached to a caregiver who is a relative (Families and Work Institute, 1994). The

Table 6.1. Types of Child Care: A Comparison

	Advantages	Disadvantages
In-Home Care	Familiar setting 1:1 caregiver–child ratio Convenient for parents	Most costly care No backup if caregiver is ill or quits Well-trained and experienced caregivers difficult to find
Family Day Care	Homelike setting; especially attractive for infant care Shared care keeps costs relatively low Exposure to other children can provide social benefits	No backup if caregiver is ill or quits Type of care least likely to be licensed Exposure to other children can promote shared illnesses Hours might not match parents' work hours Might not take school-age children or transport them from school
Center	Shared costs can be lower than in-home care Backup caregiver in case of regular caregiver's illness or absence Least homelike setting Environment and materials child-oriented Social setting and group activities	Staff likely to have at least some training Highest staff turnover Exposure to other children can promote shared illnesses

explanation for this finding could be rooted in the fact that 65 percent of the relative caregivers identified were living in poverty, the stresses of which can have negative consequences for the child as well as the caregiver. Relative caregivers also are not likely to be providing child care because they want to, or to see child care as their chosen profession. Research links good child-care outcomes to caregivers who love taking care of children and are invested in this activity both personally and professionally, conditions that are rarely met when extended family members assume child-care responsibilities.

Family Day-Care Homes

The most frequently used type of child care for the young children of working mothers is family day care. A full third of employed mothers with children under 5 rely on care arrangements in which the caregiver takes care of several children in her own home (Casper, 1997; Families and Work Institute, 1994). In fact, the number of families using family day care has increased by 50 percent over

The Underground Child-Care Economy

In 1993, Zoe Baird, a noted lawyer and a mother of two, was nominated for the post of U.S. attorney general. The nomination was scuttled in the wake of "Nannygate": It came to light that Baird had hired an illegal Peruvian couple as domestic help and never paid Social Security tax for them. Publicity surrounding the hearings served to expose the widespread "underground economy" of child care.

There are two general profiles of this underground economy. On the one hand, there are wealthy individuals, such as Zoe Baird, who hire nannies and do not obey the tax laws. On the other hand is what might be called the poor family's nannygate, where thousands of day-care providers operate without licenses or official oversight; many of these operate in the nation's urban working-poor neighborhoods.

What is to be gained from this underground system? In addition to sidestepping accreditation or licensing requirements for home- or center-based day care, the gains are largely financial. Typically, employer and employee deal strictly in cash, do not pay Social Security tax, and do not pay or report income tax. Many such employees do not have medical or disability benefits. By keeping the arrangement off the books, illegal immigrants, welfare recipients, and others can work without reporting the income. Parents, as employers, can pay less for child care than if they used formal services or accredited center-based care.

Unfortunately, the lower fees charged by unregistered or nonaccredited home- or center-based day cares are often reflected in care that is of questionable quality. While the lack of a license does not *necessarily* indicate substandard care (just as

being licensed does not mean the care is the best), quality at these centers is more likely to be lower. Unregulated day-care providers might not be certified in first aid and CPR, might avoid employee background checks, and often lack training in basic child safety. They might be caring for a dangerously high number of children, or might even have a history of abuse or neglect. Unregulated facilities are less likely to have safety features, such as fenced-in play areas and smoke detectors, and might not meet fire and safety codes. According to a 1991 study, there are from 550,000 to 1.1 million unlicensed family day-care homes nationwide (Willer et al., 1991).

Even though the IRS has vowed to crack down on the underground child-care system, financial realities for many families all but guarantee its survival: households with incomes under $15,000 spend an average of 23 percent of their income on child care, while families with incomes over $40,000 spend an average of 6 percent (Willer et al., 1991). Even though some day-care subsidies are available for low-income families, funds are severely limited, and only 1 in 10 eligible families who need help receive it (Children's Defense Fund, 1998a).

More than at any other time in history, working parents are in desperate need of high-quality, affordable child care. Too often, this is an oxymoron. Until quality care is made affordable, the underground child-care economy is sure to thrive. The lack of regulated care implicit in the underground will continue to put too many children at risk, and the failure of private employers to pay social security and benefits will continue to put their nannies at risk.

the last three decades. The overwhelming majority of such care is provided by women, many of whom include their own children in the care arrangement.

The actual definition of family day care varies, though it typically refers to a private home in which the resident provides day care for 4 to 6 children. Actual numbers vary; in the state of Idaho, for instance, family day-care workers may legally care singlehandedly for up to 12 children, any number of whom may be infants (Butts, 1993). The implications of such lax regulations will be discussed in detail later on, but it should be clear to any reader that the optimal development—indeed, the basic safety—of any child being cared for under such circumstances is being gravely compromised.

Family day care can be licensed or not, and can be provided by a relative or a nonrelative. In general, the quality of family day care tends to be merely adequate, neither hindering child development nor optimizing it (Fischer, 1989; Howes, Keeling, & Sale, 1988; Families and Work Institute, 1994). But a recent study by the Families and Work Institute of family day-care settings around the nation found that the quality of care in such settings is extremely variable (Families and Work Institute, 1994), and little evidence has emerged over the last three decades to gainsay the grim findings of a now-classic study of family day care, *Windows on Day Care* (Keyserling, 1972). Keyserling found that the worst kinds of child neglect and abuse are possible in such settings.

Certainly, there are family day-care homes that provide high-quality child care, where children engage in planned and structured activities and caregivers are adequately trained, warm, and caring. Such arrangements are far more likely to be found in *licensed* family day-care homes (Families and Work Institute, 1994; Goelman & Pence, 1987). Children in unlicensed homes engaged in solitary play significantly more and watched television twice as often as children in licensed homes. Licensed caregivers are more likely to take in smaller numbers of children and to have some training in child development (Zigler & Lang, 1991). In both licensed and unlicensed family day-care homes, however, caregivers engage in fewer "informational" activities with children (Goelman & Pence, 1987) than do caregivers in centers. Informational activities are not formal academic exercises, but merely activities in which caregivers convey information. Naming the colors of the crayons as a toddler scribbles at the kitchen table, or talking with the children about which days of the week they come to day care, would both be considered informational activities.

Regulations for family day-care homes vary widely from state to state. In some states, certain family day-care arrangements may legally operate without being regulated. This is largely dependent on the number of children being cared for; in some states the caregiver's own children may be present without being counted toward the maximum allowable number of children attending.

Child-Care Centers

Approximately 29 percent of the children in supplemental care arrangements are in day-care centers, which constitute the third major child-care option. Center care is the most popular form of care for children ages 3 to 5. Over 40 percent of

3- and 4-year-old children with employed mothers attend day-care centers, as opposed to about 23 percent of 1- and 2-year-old children, who are more likely to be in in-home or family care arrangements (Families and Work Institute, 1994).

Center care typically consists of group care arrangements involving a dozen or more children, but settings vary, and include both for-profit arrangements (like national or regional chains, Kinder-Care being a good example) and not-for-profit centers like those often found in church or synagogue basements. Center care provided or subsidized by some businesses for their employees (such as Ben and Jerry's Homemade, Inc., in Vermont, and Lego Dacta in Connecticut) also fit into the not-for-profit category. A few family day-care homes, called large or group family child-care homes, that take in larger than usual numbers of children may also be counted as small child-care centers and be required to meet state regulations pertaining to center care.

THE COST OF CARE

Costs vary widely across and even within geographic regions, across type of care, and across age groups, but it is safe to say that child care in the United States is expensive. Annual rates for care for preschool children average from $4,000 to $8,000. High-quality infant day care can cost $10,000 or more per year. In virtually all states, the cost is as least as high as a year's tuition at a public university (Child Care Information Exchange, 1996; Children's Defense Fund, 1998i).

As a rule, the cost of care goes down as the age of the child increases. School-age child-care programs (which are described in detail later in this chapter) are less expensive than preschool child care, which in turn typically costs less than supplemental care for infants and toddlers. Among family day-care homes that provide care for school-age children, costs average about $38 per week, as opposed to about $65 for preschoolers and $72 for infants (Families and Work Institute, 1994).

This economic burden weighs more heavily on poor than on middle- or upper-income families. Middle-income families spend approximately 10 percent of their annual earnings on child care, and families with household incomes of $40,000 or more annually spend an average of only 6 percent of their income on child care. Poor two-parent families spend almost a quarter of their income in this way, and poor single mothers can spend up to half of their annual income on child care (Higgenbotham, 1993; Hofferth, 1989; Stolley, 1993; Zigler & Lang, 1991).

CHILD-CARE OUTCOMES: QUALITY IS THE KEY

Decades of child-care research have shown that true effects of child care are not homogeneous. They are mediated by such variables as the child's gender, family makeup, family attitudes toward maternal employment and child care, and the child's temperament. Most research on the effects of child care, however, have focused on one variable as being the most salient: the *quality* of care. Dozens of studies indicate that children in higher-quality caregiving settings perform higher on measures of both social and cognitive development. Children from such settings have more highly developed language skills and are more sociable and considerate (McCartney, 1984), are more compliant and demonstrate greater self-control (Howes & Olenick, 1986), and are less hostile (Howes, 1990) than children from poor-quality settings. Poor-quality care is generally associated with negative behavior patterns that can persist into the early school years and beyond (Hayes et al., 1990).

Most major studies of quality child care in the United States indicate that the average U.S. child-care experience is *adequate*—that is, it does not appear to harm the child, but neither does it demonstrably promote growth (Families and Work Institute, 1994; Goelman, Shapiro, & Pence, 1990; Howes, Keeling, & Sale, 1988). Only 9 percent of care was found to contribute to optimal growth and development. These far-from-glowing assessments are made largely on the basis of research on *regulated* child-care settings; the quality of unregulated care is largely unknown.

Other researchers are even less sanguine about the overall quality of child care, insisting that approximately 70 percent of our child care is poor quality or worse (Lamb, Sternberg, & Prodromidis, 1992). Many child-care settings not only fail to meet conditions conducive to optimal child development, but have serious health and safety hazards. A survey of unlicensed family day-care homes in New Jersey, for instance, revealed a high incidence of fire and electrical hazards, improperly stored toxic materials, and other dangers (Children's Defense Fund, 1992a).

What is actually meant by "quality of care"? The components of high-quality care for young children have been known for years. The Federal Interagency Day Care Requirements (1980), along with requirements suggested by the Child Welfare League of America (1984) and the National Association for the Education of Young Children (Bredekamp, 1987b), are strikingly similar in their recommended standards for the basics of quality child care. Good-quality settings are characterized by low child–staff ratios, low staff turnover, decent wages, appropriate staff training, and relatively small classroom size (Ontario Ministry of Community and Social Services, 1991; Phillips & Howes, 1987; Ruopp et al., 1979; Whitebook, Howes, & Phillips, 1989).

Staff–Child Ratios and Group Size

The National Day Care Study (Ruopp et al., 1979), which remains one of the most comprehensive studies of the components of high-quality center care, found that the most important marker of quality in center care for preschool children was group size. In larger groups, staff behavior became more restrictive and more oriented toward behavior management, with a corresponding decrease in social interaction behaviors and verbal interaction with the children in their charge. In response, children became increasingly apathetic and demonstrated more overt distress.

For infant care, the National Child Care Staffing Study (Whitebook, Howes, & Phillips, 1989) found that staff–child ratio was the most significant predictor of both caregiver behavior and child outcome. The importance of both ratios and group size has been replicated repeatedly in smaller studies in a variety of settings. For example, in child-care centers, higher ratings on overall quality of care have been associated with higher staff–child ratios (Burchinal et al., 1996; Scarr, Eisenberg, & Deater-Deckard, 1994). Research in both centers and family day-care homes reinforces the findings that caregiver behavior is more positive and nurturant in smaller groups (Howes, 1983; Stith & Davis, 1984) and that children are more likely to form secure attachments to their caregivers in settings with more appropriate staff–child ratios (Howes, Keeling, & Sale, 1988). Children in smaller groups are talked to and played with more often than children in larger groups are (Howes & Rubenstein, 1985) and have been found to be more positive in their affect (Cummings & Beagles-Ross, 1983).

On the basis of findings such as these, child development experts agreed more than 20 years ago (Phillips & Zigler, 1987; National Center for Clinical Infant Programs, 1988) that an appropriate staff–child ratio for infant care should be no less than 1:3, for toddlers 1:4, and for preschoolers no greater than 1:5. Only three states presently meet the proposed infant care standard, four states meet the ratio recommendation for toddler care, and none meets the preschool standard. No state meets all three (Holcomb et al., 1998). Ratios of 1:6 or lower are common, and ratios as extreme as 1:17 (for preschoolers) are lawful in some states (Holcomb et al., 1998). Policies such as these institutionalize child neglect, because one person cannot provide even basic safeguards for this many children at once, let alone the warmth, attention, and stimulation essential for healthy and optimal development.

Staff Level and Training

High-quality child care is indistinguishable from developmentally appropriate early childhood education; we should therefore train and compensate child-care staffers as befits their important role in the lives of our children. In programs with trained caregivers, caregiver–child interactions are more frequent and positive and the caregivers provide a greater amount of verbal stimulation (Zigler & Lang, 1991); these caregiver behaviors are associated with greater social competence (Clarke-Stewart, 1987) and decreased apathy on the part of the children (Ruopp et al., 1979). The National Child Care Staffing Study (Whitebook, Howes, & Phillips, 1989) also found that child-care staffers provided more "sensitive and appropriate caregiving" when they received more formal education, including work in early childhood education.

Despite such findings, 39 states allow family day-care providers with no prior training in child-care to operate, and the majority of child-care providers lack appropriate training or experience (Azer & Capraro, 1997). In part this reflects pervasive public attitudes that child-care providers are merely "babysitters." One way to improve the caregivers' public image and serve the best interests of children and parents at the same time is to provide proper caregiver training. In 1972 the Child Development Associate (CDA) program was initiated with federal funds to train and assess caregivers and to bestow accreditation on those who have proved capable of taking care of groups of children (National Council for Early Childhood Professional Recognition, 1990). Training and assessment of CDAs is competency based; candidates for CDA certification must demonstrate their knowledge of child development and ability to apply this understanding in a child-care setting.

Staff Turnover

It is tempting to lay the blame for poor-quality child care at the feet of child-care workers themselves. But the blame should really go to a system that undervalues child-care workers. Most child-care workers—98 percent of whom are women and 33 percent of whom are nonwhite—are grossly underpaid (see figure 6.1), and many who are paid under the table lack health benefits, job security, and the opportunity to contribute to retirement plans.

In spite of findings that the quality of child care is higher when caregivers receive higher wages, the annual compensation for child-care workers is typically below the poverty level (Whitebook, Howes, & Phillips, 1989). In 1996, the average yearly pay of child-care workers providing center care was $11,780, well below the median average income level for all U.S. workers (Annie E. Casey Foundation, 1998; Children's Defense Fund, 1998b). Employment benefits such as health care and paid time off are rarely offered to child-care workers (National Child Care Staffing Study, 1998). It is scarcely surprising that between 1988 and 1991, turnover among child-care workers was 70 percent, as compared with turnover of less than 10 percent in all U.S. companies (Noble, 1993).

Developmentally Appropriate Care

There is a great deal of debate over whether there is a shortage of child care in the United States today. There are two ways of looking at this question, each of which yields a different answer. If we ask merely, "Are there as many available slots in child care settings as there are children who need care?" The answer is "Yes, almost." If we view this issue only in terms of the sheer numbers of children who require supplemental care, it is hard to argue that there is an inadequate supply of child care.

However, the issue is more complex. Instead of merely asking whether a placement exists for each child, research shows other questions are more relevant to child outcomes (Hofferth, 1989). Is there a licensed-care slot for each child? Is it truly available—that is, is it in the same area where the child lives? Is it accessible? Is it affordable? Is it of sufficiently high quality that the child's social and cognitive development isn't going to be compromised by the experience?

When we consider this more complicated question of whether the right *kind* of care is available for each child, the answer is far more likely to be negative (Willer, 1991; Zigler & Lang, 1991). Even mothers who have already found child-care arrangements express a wish for more appropriate ones. Nearly two-thirds

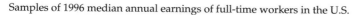

Samples of 1996 median annual earnings of full-time workers in the U.S.

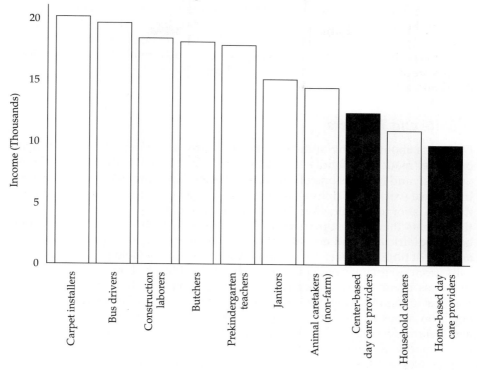

Based on a 50-week year.

FIGURE 6.1. Child-Care Wages: Who Wants This Job?
Source: U.S. Bureau of Labor Statistics, 1997.

of the mothers responding to a survey on child-care choices believed they had no alternative to the family day care they were using, and 28 percent said they would use other care if it were available. Mothers who rely on center care have similar beliefs about their lack of options. Two-thirds of these report that they have no real choices when it comes to child care. One-fourth of these said they would not use their present care arrangement at all if they had another choice (Families and Work Institute, 1994). Low-income families have still less choice than others. The Children's Defense Fund (1998) reports that families making the transition from Temporary Assistance to Needy Families (TANF) to employment and receiving child-care subsidies under the Family Support Act are often forced to place children in care of extremely low, even unsafe, quality, and are inadequately recompensed for this care.

One of the most important questions to ask about child care is whether it is *developmentally appropriate*. In other words, does the care meet the child's age-related needs? Do the caregivers understand the developmental issues relevant to the children in their care? Few parents, for instance, would engage a full-time nanny to care for a junior high school student, and no one would think of placing infants into an after-school program, but the fact remains that care appropriate to the child's age and developmental needs is far from being widely available. Two groups, in particular, have special child-care needs that are difficult to meet given our nation's present system (or lack of a system) of child care. These groups are at the opposite ends of the child-care age continuum: infants and toddlers, and school-age children.

Infants and Toddlers

Decisions about placing an infant into child care are among the most difficult ones ever made by a family. Deciding to trust a stranger with the care of their own flesh and blood is one of the most difficult things any parent will ever do. In an ideal world, decisions about whether and when both parents should be in the paid labor force following the birth or adoption of a child would be made by the parents themselves, perhaps in consultation with friends or family members, pediatricians, and employers. Parents would take into consideration the amount of time necessary for the mother to recover, psychologically and physically, from pregnancy and childbirth. They would think about the level of family stress involved in the transition to parenthood for the first time, or the changes in family dynamics set in motion by the arrival of a new family member. They would consider the amount of time it takes for them to get to know and feel comfortable with their new baby. In this far-from-ideal world, however, a new mother's return to the workplace—often within several weeks of birth—is more likely to be driven by economic concerns and pressure from employers than by a feeling that she is ready to feel comfortable being separated from her child. The Family and Medical Leave Act (FMLA) of 1993 was enacted to alleviate some of the pressure on new parents; however, this legislation only permits up to 12 weeks of *unpaid* leave after the birth of a child. Few families can afford to take a leave that is not paid. Moreover, the FMLA applies only to employers with staffs of 50 or more, which denies the leave to parents who work for smaller employers. Congressmember Rosa DeLauro has begun efforts to lower the employee requirement to 25; but as of 1998 the leave applies only to families whose workplaces have at least 50 workers.

Optimal care for an infant is different from that for an older child. Caring for a baby places severe physiological and psychological demands on the parent (Belsky, Spanier, & Rovine, 1983). Recovering physically from labor and delivery typically takes 12 weeks or longer (Farber, Alejandro-Wright, & Muenchow, 1988). Infants, especially when breast-fed, require feeding every few hours, often around the clock; the infant's feeding schedules might not become more like the parents' for six months or more. Approximately 20 percent of all normal infants cry excessively (colic) from the third week of life through the third month (Asnes & Mones, 1982). An infant's immune system, too, is immature and not fully functional apart from the temporary immunity conferred by the mother during pregnancy and nursing; it is important for much of the first year that the infant be given as much protection as possible from exposure to even ordinary respiratory and gastrointestinal infections.

An infant arrives in the world outfitted with tools that equip him to learn that the world is a stable and predictable place in which these needs can be met. The young child prefers faces over random visual patterns. He prefers human speech sounds (especially female voices) to other noises. He is able to see most precisely objects at a distance matching the distance between the mother's breast and his face. These and other skills prepare him to learn to recognize his caregivers at a very early age (Lieberman, 1994).

Much of the time that an infant and her caregivers are together is spent in establishing a sense of rhythm and reciprocal communication. Once called "bonding," the growth of such a sense of attachment is now often spoken of as "attunement" (Stern, 1977), reflecting the fact that the parents and the infant have come to expect and understand one another's verbal and nonverbal cues. When the baby cries, for instance, the parent responds by quickly offering comfort. When the baby smiles or laughs, the parents answer with smiles of their own, with a gentle touch, or a few soft words of praise and delight. Before too long the parent can tell a hungry cry that says "Bring on the milk!" from a discomfort cry that means "I've kicked off my blanket and I'm cold" to a fretful cry that means "I'm bored—play with me!" The child learns that parental behaviors do not just occur randomly, but are connected in meaningful ways to her own behavior. These little bits of behavioral dialogue rarely take more than a few moments, but as they occur over and over again in the early weeks and months of the baby's life with the same person or small group of people, the new family develops its own special form of communication.

If the child often finds himself with different caregivers, especially those who frustrate his attempts at communication by not knowing or responding to his cues, his growing sense of comfort and trust is thwarted. Thus one of the most critical features of a young child's emotional environment is *continuity of care*—the same person or few persons need to care for the baby most of the time. Because of the importance of the infant's or toddler's relationship to parents and caregivers in promoting healthy development, it is this relationship that social scientists most often explore in their research on the effects of early supplementary care. **Attachment** is an emotional bond—a sense of security and love—that a child who experiences consistent and stable caregiving develops with the people who care for and love him. Attachment status is related to how the child functions later in life. Securely attached infants, for instance, are more likely to be compliant and cooperative as preschoolers (Matas, Arend, & Sroufe, 1978).

Toddlers, too, have important developmental needs that must be considered in making child-care arrangements. The rapid pace of development during the early years requires continuous changes in what constitutes an appropriate caregiving environment, so infants and toddlers are often grouped together for the purposes of legislating child-care standards. Each age group has its own special characteristics and needs, however. Toddlers have the same needs for warmth, attention, and consistency as infants do, but the toddler's caregiver must take her mobility into account, as well as her growing sociability with those other than her mother and other family members, and her interest in toys, books, and other features of the physical environment.

The hallmark of toddlerhood is the dichotomy between growing independence and a continued need for a secure and stable source of care and love. Toddlers are pulled in many directions at once. Exploratory behavior cannot be carried out without a strong, stable base to which to return—typically the mother, but perhaps another supportive, attentive caregiver. A securely attached toddler at the beach with his mother, for instance, sticks close by her side for a while, then ventures farther—first just beyond the beach blanket, then, after checking visually with his mother to make sure she is watching him, a few yards away to investigate a seagull. Its squawk sends the child running back to his mother for a hug and reassurance, after which he is off again, this time going a little farther than the last time before coming back for a refueling moment in his mother's lap.

The Consequences of Early Child Care

Expert opinion on the specific effects of nonmaternal care for infants varies widely (see, e.g., Belsky, 1986, 1987; Phillips et al., 1987; Scarr, Phillips, & McCartney, 1987). A 1987 conference convened by the National Center for Clinical Infant Programs, the National Academy of Sciences, and the Institute of Medicine featured a panel of experts on the effects of substitute care during early childhood. In spite of significant variation in their beliefs and the research findings presented at the conference, the participants were able to reach a consensus quickly on two points. The first was that the quality of the child-care environment is directly related to measurable child development outcomes; below a certain threshold of quality, we are compromising our children's development. The second was that much research remains to be done (National Center for Clinical Infant Programs, 1988). Most of the research on the effects of nonmaternal care on infants and toddlers has focused on assessing the child's attachment to the mother, using the Strange Situation paradigm (Ainsworth et al., 1978; Bretherton, 1987; Schachere, 1990). Most such studies indicate that infants of working mothers prefer their mothers, to whom they are securely attached, over their other caregivers (Barton & Williams, 1993; Chase-Lansdale & Owen, 1987; Clarke-Stewart, 1989). Lamb and his colleagues (Lamb, Sternberg, & Prodromidis, 1992) conducted a **meta-analysis** of the effects of child care and found that although children who had experienced exclusively maternal care were significantly more likely to be securely attached than infants who had been in substitute care for more than five hours a week, the rate of secure attachments in both groups was high—71 percent and 65 percent, respectively. They point out, however, that this effect is likely to be mediated by quality of care, as all of the families were middle-class, two-parent families that were able to afford good-quality child care. Less is known about the effects of poor-quality child-care arrangements, even though such care is probably more prevalent than high-quality care.

Other workers note that the effects of child care on very young children are likely to be mediated by other factors besides type and quality of care arrangement. Families who use supplemental child care might experience more stress (independent of the child care) than do families in which a parent is able to stay at home with the children (Harwood, 1985; Hock, 1990). Some research indicates that this stress interacts with child-care usage, such that supplemental child care during the first year of life increases the likelihood of insecure attachment relationships among children from high-stress families (Gamble & Zigler, 1986; Vaughn, Gove, & Egeland, 1980). They further note that insecure attachment during infancy makes the child more vulnerable to stresses encountered later in life (Zigler & Finn-Stevenson, 1993). In addition, child characteristics such as gender (Belsky & Rovine, 1988) and temperament (Zigler & Hall, 1994) are also potential mediators of an infant's child-care experience.

Child-Care Quality and Outcomes

In 1991, the National Institute of Child Health and Development (NICHD), under the direction of Dr. Duane Alexander, launched a major study on early child care that involved over 1,300 children in 10 study sites. The study has followed most of the children's development over the first seven years of their lives, and results of the study have begun to appear. There were several significant initial findings. For example, family characteristics like mother's education and family income were strong influences on child outcomes, for both children primarily in maternal care and children who spent many hours in child-care settings (NICHD, 1997). Higher-quality child care was associated with better mother-child relationships, lower likelihood of insecure attachments in infants whose mothers were low in sensitivity to their children, fewer reported behavior problems, higher levels of cognitive and language development, and greater school readiness (NICHD, 1998). Not surprisingly, lower-quality care was associated with less harmonious mother-child relationships, more problem behaviors, and a greater likelihood of insecure attachments among children whose mothers had lower levels of sensitivity.

Center care was associated with better language and cognitive development and higher school readiness than other forms of care of similar quality. Instability of care (the number of new care arrangements experienced by the child) was associated with higher likelihood of insecure attachment if the mother was not providing sensitive and responsive care to her children. Overall, the NICHD study has clearly revealed the significance of the interaction between child-care quality and the quality of the mother-child relationship, as well as the characteristics of the individual family. All these influences combine in subtle ways to affect child outcome. Over the next several years, the NICHD study will continue to release its findings, and we will learn more about the lasting effects of child care.

Another major research effort, the Cost, Quality, and Outcomes Study, looked at 401 child-care centers in four states in spring 1993, and observed a sample of 826 preschool children who attended the centers. The sites had a diverse array of demographic and economic characteristics and varied licensing standards. The study team found that child care at most centers was poor to mediocre; however, about 50 percent of the infant and toddler rooms of such centers were of poor quality (Cost, Quality and Outcomes Study Team, 1995). They determined that child-care quality is primarily related to higher staff-to-child ratios, staff education, and prior experience of administrators. The characteristics that tended to distinguish poor, mediocre, and good-quality centers in the Cost, Quality and Outcomes Study were teachers' wages, education, and specialized training. Only 1 in 7 of the centers were found to provide a level of quality that promoted children's healthy development. Seven in 10 of the centers were providing mediocre care, putting the children's school readiness at risk. Unfortunately infants and toddlers fared worse in the study. Only 1 in 12 of the centers had infant and toddler rooms that provided developmentally appropriate care. Forty percent of these infant and toddler rooms were considered poor enough as to jeopardize children's health and safety (Cost, Quality and Outcomes Team, 1995).

School-Age Child Care

When most people think of child care, they tend to think of infants, toddlers, and preschool children. Because many mothers delay workforce participation until their children enter school, many more children of school age than younger children are in supplemental care. Approximately two-thirds of the children in child care are between the ages of 5 and 13. Over 1.5 million children between kindergarten and eighth grade are in school-age child-care programs, of which there are almost 50,000 in the United States (Cohen, 1993b).

Parents who look forward to leaving child-care problems behind when their children are old enough for school soon realize they have merely traded one set of child-care concerns for another. They might find that the family day-care home on which they have come to rely takes only preschoolers. For half of all U.S. kindergartners, kindergarten programs last only a half day (Olsen & Zigler, 1989), and the neighborhood child-care center might take children for full days only. Even in school districts that provide all-day kindergarten, parents who are employed full-time must still make arrangements for the late afternoon and early evening. Perhaps the school bus company will not transport children between school and the local child-care center, or perhaps the after-school program is full—or nonexistent. Just as the needs of preschool children are often ignored when school facilities and programs are being planned, the child-care needs of school-age children are often overlooked when the supply and quality of child care are at issue.

School-age child-care arrangements vary widely. Some family day-care homes take school-age children (although many others do not), and some day-care centers also provide before- and after-school care, though transporting children from the center to school and back again can be problematic. A recent federal study of school-age child-care settings finds that such programs are more likely to be located in schools than in any other setting. School-based after-school programs account for 28 percent of all such programs and 35 percent of all en-rollments in such programs. Not all school-based programs are run by the schools; many schools enter into cooperative agreements with towns, communi-ties, and other organizations in which the school provides the physical setting for the program, which is then administered and staffed under the aegis of town government or local youth organizations (Cohen, 1993a; Seligson et al., 1990). School-age child-care programs are also run by for-profit and nonprofit child-care facilities, private schools, state, county, and local government organizations, youth organizations, parent groups, and colleges and universities. Before-school programs are not as common as after-school programs, and very few provide child care on school holidays or during the summer months (Cohen, 1993b).

The nature and quality of school-age child-care programs vary tremen-dously. School-based programs, for instance, vary in the extent to which they have access to all school facilities, and in the types of activities offered. In some cases children have access to a wide menu of structured and semistructured ac-tivities, such as dramatic play, play with cards or board games, computer or video game play, movies, and supervised help with homework. Others are basi-cally regimented baby-sitting programs in which children might simply sit at cafeteria tables for hours on end (Cohen, 1991). The children in one-quarter of all school-based programs have no access to a playground or park. Fewer than two-thirds of such programs offer placement to children beyond the third grade; of these, fewer than half offer any structured activities (Cohen, 1993b). Some programs allow parents to use the facilities on a drop-in basis; others require full-time registration or a combination of regular hours plus drop-in care as needed (Seligson & Coltin, 1991; Seligson & Fink, 1989).

The average hourly fee for all types of school-age child care is about $1.77, with for-profit child-care facilities charging more than nonprofits. Approximately one-third of school-based programs receive some government subsidy, but tuition payments still account for 80 percent of the budgets of these programs. Even though the **Child Care and Development Block Grant** provides subsidies for school-age child care in at least 14 states, enrollment by poor children is still lim-ited by economic constraints (Cohen, 1993b). The same low pay scales and high staff turnover rates that plague child care for younger children characterize school-age child care as well. Turnover in these programs averages 35 percent per year and is almost twice that high for some programs. With staff earning an aver-age of $6.77 per hour, this should hardly be surprising (Noble, 1993).

The quality criteria for school-age child-care programs are similar to those for child care for younger children. First and foremost, high-quality programs for older children should provide a safe environment. Staff members should be well qualified and knowledgeable about the developmental issues of middle child-hood, and should provide a balance between structured and unstructured, and teacher-directed and child-initiated activities. Efficient administration, strong links between parents and staff, and the communication of clear limits and con-sistent expectations for children are important in both types of settings (Baden et al., 1982). Recommended staff–child ratios for school-age programs tend to fall at around 1:10 for children age 6 and under, and 1:12 for those over 6 (Cohen,

1993b). Safe and welcoming physical environments offering a variety of child-directed activities are as important here as in child-care facilities for younger children. Elementary school principals are beginning to take a large part of the responsibility for establishing quality standards for school-based child care. A 1993 report by the National Association of Elementary School Principals recommends standards for such programs and offers tips for starting school-based programs (Cohen, 1993a). Even so, such programs are typically not considered an extension of the school day, but a separate program with the emphasis on safety, supervision, and a range of recreational—rather than educational—activities. Similarly, the National Association for the Education of Young Children offers accreditation to some child-care centers that serve children through age 8.

Consideration of the developmental needs of the school-age child is as important as remembering those of infants when choosing child care. The school-age child is blossoming socially as well as intellectually. Interaction with peers is an important component of preparing for independence later in life. Such contacts also enhance children's abilities to take the perspective of others (Medrich et al., 1982; Selman, 1981). In addition, the growth of new interests makes extracurricular activities like music classes and sport activities an important part of the child's life. Fitting these into a child-care arrangement—or fitting a child-care arrangement around such interests and activities—is bound to entail a certain amount of conflict and compromise within families.

Home Alone

Between 5 and 10 million children, many of them as young as 5 years old, are frequently left in what is euphemistically termed "self-care," which is to say that they are left alone to care for themselves while parents go to work, look for jobs, or attend school. This figure can be given only as a range. It is likely that parents are reluctant to be accurate about how often they leave their children home alone, which is an illegal thing to do in many states. Further, such a figure does not account for the discrepancy between the large number of employed mothers of school-age children and the relatively small number of school-age child-care slots. The true number of these "latchkey children"—so-called because of their practice of wearing their house or apartment keys on strings around their necks—is probably closer to 10 million (Wellesley College Center for Research on Women, 1996).

A Boston-area survey conducted by the School Age Child Care Program (SACCP) showed that the supply of school-age child care available could accommodate only 5 percent of the area's school-age population. A full three-quarters of the respondents who were employed or attending school were unable to be home when their children arrived home from school, but fewer than 14 percent of them had access to formal after-school programs. Over two-thirds of these children were cared for only by a sibling; 13 percent were home alone at least part of the time (Seligson et al., 1990). Only one-third of schools in low-income areas offer before- and after-school care (National Center for Education Statistics, 1993).

Many parents feel they have little or no choice about leaving children alone. Nearly half of the respondents to the SACCP survey (mothers *and* fathers) reported that workplace policies are so rigid that they are not even allowed to call their children from work to make sure they arrived home safely from school; many were not allowed to take calls from their children, even in an emergency (Seligson et al., 1990).

The day-to-day experiences of latchkey children are clearly not conducive to optimal development. Parents often attempt to provide structure for their children when they cannot be with them. They might leave notes asking the children to do their homework, or start dinner, or stay home with the doors locked and be careful. Many children do not have even the limited benefits of this type of attention.

The risks of such arrangements are threefold. First, normal activities are extremely limited for children in self-care. Often expected to stay at home alone behind locked doors, they are unable to visit friends or have company, to play outside or participate in sports or extracurricular school activities. Self-care children tend to watch more television and to snack more than their appropriately supervised peers (Zigler & Lang, 1991).

Second, such children are at greater risk of physical injury from accidents and fire, and are more vulnerable to crime (Select Committee on Children, Youth and Families, 1984). One study of eighth-grade students in self-care indicated significantly higher rates of cigarette smoking, consumption of alcohol, and use of marijuana among these children than among peers in adult-supervised after-school settings (Dwyer, 1990). Some communities offer self-care programs. They might provide telephone lines that children can call when they are home alone for homework help or for reassurance when they are frightened. In some neighborhoods, block parents are trained to cover emergencies encountered by these children. It would be a mistake, however, to rely on such programs to take the place of the care and supervision missing in these children's lives. And few, if any, services are available that would prevent crises.

Finally, we must recognize the psychological consequences of this form of neglect. Placing a child in self-care represents an erosion of a significant portion of that child's environment and thus of her optimal development. Children in self-care do not learn to organize their own time, to become independent, and to explore the world from the safe base of consistent, caring, adult supervision. Instead, adult responsibility is thrust upon them before they are prepared for such a role (Zigler & Lang, 1991; Elkind, 1981). Some researchers have found no ill effects of self-care (e.g., Vandell & Corasaniti, 1988); others have found measurable negative consequences from self-care. In a study of supervised and unsupervised inner-city African American children, unsupervised girls were more likely to exhibit personal and social difficulties than were appropriately supervised girls (Woods, 1972). Numerous studies conducted by Long and Long (1982) and others (Galambos & Garbarino, 1985; Rodman, Pratto, & Nelson, 1985; Steinberg, 1986) indicate that latchkey children are bored, frightened, and lonely. They are often prematurely sexually active, and are more likely than their supervised peers to engage in antisocial behaviors (Richardson, Dwyer, &

McGuigan, 1989). Coolson, Seligson, and Garbarino (1985) sum up the dangers to latchkey children this way: they are at increased risk of feeling bad, behaving badly, developing badly, or being treated badly.

CHILD-CARE REGULATION

Despite the fact that an increasing number of families depend on out-of-home care for their children, child care has been, and continues to be, regarded as an individual family problem, to be addressed by parents. This is evident in the fact that the majority of businesses in America do not make provisions for facilitating work and family life by making available parental leaves of absence, flexible work schedules, or child-care services. The same attitude is also evident in the lack of government initiatives to address the problem (Zigler & Finn-Stevenson, 1989).

Federal Versus State Responsibility

Extensive research enables us to postulate that a large proportion of our nation's children are receiving child care of demonstrably poor quality, often from a very young age, and are at risk of suboptimal development. The shortage of appropriate, high-quality child care is also related to a loss of productivity among women in their childbearing years, many of whom indicate that the lack of child care impedes their ability to seek and maintain employment (U.S. General Accounting Office, 1992). Parents who received support in the form of child care while participating in job-training programs funded under the Title II-A Job Training Partnership Act, for instance, performed better than those without such support, more often completing training and finding jobs. It is clear that we need a uniform system of child care that meets both children's developmental needs and the needs of working parents. The patchwork arrangements so many families must make for child-care coverage are reflected on a larger level in the disarray in U.S. child-care policies.

The federal government has largely ceded its responsibility to provide safe, high-quality child care to individual states. Attempts to regulate child care at the federal level have been made since 1941, when the Office of Education first recommended staff–child ratios for child care (which, at 1:10 for preschoolers, were far less conservative than minimal requirements recommended by today's experts), along with staff training in child development, nutrition, and health (Children's Bureau, 1942). The first Federal Interagency Day Care Requirements (FIDCR) were proposed in 1968 (FIDCR, 1968), with subsequent revisions put forth in 1972 and 1980 (FIDCR, 1972, 1980) . The 1980 version recommended standards for health, safety, staff training, social services, and other features of child care, with ratios of 1:3 for infant care and 1:4 for toddlers forming the centerpiece of this proposal. The FIDCR have never been enforced, largely a casualty of conflict between proponents of low-cost care and advocates of high-quality care (Phillips & Zigler, 1987).

In 1971 the Nixon White House proposed a major effort—the Family Assistance Plan—to move welfare recipients into training and jobs programs and off of the welfare rolls. To facilitate this transition, the plan made provision for the expenditure of hundreds of millions of dollars on child-care services. Congress was working on its own Child Development Act at the time and combined the two plans and passed the legislation, which provided for expanding the number of child-care facilities, subsidizing child-care costs for families on welfare, and allowing tax deductions for other families using child care. At that point, however, events took an unexpected turn as right-wing groups mounted a high-pressure campaign that ultimately convinced President Nixon that the plan advocated communal rearing of children and encouraged Communism. Although neither of these charges was true , Nixon vetoed the act (Nixon, 1971). The 1980 FIDCR, never enforced, currently represent the last attempt at federal regulation of the quality of child care.

Special interest groups have also lobbied against the enactment of adequate federal child-care standards. These groups include both large for-profit child-care centers and small "mom and pop" centers, both of whom are concerned about the expense associated with meeting stricter government standards. Although operating costs would be higher for providers, these costs would ultimately be passed on to parents. One fear is that parents who could not afford the greater expense would be driven into poor-quality, "underground" child-care settings. Unfortunately, the

---

 ## *Child-Care Milestones*

1971 President Nixon vetoes the Child Development Act.

1981 New tax law allows parents to use pretax dollars to pay for child care.

1982 SAS Institute, Inc., opens the first free on-site child-care center.

1983 Child Care Action Campaign launched.

1986 For first time in U.S. history, over 50 percent of all mothers with children under age 3 are in the paid labor force.

1990 President Bush vetoes the Family and Medical Leave Act for the first time.
Congress authorizes $2.5 billion in Child Care Development Block Grants.

1991 For first time, over 50 percent of all mothers with children under age 1 are in the paid labor force.

1992 President Bush vetoes the Family and Medical Leave Act for the second time.

1993 President Clinton signs the Family and Medical Leave Act into law.

1993 "Nannygate"—the appointments of Zoe Baird and then of Kimba Wood as U.S. attorney general are axed by admissions that both women paid child-care workers "off the books."

1996 Public Law 104-193, welfare reform law, introduces Temporary Assistance to Needy Families (TANF); limited benefits and new work requirements raise demand for child care.

Source: Information derived from Wilburn & McMorris, 1994, and U.S. Department of Labor, 1992.

reality is that there is always a trade-off between child-care quality and cost. In addition, the State Governors' Association has been an impediment to the enactment of federal child-care regulations. This is an issue not only of sovereignty—of who has jurisdiction over child-care regulations—but also of economics. Under recent federal legislation, Child Care and Development Block Grants are available to the states to help families pay for child care and related programs, with priority given to economically marginal families (Budget Reconciliation Act of 1990). Individual states must match these funds and fear that available child-care monies will not go as far if they must be spent to mount and administer programs of higher quality than are currently typical. These cost-related concerns are not entirely unfounded; high-quality child care does cost more to provide than poor-quality care. Even families often resist the notion of federal child-care standards on these grounds; many are already paying in more than $5,000 per year for infant care (Children's Defense Fund, 1990).

The States' Role

In place of uniform national standards for child-care quality, there currently exist fifty separate sets of child-care legislation, one for each state (Holcomb et al., 1998; Zigler & Young, 1987). These state standards vary with respect to required ratios, staff training, rules regarding exemption from compliance (e.g., because of small enrollments in family day-care homes or affiliation with a religious organization) (Higginbotham, 1993), immunizations required, and other variables. Block grant funds available to states to support child care are inadequate to guarantee universal access to care. Many states have dropped previously eligible families from waiting lists for subsidized care by lowering eligibility income levels; even many poor families with one or more working parents are unable to afford the fees or co-payments even for subsidized care (Children's Defense Fund, 1998c).

A recent study of the regulatory status of center-based infant and toddler settings presents a bleak picture. Not one state had regulations that met the criteria for optimal or good child care (Young, Marsland, & Zigler, 1997). Only 17 states had regulations rated as "minimally acceptable," 30 states had regulations that received overall ratings of "poor," and 4 states had no infant and toddler regulations or the ones they had were rated as "very poor." Even in states with adequate legal requirements for center and family day care, inspections to guarantee compliance are few and far between, and many states make no provision for enforcing standards. Clearly, the principles of child development do not vary from state to state; requirements safeguarding children's development should not either.

Local Government

With a virtual vacuum of adequate provisions for high-quality child care at the national or state level, some towns and communities have stepped in to fill this need (Seligson et al., 1990). A promising model is emerging in which after-school care, in particular, is administered at the local or municipal level, often in conjunction with local boards of education. Child-care programs for younger children might also be administered and subsidized at the level of town or community government.

The Role of Business and Industry

Employers in large and small companies alike are learning that providing for the family-based needs of their employees is more than mere altruism. When child-care crises are the number one reason for employee absences in many companies (Dumas, 1994; Gardner, 1994), providing employees with help finding, and even paying for, child care makes good business sense. Furthermore, as one industry

---

 Child Care in the School of the 21st Century

The School of the 21st Century (21C) program was launched in 1988 to meet the need for affordable, high-quality child care. Designed by Professor Edward Zigler, the program places school-age child care as a second system within the public school building, and includes other family support programs designed to address community needs and ensure that children arrive at school ready to learn. Since 1988, more than 500 schools in 17 states have implemented the program, which continues to grow as public interest in child development increases.

The 21C program (known as Family Resource Centers in some communities) is a flexible model, allowing schools to tailor the program to suit local needs. In some communities, the 21C program serves as an umbrella for an array of family support services: adult education, social services, youth services, and the like. The school building remains open for the hours of the full workday, to accommodate the needs of working parents. Sliding-scale fees allow all parents access to services, and no programs are compulsory.

Core Components of the School of the 21st Century

Child care for preschoolers
High-quality child care for children ages 3 to 5

Support and guidance for new parents
Family outreach for parents of children 0 to 3 years, based on the Parents as Teachers (PAT) program

Support and training for child-care providers
Workshops, training, and support for local child-care providers

School-age child care
After-school care; vacation care

Information and referral services
Educating parents about services in their communities

Health education and services
Collaboration with providers to offer nutrition education, developmental screening, and mental health services

executive has noted, "Industry will need confident, independent self-starters with high self-esteem and motivation. . . . You are not going to be able to get that from a population of children who have grown up in mediocrity" (Yetter, 1991).

Companies that provide child-care benefits of any sort are still in the minority, but an increasing number of employers now provide child care (11 percent) or resource and referral services (20 percent) (Families and Work Institute, 1998). IBM, for instance, allocated $22 million in the early 1990s for child-care support services for its employees. DuPont, Fannie Mae, Bayer, S. C. Johnson, Citicorp, and others all offer a variety of child-care assistance programs ranging from on-site child-care centers to sick-child-care options to pretax child-care spending accounts. Other companies purchase or subsidize child-care slots in facilities near the workplace, offer resource and referral services for parents seeking child care, offer **flex time** and job-sharing programs that enable parents to minimize their use of supplemental care or to make scheduling appropriate care easier. Smaller firms, too, are beginning to take a similar approach, as employers realize that high turnover related to childbirth and high absenteeism related to child-care problems have a negative impact on company productivity. Assisting parents with their child-care-related needs lowers turnover, raises morale, and improves productivity (Gardner, 1994; Yetter, 1991).

Some companies offer more than just human resources policies to families in need of child care. Some leaders of business and industry have mounted or participated in coalitions to promote high-quality child care. The Hewlett Packard Corporation, for instance, loaned a senior executive to help mount a school-age child-care program in California. Coors Brewery mounted a public awareness campaign to support area school-age child-care programs (Seligson et al., 1990). The American Business Collaboration for Quality Dependent Care is a joint effort of 145 companies that have spent millions of dollars on child care for employees and community members in almost 300 communities across the nation (Shellenbarger, 1993a). And the on-site employee child-care facility at Arnold and Porter, a Washington, D.C., law firm, offers assistance to child-care providers in surrounding communities and is working to update child-care licensing requirements for the District of Columbia.

Families: Child-Care Consumers

In spite of the rising numbers of families who rely on supplemental child care, and in spite of feelings among families that government should take more responsibility for the provision or regulation of child-care services (Zinsser, 1989), child care continues to be widely regarded as an individual family problem that should be addressed by parents. With no uniform national standards for child care, and with state standards that often fail to fully address the developmental needs of young children, parents have to be their children's best advocates. The parents' role can be twofold: first, to select the best-quality care available, taking into consideration the differing types of care and differing needs of infants, toddlers, preschoolers, and school-age children, and second, to use their power as consumers to lobby for better child care.

There are several impediments to the fulfillment of these roles, however. For families whose time is already filled to capacity by the demands of juggling child rearing and employment, researching child-care standards and weighing the available options is unfeasibly taxing. Furthermore, the available options are often so limited, and of such poor quality, as to make evaluations of them essentially meaningless. Which is the better choice, for instance, for a middle-income single parent with a 6-month-old infant: the affordable neighborhood center in which babies are kept in cribs for much of the day and the smell of diapers pervades the nursery, the day-care home with the loving provider who thinks she might have an opening for an infant in a few months, or the high-quality center that has an opening but costs more than the parent can comfortably afford and is located on the other side of town?

Parents have also not been well informed about the optimal standards for child care or about what standards truly mean. When parents were polled by the Families and Work Institute about whether they sought **licensed** child care, fewer than one-third of respondents felt that licensing was very important and almost 20 percent felt that licensing didn't matter at all (Carroll, 1993). When asked what the most important qualities of child-care were, parents using in-home, family, and center care all responded in the same way. When asked how they define child-care quality, however, parents describe a wish list that prominently features child safety, parent-caregiver communication, warm child-caregiver interactions, consistent disciplinary practices, experienced caregivers, and high staff–child ratios. Although licensing is no *guarantee* of high-quality care, regulated settings are far more likely than nonlicensed settings to feature just these qualities.

Child-Care Funding

Although advocates have so far been unsuccessful in getting the federal government to take responsibility for child-care quality, they have met with a small measure of success in having the government partially address the high cost of care. This problem is addressed in a two-pronged approach: the dependent care income tax credits for the middle class and child-care subsidies for low-income families.

The dependent care tax credit represents the largest source of federal assistance to families with child-care needs. In excess of $3 billion it has benefited close to 10 million families, the majority of whom earned more than $25,000 a year (Lindsey, 1988). The tax credit is not refundable, so it is applicable only to those who owe taxes and thus cannot be used by families with very low incomes, those who are most in need of help. In 1997, Congress passed a new $500 per child tax credit that is automatically given to families, even those without child-care expenses, but this credit also is nonrefundable. Taking this credit into account, a two-parent family would have to make at least $31,000 a year before it would receive the full benefit of the Dependent Care Tax Credit (Parrot, 1998). There is a movement to make the credits refundable and usable by lower-income families, but thus far the effort has been unsuccessful.

Block grants, funds generated at the federal level and awarded to the states, who allocate and administer them, also provide some subsidy for child care for lower-income families. Child Care and Development Block Grants (CCDBG), funded at $2.87 billion in fiscal year 1997, require states to match funding and are available to families with incomes below 85 percent of state median income, though individual states may set levels lower than this—effectively reducing the number of eligible families—at their discretion.

Title XX/Social Services Block Grant (SSBG) makes federal funds available to states for a variety of social service uses, only one of which is child care. Funding for SSBG has declined from $2.8 billion to $2.5 billion in recent years. Advocates believe that only about 20 percent of SSBG monies are spent on child care; the amount varies from state to state, but in no case is it sufficient to make high-quality child care affordable to every family that needs it (Children's Defense Fund, 1998b, 1998f; Sugarman, 1988). Some states have responded creatively to cuts in Title XX funds. California, for instance, has established an impressive statewide resource and referral network, which provides subsidies and vouchers for child care, information and referral services, and provider training and recruitment. As an additional means of making the most of limited child-care funds, a consortium of government agencies and businesses in California was able to raise $700,000 to fund child-care pilot projects and to train family day-care providers (Zigler & Finn-Stevenson, 1989).

In addition, a promising new avenue for funding an integrated programmatic model lies in the Human Services Reauthorization Act of 1990, which allocates funds for the purpose of developing a network of family resources and support programs within communities.

THE FUTURE OF CHILD CARE

The economic/social reality is that demand for child care cannot be ignored; many questions remain to be answered, but the one given is that parents must use substitute care. If we are to construct a satisfactory, cohesive national child-care system, we must observe seven principles: (1) Such a system must be reliable and stable, and tied to a major institution that is well known throughout American society. (2) It must guarantee universal access to all services, and integrate all ethnic and social groups in the provision of these services. (3) It must be of sufficiently high quality to promote optimal child development. (4) Any such system should provide services to families even *before* the birth of a child, and must continue them at least through the first 12 years of life, if not beyond. (5) Such a program must address not only cognitive but also personal and social development. (6) Such a system must necessarily both rely on and hold as sacred the relationship between caregivers and parents. (7) It must reflect the value of those caregivers by both demanding better training and providing wages and benefits befitting workers of high status (Zigler, 1987).

The first component of such a program should be a strong national parental leave policy. Allowing at least one parent to remain at home with a new baby for a large part of the first year goes a long way toward simultaneously minimizing family stress and getting the infant off to a good start by creating an environment conducive to the development of a strong sense of trust, a secure parent-child attachment, and a head start on both social and cognitive development (Hopper & Zigler, 1988).

SUMMARY

Finding accessible, affordable, good-quality child care is one of the largest challenges facing today's parents. Well over half of all U.S. children spend some portion of their time in the care of someone other than a parent. Changes in employment patterns, with more women in the paid workforce than ever before in U.S. history, the increase in the number of single-parent families, and increasing workplace demands have all contributed to this phenomenon. Child-care arrangements vary wildly, but most fit into one of three categories.

In-home care arrangements are those in which the child is tended by a babysitter, nanny, or nonparent relative in the child's own home. In family day care, individual children or small groups of children are cared for by a relative or nonrelative in the caregiver's home. In center care, groups of children are cared for, typically by nonrelatives, in for-profit or not-for-profit commercial establishments ranging from small nurseries sponsored by religious or community groups, to small commercial mom-and-pop facilities, to large commercial daycare chain centers. Many families who are unable to find a single arrangement that fits their schedule, budget, and child's developmental needs develop a patchwork arrangement in which they juggle different caregiving situations on different days, or must change caregivers frequently because of caregiver turnover, incompatibility, or financial constraints.

Quality of care also varies widely within each of these arrangements. Quality is one of several important variables contributing to the developmental outcome of care. The availability of warm, predictable, stable care from a very small number of caregivers who are responsive to her needs lays the groundwork for the child's development. The ability to form trusting relationships with others and the capacity to see the world as a stable, predictable, well-ordered place form the foundations for healthy social and cognitive development. The lack of continuity of care and the prevalence of poorly trained caregivers with little understanding of child development are of concern to both parents and experts familiar with the components of healthy child development. Today's social and economic realities have forced many parents to make use of suboptimal child care.

We know what constitutes high-quality child care, and we know how to achieve it. Quality of care is affected by staff–child ratios, by caregiver training and turnover, by the number of children being cared for at once, and by the safety and comfort level of the facility. Other variables contributing to child outcome include the child's age at the time of entry into supplemental care, the child's gender, and a variety of parental variables contributing to the stability of the child's daily life. High-quality care costs more than poor-quality care. In addition, the federal government has failed to pass uniform standards for child care, and state licensing standards vary from state to state with respect to caregiver training, staff–child ratios, health and safety regulations, and enforcement of these.

Federal, state, and local governments continue to wrangle over who should have responsibility for meeting the child-care needs of children and parents. Some employers have begun to provide on-site child-care facilities or child-care subsidies for workers, but such benefits are available only to a tiny minority of parents. Changes to federal and state welfare policies during the late 1990s have contributed to the child-care crises by precipitously increasing the demand for child care without providing adequate supports in the form of either appropriate child-care placements or reasonable subsidies for parents forced by law to find child care. In spite of the large numbers of children in supplemental child care, policies regulating and subsidizing the quality of care continue to lag far behind demand.

CHAPTER 7

Child Health

Although America spends more money per capita on health care than any other nation, millions of U.S. children continue to suffer from completely preventable and treatable illnesses, lack access to adequate health care, and suffer from the direct or indirect effects of pervasive public health problems. Child health statistics read like a grim litany. Each year, nearly 40,000 U.S. children die before their first birthday; the majority of these deaths could be prevented. Underinsurance is a major problem for children, even for those whose parents are employed full-time. Preventable and treatable childhood diseases continue to kill American children at rates unknown in other industrialized—even in some developing—nations. Low birthweight, which is almost entirely preventable, continues to lead to death or persistent health and cognitive problems in too many infants. Policy responses to these issues in recent decades have swung between informed commitment and determination to a willingness to overlook the serious implications of America's child health problems in the interest of focusing resources on other priorities.

Perhaps most disturbing of all, the inequity inherent in our present health care system accounts for gross differences in health and health care provision among different groups of American children; poverty, for instance, is everywhere implicated in the poor health of children. In this chapter we will look at each of these problems in some depth, and discuss how policy of various sorts and at various levels is addressing these issues—sometimes effectively, sometimes not.

THE BIRTH OF CHILD HEALTH POLICY

Certainly significant progress has been made in improving child health. Two hundred years ago, childhood mortality in the United States stood at no less than 50 percent. One hundred years ago there had been little improvement: Over 50 percent of all deaths in New York City in 1869 were of children under 5 years of age (Kopp, 1983). Congenital problems, infectious diseases, poor diet, and unsanitary living conditions caused the greatest proportion of these deaths (Kopp, 1983). Even as recently as World War II, three American infants died for every two soldiers killed in action (U. S. Department of Health, Education, and Welfare, 1976). Change came slowly, fostered by doctors like Abraham Jacobi, recognized as the father of American pediatrics for his insistence that the medical treatment of children is not simply a miniature version of the treatment of adults.

Child health was one of the first family-related topics to draw the attention of policy makers and child advocates. In 1912, at the urging of the 1909 White House Conference on Children, President Taft founded the U.S. Children's Bureau and appointed Julia Lathrop as its director. Lathrop, the first woman in U.S. history to be selected by a president to head a federal statutory agency, assumed as her first tasks the investigation of infant mortality and the establishment of a registry to document the births of all U.S. children.

Lathrop also commissioned a pamphlet of information on prenatal care and infant care for parents. The result was *Infant Care*, (West, 1914) which first appeared in 1914 and became the government's all-time best-selling publication.

Infant Care was revised yearly until its publication was discontinued during the Reagan administration, and it was influential in encouraging women from all socioeconomic groups to obtain early prenatal care, to breast-feed their infants, and to have them immunized against preventable diseases.

CHILD HEALTH GOALS

Let us imagine that we are grading the United States on its performance in the area of promoting and protecting child health. Our first step would be to establish goals and criteria for assessing changes in child health. Such goals are in fact set for child health by a number of groups. Players and advocates in the child health arena include foundations like the Carnegie Corporation and the Robert Wood Johnson Foundation, government agencies like the U.S. Department of Health and Human Services (USDHHS) and the Department of Agriculture, advocacy groups such as the Children's Defense Fund and the Center for Children in Poverty, and professional associations like the American Academy of Pediatrics, as well as lawmakers at the federal, state, and local level. In addition, representatives of business and industry—especially health care—community groups, religious organizations, and individual citizens are all instrumental in defining child health goals, implementing solutions to address them, and assessing the progress (or lack thereof) in achieving them. Each of these plays a role in setting and working to meet our child health goals.

One list of child and maternal health goals has already been defined by the USDHHS in its "Health 2000" objectives (see table 7.1). Additional goals proposed by other agencies address social support for isolated parents, improvements in day-care quality, immunizations, poverty, equitable distribution of medical services, maternal and pediatric HIV/AIDS, gun control, violent crime, nutrition, access to health care, family planning services, catastrophic health care, and health education (Carnegie Corporation, 1994; Ehrenhaft, 1987; Johnson, 1993; Klerman, 1996; Klerman, 1991; Schroeder, 1993).

Such lists remind us that there are two ways of looking at child health. The first is to see the preservation of child health largely as a matter of disease prevention and eradication. This was certainly the model for child health policy during the better part of our country's first 200 years (U.S. Department of Health, Education, and Welfare, 1976). More recently, however, our conception of child health has broadened to include such factors as child safety and nutrition. Pervasive violence, poor housing, substandard child care, inadequate educational opportunities, and drug abuse are also among the topics now viewed as public health concerns.

Child Health and Poverty

Among near-poor families, only about 39 percent of parents said that their children were in "excellent" health, compared with almost 64 percent of families with incomes of $35,000 or more (Adams & Benson, 1990). Poor children in

TABLE 7.1. Child Health Goals for the Year 2000, as Defined by the U.S. Department of Health and Human Services

- Reduction of infant mortality
- Reduction of the fetal death rate
- Reduction of maternal mortality rates
- Reduction of the number of babies born at low or very low birthweights
- Improvement in the number of women who gain weight appropriately during pregnancy
- Reduction in the rate of severe complications of pregnancy
- Reduction of the cesarean delivery rate
- An increase in the percentage of women who breast-feed their babies
- A decrease in the percentage of Americans who use tobacco products
- A decrease in the rate of fetal alcohol syndrome
- An increase in the percentage of women receiving prenatal care beginning in the first trimester of pregnancy
- An increase in the percentage of those seeking preconception counseling
- An increase in the percentage of expectant parents receiving counseling on fetal abnormalities
- Improved primary care for infants
- Improved care appropriate to the risk level of the child in question
- Increased screening for galactosemia and sickle cell anemia

Source: U.S. Department of Health and Human Services, 1992.

America are far more likely to suffer from health problems and are far less likely to receive appropriate, regular, and preventive health care than are the children of middle- and upper-income families. During 1991, 8 percent of white and nearly 10 percent of black children between 1 and 4 years of age had not been seen by a physician; poor children were more likely to receive medical care in hospitals and less likely to get their medical care in physicians' offices than children with family incomes above poverty (USDHHS, 1992).

Because poor children are less likely to receive acute care in a timely fashion, they often need hospital admission to treat illnesses that might have been treated on an outpatient basis had they been detected earlier. Hospital admissions for the treatment of asthma, bacterial pneumonia, cellulitis, dehydration, and gastroenteritis are frequent among low-income populations; asthma-related admissions, for instance, are four times higher among economically disadvantaged children than among children from higher socioeconomic strata (Schroeder, 1993). Further evidence that poor families are more likely to delay seeking medical care for their children is found in the longer hospital stays experienced by poor children. Children with family incomes under $20,000 averaged nearly twice as many days in the hospital in 1991 as children from higher-income families (USDHHS, 1992).

A number of chronic conditions and infectious diseases are disproportionately associated with poverty. Among these are asthma, rheumatic fever, hemophilus influenza, meningitis, gastroenteritis, parasitic diseases, measles, and other communicable diseases (Wood et al., 1990). Anemia, which is also associ-

Getting the Lead Out

The production of lead-based paints was halted by law in the United States in the early 1970s, but in spite of cleanup efforts in the intervening years, the Centers for Disease Control (CDC) reports that 57 million housing units, many occupied by young children, still contain dangerous amounts of lead (U.S. Department of Housing and Urban Development, 1990). Three to 4 million children (close to 1 in 6) have dangerously high blood lead levels, and it has been estimated that 4 million fetuses will suffer toxic effects of lead exposure before the year 2000 (CDC, 1990). Ingestion of lead-coated paint chips has long been blamed as the primary source of elevated lead levels among young children, but simple exposure to the lead-laced dust that accumulates as a matter of daily wear in older houses poses more of a threat.

Lead toxicity is a problem to which children at all income levels are susceptible, particularly as gentrification of older and poorer neighborhoods results in the release of lead during old house renovation. However, low-SES children are far more likely to be affected than are children from more affluent families (Klerman, 1991). Black children are disproportionately represented among those with elevated lead levels; among children under 5 with family incomes under $6,000 in 1988, for instance, black children were almost four times more likely to suffer from elevated lead levels than were white children (Agency for Toxic Substances and Disease Registry, 1988).

Among all socioeconomic and ethnic groups, infants, toddlers and preschoolers are at particularly high risk of lead poisoning, both because they spend more time playing and crawling on floors where lead-contaminated dust settles, and because of their tendency to mouth objects. Further, lead exposure during this stage of rapid brain development appears to have greater ramifications for child health than exposure at later stages. Lead also crosses the placental barrier and poses a prenatal risk. Fetal lead poisoning can result from environmental exposure experienced by the mother, or, if the mother herself had high lead levels as a child, by the release of lead stored in her own skeletal system as her body releases lead along with the calcium needed by the fetus.

What are the effects of lead poisoning in early childhood? Lead appears to interfere with the developing neural circuitry in the young child's brain and can lead to learning disorders, speech and language disabilities, and school failure. Prenatal exposure to lead shortens gestation, lowers birthweight, and can lead to attenuated mental development. Environmental exposure during early childhood can lead to a great variety of problems, including chronic irritability, fine motor difficulties, stunted cognitive development, short stature, loss of hearing acuity, kidney disorders, comas, convulsions, and death. Chronic anemia exacerbates the effects of lead poisoning, so children with poor diets are at an increased risk (Bellinger et al., 1987).

Today, lead poisoning can be treated with drugs that bind with the lead in the bloodstream so that it can be excreted from the child's body. But lead in the bones is more difficult to remove, and elevated lead levels in the brain, and the damage associated therewith, appear to be irreversible.

Lead poisoning is not a new problem, but it is one for which we have yet to find a workable solution. The use of lead by industries, utilities, fuel companies, and others—often carelessly and with little thought to the environmental or public health consequences—has gone on for centuries. Lead poisoning among children was first documented in Australia around 1900 and began to be reported in the United States during the 1920s.

In spite of a high incidence of problems associated with lead exposure, however, the U.S. government took no action until the surgeon general's report "Medical Aspects of Childhood Lead Poisoning" was released in 1970 (Goldman, 1998). In 1971, the Lead-Based Paint Poisoning Prevention Act (PL 91-695) was passed, authorizing federal assistance to communities to mount and carry out both screening and prevention measures. In 1992, the Maternal and Child Health Services Block Grant Act (MCH), and the Omnibus Budget Reconciliation Act of 1981 transferred responsibility for lead-poisoning prevention efforts to the MCH program in the U. S. Public Health Service, and gave each state the power to set priorities and make decisions about the use of these funds. Turning lead-elimination and treatment oversight over to the states has had little impact on the outcomes for children. A few states do not even have basic lead-screening programs. And even though the technology exists to clean every house in the nation of lead within a few decades, the cost of such an operation is often deemed to be prohibitive, and in many cities an investigation of suspected environmental lead cannot even be launched unless it can be proved that the children residing in these environments have already been poisoned. A number of **lobbying** groups, convinced that the elimination of lead poisoning as a childhood hazard is both worthwhile and attainable, have sprung up to work toward the elimination of environmental lead hazards, and to alert parents and housing administrators to the fact that the dangers of lead haven't gone away.

ated with lower maternal education and young maternal age (Yip et al., 1987), and elevated blood lead levels (Bellinger et al., 1987; Klerman, 1996) are also strongly associated with childhood poverty.

Poor children have more vision and hearing problems, and these are more likely to go undetected and untreated for longer periods than in nonpoor children. Children living in poverty are also more likely to experience psychosocial and psychosomatic problems and learning disabilities (Egbuono & Starfield, 1982; Klerman, 1991; Zill & Schoenborn, 1990) and to miss more days of school each year than children at higher income levels (Schroeder, 1993). Dental care, too, is relatively inaccessible for low-SES children, two-thirds of whom have never seen a dentist before beginning kindergarten. Among poor school-age children, only about half (as opposed to 83 percent of nonpoor children) saw a dentist during 1989. The long-term ramifications of such neglect become apparent when we consider that one-half of poor elderly Americans have lost all of their teeth (Schroeder, 1993).

Child Health in a Global Context

The United States also does poorly in other areas, compared to other nations (see table 7.2). Some 70 nations worldwide provide full medical care and financial assistance to all pregnant women; the United States does not. Sixty-one nations ensure basic medical care for all workers and their families; the United States

TABLE 7.2. How the United States Compares with Other Nations in Meeting Child Health Care Goals

Goal	Rank of United States*
Immunization of all children against polio—all races, by age 1	17
Immunization of all children against polio—nonwhite	49
Prevention of infant mortality	18
Prevention of mortality to children under 5	18
Prevention of low birthweight	17

*Among industrialized nations
Source: Children's Defense Fund, 1998g.

does not (Children's Defense Fund, 1992b). Only 75 percent of U.S. children have received the recommended DPT(diphtheria, pertussis, and tetanus) immunizations; the corresponding figure for children in the Netherlands is 97 percent (Harvey, 1990).

In some areas these figures are improvements (e.g., prevention of mortality in children under 5), but in other areas we are losing ground. In 1950, the United States was ranked third in the world in the prevention of postneonatal infant mortality (prevention of mortality from the end of the first month to the end of the first year); today we rank behind 17 other nations on this variable (Harvey, 1990; Children's Defense Fund, 1998g). In contrast, infant mortality in France dropped from 32 percent to 10 percent during the same period (Manciaux et al., 1990).

Child health services in many other nations are received largely through comprehensive, free systems in which children are tracked from birth through childhood by home visitors, public health personnel, and pediatric caseworkers. In England and Wales, for instance, the National Health Service and Social Security are responsible for the standardization and provision of child health services, which are overseen at the local level, first by a system of health visitors, then later by school nurses (Goodwin, 1990). In Canada, responsibility for health care is shared by the provincial and federal governments; through this system, health care is provided to all citizens. As a percentage of gross national product (GNP), the total expense for the Canadian health care system amounts to less than 9 percent; the United States spends 11 percent of its GNP and does not guarantee coverage for the entire populace (Pless, 1990).

French children, too, receive free health care up to age 6, and many families receive cash allowances to help them care for their young children (see chapter 5 for more on family allowances). Care is provided through home visits and special maternal and child health clinics; parents who wish to use private pediatricians may do so and are later reimbursed completely for these services. Once the child reaches age 4 and attends nursery school, a school nurse assumes responsibility for tracking the child's health and providing care. Children with special medical needs are given free care in specialized outpatient clinics called Centers for Early Medico-Social Action. Some groups in France—**migrant families** and teen mothers, for instance—are still underserved, but the French system succeeds in meeting many of the child health goals, particularly regarding pregnancy and early childhood, that the United States has yet to meet (Manciaux et al., 1990).

What accounts for the disparity between our nation and others with respect to the provision of comprehensive child health care? Some argue that this is a factor of the racial and ethnic heterogeneity of the U.S. population, but even our health indicators for white children tend to be poor. Others suggest that the dense population status of most European nations makes its citizenry easier to reach with health services. Norway, however, is more rural than any state in our nation, and yet 80 percent of Norway's children receive DPT immunization by age 3 (Harvey, 1990).

Conferees at an international pediatric meeting on the provision of child health care worldwide concluded that the individualistic philosophy of the United States tends to view children as the private property of their families, whereas Europeans are more likely to believe that children are a national resource, the responsibility for which falls to the entire nation (Harvey, 1990).

ACCESS TO HEALTH CARE

Unlike Canada, France, England, and other countries that have comprehensive health care systems administered at the national level, the U.S. system of health care is hardly a system at all. A large percentage of Americans essentially are denied health care because they lack the insurance coverage to afford it. In some areas the problem is compounded by a shortage of medical services. In all areas, the problem affects children more seriously than other age groups, partly because of the lifelong health ramifications of being denied adequate medical care early in life, but also in part simply because the young are overrepresented among the underinsured.

Almost 12 million children in the United States are uninsured. They are the largest and fastest-growing group of uninsured persons in this country (American Academy of Pediatrics, 1998a, 1998g; Children's Defense Fund, 1998d; U. S. Bureau of the Census, 1997). Among children whose family incomes are below the poverty level, nearly 23 percent lack medical insurance (Medicaid notwithstanding); over 27 percent of near-poor children have no insurance (Klerman, in press). Approximately 7 million American children, without coverage from either Medicaid or private insurance, are essentially denied access to routine medical care (American Academy of Pediatrics, 1998a).

This is by no means a problem restricted to poor children alone. More than 90 percent of uninsured children live in families in which one or both parents are employed. Only 1 uninsured child out of 3 lives below the poverty level, though 70 percent live within 200 percent of poverty (U. S. Bureau of the Census, 1997). In most of these cases, parents make too much to qualify for Medicaid but are unable to afford private insurance. In 1980, most medium and large companies paid 100 percent of family health insurance costs; today only a quarter do, and not all of these offer dependent care coverage, leaving children uninsured (U.S. Department of Labor, 1980, 1994b). Even when employers foot part of the health care bill, the employee's share of a family HMO policy can range from approximately $4,000 to almost $10,000 a year, well beyond the reach of many families (Children's Defense Fund, 1998d).

Lack of insurance affects nonwhite children in disproportionate numbers. Among whites, 70 percent are insured, but only 44 percent of black children and 38 percent of Hispanic children are (Children's Defense Fund, 1997d). Hispanic children are less likely than blacks or non-Hispanic whites to be covered by employer-provided insurance, even though they are about as likely to be employed. Although 87 percent of Hispanics are employed (as compared with 91.2 percent of all Americans), only 36.4 percent of Hispanics (versus over 60 percent of all Americans) have employer-provided insurance (Children's Defense Fund, 1998b).

Medicaid

The largest single source of U.S. health care coverage for pregnant women and babies is the Medicaid program. Established in 1965 as a tool in President Johnson's War on Poverty, and administered by the U.S. Department of Health and Human Services (USDHHS), as well as by individual states, Medicaid provides health coverage to pregnant women and infants from low-income families; disabled persons are also covered under Medicaid. Although the largest percentage of the funding is allocated for the care of the elderly, the largest number of Medicaid recipients are women and children (Klerman, 1996).

Expansions in the 1990s have improved coverage for children, especially for infants and preschoolers, but because of inconsistencies from state to state in the administration of the program, over 60 percent of all poor children still do not receive coverage (American Academy of Pediatrics, 1997b). Preschool children covered by Medicaid averaged 6 physician visits each per year; in contrast, children with no insurance see pediatricians an average of 2.8 times yearly and privately insured children make 3.4 pediatric visits a year (Schroeder, 1993).

Medicaid is a reimbursement program—the health care provider is reimbursed for services rendered. The program is frequently criticized by care providers for its complexity, the amount of paperwork required of physicians before they can be paid for their services, the number of claims that are denied and must be filed again, and low rates of reimbursement (Klerman, 1996).

In addition, Medicaid has come under fire for its lack of uniform standards and practices from one state to another. For instance, in 1987 in California, Medicaid covered all children below 109 percent of poverty; in Alabama during that same year, only selected groups of children below 16 percent of poverty were covered (Johnson, 1993). Since then, expansions have resulted in somewhat more uniform coverage, especially for infants and preschoolers, but health care policy analysts still cite such inconsistencies as one of the program's major weaknesses (Schroeder, 1993).

About 70 percent of U.S. pediatricians take Medicaid patients. Compared with physicians in other specialties, this is a relatively high rate of participation, but many of these are no longer accepting new Medicaid patients. More

Medicaid-participating pediatricians are badly needed, particularly in economically disadvantaged communities; low-income areas have 44   percent
fewer pediatricians than more affluent areas. This trend shows no sign of re-
versal within the near future: pediatricians are locating practices in poor areas
at much slower rates than they are in higher-income communities. Some states
have recently raised provider fees in order to encourage Medicaid participation
and thus satisfy legislated requirements that states demonstrate adequate coverage for children under Medicaid (Schroeder, 1993). Even so, advocacy groups
like the American Academy of Pediatrics have recommended that further incentives be offered to encourage pediatricians to locate in low-income areas
and accept Medicaid patients (Lowe, 1993).

Even with recent reforms to the Medicaid system, critics argue that Medicaid perpetuates a two-tiered system of health care for children. Eligibility, reimbursement, funding levels, and services covered vary from one state to another.
Testimony before Congress by representatives of the American Academy of Pediatrics emphasized as well the stigma that Medicaid reflects:

> Medicaid has perpetuated a two-tiered system of care in which eligibility, ben-
> efits and reimbursement limited by lack of funds, vary from state to state. Med-
> icaid still entails a welfare stigma and must be applied for with a means-test ad-
> ministered by the public aid system. Working class families struggling to stay
> independent find this aspect of the program distasteful and resist enrolling their
> children. (Lowe, 1993)

Early and Periodic Screening, Diagnosis, and Treatment

In 1967 an amendment to Medicaid legislation made all families who qualified
for Medicaid coverage eligible for periodic health-screening services for their
children. The Early and Periodic Screening, Diagnosis, and Treatment Program
(EPSDT) mandates that any condition requiring treatment that is found during
the course of this screening be addressed through diagnostic and treatment procedures reimbursable (to the care provider) through Medicaid. Unlike routine
health care provided under Medicaid, EPSDT is distinguished by its mandate to
actively seek out children who would benefit from such screening procedures.
Unfortunately, the program has not been fully implemented and coverage differs widely from state to state (Markus, 1997).

Maternal and Child Health Services Block Grant

A small but historically important program for the provision of health care to
women and children is covered by the Maternal and Child Health Services
Block Grant (MCH). Originally established by the U.S. Children's Bureau as Title V of the 1935 Social Security Act, this program provides less than $250 mil-
lion in funding, 85 percent of which is allocated to state departments of health
(the remaining 15 percent remains with the Maternal and Child Health Bureau
and helps to pay for research, training, and demonstration projects). The Balanced Budget Act of 1997 offers states $20.3 million in the form of child health

Barriers to Health Care Access

The economic aspect of providing child health care is only one barrier to the receipt of regular, appropriate care. Although many people assume that the much-touted concept of "universal access" to health care refers primarily to making health care affordable, access actually has many components (Johnson, 1993):

- *Affordability.* In addition to the 12 million uninsured children in the United States, there are millions of others who are underinsured. Many services are not covered, and co-payments for pediatric care or prescription medications can be prohibitive for many families.
- *Availability.* Even for those who can afford health care, it might not be available. One barrier to universal health care coverage is the inadequacy of supply and distribution. If an inner urban area lacks pediatric services, for instance, or if one obstetrician is responsible for covering two or three whole rural counties, no amount of insurance coverage for a given family or child is going to result in adequate medical care.
- *Transportation.* Health care access is also at stake when the clinic is miles from the families it is intended to serve, if few families own automobiles and public transportation is scarce or prohibitively expensive. A similar problem is faced by employed parents who have inflexible schedules that do not coordinate easily with clinic hours. Increasing numbers of pediatric clinics are increasing their evening and weekend hours to address this problem.
- *Appropriateness.* If acute care services are covered under a given plan, but

preventive care is not, or if prevention and routine care are provided but there is no provision for coverage for children with medical conditions that place them in high-risk categories, then the available care is not fully appropriate, and the children in question cannot be said to have full access to health care.
- *Language barriers and cultural issues.* Many clinics, particularly in urban areas, try to hire physicians, nurses, and support staff who speak Spanish or an Asian language. However, not many can offer the range of languages spoken by the ethnically and culturally heterogeneous clientele in many American cities today. Furthermore, even if a physician speaks the same language as her patients, she might not fully appreciate all the cultural nuances associated with parenting and child care or with the reluctance to discuss intimate or personal matters with strangers. As a result, misunderstandings and resentments can arise that are barriers to the parent seeking health care for his or her child or to the pregnant woman in need of prenatal care (National Commission for the Prevention of Infant Mortality, 1992; Carnegie Corporation, 1994).
- *Legal and ethical issues.* Special barriers exist for some patients. Ambivalence or negative feelings about pregnancy, particularly for unmarried women, are strongly associated with late or no prenatal care (Children's Defense Fund, 1998a, 1998f). Forty percent of women with unwanted pregnancies put off seeking prenatal care until the second or even the third trimester (Schroeder, 1993).

block grants. This money may be used to expand Medicaid coverage or to establish or supplement other child health insurance programs (Mann & Guyer, 1997). Administered by the U.S. Department of Health and Human Services, this program is funded by both federal and state appropriations. The bulk of the funding provided through state health departments helps to pay for immunizations and prenatal care, though acute care may also be provided.

THREATS TO CHILD HEALTH

Early Care and Later Development

During the nine-month gestation period, many factors interact to determine outcomes for the newborn. Some reproductive risk is determined genetically; many other factors are more malleable and can be controlled through appropriate diet, medical care, and the mother's avoidance of behaviors that put her own health and that of her child at risk (see table 7.3). Genetics plays a part, here, too, helping to determine an individual's susceptibility to damage from exposure to a disease such as rubella or a **teratogenic agent** like lead, nicotine, or heroin.

Toxins and infections are not the only dangers. New information about brain development indicates that the prenatal period is a critical developmental period that has lifelong ramifications for social, emotional, and cognitive development. Adequate maternal nutrition, rest, abstention from drug, alcohol, and tobacco use, and even freedom from excessive stress are optimal components of a healthy prenatal environment. Risk factors associated with poverty, health care barriers, and other variables can weigh against good perinatal outcomes, but early and regular prenatal care contributes to the likelihood that a pregnant woman's overall health status will be monitored regularly, and that any necessary medical intervention can be provided (Begley, 1997; Chugani, 1993; National Public Radio, 1998).

Early and consistent prenatal care is essential for monitoring the variables that are known to have an impact on brain development, for screening expectant women for the presence of genetic and disease factors that can affect pregnancy outcome, and for educating women to help them monitor their own health and that of their baby. In fact, such care should ideally begin even *before* conception; it is becoming clear that the mother's own health and nutritional status can have serious implications for fetal and later child development. Adequate folic acid in the mother's diet, for instance, is linked to a lowered risk of her child having a neural tube defect like spina bifida. The critical period for this interaction, however, appears to be within just a few days of conception, before a woman would typically have any signs at all that she was pregnant, and thus long before prenatal consultations would be helpful. Research indicates that women who attend fewer prenatal checkups have babies with lower birthweights and poorer survival rates than women who received regular prenatal care (Begley, 1997).

TABLE 7.3. Threats to Child Health That Are Preventable or Treatable Through Prenatal Care

Threat	Possible Effects
Alcohol abuse	Mental retardation; facial and skeletal anomalies; heart defects
Nicotine abuse	Low birthweight; prematurity; stillbirth; increased risk of sudden infant death syndrome (SIDS)
Drug abuse	Varies with drugs used; can include drug dependency/ withdrawal in the newborn; respiratory distress; low birthweight; hyperirritability; poor state regulation; neonatal death
Gestational diabetes	Toxemia (maternal); abnormally large fetus; elevated risk of cesarean delivery
Syphilis	Blindness; deafness; physical malformations; mental retardation; stillbirth
Elevated blood pressure	Preeclampsia; convulsions; maternal death
Maternal herpes, type II	Neonatal death
Maternal malnutrition	Low birthweight; prematurity; infant mortality

Child development experts, health care professionals, and policy makers all have a stake in optimizing child development, but policy has not kept pace with our growing understanding of the full significance of prenatal care for achieving that optimization. Knowledge of brain development during the pre- and **perinatal periods,** and of its significance for a child's later functioning, has immediate and direct implications for health policy. Recent technological developments in medical imaging allow scientists to assess brain development even in the prenatal period, and to gauge more accurately than ever before the impact of environmental influences on brain and central nervous system development (Chugani, 1993; Chugani, Phelps, & Mazziotta, 1987; Kolb, 1989). As a result, experts now understand that not just the physical structures of the brain, but the complexity and variety of the neural connections among them, are laid down much earlier in life than we had heretofore understood, and are much more strongly linked than we had understood before to early care and health status (Chugani, 1993). Brain growth and development continue to take place well into the adolescent years. It is clear now that the efficacy and sophistication of human brain functions are determined to a greater degree than understood before by what takes place during the prenatal period and the first three years of life (Carnegie Corporation, 1994).

Such findings clearly imply that delivery of early, consistent, high-quality prenatal care has lifelong implications for child development and for health care and education expenditures in both the public and the private sector. The implications of providing (or neglecting to provide) such care will be continually revised as more and more information on neurological development and its ramifications becomes available, but it is clear already that this information must figure into policy debates that have an impact on whether all women are eligible to receive the prenatal care they need, and whether it is fully available to all women who are eligible.

In spite of the critical importance of prenatal care, 1 in 5 U.S. women receive no prenatal care at all during the first trimester (Children's Defense Fund, 1998a). More than 4 percent receive no prenatal care until the third trimester. Ethnicity and maternal age are also risk factors for delayed care; white women are more likely to receive early prenatal care than are black mothers, of whom only 70 percent get prenatal care during the first trimester, and only 21 percent of pregnant adolescents receive early care (Children's Defense Fund, 1998b). Other variables associated with delay of prenatal care are poverty, single marital status, and low educational attainment (USDHHS, 1992).

One of the most potentially dangerous anomalies of pregnancy is toxemia, also called eclampsia. Eclampsia is almost entirely preventable or treatable with appropriate prenatal care. Although slight variations in blood pressure during the course of pregnancy are normal, a sudden extreme rise in blood pressure, along with sudden weight gain and swelling of the hands, face, and feet, can signal the onset of preeclampsia. If undetected and unchecked, the mother's condition continues to worsen rapidly. Symptoms at this stage can include headache, blurred vision, and abdominal pain; in severe cases the mother might experience convulsions, lapse into a coma, or even die. If early signs of eclampsia are detected, however, the condition is treatable; bed rest (at home or in the hospital) is recommended, and medication might be prescribed; in such a case the prognosis is excellent for both mother and child.

Early prenatal care also provides an opportunity for diet and nutrition counseling, and for the prescription of nutritional supplements as necessary. Approximately one-third of U.S. women do not gain weight adequately during pregnancy; pregnant adolescents and African American women are particularly likely to gain weight inadequately and thus risk having a low-birthweight baby (National Commission for the Prevention of Infant Mortality, 1992; Institute of Medicine, 1990). Low-income women might qualify to receive food supplements through the Women, Infants and Children (WIC) program of the USD-HHS, which distributes milk, formula, baby foods, cheese, and other products to pregnant women and teens, infants, and nursing mothers.

Substance-abuse counseling is an essential part of prenatal care; the use of even alcohol and nicotine products should be avoided during pregnancy, and prenatal visits are an excellent forum for providing the health education and support many women need to avoid engaging in behaviors like these that place fetal development at risk. Maternal drug use during pregnancy can result in fetal addiction; babies born to drug-addicted mothers tend to be irritable, out of synchrony with caregiver behaviors, and poorly organized neurologically. Such infants might demonstrate behavioral problems or cognitive delays as they grow older (National Commission for the Prevention of Infant Mortality, 1992). Substance abuse during pregnancy contributes to the high cost of medical care, as well. Drug-addicted newborns require longer hospital stays and ring up larger health care bills. Approximately $504 million a year is spent on perinatal care for cocaine-exposed infants (Howard, 1990; Zuckerman, 1991).

One national health objective for the year 2000 is to lower the incidence rate for fetal alcohol syndrome (FAS), a disorder affecting children who were exposed prenatally to excessive amounts of alcohol. The severity of the disorder varies, but infants with FAS typically have small brains and heads, and some degree of central nervous system impairment and permanent mental retardation; approximately 20 percent have facial deformities that include a short, wide nose, a flattened midface area, and epicanthal folds of the eyelids. FAS occurs in slightly over 1 per 10,000 live births. Another national health goal is abstinence from tobacco use among at least 90 percent of pregnant women. Because of the lack of addiction treatment options available in general, and to pregnant women in particular, it is unlikely that either of these goals will be met.

Finally, prenatal care provides an opportunity for genetic counseling and screening. Detection of genetic disorders can provide expectant parents with information that will help them to make decisions about any treatments available for their child or whether to continue the pregnancy in the case of severe disorders, and to be prepared—both emotionally and with respect to marshaling medical and economic resources—for the birth of a child with special needs.

Infant Mortality

Each year in the United States approximately 40,000 children die before their first birthday (Children's Defense Fund, 1998g); during 1997, between 8 and 9 out of every 1,000 live births resulted in an infant death. **Congenital abnormalities** account for the greatest proportion of infant deaths; low birthweight, anomalies resulting from **prematurity** (e.g., respiratory distress syndrome, which results from the immaturity of the premature infant's lungs), and sudden infant death syndrome (SIDS) are also leading killers of children in the first year of life (Centers for Disease Control and Prevention, 1998; Klerman, 1996; March of Dimes, 1994).

Although our infant mortality rate is at its lowest ever, continued improvement in this area is one of the most important of the maternal and child health-related goals of the Health 2000 goals program established by the U.S. Department of Health and Human Services. Not only are we failing to meet this goal, we are actually *losing* ground in areas related to the preservation of infant life. As figure 7.1 shows, infant mortality rates remain roughly stable, on the average, but infant mortality rates for black Americans are rising; today 17 out of every 1,000 black infants die during the first year of life (Children's Defense Fund, 1998g). Infant mortality rates for all Latino subgroups in the U.S. are also higher than those for white Americans (see figure 7.2). In addition, the percentage of infants born at low or very low birthweight is also on the rise, and no progress is being made in curbing the postneonatal infant mortality rate or in increasing the percentage of babies whose mothers received prenatal care during the first trimester (Children's Defense Fund, 1998a). Approximately two-thirds of these deaths occur during the **neonatal period** (i.e., during the first 28 days of life), and many could be prevented with adequate medical care, nutrition, and appropriate prenatal care for the mother.

Infant deaths per 1,000 live births

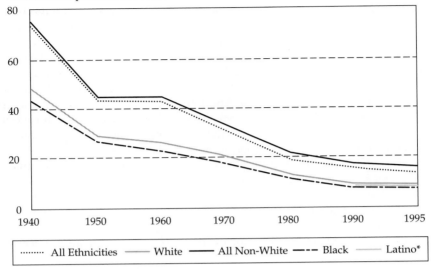

Infants are children under 1 year of age
*Data for Latinos only available since 1990

FIGURE 7.1 Historical infant mortality rates in the United States by ethnicity, 1940-1995.
Source: National Center for Health Statistics, 1997.

Rates per 1,000 live births among infants less than 1 year old.

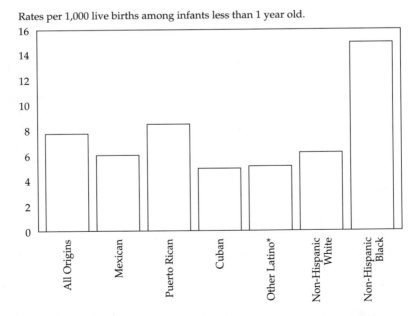

* Includes Central and South American, other, and unknown Hispanic origins.

FIGURE 7.2 Infant mortality among Whites, Blacks, and Latino subgroups in the United
States, 1995. *Source:* National Center for Health Statistics, 1997.

In 1987, Congress established the National Commission to Prevent Infant Mortality and appointed Florida Governor Lawton Chiles to oversee its creation of a comprehensive plan to reduce infant mortality. A report of their initial findings was issued to Congress in 1988; among their recommendations were universal access to primary and preventive care for all children, improvements in immunization coverage, and Medicaid reforms. A panel of the American Academy of Pediatrics (AAP, 1990) concluded that at least 1 infant death out of 4 could be prevented with adequate health care, and noted in their findings that the lack of insurance coverage for many families affects children in devastating ways even before birth. Fourteen million women of childbearing age have no coverage for prenatal and delivery care. The AAP concluded that high U.S. rates of low-birthweight deliveries and infant mortality are directly linked to this lack of insurance.

Low Birthweight

One of the leading causes of infant mortality in the United States is also the most preventable with the provision of early and regular prenatal care. Poor nutrition, illness, and the use of nicotine, alcohol, and other drugs are all associated with low-birthweight deliveries; each of these factors can be addressed and largely ameliorated through appropriate prenatal care. Infants born at low birthweight are 40 percent more likely to die during the perinatal period than infants born at an appropriate weight. Low-birthweight infants constitute just over 7 percent of all infants born in the United States, but 60 percent of those that die within the first year (National Commission for the Prevention of Infant Mortality, 1992). Thirteen percent of black infants in the United States are born at low birthweight, a statistic that has not improved in 20 years. The United States lags behind 16 other nations in its prevention of low birthweight (Children's Defense Fund, 1998g).

The problems posed by high rates of low-birthweight deliveries are not merely medical or ethical, but are also economic. The average cost for the post-delivery hospital stay for a low-birthweight infant is $20,000 (almost 10 times higher than the cost of caring for a newborn of normal birthweight). In 1990 alone, hospital costs of caring for low-birthweight newborns came to over $2 billion (National Commission for the Prevention of Infant Mortality, 1992). Over a lifetime, the medical costs for such a child average $400,000 (Carnegie Corporation, 1994). Approximately half of the infants who must spend time in a newborn intensive care unit (**NICU**) are low-birthweight babies. Rapid technological advances save many thousands of infants each year who would not have survived had they been born under similar conditions even a decade ago, but such care is extremely expensive.

Four to 6 percent of all infants born in U.S. hospitals are treated every year in NICUs; at least half of these—some 75,000 to 100,000 newborns—are born at low birthweight, and these are among the most expensive of all hospital admissions. A health technology study from the federal Office of Technology Assessment concluded that hospitalizations for very-low-birthweight infants, whose representation in the NICU is on the rise, average almost 100 days and can cost over $150,000. Because these hospitalizations are more likely to be associated with low-income mothers, a large proportion of this cost is born by the public. Furthermore, Medicaid payments typically do not cover the full cost of neonatal intensive care (Ehrenhaft, 1987).

The high cost of caring for these infants does not end when they leave the hospital. Low-birthweight and very-low-birthweight infants are at high risk of developing hearing, vision, and learning problems requiring special services for many years, even for a lifetime. Over 15 percent of very-low-birthweight infants (as opposed to 4.7 percent of low-birthweight babies and 4.3 percent of infants born at normal weight) require special education and 19.6 percent of low-birthweight children (versus 13.5 percent of normal-birthweight infants) will ultimately experience some school failure (Newman & Buka, 1991).

National health objectives for the year 2000 in this area are to reduce low-birthweight deliveries to 5 percent and very-low-birthweight deliveries to 1 percent (averaged across all ethnic groups; corresponding goals for black newborns are 9 and 2 percent, respectively). At current rates, this goal will not be reached; in fact, the United States is slipping backward in this area (National Commission for the Prevention of Infant Mortality, 1992). (See table 7.4.)

Maternal Mortality

Pregnant women are also at risk because of policies that limit access to adequate prenatal care. In 1990, 343 women died in the United States as a result of complications of pregnancy or childbirth. Among white mothers, the rate of maternal death is 5.4 out of every 100,000 live births; among black women the rate is more than four times higher (USDHHS, 1992). There has been a striking decline in the rate of maternal mortality linked to childbearing during the past three to four decades, and the U.S. Department of Health and Human Services has listed the further reduction of maternal mortality rates as a "Health 2000" goal. Even so, statistics indicate that maternal mortality rates are not declining as rapidly as they have in previous decades.

TABLE 7.4 Low-Birthweight Deliveries in the United States, by Mother's Ethnicity

Mother's Ethnicity	Incidence of Low-Birthweight* Delivery
White	6.3%
African American	13.0
Native American	6.5
Asian or Pacific Islander	7.1
All	7.4

*Less than 5 1/2 pounds (2,500 grams)
Source: March of Dimes Birth Defects Foundation, 1999.
Figures reflect percentages in 1996, the most recent year for which data are available.

The Politics of Breast-Feeding

Though it is certainly possible for parents who feed infant formula to their babies to have close, loving relationships with their children, no pediatrician would dispute the superior health benefits of breast-feeding. The advantages of breast milk over artificial formulas are well documented; among the most important of these is a significant immunological benefit. Breast-fed infants are less likely to develop sepsis, infections (including ear infections), or diarrhea ("A Warm Chain for Breastfeeding," 1994). Recent research even credits breast-feeding with a diminished risk of minor neurological disorders (Lanting et al., 1994). Health benefits to mothers, including wider spacing of births and lower levels of ovarian cancer and some breast cancers ("A Warm Chain for Breastfeeding," 1994; Newcomb et al., 1994).

Most important, breast-feeding is associated with dramatically lower rates of infant mortality (Wirpsa, 1994). Even in areas with low rates of infant mortality, infants who are bottle-fed are five times more likely to require hospitalization; formula-feeding is also more likely than breast-feeding to be associated with SIDS ("A Warm Chain for Breast-feeding," 1994). Former U.S. Surgeon General Joycelyn Elders estimates that if all mothers breast-fed their infants, even for as little as three months, U.S. infant mortality would drop by some 10 percent ("Surgeon General Elders Urges . . . Breast-Feeding," 1994). In nations with high rates of infant mortality, artificially fed infants are 14 times more likely to die from diarrheal diseases during their first year of life than are breast-fed babies, and they are four times more likely to die of pneumonia ("A Warm Chain for Breastfeeding," American Academy of Pediatrics, 1997a,b; 1998a, 1998b, 1994).

If breast-feeding is so healthy, why don't all new mothers do it? Lack of information, encouragement, and support are probably the main reasons. Health care providers and others who are in contact with women who might breast-feed if provided with education and support, often do not promote it. Of its $450 million budget, for instance, the WIC program spends only $8 million to promote breast-feeding, a practice that would not only bolster infant health but might save millions of dollars in tax expenditures for nutritional supplements and health care (Wirpsa, 1994). Many hospitals support breast-feeding by providing new mothers with practical help and information; some even offer nursing mothers telephone "warm lines" staffed by lactation consultants. Many others, however, subtly discourage nursing by bottle-feeding newborns in the nursery with water or sugar water solutions, and by sending all new mothers home with gift packs of formula samples (often attractively packaged with infant toys and manufacturer's coupons) provided by formula companies. Formula producers have also drawn criticism for undermining breast-feeding and promoting the sale and use of infant formulas in third-world countries, where breast-feeding would be a healthier and more economic alternative (Catholic Institute for International Relations, 1993; Wirpsa, 1994).

Further, in the United States, societal attitudes do not encourage breast-feeding. Women have been arrested for nursing in public places (Widner, 1993), and few employers provide the kind of simple supports a new mother might need to continue nursing after returning to work: two or three short breaks throughout the day, a quiet place to express breast milk with a manual or electric pump, and a re-frigerator for storing milk. Recently a group of health care providers, policy makers, representatives of state and local government and others instituted a com-prehensive breast-feeding support pro-gram in Colorado. The program takes a multilevel, multidisciplinary approach that includes education of clinic and hos-pital staff, use of the media to promote breast-feeding, public health education materials that target both mothers and fa-thers, a massive public awareness cam-paign, and representation by and liaison with Colorado employers. As a result, breast-feeding rates in Colorado have soared: 72.6 percent of new mothers in Colorado chose nursing, as opposed to only about 53 percent nationwide (Wid-ner, 1993).

Even more than ethnicity, maternal age is a risk factor for maternal mortal-ity. With age held constant, women over 35 have more than twice the risk of ma-ternal mortality than women aged 20 to 24. Again, appropriate prenatal care is a critical element in the prevention of maternal death: early detection of elevated blood pressure, for instance, can lead to treatment before the onset of eclampsia, and consistent monitoring of maternal health can prevent or control conditions associated with increased risk of surgical delivery (e.g., gestational diabetes).

CHILD SAFETY

The major cause of death among children at ages 1 to 19 is not disease, but acci-dental injury (USDHHS, 1992). The major cause of these accidental deaths is au-tomobile accidents; following these, burns and drowning are the most prevalent causes, especially among children under age 5. Deaths from injury are also among the most preventable of all childhood deaths; these occur at a much higher rate in the United States than in many other countries, and occur dispro-portionately among poor children. Safety-oriented policy has significantly re-duced accidental injury and death among children, but there is yet much room for improvement.

Approximately 22 per 100,000 children between the ages of 1 and 4 die as a result of injuries. Almost 1 parent out of 10 reports that their child was involved in an accident, injury, or poisoning incident within the previous year (Dawson, 1991). Traditional health care (oriented to prevent disease) has little effect on these rates. Instead, health care professionals must turn their attention, and their energy, into health- and safety-oriented public education, often using such non-traditional medical tools as television commercials and other public awareness forums.

Legislation mandating safety standards does prevent injury and reduce childhood mortality, but such legislation would be more effective if it empha-sized public education and subsidized safety-promotion devices like car safety seats, home smoke detectors, bicycle helmets, and upper-story window guards (Klerman, 1996). For instance, legislation mandating the use of approved car safety seats for children under age 4, which was first enacted in Tennessee in

1978 and rapidly adopted by other states, has radically reduced the number of childhood fatalities resulting from automobile accidents. Research indicates, however, that among Medicaid-eligible families, children are far less likely to be restrained appropriately when traveling in automobiles. The cost of child safety seats might be prohibitive for some populations, but it is likely that public awareness and education campaigns would help to effect positive behavioral change among this population (Sharp & Carter, 1992).

Local-level campaigns often seem more effective in such cases than federal mandates, particularly when they consist of or are coupled with concrete, practical actions. Hospitals, for instance, might loan, or sell at a discount, automobile safety seats to parents of newborns; some employers even offer child safety seats as bonuses to employees expecting a baby—sometimes as an incentive or reward for receiving regular prenatal care (Noble, 1994). Playground safety campaigns are seeking to reduce the 170,000 annual playground-related injuries. These campaigns are mounted by consumer safety groups like the U.S. Public Interest Research Group and the Consumer Federation of America and are promoted by the manufacturers of playground equipment ("Playground Safety at Issue," 1994). Safety campaigns might also be emphasized at the local level; the effectiveness of a 1993 Connecticut law mandating the use of bicycle safety helmets by children age 12 and under was enhanced by the public education campaigns mounted by local police forces in some Connecticut towns.

PRIMARY HEALTH CARE AND DISEASE PREVENTION

Preventing childhood disease is far more cost effective and more conducive to healthy child development than providing secondary health care—that is, treating acute illnesses once they appear. Beginning in the 1940s with the introduction of widely available antibiotic medications, childhood mortality and morbidity due to illness began to decline precipitously, and the focus of pediatrics shifted from disease treatment to disease prevention and the optimization of childhood growth and development (Hall, 1991). U.S. childhood mortality rates have declined in the mid to late twentieth century largely because of the availability of affordable, effective, safe immunizations. Such killers of children as measles, pertussis (whooping cough), and polio are now completely preventable; smallpox has been eliminated altogether, as other diseases might be if all children were immunized.

During the late 1980s and early 1990s, however, disease prevention trends slowed; some even reversed. Cuts in vaccination funding during the Bush administration alone came to $35 million (Chan & Momparler, 1991). Preschool-age children today are less likely to be up-to-date on their polio and DPT (diphtheria, pertussis, tetanus) inoculations than were preschoolers in the 1970s. Children who are members of racial and ethnic minority groups were even less likely to be protected; in 1970, 69.2 percent of white children and 50.1 percent of nonwhite children were fully immunized against polio, but by 1990 those figures were 52.7 percent and 42.1 percent, respectively (Schroeder, 1993).

The cost of a complete set of vaccinations for a young child rose from $28 in the early 1980s to $270 by the mid 1990s. This increase, along with the increase in numbers of uninsured children, prevented immunization rates from climbing higher. A measles epidemic between 1989 and 1991, which affected 55,000 children and killed 130, prompted an enhanced focus on public education efforts and was in part responsible for the Clinton administration's expanded efforts to improve immunization rates. In 1993, the Vaccines for Children (VFC) program was enacted to promote and fund immunizations for children on Medicaid and for those whose private insurance did not cover the cost of vaccinations. By 1996, 78 percent of U.S. 2-year-olds were fully immunized, as compared to only 37 percent in 1991 (Children's Defense Fund, 1997c, 1998g).

Appropriations for inoculations are still inadequate to guarantee millions of children complete protection from preventable diseases (Carnegie Corporation, 1994). The childhood immunization goal for the year 2000 is to have at least 90 percent of preschoolers fully up-to-date with their vaccinations, a rate reached years ago by most European nations (Harvey, 1990). At current rates, we will fall far short of reaching this goal (USDHHS, 1992). Table 7.5 shows the recommended schedule of childhood vaccinations.

SUBSTANCE USE AND ABUSE

The "drug problem" is increasingly viewed as a crisis affecting not just teens and young adults, but also preadolescent and even younger children. Young children are believed to suffer particularly pernicious effects of substance abuse, ranging from prenatal insults directly and indirectly associated with drug use (e.g., teratogenic effects of exposure in utero, substandard prenatal care), family violence, child abuse and neglect, malnutrition, and caregiving deficits, as well as the ill effects of early drug use itself (Lecca & Watts, 1993). Thus it makes sense to discuss the problems associated with drug use in America in a public health context.

Drug use among young people declined during the 1980s but is on the rise again. Illicit drug use increased significantly for young adolescents between 1996 and 1997, and the use of marijuana by youth 12 to 17 more than doubled between 1992 and 1997, with the average age of first use declining from 17 to 13.

TABLE 7.5. Recommended Childhood Immunization Schedule

Hepatitis B	Birth–2 months
DPT	2 months, 4 months, 6 months, 12–18 months, and 11–16 years
H. Influenzae	
Type B	2 months, 4 months, 6 months, 12–15 months
Polio	2 months, 4 months, 6–18 months, 4–6 years
MMR	12–15 months, 4–6 years, *or* 11–12 years
Varicella	12–18 months

Source: Advisory Committee on Immunization Practices, the American Academy of Pediatrics, and the American Academy of Family Physicians, 1998.

The rate of marijuana use, however, still remains significantly below the level of use in 1979 (Hall, 1998; SAMHSA, 1998).

The costs associated with both drug use and the battle against it are staggering. Direct health care costs related to substance abuse, for instance, were estimated at $150 billion for 1997 (Office of National Drug Control Policy, 1998). The National Drug Control Budget (see table 7.6), for which over $17 billion has been requested for fiscal year (FY) 1999 (Executive Office of the President, 1998) is distributed among no fewer than 16 federal offices, including the Department of Justice, the Department of the Treasury, the Department of Agriculture, the Department of Labor, and the Department of Education.

Whether we as a nation have gotten our money's worth out of this effort is a topic of ongoing debate. Proponents of this war on drugs claim responsibility for a recent decline in drug use among the general population; detractors note that changing demographics of drug use—the rise of drug use among school-age children (SAMHSA, 1998) and the concentration of the majority of use among a small section of the population (Horgan, 1993)—are grounds for trying a new approach. Both supporters of a traditional war on drugs and those who question the efficacy and/or ethics of current policies tend to agree that massive efforts to stop drug use in the United States have not yet been successful (Children's Defense Fund, 1998g; Hall & Zigler, 1997; Lindesmith Center, 1998; Pakroo, 1997; Research Triangle Institute, 1997a, 1997b; SAMHSA, 1998; U.S. General Accounting Office, 1997).

Public outrage over substance abuse is particularly high when children are affected, and public trust in prevention efforts is similarly high. Drug-use prevention efforts account for approximately 13 percent of the nation's drug-fighting budget, the third largest share after law enforcement and treatment (Executive Office of the President, 1998). These dollars are spent largely on education efforts for children as young as preschool age; private and foundation monies further support drug education. Drug-abuse education efforts have traditionally followed four patterns: (1) exaggeratedly frightening films and literature on the potential negative effects of drugs (e.g., the 1930s film *Reefer Madness*), (2) educational shock films of the 1960s; (3) resistance skills training (e.g., the "Just Say No" media campaign of the 1980s, the Drug Abuse Resistance Education program of the 1980s

TABLE 7.6. FY 1999 Drug Budget (Requested), by Function

Criminal justice system	$8,544.0*	50%
Drug treatment	3,092.2	18.1
Drug prevention	2,158.8	12.6
International expenditures	548.1	3.2
Interdiction	1,805.2	10.6
Research	752.1	4.2
Intelligence	196.5	1.2

*Millions

Source: Executive Office of the President (1998). FY 1999 drug budget program highlights. Washington DC: U.S. Government Printing Office.

and 1990s); (4) programs purporting to increase drug-avoidance behavior through the enhancement of self-esteem in young children (Falco, 1992; Hall & Zigler, 1993; Hall, 1996; Musto, 1983). Although a few educational program evaluations demonstrate short-term behavior modifications with respect to drug use, not one of these efforts has been shown through rigorous empirical evaluation to have significant long-term effectiveness (Falco, 1992; Hall, 1996; U.S. General Accounting Office, 1998).

Thirty years of research findings indicate that a more effective way to implement positive changes in children is to intervene first with families. The most promising intervention/prevention efforts are likely to be those that are truly ecological in nature: those that target not children in isolation, but children within the context of their families (e.g, two-generation programs like Head Start—see Smith, 1991), and those that address children and families within a community context (Hawkins & Catalano, 1992). Furthermore, the most effective interventions are likely to be those that target very young children, long before the likelihood of drug use looms very large.

A two-pronged attack on problems related to drug use might employ such family programs along with a focus (and concomitant commitment to spending) on addiction research and treatment; and on the provision of services for the children of drug-addicted parents. These might include not only basic child protective services, but child psychotherapy, home visitation, and oversight of supportive, consistent child-care placements as needed (Besharov, 1995).

VIOLENCE AS A PUBLIC HEALTH ISSUE

Societal violence has become a public health issue for children and families. A recent comparison of the homicide rate in 21 developed countries indicated that the United States has the highest rate in the world, with a rate more than four times that of the next highest country, Scotland (Fingerhut & Kleinman, 1990). In Chicago alone, the rate of "serious assault" increased 400 percent from 1971 to 1991(Garbarino et al., 1992).

The growing use of firearms has made children more frequent victims, witnesses, and even perpetrators of violent behavior. During the mid to late 1980s, firearms accounted for 96 percent of the increase in U.S. homicide rates (Centers for Disease Control, 1990a, 1990b). The one year from 1991 to 1992 saw an increase of more than 21 percent in the number of reported violent crimes involving handguns. Handguns were used in nearly 931,000 murders, rapes, robberies, and assaults in 1992, as compared to 772,000 in 1991 (Worsnop, 1994).

Children as Victims

Recent reports indicate staggering levels of deadly violence among young people. Between 1987 and 1990, the rate of gunshot wounds in children under 16 doubled (Gibbs, 1993). Among American children less than 1 year of age, the major cause of death is physical abuse, and homicide accounts for 10 percent of all deaths of children between 1 and 4 years (Osofsky, 1994). Homicide is the second-leading cause of death among all 15- to 24-year-olds in the United States (National Center for Health Statistics, 1993). Gunshot wounds are the leading cause of death for both African American and white teenage boys (Koop & Lundberg, 1992). Even though violence is pervasive among both groups, one survey indicates that African American young men are murdered at a rate more than seven times that of their white counterparts (Fingerhut & Kleinman, 1990).

Several authors (i.e., Cicchetti & Lynch, 1993; Garbarino et al., 1992) have lamented the paucity of research documenting the tragic effects that high levels of community violence must be exerting on our nation's children. Pending such studies, no definitive evidence links children's increased exposure to violence to young people's increased participation in violent acts. Very recently, however, several researchers have made strides toward understanding the specific developmental consequences of our violent society (i.e., Bell, cited in Garbarino et al., 1992; Cicchetti & Lynch, 1993; Garbarino et al., 1992; Martinez & Richters, 1993; Osofsky, 1994; Osofsky & Fenichel, 1994; Richters & Martinez, 1993a, 1993b). Children exposed to chronically high levels of environmental violence might experience symptoms ranging from increased levels of fear, anxiety, stress, and depression, to diagnosable forms of psychopathology such as posttraumatic stress disorder (Emens et al., 1996).

Societal Factors

Although no single factor is determinative, poverty and its concomitant problems are major determinants of violence: poverty predicts a greater likelihood of perpetrating, experiencing and witnessing violence (American Psychological Association [APA], 1993). Children are the poorest Americans, and nonwhite children are even more likely to be poorer than their white counterparts (American Bar Association [ABA], 1993; APA, 1993). Adult unemployment, low wages for parents who work, and lack of affordable housing all contribute to violence and delinquency. The culture of poverty can breed an atmosphere of fatalism, where young people believe they can look forward only to death or jail (ABA, 1993). Other community factors, including quality of education and a low sense of community cohesiveness, also affect emotional and behavioral outcomes (Hawkins, Catalano, & Miller, 1992; Hawkins & Catalano, 1992; Murray & Perry, 1985; Yoshikawa, 1994).

Policy Factors

As with other threats to child health discussed in this chapter, violence falls outside the sphere of traditional health care, and so must solutions to this problem. A wide range of social policies influence children's developing social competence, sense of well-being, and, indirectly, their risk of delinquency. Such factors include the quality and availability of child care, preschool, and public schooling, the economic and emotional impact of high unemployment rates, limited housing opportunities and health coverage, and the availability of guns and regulation of their ownership. Recent studies show that restriction of handgun access also reduces firearm homicide rates (Yoshikawa, 1994).

Violence in Schools

Violence by and against young people is a problem increasingly likely to garner media attention; headline-making incidents such as school-based shootings of youth by other youth in Colorado, Washington, Kentucky, Arkansas, and other states in recent years spur calls for a means to stem what is viewed as a rising tide of random violence (Brauer & McCormick, 1998; Dickinson, 1999; Cloud, 1999, 1998). Guns and other violence in schools, however, is neither a new problem nor one that necessarily is on the rise. A report from the Center on Juvenile and Criminal Justice in Washington, D.C., indicates that the risk of being killed at school is less than one in a million, and that numbers of shooting deaths at school—in contrast to child deaths from shootings in the home or community—have actually fallen since the early 1990s (Center on Juvenile and Criminal Justice, 1992). As serious as any violence against children is, there are dangers inherent in overreacting to isolated major incidents. Using overburdened school budgets to fund security measures that have not been proven useful, increasing school suspensions and expulsions, and proposing the elimination of essential after-school programs based on ill-founded fears eliminate other services children need (Lantier, 1998).

Even if school-based violence is not increasing, school administrators in urban, suburban, and rural settings, as well as groups like the National Association of School Psychologists, are looking for ways to predict and eliminate violent and disruptive behavior on school grounds. The need to predict and control such behavior has spawned a violence prevention curriculum industry. A two-year study of 84 youth violence prevention curricula, however, indicates that only 10 such programs meet criteria that indicate promise; none of them have been subjected to empirical testing that would demonstrate their long-term usefulness (Alexander, 1988; Drug Strategies, 1998).

Media reports typically decry school violence as senseless and inexplicable, but researchers who study youth violence point to a culture in which violence is sanctioned as a means of self-expression and problem solving, and to the ease with which even very young children and adolescents are able to obtain guns and other weapons whose deadly potential is incompatible with the developmental level of their young users (Garbarino, 1998). A recent study by the Centers for Disease Control and Prevention noted that 1 out of every 5 adolescents carries a weapon—a gun, knife, or club—every day, often during school. Children as young as 5 have attended school armed with guns and other weapons ("Kindergarten Student Faces Gun Charges," 1998).

In addition to the few potentially effective curriculum-based programs identified by the Drug Strategies study, and in addition to gun control measures advocated by many psychologists and legislators, researchers point to the potential for early intervention and family support programs to provide useful, long-term violence reduction among young people, both in the community and at school (Emens et al., 1996).

Nutrition and Child Policy

Inadequate diet, both in utero and during infancy, is associated with problems of physical and cognitive development, and with behavioral problems. Programs that target child hunger have been shown to improve perinatal outcome and school performance, and to save money on child health care.

Even in the face of widespread awareness of the consequences of undernutrition, however, 29 percent of U.S. children are at chronic risk of hunger (Food Research and Action Center, 1998c; Nation's Health, 1998; Sidel, 1997). The U.S. Conference of Mayors has documented an increase in the need for emergency food assistance every year since 1983. Although private agencies provide emergency food to millions of families every year, the federal government remains the major supplier of nutritional supplements and subsidies (Food Research and Action Center, 1998c). The three main government programs that target hunger are the food stamp program, the school lunch program, and the federal Social Supplemental Food Program for Women, Infants, and Children (WIC). Each of these programs has gone a long way toward alleviating hunger among poor children and near-poor children, but continued budget cuts mean that not all of those who meet eligibility requirements receive services.

FOOD STAMPS

The federal food stamp program was first implemented for a brief period between 1939 and 1943, and was repiloted in the 1960s, but was not offered nationally until 1974. In 1997, approximately 22.8 million people received food stamps in any given month; 60 percent of the households receiving food stamps contain children. The average length of program participation is less than two years, with half of all recipients leaving the program after six months or less. Federal funds account for 100 percent of food subsidy costs; administrative costs are split evenly between federal and state governments.

Although there are strict eligibility requirements for participation in the food stamp program, critics argue that black-market trafficking in food stamps undermines the program's effectiveness. An electronic benefits tracking system in the works, which would replace a recipient's paper coupons with a plastic debit-type card, could significantly reduce food stamp fraud (Food Research and Action Center, 1998a, 1998b, 1998c).

WIC

The WIC program, which is administered by the federal Department of Agriculture, provides food supplements, medical referrals, and nutrition education to low-income pregnant and breastfeeding women and to infants and young children. Program evaluations indicate that WIC reduces malnutrition and anemia, and saves $3.50 in special education and Medicaid costs for every $1 spent on prenatal nutrition (Food Research and Action Center, 1998f; Gleick, 1995). Even so, only about 7.4 million eligible participants are currently being served; for the first time ever, Congress rejected administration appeals to expand coverage in FYs 1997 and 1998 (Children's Defense Fund, 1998g). At present, individual states also have the option of refusing WIC benefits to women, infants, and children whose immigrant status is undocumented.

THE NATIONAL SCHOOL LUNCH PROGRAM

The NSLP, which was created in 1946, provides funding directly to schools to enable them to provide free or reduced-cost lunches to approximately 26 million children whose family income falls below 185 percent of the federal poverty level. Approximately 7 million children receive breakfast at school through a similar program begun in 1966. Although research indicates that these programs decrease absenteeism and improve academic performance, the programs regularly face budget hurdles. During the Reagan administration, for instance, attitudes toward school meal programs were characterized by a cost-cutting attempt— ultimately unsuccessful—to reclassify pickles and catsup as vegetables. Periodic attempts are also made to shift responsibility for hunger alleviation measures to the states, who would receive block grants from which all WIC, school meal, and a similar day-care nutrition program would be funded. Advocates of such a plan project that billions of dollars could be saved in administrative costs. Child advocates warn that such a shift could result in the loss of coverage for millions of children.

HEALTH CARE REFORM

Virtually all of the private and government-sponsored reports on U.S. child health during the past several decades have emphasized the need for health care reform (e.g., Carnegie Corporation, 1994; Children's Defense Fund, 1998b; National Commission on Children, 1990; National Commission on Infant Mortality, 1992). Virtually all of these have proposed some fundamental reorganization of the system that includes medical care providers, health care administrators, insurance companies, employers who contribute to medical insurance plans, and private citizens.

During 1993 and 1994, Congress considered no fewer than six such plans, including President Clinton's own "health security plan" (Children's Defense Fund, 1992a; Clymer, 1993; March of Dimes, 1994). The broad public support at the beginning of this debate for a plan that would provide universal health care coverage ultimately subsided somewhat as concern for health care cost containment took precedence over concern for universal coverage. Congress ultimately failed to pass any of the six plans when no compromise could be reached on such fundamental issues as plan provisions, scope of coverage, and funding mechanisms (Klerman, 1996; Knitzer, 1996; March of Dimes, 1994; Van Biema, 1993).

In spite of the lack of consensus on how, or even whether, the government should guarantee universal access to health care, one point of agreement emerged from the health care debate: the need to provide affordable health care for children. Accordingly, the Balanced Budget Act of 1997 made provision for approximately $24 billion to be made available to states, over a 10-year period, in the form of child health block grants. Title XXI of the Social Security Act thus established the state Child Health Insurance Program, or CHIP (Ullman, Bruen, & Holahan, 1997).

Under the provisions of CHIP, each state is allotted funding in proportion to their share of uninsured U.S. children. States may use the money to expand Medicaid coverage and/or to provide health insurance to uninsured children with family incomes under 200 percent of the federal poverty level but still too high for

Medicaid eligibility. No more than 10 percent of the funds may be used for administration; the remaining 90 percent must go directly toward the provision of health care. To be eligible, each state must contribute matching funds and maintain existing Medicaid eligibility levels (Children's Defense Fund, 1998b, 1999).

The focus of CHIP is on providing health care for the children of working poor families. The funds provided under this plan are the largest increase in child health care spending since the original enactment of Medicaid in 1965, and are a significant step forward in expanding health coverage for U.S. children. Even so, the plan has some limits. First, not all children who meet income eligibility will receive care under CHIP. Allotted funding is sufficient to protect 6 million uninsured children under 200 percent of the poverty level, leaving almost 3 million others without coverage. In addition, another 3 million children live in families with incomes above poverty but still lack access to affordable health care. Third, CHIP provides no incentives for states to increase Medicaid participation among Medicaid-eligible children. Finally, even when children are covered by CHIP, attendant out-of-pocket costs to families can still be prohibitive: states are allowed to require sliding-scale fees from families with incomes higher than the poverty level.

SUMMARY

U.S. children today are far healthier overall than they were in the early years of our history. Two hundred years ago, fewer than half of all children survived into adulthood, and improvements in this area came slowly until the early years of the twentieth century, when medical advances related to sanitation, nutrition, and disease prevention and treatment carved the mortality rate back. Health issues were among the first to draw policy attention to children's concerns. The founding of the U.S. Children's Bureau by President Taft in 1912 addressed the need to study infant mortality. Radical advances in health sciences and technologies in the years since World War II have given us the capacity to have the healthiest children on earth.

In spite of such improvements, however, U.S. children continue to suffer unduly from completely preventable and/or treatable illnesses, tend to be underinsured, and often have difficulty obtaining access to health care. Like too many other problems facing children and families, virtually all health care statistics are disproportionately worse for poor children than for wealthier ones, and for those from ethnic minority groups as compared to white children. Fully preventable and treatable childhood diseases continue to kill American children at rates unknown in other industrialized, even in some developing, nations. Low birthweight, which is almost entirely preventable, continues to lead to the death of too many infants and to leave others with persistent health and cognitive problems.

America spends more money per capita on health care than any other nation, but children continue to bear the burden of a system that neglects our youngest and poorest citizens. In spite of recent attempts to improve health care access for low-income children, almost 12 million U.S. children are uninsured.

Affordability is the most serious barrier to health care access, but other barriers include lack of proximity, lack of transportation, lack of coverage for specific (often preventative) services, and cultural barriers.

Compared with other nations, and relative to its economic power, the United States has worse rates of disease, immunization, infant mortality (in which our standing has slipped radically since the 1950s), low birthweight, health care access, delivery of prenatal care, and protection of children from violence. In these and other areas, poor children receive the poorest care. Poverty is associated with higher levels of chronic conditions like asthma, anemia, and elevated blood lead levels, and with acute illnesses like measles. Poor children are less likely to receive dental care and to have vision and hearing problems detected and treated. They are far less likely than nonpoor children to receive their health care from a primary care physician, to receive routine well-child check-ups, and to have follow-up care after an illness. Poor children are more likely to receive their health care in hospitals and emergency facilities; they spend a greater average number of days in hospitals, and miss more days of school because of health problems than do nonpoor children.

Provision of adequate prenatal care would lay the foundation for better health among all U.S. children. The first trimester of pregnancy is, in most respects, the most critical stage of pregnancy. The development of all body structures and organs, including the brain and central nervous system, is highly susceptible at this stage to the deleterious effects of poor maternal nutrition and to exposure to teratogenic substances ranging from disease-causing organisms to drugs to chemicals in the environment, many of which can be linked to later cognitive deficits, low birthweight, miscarriage, or perinatal mortality. The first trimester also presents an opportunity to detect and correct a host of medical conditions that, if left untreated, can have wide-ranging and persistent harmful consequences for the child's health and development. In spite of this, approximately one-fourth of all U.S. pregnant women receive no prenatal care at this important time.

Low birthweight, associated with poor prenatal care and other factors, affects approximately 100,000 infants a year in this country. In addition to the medical problems associated with low birthweight, the problem has significant economic ramifications: low-birthweight babies typically spend 100 days in the hospital after birth, at an average cost of $150,000 per child. Even after being released from the hospital, low-birthweight babies are more likely to suffer a host of other physical, psychosocial, and educational deficits that have personal and economic costs.

Policy responses to these issues in recent decades have swung between informed commitment and determination to a willingness to overlook the serious implications of America's child health problems in the interest of focusing resources on other priorities. Legislative and executive attempts during the 1990s failed to implement significant health care reform. As of this writing, small improvements have been made in the delivery of services to children living in poverty, but millions of U.S. children are still without health care coverage.

CHAPTER 8

Child Abuse and Neglect

Elizabeth Gilman

Child maltreatment has a long and varied history. Only recently, however, has it become a major focus of public concern, debate, and scientific study. Until the 1960s, comparatively few professionals considered child abuse to be a serious social problem. For centuries children have suffered many forms of maltreatment, including abandonment, mutilation, murder, beatings, and forced labor, often within social environments that found such practices acceptable or even desirable (Ariès, 1962; Boswell, 1988; Greenleaf, 1978; Zigler & Hall, 1989). By starting with a brief examination of this history we can begin to understand the underpinnings of today's attitudes and laws about child abuse.

CHILD MALTREATMENT IN HISTORY

The Bible contains accounts of calculated slaughters of infants—first during the time of Moses, and later by King Herod when the birth of Jesus was foretold. The Bible frequently refers as well to ritual killing, as in the stories of Solomon and Abraham, and the sacrificial burning of children in the valley of Hinnon (the source for classical views of Hell as a burning pit) as a sacrifice to the god Moloch (2 Chron. 28:3). Moreover, interment of live newborns in the foundations of buildings also has a considerable history that spans centuries and cultures (Bakan, 1971; Radbill, 1974). This practice continued as late as the seventeenth century in Europe, even after it had been legally abolished. Children were buried in the dikes of Oldenberg and in the foundations of London Bridge; in India the practice lasted until the twentieth century (Stern, 1948).

Infanticide, particularly for poor or defective newborns, females, or children in large families, was also common practice in ancient Greece, Rome, Arabia, and China. By law, a father in Rome had the right of possession over his child; he could sell, mutilate, castrate, or murder the child with impunity (Lee, 1956). Widespread poverty during the Middle Ages only exacerbated the plight of children, who had become for many families an economic liability. Many children were abandoned, sold, or deliberately mutilated to render them more effective as beggars. In Scandinavia, fathers had legal power over the lives of their newborns; until a father consented to take his child into his arms, it could not be fed or baptized. This right persisted in law until the 1850s in Norway and Denmark (Werner, 1917).

Children who were fortunate enough to attend school were no safer. Up to about the fifteenth century, corporal punishment in schools was framed as a facet of monastic self-abnegation; subsequently, as Ariès (1962) has theorized, the beatings and abuses inflicted on students took on a tone of brutality and humiliation. So-called "scholastic punishment" was inflicted on children of all ages and social stations in the European school system, even in Jesuit schools, where the beatings were administered not by the faculty but by fellow students (Ariès, 1962), the idea of academic discipline enforced through physical beatings had become entrenched.

Child labor, particularly during the industrial revolution in both Europe and America, placed the young child in another brutal environment. Even very young children of the lower classes worked long hours under harsh and hazardous conditions. Occupational injuries, diseases, and deformities resulting from working long hours under unhealthy, often cramped conditions, were commonplace (Cahn & Cahn, 1972; Hanway, 1785).

Voices of Reason

Alongside the many who have condoned brutality against children throughout history have been individuals who advocated protecting the young. In the ancient world, Tertullian spoke out against the killing of children, as did the emperors Constantine, Valens, and Theodosius. The code of Hammerabi in ancient Egypt specified severe punishments for a mother who murdered her newborn child (Garrison, 1965), and the Roman Emperor Tiberius set the death penalty for those who sacrificed children to Moloch (Ariès, 1962). Jewish, Christian, and Muslim law have long prohibited infanticide.

As early as the second century A.D., orphanages and hospitals for abandoned children began to appear. Pope Innocent III established a system of foundling homes in the thirteenth century to care for the children born out of wedlock during the Crusades. Other such institutions were established by Empress Catherine II of Russia and throughout European nations (Radbill, 1974). Laws protecting children also arose in Europe beginning in the sixteenth century: Henry II of France and James I of England passed laws prohibiting the concealment of a child's birth (Radbill, 1974), and the late 1800s saw the passage of laws protecting abandoned or abused children and infants sent out to nurse (Ariès, 1962). In England in the nineteenth century, however, child murder continued to be so prevalent that the House of Commons established a committee on the subject, and infanticide was still considered a problem throughout Europe (*Encyclopaedia Britannica*, 1890; Zigler & Hall, 1989).

The Middle History: Child Abuse and Policy

In the United States, the case of Mary Ellen Wilson marks the first public acknowledgment of child maltreatment to gain widespread attention. Eight-year-old Mary Ellen was found starved, chained, and beaten by her adoptive parents in New York City in 1874. Because no existing law addressed abuse carried out by a child's caretakers, the police department refused to take any action. Henry Bergh, founder and president of the Society for the Prevention of Cruelty to Animals (SPCA), intervened and saw the case brought to trial. Contrary to popular myth, the SPCA itself was not involved. Mary Ellen was placed in an orphanage; her adoptive mother was jailed for one year. A secondary result of the trial, which was well publicized in the newspapers of the time, was the founding in 1875 of the Society for the Prevention of Cruelty to Children. During the same period, a number of other organizations were founded to care for children, including charity homes for homeless or abused children, child protection agencies, and foundling hospitals (Bremner, 1971a).

With the development of more advanced diagnostic techniques, particularly pediatric radiology, child maltreatment as a cause of injury finally began to move to the foreground. Nevertheless this movement has been very slow. Even though the radiology of the 1940s made such abuse-related injuries as subdural hematoma detectable, these were not always attributed to maltreatment. For example, in Caffey's important paper of the time, little mention is made of intentional ill treatment (Caffey, 1946). Not until the 1960s, when Kempe and his colleagues coined the term *battered child syndrome* (Helfer et al., 1962), were particular types of injuries seen as the signs of deliberate child abuse. Thus the origins of today's child maltreatment field, in terms of its fundamental definitions, diagnoses, and policies, are comparatively recent. For this reason, it is not too surprising that this important area of study remains very much in a state of growth and pervasive controversy.

DEFINITION, DEMOGRAPHICS, AND DEVELOPMENTAL PERSPECTIVES

Child abuse is difficult to define. At least 9 parents out of 10 in the United States continue to use corporal punishment and believe physical discipline is necessary and even desirable for children's well-being, in spite of mounting evidence that spanking is ineffective and strong argument that it is inhumane. Approximately 90 percent of the parents of toddlers, and nearly 50 percent of the parents of adolescents use corporal punishment as a disciplinary technique ("Childhood Spanking and Increased Antisocial Behavior," 1998; Brett, 1998). Most child development experts oppose the use of any corporal punishment by parents. Some point to research that physical punishment of children not only is ineffective (Maurer & Wallerstein, 1987), but might even have an effect opposite to that intended. Many note a correlation between corporal punishment and increased anger and resentment in children (American Academy of Pediatrics, 1988; Baler, 1988; Lerner, 1998; Weininger, 1998); at least one study reveals that 100 percent of inmates at San Quentin prison incarcerated for violent crimes were spanked or beaten as children (Maurer & Wallerstein, 1987).

Corporal punishment—even when intended only to discipline or "teach a lesson"—is often associated with injury to children. At least 60 percent of physical abuse is associated with an attempt to discipline or punish the child (Zigler & Hall, 1984). Muscular and skeletal damage, central nervous system hemorrhage, spine and sciatic nerve damage, and even blood clots can result from "paddling," spanking, or blows to the buttocks, face, hands, or other body parts. (American Academy of Pediatrics, 1988; University of Alabama, 1998). More than a thousand children are known to have died from maltreatment in the United States in 1996 (the most recent year for which statistics are available). Such deaths are the result of actions including shaking (particularly of infants); injury to the head, chest, or abdomen; scalding; drowning; suffocation; and poisoning. It is likely that many other deaths are the result of abuse but cannot clearly be identified as such (National Clearinghouse on Child Abuse and Neglect Information, 1998; U.S. Department of Health and Human Services, 1998a).

Even so, spanking and even more extreme forms of punishment—most often by parents who never mean to cause their children harm—are so firmly ingrained in our society that there is still debate about how and where to draw the line between discipline and child abuse. A Temple University study of the antecedents of spanking behavior indicate that most parents who spank or use other forms of corporal punishment do so because they are modeling the behavior of their own parents (Maurer & Wallerstein, 1987).

Types of Abuse

The passage of the Child Abuse Prevention and Treatment Act (CAPTA) in 1974, and its revision in 1996 (PL 104-235) represented progress in the establishment of a more rigorous definition of child abuse. The provisions of this act define child abuse and neglect as any action or lack of action

> resulting in imminent risk of serious harm, death, serious physical or emotional harm, sexual abuse, or exploitation . . . Of a child . . . under 18 . . . By a parent or caretaker (including any employee of a residential facility or any staff person providing out-of-home care) who is responsible for the child's welfare. (PL 104-235, 1996)

Such actions that cause injury to a child, such as shaking, kicking, hitting, beating, biting, or burning, need not have been deliberate or intended to cause harm. Indeed, many injuries to children result from what parents describe, in essence, as overdisciplining or overpunishing the child.

Child neglect is a more amorphous category, but one of the most serious and dangerous forms of child abuse. Accounting for 65 percent of maltreatment reports, child neglect can involve leaving young children unattended, failing to seek or provide adequate medical care, food, or water, or shelter to a child, or abandonment (DiLeonardi, 1993). The National Incidence Study of Child Abuse and Neglect (NIS-3) found that over 300,000 U.S. children were harmed by neglect annually (Sedlak & Broadhurst, 1996).

Sexual abuse is probably the most consistently underreported form of child maltreatment. Under the CAPTA definition, child sexual abuse is described as

> Employment, use, persuasion, inducement, enticement or coercion of any child to engage in, or assist any other person to engage in, any sexually explicit conduct or any simulation of such conduct . . .; or rape, as in cases of caretaker or inter-familial relationships, statutory rape, molestation, prostitution, or other form of sexual exploitation of children, or incest with children. (PL 104-235, 1996)

Such a definition also includes commercial exploitation through prostitution or the production of materials held to be pornographic.

Emotional abuse is the most recent form of abuse to be acknowledged specifically in legal and clinical practices. Again, the definition cites practices "that have caused, or could cause, serious behavioral, cognitive, emotional, or mental disorders . . . [ranging from] extreme or bizarre forms of punishment, such as confinement of a child in a dark closet [to] . . . habitual scapegoating, belittling, or rejecting treatment" (National Clearinghouse on Child Abuse and Neglect Information, 1998). Reports of such practices are often difficult to substantiate, but strong suspicion of extreme emotional abuse can be sufficient to warrant the intervention of child protective services.

The Difficulty of Definition

Clearly, any definition of maltreatment has major implications for the legal, medical, political, and social response to the phenomenon. The definition affects how instances of abuse are identified, counted, and treated, both psychologically and legally. Are perpetrators to be seen as criminally liable for their actions? as members of a subculture with mores incompatible with mainstream society? as impaired individuals requiring psychological services? In shaping our definitions, should we focus on the outcomes for the child in a given situation, or on the perpetrator and his or her intent?

Though CAPTA guidelines set the standards for child maltreatment definitions, each state has its own set of current definitions, and these range considerably in their scope from very broad to quite narrow. Disagreement as to the inclusion of specific forms of maltreatment within the definition begins to appear as the behaviors in question become more subtle. Most states, for example, include physical abuse, sexual abuse, and physical neglect within the definition of child maltreatment, but such areas as inadequate supervision and psychological abuse are controversial and elude uniform legal definition (Barnett, Manly, & Cicchetti, 1993). A broad definition might include anything that interferes with a child's optimal development, a narrow one only the harsher forms of physical abuse and deprivation. As a policy matter, the sort of working definition employed by agencies has major implications for service delivery, in that a narrow definition will allow fewer children and families to qualify for assistance (Zigler, 1980).

Estimates of Incidence

Over 2 million cases of child abuse or neglect, involving over 3 million children, were reported in 1996, according to the third and most recent National Incidence Study of Child Abuse and Neglect (NIS-3) (U.S. Dept of Health and Human Services, 1998a). NIS-3 estimates that approximately 44 children out of every 1,000 are reported as maltreated every year; approximately 2,000 deaths a year are attributed to maltreatment. The **incidence** of abuse and neglect is increasing: the number of cases reported in 1996 was 18 percent higher than in 1990 (U.S. Dept of Health and Human Services, 1998a). It must be borne in mind, however, that not all cases of abuse are reported, and that all reported cases are not necessarily genuine instances of mistreatment.

Profiles: Victims of Abuse and Neglect in 1996

- Over half of reported victims were 7 or younger; 25 percent were 4 or younger; 26 percent were 8 to 12; 21 percent were 13 to 18.
- Children 3 and under account for 75 percent of fatalities attributed to child abuse or neglect.
- Reports of sexual abuse were more likely to involve female children (77 percent), as were reports of emotional abuse (53 percent).
- Reports of neglect (51 percent), physical abuse (52 percent), and medical neglect (52 percent) were slightly more likely to involve boys.

- 53 percent of child abuse or neglect reports involved white children; 27 percent, black; 11 percent, Hispanic; 2 percent, Native American; 1 percent, Asian American.
- Children from homes in which family income was $15,000 or less were 25 times more likely to be reported as abused as were children from families earning $30,000 or more.

Source: U.S. Department of Health and Human Services (1998a). *Child Maltreatment 1996: Reports from the States to the National Child Abuse and Neglect Data System.* Washington, DC: U.S. Government Printing Office.

Profiles: Perpetrators of Abuse and Neglect

- 77 percent of child abuse and neglect takes place at the hands of the child's own parents.
- 11 percent of alleged abusers are relatives other than parents.
- 2 percent are other, nonrelative caregivers, such as child-care providers or foster parents.
- In 10 percent of cases, the alleged perpetrator is not known to the child.
- 61 percent of perpetrators are female, though 75 percent of perpetrators in sexual abuse cases are male.

- 81 percent are under 40.
- 50 to 80 percent of substantiated parental child abuse cases involve some form of substance abuse by the parent.

Source: U.S. Department of Health and Human Services (1998a). *Child Maltreatment 1996: Reports from the States to the National Child Abuse and Neglect Data System.* Washington, D.C.: U.S. Government Printing Office.

Estimating Unreported Maltreatment

With the advent of mandatory reporting of child abuse in the late 1960s, public awareness of maltreatment as a major concern rose dramatically, as did the number of reported cases. The nation's reports of alleged abuse and neglect climbed from an estimated 669,000 in 1976 to 2,163,000 in 1987. This is an average increase of 10 percent per year (Finkelhor, 1993). In light of these distressing figures, a national child-abuse emergency was proclaimed (U.S. Advisory Board on Child Abuse and Neglect, 1990a). The increase in cases has continued unabated and obviously accounts for only those cases for which reports are filed. Some estimates have suggested that the actual number of cases is much higher, with abuse occurring in as many as 3 to 4 million households each year (Gelles & Straus, 1988; National Center on Child Abuse and Neglect, 1988).

Despite the increase in reports, and at least the possibility that these underestimate the prevalence of maltreatment, a controversy exists regarding both the true number of cases and whether the rise is attributable to more reporting or to an increase in maltreatment. Considerable research supports the idea that the increase is due to heightened awareness and consequently higher rates of reporting (Finkelhor et al., 1990; Peters, Wyatt, & Finkelhor, 1986). Nevertheless, many researchers and clinicians also believe that much of today's child maltreatment does not appear in our statistics (Finkelhor, 1993). This conclusion is based in part on the results of the National Incidence Study (NIS) (Sedlak, 1991a), which looked at the number of cases known directly to professionals within communities throughout the United States and compared these numbers with those generated by the local protective service agencies. The comparison revealed that 65 percent of all maltreatment and 60 percent of the most severe cases known to professionals (including serious injuries and impairments resulting from abuse and neglect) were not getting into the child protective service (CPS) system (Sedlak, 1991b).

David Finkelhor (1993) points out that the NIS figures also underestimate the likely true number of cases, in that they reflect only those cases that come to the attention of professionals. He suggests that one way of roughly determining the true magnitude of the problem is by comparing the percentage of adults who report having been abused as children with the number of today's reported cases. By way of example, he notes that if 15 percent of women and 5 percent of men say they were sexually abused as children, this would indicate there are actually 300,000 to 400,000 additional child victims each year, a number that is 2 to 3 times higher than the figure currently reported (Finkelhor, 1984; Finkelhor et al., 1990).

In opposition to this view is one advanced by Douglas Besharov (1988a), who believes that the increasing number of abuse reports indicates not a rise in cases or in reporting efficiency but an overreaction on the part of professionals. The policy that would follow from this view would be one establishing more rigorous criteria for reporting and a narrower definition of what constitutes child maltreatment (Finkelhor, 1993; Besharov, 1988b). Besharov has argued that 80 percent of all substantiated cases are in fact those that do not pose serious physical danger to the child; in this category he places excessive corporal punishment, minor physical neglect, emotional maltreatment, and educational neglect (Besharov, 1988a, 1988b; Solnit, 1980).

If we were to favor using serious physical danger as the criterion for abuse, we might conclude that overreporting is a problem; however, it is easy to see from this debate the significant influence that definition of abuse has on statistics, policy, and treatment. Based on the NIS, for example, sexual abuse is the area in which case reports have grown most rapidly: while all abuse cases grew 57 percent between 1980 and 1986, sexual abuse cases more than tripled (Sedlak, 1991a). It might be that sexual abuse poses no major physical harm in some instances, yet to define it in a way that places it beyond the

purview of reporting laws does not address the major psychological injury that sexual abuse can inflict on children.

In attempting to calculate the true number of sexual or other abuse cases, we do not know for certain whether adults' retrospective reports of childhood abuse are accurate, yet the discrepancies such reports may reveal in our statistical accounts, along with the NIS results, at least bear consideration. The NIS study director concluded that more than half of the very serious maltreatment cases do not come to the official attention of protective service agencies (Sedlak, n.d.). As our systems of reporting and analytical methods increase in sophistication, we might be able to determine with greater accuracy the true incidence of child maltreatment.

DEFINING RISK: THE PROBLEM OF PREDICTION

No single constellation of variables will foretell with precision which children will be vulnerable to abuse. We have access to reliable, reasonably recent demographic data on abused and neglected children, their perpetrators, and the circumstances and settings in which the maltreatment took place. In addition to the information in the boxes here, we know that abuse is more likely to take place when family size is large, when parents are undereducated, when poverty or other environmental stressors are present, or when children have special needs or characteristics, such as prematurity, infant colic, or mental retardation. The danger, however, is that such statistics will be used to stereotype, not support, families. Clearly, failing to predict when child abuse might occur or recur puts children at risk of injury or even death. Erring on the side of conservatism by falsely labeling a family as abusive or potentially abusive, even when this is done in the spirit of protecting the child, leads to its own set of problems.

Risk Assessment

Some prevention efforts have focused on attempts to quantify a child's level of risk for maltreatment. Supported by the National Center on Child Abuse and Neglect (NCCAN), these efforts have resulted in the development of assessment instruments designed to help protective service staff identify potential child abuse. Unfortunately, the instruments have proven to be of limited value: 75

percent of a group of 328 surveyed workers found that the instruments offered little benefit (American Humane Association, 1993).

Other research has attempted to determine the correlates associated with maltreatment in order to describe the characteristics of a typical abused child and a typical perpetrator. Generally, even though we can look to statistical averages that describe child abuse victims and perpetrators, there is no such average child or average case of child maltreatment (Zigler & Hall, 1989). When the field of child maltreatment research was still relatively young, Gil (1970) undertook a major study that included child-abuse registry data from all 50 states, Washington, DC, and the Virgin Islands for the years 1967 and 1968. The study has been criticized (Spinetta & Rigler, 1972) for underestimating the incidence of abuse and for overidentifying child maltreatment with poverty. It should be noted that the manner in which child maltreatment comes to the attention of authorities tends to insulate abuse in middle- and upper-class families from detection: reports come generally from hospitals, public agencies, and police—all of which have more contact with the poor (Pakizegi, 1985). Also, the more spacious single-family houses and stricter adherence to privacy in upper-class life has been cited as another reason for a lower rate of detection (Parke & Collmer, 1975). Nevertheless, when the results of the Gil study are taken together with subsequent surveys (e.g., Anderson et al., 1983; Junewitz, 1983), we are able to speak with some insight about factors associated with child abuse.

Although research into risk factors has tried for the most part to identify the relative importance of such components as poverty, social isolation, prior history of abuse, and parent characteristics and expectations, researchers have given relatively little attention to *interactions* among these many variables (National Research Council, 1993). Current attempts to predict the occurrence of abuse have had mixed results; the range of accuracy varies widely. Two goals are useful in this analysis: (1) sensitivity, the accuracy of identifying those who will actually have parenting problems (true positives); and (2) specificity, the accuracy of the prediction of those who will ultimately not have these problems (true negatives) (Pakizegi, 1985). Most such studies have used **cluster analysis** and distributive function analysis to reveal patterns in a set of data.

Among the better predictive studies, the accuracy of identifying families as high or low risk is around 75 percent (Pakizegi, 1985). A sampling of the research, however, will give us an idea of how complex the interpretation of these individual findings can be. For child characteristics taken in isolation, no **predictive validity** has been found (Anderson, 1977). Other factors—such as spouse abuse, frequent pregnancies, and single parenthood—have been found to be somewhat valid predictors of abuse, and many have proposed developing a scale which would take into account the *interaction* of these variables. An interaction between stress in the mother's childhood and current environmental stress factors, for instance, showed a 70 percent sensitivity (Newberger et al., 1977). More research into this approach might yet yield a workable instrument, but for the time being, caseworkers have to rely on some combination of reporting and human intuition.

Family Profiles and the Myth of Intergenerational Transmission

One theory about child abuse that has led to debate and both media and scholarly distortion is the idea of intergenerational transmission. In 1962, Kempe and his colleagues published a paper observing that many parents who abused their children had themselves suffered abuse in childhood. Numerous subsequent writers made a similar observation, so many that one reviewer of the literature concluded that the idea of the transmission of abusive treatment through the generations had become virtually a precept of the field (Spinetta & Rigler, 1972). The theory reached this status without adequate supporting evidence, however, and there are growing indications that the existing intergenerational literature is limited in its applicability (Kaufman & Zigler, 1989, 1996; Dubanoski, 1981; Gelles, 1979a, 1979b; Gelles & Cornell, 1985; Giovannoni & Billingsley, 1970; Hunter & Kilstrom, 1979).

Moreover, a number of more recent studies have determined that many parents who were abused as children do not subsequently maltreat their own children. This is so despite the estimate reported by Kaufman and Zigler (1989) that a person who was abused is six times more likely than a nonabused individual to become an abusive parent. But as Kaufman and Zigler have pointed out, a greater likelihood is not the same as an inevitability; in fact, they surmised that most individuals who have been abused do not grow up to abuse their children. For example, Hunter and Kilstrom (1979) determined that 82 percent of the parents they studied were able to avoid repeating the cycle of abuse. A study conducted by Egeland and Jacobvitz (1984) found that 70 percent of the parents they followed had avoided participating in abuse. Interestingly, in both groups, it was found that parents who had come to terms with their own abusive childhoods were in fact more likely to refrain from repeating an abusive pattern than those parents who had denied what had happened to them as children or who held idealized images of their parents. The nonabusive parents had several other characteristics in common: they had fewer life stresses, more readily available social supports, healthier babies, and, in the Hunter and Kilstrom study, less ambivalence about their children. Such factors as these should clearly be taken into account as we attempt to design intervention programs to treat the problem of child abuse.

THEORETICAL PERSPECTIVES

As with other complex behavioral phenomena, child maltreatment does not take place in a social vacuum. The child has a place within the family unit, and both child and caregivers are situated within several contexts: neighborhood, school, community; perhaps they are members of a distinct subculture as well. As scientific conceptualization of child abuse has evolved from its inception in the 1960s, such ecological factors have played an increasingly greater role as we have devised working models. Clearly the use of an individual or an environmental approach will influence the manner in which society addresses this problem.

There are several ways to conceive of child maltreatment: as a form of pathology based in the character traits and/or the psychodynamics of the individual perpetrators; as a sociocultural phenomenon in which the stressful nature of the abuser's own environment precipitates abuse; or as a combination of individual and social factors in which child and perpetrator characteristics are aggravated by other factors in the environment to produce abusive behavior (Zigler, 1980; see, e.g., Belsky, 1978; Cottle, 1975; Daniel & Hyde, 1975; Garbarino, 1976; Gelles, 1973; Gil, 1979; Kempe et al., 1962). Among the situational influences most often cited as having great impact on family functioning are poverty, isolation, and lack of adequate social supports for parents (Zigler, 1980). Investigators consistently report that child maltreatment occurs most often among single-parent families, families with unemployed fathers, substance abusers, nonbiological parents, and families who are poorly housed or living in poverty (Gelles, 1989; Gil, 1970; Straus, Gelles, & Steinmetz, 1980). Increasingly, theorists and researchers regard the course of child maltreatment as originating from multiple factors (Belsky, 1980; Cicchetti & Lynch, 1993; Cicchetti & Rizley, 1991; Garbarino, 1977).

Though individual psychopathology might account for a certain number of cases, it is evident that a policy that relies solely upon an individual treatment approach will fail to eradicate child maltreatment. First, study of the **etiology** of abuse has revealed that the problem has deep and far-ranging origins that spring from social and situational forces largely unaffected by individual modes of treatment (Zigler, 1980). Moreover, society simply does not have the resources to implement a program of individual treatment on a national scale. Although peer self-help groups like Parents Anonymous and telephone help lines serve a valuable function in providing social supports for abusive or potentially abusive parents, these forms of assistance are inadequate to address on a sustaining basis the often overwhelming emotional and environmental stressors present in the daily lives of these families. A successful explanatory (and ultimately a treatment) model must recognize and address the social context in which child and caregiver are embedded.

For the above reasons, an interactive, **ecological** model offers us the greatest opportunity for both understanding and addressing the maltreatment problem. Such a model sees the child abuser as an individual possessing certain characteristics who is a member of a family of a particular type that is itself part of a larger social, political, and economic structure within a community (Zigler, 1980). Clearly a paradigm of such complexity is difficult to comprehend fully and daunting in terms of our efforts to formulate effective forms of intervention. Nevertheless our willingness to acknowledge the scope of the problem is essential if we are to design the sort of comprehensive solutions it demands.

Developmental Issues

A theoretical framework that utilizes an interactive approach permits us to include in our analysis important aspects of healthy human development that must be incorporated in any effective plan to enhance the lives of children and families. By framing policies that deal with maltreatment in terms of a healthy developmental course, we are better equipped to design interventions helpful to families with children who are infants, preschoolers, school-age, or adolescents (National Research Council, 1993).

Each of the life stages of a child makes particular demands on the caregiver, and each stage brings with it a set of specific developmental needs and vulnerabilities. Because the child is in fact a changing and developing system, we must take a developmental perspective in understanding, defining, and acting to ameliorate the effects of child abuse (Aber & Zigler, 1981). Clearly the challenges of protecting and nurturing an infant are vastly different from the skills required to successfully parent an adolescent. As the child grows, she moves into experiential realms of increasing complexity; at the same time the tasks of parenthood are altered and become correspondingly complex. Thus the repertoire of caregiving skills that are adequate at one stage of a child's development might not suffice as the child matures. Under these circumstances, children and parents or other adults in the family environment can be susceptible to different forms of maltreating behaviors at different points in the life cycle. An analytic perspective that operates from a developmental, as well as an ecological standpoint offers us the greatest opportunity to understand more fully the **epidemiology** of child maltreatment as well as the varying consequences certain forms of maltreatment may have, depending on where they occur on the continuum of the child's life. For children at various ages, specific coping mechanisms are present that can either facilitate or inhibit their ability to adapt to diverse environmental demands, including those created by abuse and neglect (National Research Council, 1993). To have maximum effect, interventions aimed at preventing or treating specific forms of maltreatment in children of differing ages must take developmental issues into account.

The Social Context

Child abuse cannot be narrowly understood as an aberrant phenomenon apart from the social substrate of families, one in which parents are socialized to behave in certain ways toward their children. Parents receive many cues telling them it is acceptable to use aggression in dealing with children. American society as a whole has provided little outside support to strengthen families (Hall, Zigler, & Kagan, 1996), but it provides plenty of support for behavior conducive to child abuse. Nicholas Hobbs (1980) has expressed the problem by describing child abuse as "a swatch from the fabric of a violent and abusing society" (p. 280).

Violence is a pervasive social problem in America. Compared to other nations, the United States is characterized by extremely high rates of interpersonal violence (Children's Defense Fund, 1998k). Violence is often tolerated as a means of self-expression at sport events, as a marketing tool in television and other entertainment media, and as a means of conflict resolution. A number of scholars have argued that social approval of violence legitimizes and reinforces its use (Emens et al., 1996). Although socialization typically requires that violent

Corporal Punishment in Schools

School corporal punishment is prohibited by nearly all industrialized nations; the exceptions are the United States and South Africa, and parts of Canada and Australia. Many countries in Europe banned the practice during the latter nineteenth century; by 1990, these had been joined by Switzerland, Germany, Greece, China, New Zealand, Ireland, and the United Kingdom (Feshbach, 1980; National Coalition to Abolish Corporal Punishment in Schools, 1991). The U.S. Supreme Court has upheld the right of state school authorities to administer physical punishment, even, as in the case of *Baker v. Owen* (1975), when this violates a parent's written instructions to the contrary. In the case of *Ingraham v. Wright* (1977), where a junior high school boy was injured in the course of being beaten by two teachers using a two-foot wooden paddle, the highest court held that this action did not constitute cruel and unusual punishment, nor did it violate the boy's due-process rights. Approximately 610,000 children were subjected to physical punishment in American schools in 1993 (Children's Defense Fund, 1994b).

This situation has led some thinkers to conclude that state law permitting corporal punishment in schools provides a social model encouraging parents to use physical violence against their offspring; the fact that education professionals would be administering the punishment lends an inappropriately official imprimatur to the practice, say critics (Feshbach, 1980). One scholar notes that state laws prohibit violence against convicted felons but not, at least in some states, against children (Prescott, 1979). Harsh disciplinary practices in general appear to be causally related to a style of processing social information that leads to aggression; this finding suggests that severe physical punishment encourages the child to develop more aggressive behavior (American Academy of Child and Adolescent Psychiatry, 1998; American Academy of Pediatrics, 1991; Weiss et al., 1992). The American Civil Liberties Union has stated that using "physical violence on school children is an affront to democratic values and [an] infringement of individual rights" (Reitman, Follman, & Ladd, 1972, p. 36).

In recent years, numerous professional and private citizen organizations in the United States have been active in attempting to end corporal punishment in schools. Among these are the National Center for the Study of Corporal Punishment and Alternatives, the Committee to End Violence Against the Next Generation (EVANG), the National Coalition to Abolish Corporal Punishment in Schools, and the Center for Effective Discipline. For example, since 1987 the Center for Effective Discipline, in Columbus, Ohio, has assisted the National Committee to Prevent Child Abuse, EVANG, and the National Coalition to Abolish Corporal Punishment in Schools in planning annual national conferences on school corporal punishment. In part through the efforts of these and other organizations, nine states and a number of municipal governments in other states have enacted legislation prohibiting this form of punishment in schools, and similar legislation is pending in four additional states (American Academy of Child and Adolescent Psychiatry, 1998).

urges be restricted to specific settings, as in boxing or other sports, socially and legally sanctioned violence spills over into schools that permit corporal punishment, military and legal agencies that employ it both in training personnel and in enforcement, and into private homes where it is used against children and other family members. More violence takes place in the American family than in any other social group in this country (Allan, 1978)—recall that at least 90 percent of U.S. parents use corporal punishment against their children, often starting when the children are infants or toddlers, and that such punishment often leads to injury ("Childhood Spanking," 1998; Zigler & Hall, 1984).

As long as physical punishment of children is permitted (Feshbach, 1980; Gelles, 1973; Gil, 1970; Reid, 1983; Zigler, 1980), it seems unlikely that such acts, unless they lead to serious injury or death, will be considered criminal in the United States in the foreseeable future. Imposing further legal limits on physical punishment of children appear desirable, however. We do have evidence that cultures with a low incidence of child abuse—including Sweden, Finland, China, Japan, and Tahiti—also tend not to use physical punishment, but we cannot say for certain that this is a direct causal relationship (Belsky, 1980; Rogers, 1979).

Sweden's Ban on Corporal Punishment of Children

In July 1979, Sweden instituted a legal ban on the corporal punishment of children by their parents or other caretakers. This prohibition was the first—and until 1984, the only one—of its kind among the industrial nations (Deley, 1988; Durrant, 1996;) to give legal force to the recommendations of pediatricians, psychologists, and other social scientists who believe physical punishment of children should be avoided (Ziegert, 1983). The text of the law is as follows:

The parent or guardian should exercise the necessary supervision in accordance with the child's age or other circumstances. The child should not be subjected to corporal punishment or other injurious or humiliating treatment. (Saltzer, 1979, p. 3)

The Swedish law has its origins in an assumed connection between corporal punishment, child abuse, and domestic violence in general. Its legislative intent—since followed by several other nations—apparently was to provide parents with behavioral guidelines for child rearing (Ziegert, 1983), as well as to establish a norm against all forms of physical punishment (Deley, 1988). An additional purpose noted by supporters of the law was to allow for ease of conviction under the Swedish criminal code for injury of a child: with the law in place, a parent could not argue that the injury resulted accidentally as the child was being punished (Adamo, 1980).

In Sweden, physical punishment was legally permissible and even considered necessary until the early twentieth century; with the rise of democracy, however, attitudes began to change. In 1966, sections of the Parenthood Law supporting a right to spank children were deleted (Deley, 1988). In 1970, a government study documenting a substantial number of injuries to Swedish children was released; this study may have been instrumental in the subsequent passage of the ban on corporal punishment (Oster, 1979). Despite some public debate when the law was proposed, the prohibition passed in the Swedish Parliament by a majority of 259 to 6 (Deley, 1988).

Due in part to a widespread public information campaign launched by the Swedish government, virtually all adults in Sweden were aware of the law by 1981 (Ziegert, 1983). Prior to its passage, public opinion polls indicated that a steadily declining number of the Swedish people favored occasional corporal punishment; this number continued to decrease with the passage of the 1979 ban (Ziegert, 1983). Despite the relatively homogeneous character of the Swedish population, various immigrant groups and other subcultures within Swedish society who maintained a tradition of corporal punishment presented a challenge to enforcement and ultimate acceptance of the ban. To a great extent, this public awareness and acceptance has been accomplished through the action of Sweden's powerful private child protective organizations and through an information and public education campaign carried out by the school system and the government's network of social service agencies (Ziegert, 1983).

The Legal Context

Although the society as a whole has an interest in protecting the young from harm, this function is counterbalanced by fundamental rights that accrue to all citizens, including parents (Melton & Thompson, 1987). Such rights include Fourteenth Amendment due-process and equal-protection guarantees, as well as those protections set forth in the Bill of Rights. Because these rights are considered fundamental, they cannot be abridged by legal action unless a legitimate, compelling state interest for the intrusion can be demonstrated. Against this backdrop, the legal tension between protecting a child from harm at the hands of a parent and maintaining the parent's fundamental interest in autonomous parenting becomes clearer, as do the legal impediments to such measures as a law prohibiting corporal punishment. Even when a parent has been found to be neglectful or abusive, a high standard of proof is needed to terminate parental rights in the child. The state may, under certain circumstances, intervene to protect the health and welfare of children, but these state involvements in family life must be legally specific as to the nature of the parents' alleged maltreatment or neglect, and the state must observe the standards governing due process in its dealings with the parents.

An additional legal issue in proceedings involving fundamental rights is that the state's activity, in this case in the child maltreatment arena, must be reasonably related to child welfare and must not be broader in scope than is absolutely necessary to achieve the specific protective purpose. This requirement has major implications for policy development, because it is likely to limit the state's use of many sweeping child maltreatment prevention methods, like compulsory, universal parent training for teens or welfare recipients, on the grounds that they are insufficiently tailored to the state's interest in child protection while intervening in the lives of large numbers of parents who have not been adjudicated as abusive (Thompson, 1993).

The Problem of a Child Witness

In the face of an accusation of child maltreatment, an adult's right to fair adjudication of the case necessarily includes confrontation of the primary witness lodging the allegation, often the adult's own offspring. Unfortunately, this situation can doubly traumatize the child, who, having been abused by a trusted adult, is now required to speak out against this selfsame significant person in his life and one to whom he usually maintains a profound attachment. It has therefore been observed that state interventions motivated by child protection frequently have the unintended result of causing the child more suffering than the abuse itself, particularly when protection involves removal from the home (Thompson, 1993). Psychological conflicts engendered in the child can be exacerbated when the child is urged by one parent to testify against another, or when the child is aware that his testimony will likely result in the loss of a difficult, but still valued, way of life for himself or for his parent. Consistently, research has shown that testifying in court is associated with adverse effects for maltreated children; moreover, clinical symptoms have increased dramatically with the need to testify multiple times (Goodman, Batterman-Faunce, & Kenney, 1993; Goodman et al., 1992). These sequelae typically include such symptoms as nightmares, bed-wetting, depression, anxiety, tantrums, and flashbacks.

In an effort to alleviate some of the stresses experienced by abused children, Congress passed the 1990 Victims of Child Abuse Act (42 U.S.C. 13001-1990), through which states are provided with grants to expand programs assigning court appointed attorneys (guardians ad litem) and/or court-appointed special advocates (CASAs) for abused children. These advocates are volunteers who help to support the child during court proceedings and who work to safeguard the child's rights and to meet her needs. The 1990 act also provides funding for such purposes as court personnel training and the purchase of equipment to record children's testimony (Kaufman & Zigler, 1996). To date, 48 states have adopted legislation allowing either an attorney or a CASA volunteer to act as a special support to a child victim during court trials; however, other reforms, such as permitting special court procedures in child-abuse trials, or special hearsay rule exceptions, have not been as widely adopted (Howell, 1993).

In an effort to minimize the psychological trauma inflicted on a child required to appear in court, 18 states have adopted laws to ensure a speedy trial in abuse cases; 17 states require a closed courtroom for child-abuse trials. A technique called "vertical prosecution" is used in 8 states to spare the child the experience of having to repeat testimony. In this method, only one prosecutor handles the matter from start to conclusion. In some jurisdictions, multidisciplinary teams made up of social workers, police, prosecutors, medical staff, and the like work together on a case, thereby ensuring that the child need not undergo multiple investigatory interviews (Howell, 1993).

Children have benefited from several additional reforms in the courtroom (Howell, 1993). In some states these include the admissibility of third-party statements and/or videotaped accounts of abuse, which would ordinarily violate the hearsay rule—a rule of evidence against the repetition of third-party testimony. These exceptions to the hearsay rule typically are permitted in instances where there is corroborating evidence and no leading questions are asked. Three states even permit leading questions when children are interviewed in court, in the belief that children can require this support to testify adequately. Recent research, however, tends to undermine the validity of this assumption (Ceci & Bruck, in press; Ceci et al., 1993). Thirty states will admit into evidence a child's statements recounting abuse to a professional individual like a physician or police officer (Howell, 1993).

IS THE CHILD WITNESS RELIABLE?

In recent years, heated controversy has arisen regarding the credibility and suggestibility of child witnesses. This has come about in part because of increased public awareness, and media coverage, of child abuse, coupled with a seeming rise in the number of accusations that children are being abused in preschool settings or by one or the other of their divorcing parents. Social science research has been attempting to inform the debate, which persists with many questions still unresolved.

A few general principles nevertheless have emerged from the best research (Ceci et al., 1993). Among these is the advisability of minimizing the number of times a child must recount a story and eliminating as many leading questions as possible. In addition, it is wise to conduct an interview as soon as possible following events, although this is not always feasible—months or even years can elapse before disclosure. A third important issue is the demeanor of the interviewer, in that children's errors are known to be affected by interviewer attitude. It is also important to avoid conveying or suggesting certain desired statements to a child, and to be aware that high stress and high personal relevance to a child can influence a child's understanding of events and accuracy of reporting (Ceci et al., 1993). There is considerable evidence that children will incorporate others' suggestions of minor events into their own accounts; yet we do not have sufficient knowledge of what process occurs when the events are significant to the child and others. Despite the lack of firm ground under many of these issues, we are also beginning to see evidence of individual differences among children as to their ability to recall occurrences accurately (Clarke-Stewart, Thompson, & Lepore, 1989), and efforts are being made, through interviewing techniques, to help children become more resistant to suggestion (Warren, Hulse-Trotter, & Tubbs, 1991).

Further research will undoubtedly reveal more useful information about child testimony, yet the fundamental tensions of this policy area will remain. The nation's adversarial justice system is weighted on the side of protecting the accused, not the accuser, while the child advocate or protective service worker perhaps would rather err on the side of ensuring a child's safety. A rift as deep as this is not readily bridged, and it is unlikely that research into children's testimonial accuracy will yield the degree of certainty that courtrooms require. For the time being, all we can do is proceed with good faith and maximum caution.

Child Abuse in Day Care

Owing at least in part to the lack of uniform federal standards for facilities and staff ratios and training, conditions in day-care facilities in the United States vary tremendously, from facilities that are safe and growth-enhancing to children at one end of the continuum to extremely poor and potentially dangerous facilities on the other (Children's Defense Fund, 1998k; Gilman & Zigler, 1996). Virtually every aspect of child care in the United States arouses some level of controversy, from whether children should attend and at what ages, to who should provide, regulate, and pay for such care. Beliefs and emotions related to the care of children run high, and are often compounded by parental dissatisfaction with the limited child-care options available to them.

In the 1980s and early 1990s, this picture was further complicated by a rash of child sexual abuse scandals linked to day-care settings. National statistics indicate that fewer than 2 percent of all cases of child abuse occur at the hands of child-care providers, but the media attention and hysteria associated with these cases is frequently out of all proportion to these facts. Issues pertaining to the use of children as witnesses in court cases, to the way evidence is gathered from and about young children, and to the very nature of due process and defendants' rights took center stage as several of the most lurid and controversial of these cases gained national media attention (Bikel, 1991, 1993, 1997; Eberle & Eberle, 1993; Hass, 1995; Public Broadcasting System, 1997b).

McMartin Preschool. The accusations of a 2-½-year-old boy attending the McMartin Preschool in Manhattan Beach, California, in 1986, are often cited as the trigger in a case said to have started the wave of hysteria associated with child-care-related abuse charges. In this case, the manner of collecting evidence and of soliciting the testimony of parents and young children (who spoke of sexual abuse, bizarre satanic rituals, and hidden underground passageways beneath the school—all unsubstantiated by evidence) were called into question by the media and by child psychologists. None of the seven defendants were ultimately convicted, but the 28-month-long case was, at the time, the longest and costliest prosecution in U.S. history.

Little Rascals Day Care Center. This child-care center, in Edenton, North Carolina, was at the center of a controversial case in which seven staff members were ultimately arrested and charged with 400 counts of sexual abuse against 29 children. In spite of concerns about the way evidence was collected, jurors were selected and treated, and children's testimony was introduced, and about the nature of the testimony itself (in which children spoke not only of rape, sodomy, and child pornography, but also of being abused aboard ships in outer space and in shark-infested sea waters during the school day), four of the defendants, all of whom pled innocent, served jail time.

Fells Acres Day School. Accusations of sexual abuse against a male bus driver and handyman who helped a 5-year-old boy change into dry clothes after a toileting accident sparked a Massachusetts case ultimately involving seven staff members, two trials, and multiple appeals. Physical evidence (e.g., vaginitis) introduced by the defendants' attorneys was described by expert witness as consistent with poor hygiene by young children; even so, the day-care center's owners were convicted, and a later overturning of the verdict was based less on the dubious strength of the evidence presented than on a constitutional technicality—the children had been allowed to testify while facing away from defendants, thus depriving the accused of the right to "face" their accusers.

Despite the clear need for action to remedy unsafe conditions in child-care facilities, it seems likely that the potential for child abuse in such settings has been grossly exaggerated, probably through the media coverage that occurs in situations like the ones described here. It must be remembered that most child abuse takes place in the home (U.S. Department of Health and Human Services, 1998a). Even though this is still the case, a number of legislative and other efforts have been proposed to deal with what seems to be perceived as the "major problem" of physical abuse in day care, whereas relatively little emphasis is being placed on the biggest problem in day care—guaranteeing high-quality, developmentally appropriate care.

Nevertheless, in the absence of adequate regulations that govern the operation of child-care centers or the employment of child-care providers, it is valuable to have some federal guidelines in place. A foundation for minimal protections against known child abusers has been laid by the National Child Protection Act, which was signed into law in December 1993. Under the act, states are required to report child-abuse crime information to a national background check system and must also maintain contact with the Na-

tional Center on Child Abuse and Neglect and related agencies for the purpose of exchanging technical assistance in child abuse cases. For states with poor data collection systems, the act provides funding for improvements.

Other provisions include the mandatory initiation of a study of convicted child-abuse offenders within each state, and the voluntary establishment of a system whereby qualified entities designated by the state may request, from a state agency, a national background check on child-care providers. It should be noted that this latter provision is *not* a requirement of the states, which retain the ability not to require background checking of prospective providers. Moreover, even when the state elects to participate, a provider's background may not be examined unless he or she provides a set of fingerprints and signs a statement containing provider identity data and setting forth the legal rights of the parties (National Child Protection Act, 1993). The act also does not address the issue of private child-care workers or nannies who are hired to care for children in the children's home. Thus, although this federal legislation provides a framework containing background data on child-abuse offenders, the usefulness of this information is limited unless each state enacts its own regulations.

INTERVENTION AND PREVENTION

When the federal Child Abuse Prevention and Treatment Act (CAPTA) was adopted in 1974, it required states to establish child-abuse reporting laws in order to receive federal funding. This legislation also established the National Center on Child Abuse and Neglect (NCCAN) as part of the U.S. Department of Health and Human Services. Thus, at the outset of federal involvement in child abuse, the larger portion of resources were designated for investigation than for providing assistance to troubled families (U.S. Advisory Board on Child Abuse and Neglect, 1993; Zigler, 1983). Today, the only "service" provided as a result of many child-abuse and neglect reports is an investigation (Kaufman & Zigler, 1996). Not only is this so in nonsubstantiated cases of abuse and neglect, but it occurs in an estimated 40 percent of substantiated cases as well (McCurdy & Daro, 1992). The result, in many cases, is that no services are provided for families, even when the state finds support for allegations of maltreatment.

The reasons for this emphasis on investigation over treatment are complex, but they might be related to an historical reluctance, supported by laws and social attitudes, to intervene in family matters and to allocate significant public funds for this purpose. The need for treatment for at least some abuse victims has been documented by numerous studies showing a variety of behavioral and clinical **sequelae** that can result from child abuse. These include problems in school functioning (Hoffman-Plotkin & Twentyman, 1984), peer relations (Kaufman & Cicchetti, 1989; Mueller & Silverman, 1989), depression (Kaufman, 1991; Pelcovitz et al., 1994), delinquency (Lewis et al., 1989; Widom, 1989), and post-traumatic stress disorder (McLear et al., 1994). The idea that parents have a right to control the treatment of a child is deeply ingrained, and may have given rise to a social attitude that appears to favor identification of child abusers over helping them. Solnit (1980), however, has rightly noted that it is injurious to apply labels to individuals in society without offering needed services to compensate them for the negative consequences and stresses that the label itself can bring.

Impediments to Risk Reduction

As we have noted, prediction and/or prevention of abuse with any reasonable level of precision seems to have remained beyond the present capacity of social science. Even if the state of knowledge were to expand dramatically, other aspects of the problem seriously limit our ability to make an impact on the rates of maltreatment. Two key problems plague the practice of child-abuse risk assessment and other attempts at prevention: the large size of protective service workers' caseloads and the exponential increase in the number of cases reported to protective agencies (McCurdy & Daro, 1992). In some offices, caseloads are reported to be as high as 100 or more cases per worker (*Artist v. Johnson*, 1990; Child Protective Services, 1992; *LeShawn v. Dixon*, 1991). Because of a lawsuit filed on behalf of clients by the American Civil Liberties Union, some states now have an imposed maximum number of 18 cases per worker (Kaufman & Zigler, 1996). Adequate research is lacking as to the optimal caseload size for a successful program of child-abuse intervention that would deliver high-quality diagnostic and prevention services to families while preventing worker burnout among staff members. Clearly the severity of abuse and the level of services required by the families would influence the ideal number of cases to be monitored by an individual worker.

Placement and Family Preservation

When state involvement is required in a case or suspected case of child abuse or neglect, its goal should be to determine need, not blame or risk. In this context, need should be defined broadly, to include assessment of physical health,

The Case of Elisa:
Who Should Shoulder the Blame?

Public attention has been drawn to the controversy surrounding family preservation programs by the dramatic failures in a few such programs that resulted in the deaths of children reunited with abusive parents. The case of 6-year-old Elisa Izquierdo, beaten to death by her crack-addicted mother after months of severe abuse, provides a grim illustration of what can—and often does—go wrong in child protection cases. A promising and appealing child who had been born addicted to crack but who had blossomed in the loving care of her father, who was given custody of her at birth, Elisa was thriving in his care and performing well in her Montessori school. When Elisa's father died of cancer, however, she was returned to the custody of her mother.

The warning signs that Elisa was in trouble were immediately apparent. Neighbors repeatedly reported to the New York City Welfare Administration (CWA) that they heard Elisa screaming and begging for mercy. Two other children had already been removed from Elisa's mother's home. Officials at the public school to which Elisa's mother had her transferred reported her injuries to CWA. Elisa's mother herself begged caseworkers to remove Elisa from the home; news coverage of the case indicated that they responded that they were "too busy" to investigate. Two months before Elisa's seventh birthday, her mother killed her by throwing her against a concrete wall. A police officer reported that there was no part of her body that had not been cut or bruised. He called it the worst case of child abuse he had ever seen (Van Biema, 1995). Critics placed much of the blame on budget cuts to CWA, made by the Pataki administration, that increased the case-loads of already overburdened caseworkers (Brandwein, 1995; Dina, 1995).

Budget cuts have trimmed personnel and material resources from child protection programs. As of this writing, Congress is considering a bill that would cut almost $3 billion more from child protection programs across the nation (Smolowe, 1995). At the same time, between 4 million and 10 million children are scheduled to be cut from welfare rolls as a part of congressional attempts to balance the national budget. Such cuts are likely to result in additional child-abuse cases as poverty levels and family stress increase.

Even now, social services caseworkers are overburdened and undertrained (Beck, 1996; Gelles, 1996; Van Biema, 1995). Required to make life-and-death decisions on a daily basis, caseworkers feel unappreciated when their actions do protect children, and guilty when they do not. A 1995 survey of former child protection caseworkers in Arizona revealed that two-thirds of them left their jobs because of pressure and stress (Smolowe, 1995).

At least a part of the blame, however, must fall on our historical overreliance on a philosophy emphasizing family preservation—that is, keeping biological families together as a priority that often overrides the demonstrable needs of children to be protected from those very families. Elisa Izquierdo's story is not unique. In 1989, Los Angeles county paid $18 million to settle lawsuits brought on behalf of children who were abused while in the county's custody (Hornblower, 1995). Over a thousand children are killed each year while in the custody of their parents (Beck, 1996). One of these was 15-month-old David, abused and finally smothered to death by his mother. His parents had already lost custody of his older sister because of severe abuse, and caseworkers had received reports that David was being abused. Child-abuse expert Richard Gelles (1996) blames casework loads and the philosophy of family preservation, which emphasizes the rights of biological parents over those of their children.

In child protection cases, especially when the child is suffering grievous physical or emotional harm, the welfare of the child should be the foremost concern. There are certainly many families that can improve their functioning with

the addition of supportive services to ease them through rocky times, but strong evidence indicates that not all families will be able to provide optimal or even adequate care for their children with the limited supports available. Concentration of our resources on helping a few physically abused and neglected children to remain safely at home can deflect us from the larger task of improving the lives of countless desperately deprived children whose level of *physical* danger would never result in their being removed from their homes (Magura, 1981).

mental health, substance abuse, and vocational, educational, recreational, and material needs (Kaufman & Zigler, 1996). Certainly there are circumstances in which children must be placed outside the home for their own safety. Yet we must be wary of allowing children to drift for years in foster care without any legal resolution and without a permanent home.

A number of issues have emerged in permanency planning for abused and neglected children: (1) Most of the 502,000 children in foster care today will experience more than one placement; (2) in some states, up to a third of children who enter care spend the majority of their young lives moving from one foster home to the next without ever receiving a permanent home; and (3) in many states it is difficult to terminate parental rights, even when there is clear and convincing evidence that it would be detrimental to allow the child ever to return to the care of the biological parents (Knitzer, 1996; Knitzer, Allen, & McGowan, 1978; Russo, 1991). As maltreated children have come to represent a larger share of child protection service agencies' caseloads, agency resources have been consumed at faster rates than ever, even as federal and state budget-cutting priorities have reduced funds available to them. One result has been both fewer out-of-home placements for at-risk children *and* fewer dollars available to support parents who retain custody of their children (Children's Defense Fund, 1998k; USDHHS, 1997b).

Family preservation proponents argue that children should not be removed from their homes without compelling reasons; that children might suffer harmful developmental consequences and even abuse while in foster care; and that costs of foster care can be significant. If, due to successful family support efforts, a child is not placed in foster care, the projected state savings are estimated at $27,000 (Daro, 1988). Governmental policies now favor the avoidance of foster placement through family preservation efforts, as well as the reduction of multiple placements for children who are removed from their families, and the reduction of the time period between initial removal and permanent placement for children (National Research Council, 1993).

Critics of a hard-line family preservation approach express concerns that, without adequate provision for family support services, children at demonstrable risk for maltreatment who are left with their biological families remain in danger; all-too-frequent reports of child injuries and even deaths under such circumstances bear out these concerns (Beck, 1996; Gelles, 1996; Hornblower, 1995; Leventhal & Horowitz, 1996).

Early Intervention as a Prevention Strategy

In an ideal world, our best child protective tool would be primary prevention—that is, stopping child abuse before it starts. The devastation that can afflict a child and a family in which abuse has taken place often cannot be healed completely; child abuse has emotional, social, and cognitive, as well as physical, outcomes for the child and her family; for our culture the full social, legal, and economic ramifications of this behavior are inestimable. Research has shown us that the effects of child abuse are cumulative over time, creating almost a domino effect on later development (Aber & Cicchetti, 1984; Cicchetti & Carlson, 1993). Professionals in the field of abuse are unified in their call for parent education and support programs that will not only teach parents and future parents how to care for their children, but also inform them of what to expect as their child grows (Zigler & Hall, 1989). Parents also need training in effective ways to discipline their children without recourse to physical punishment. A growing body of findings from longitudinal research indicate that early intervention and parent education programs—particularly when they operate on a parents' own turf through the use of home visits by professionals or paraprofessionals—can provide just the support parents need to avoid resorting to child abuse (U.S. Advisory Board on Child Abuse and Neglect, 1993; Gray & Halpern, 1989; Olds & Henderson, 1993; Taylor, 1997). One meta-analysis of early intervention programs providing parenting education and support indicated that training is most effective when implemented early, prenatally if possible (Gray & Halpern, 1989).

Broad-Based Family Support

In keeping with the ecological developmental approach, we believe that a comprehensive, multifaceted family support intervention offers a promising means both to prevent and to treat child abuse. This is so particularly in a context in which we have no precise means to assess exactly which members of a population are likely to become child abusers. The National Committee for the Prevention of Child Abuse emphasizes education and support services as part of a comprehensive prevention plan (Daro, 1993). Broad-based family support projects have been proliferating around the country, among them the School of the 21st Century program founded by Edward Zigler, which includes in its components a child-care system and outreach programs to assist, support, and educate parents (Zigler & Gilman, 1993). Another excellent example is the Ounce of Prevention program in Illinois, whose family support project has

Programs That Work:
Supporting Families to Prevent Child Abuse

Home visitation services are especially important (Daro, 1988) and have been endorsed by the U.S. Advisory Board on Child Abuse and Neglect as the most critical element in a comprehensive child abuse prevention program (U.S. Advisory Board, 1991). The following are some of the most promising of such programs:

- Hawaii's "Healthy Start," begun by Dr. Calvin Sia as a demonstration project in 1985, aims to prevent child abuse and neglect by improving family coping skills and functioning, promoting positive parenting skills, and enhancing healthy child development. The project, which emphasizes home visitation and continuity of health care and supportive services for families of newborns, has been extremely successful in preventing child abuse. After its first three years of operation, no cases of abuse had been reported among the 241 high-risk families served by the program (Breakey & Pratt, 1991). Healthy Start has expanded its services and gained wide acceptance and support: in 1992, the Hawaii state legislature appropriated $7 million in funding for the project, which now serves at-risk children ages 0 to 3 and their families throughout the state (Sia, 1992). The project has become the model for another program, Healthy Families America, now based in several cities across the nation, including Chicago and Washington, D.C.

- The Missouri-based Parents as Teachers program incorporates home visits, developmental screenings, group meetings, and referrals for other services to supplement their parent education lessons. In 1984, Missouri set a national precedent when it enacted legislation that mandated the use of this program in all school districts to offer parent education and support services to the parents of children under 3. The program's goal is to improve the general welfare of the children served, but increasing a parents' understanding of normal child behavior and development is a valuable tool in the prevention of child abuse (Wells, 1997).

- The Prenatal/Early Infancy Program (PEIP), based in Elmira, New York, recruited young, poor, first-time parents from an area that had New York state's highest child-abuse rates. The parents were offered child-care services, regular prenatal and well-child care, pre- and postnatal home visits by a nurse, and developmental education. The results of these studies offer the most compelling evidence to date supporting the use of prenatal and follow-up home visits as a means of fostering better child cognitive development, as well as improved maternal perceptions of child behavior, mother-child interactions, child medical care, and reduction in the occurrence of child abuse, at least for the duration of the intervention (Wolfe, 1993); in a typical program evaluation, only 4 percent of program mothers (as opposed to 19 percent of comparison-group mothers) had abused their children (Olds & Henderson, 1993). Olds and Henderson (1989) note that in order for programs to have a sustained impact, parent education services must be coupled with equal emphasis on improving conditions in the home environment.

- In a longitudinal study of a comprehensive early intervention program for first-time, high-risk parents designed by Sally Provence and Audrey Naylor at Yale University, it was determined that these services not only produced results initially, but that the gains were magnified over time (Seitz, 1985). The services included home visitation by a psychologist, nurse, or social worker; well-baby care; and child care services. In the 10-year follow-up of the sample families, it was found that the mothers achieved higher levels of education, the primary wage earner had a better employment history, and the children performed better in school, as compared with controls.

been very successful in controlling child abuse and decreasing the influence of other negative social indicators (Zigler & Hall, 1989).

Media Efforts

The media can also play a powerful role in enhancing parental knowledge and indirect prevention of child abuse. We have seen increasing use of brief, televised public service announcements (PSAs)—such as a nationally promoted "Don't Shake the Baby" campaign—to inform parents on the dangers of corporal punishment, how to diffuse anger, and where to seek help when they find themselves overly stressed. It has been difficult to conduct rigorous evaluations of the impact of such PSAs, but their use seems promising as an easily accessible and nonthreatening means of delivering parenting information (CSR, 1998).

National Efforts

The efficacy of family support in the prevention of child abuse has been recognized in the enactment of a number of federal initiatives. The Family Support Act of 1988 (PL 100-485) appropriated funds to address many of the risk factors associated with child abuse, and provides grants to develop job training, parent education, early childhood intervention, and other supportive services. Enacted in 1992, the Child Abuse, Domestic Violence, Adoption, and Family Services Act (PL 102-295) provides funds for community-based prevention and treatment demonstration projects and service programs. The ADAMHA Reorganization act of 1992 extends the 1984 National Institute of Mental Health Child and Adolescent Services Systems Program (CASSP) initiative (Kaufman & Zigler, 1996). This act offers states grants to improve cooperation and services integration among the child welfare, mental health, juvenile justice, and education systems in developing comprehensive programs for children with serious emotional disturbances. Its further goal is to assist in the development of a system of community-based, family-focused services, including home-based mental health projects.

In 1993, the Omnibus Budget Reconciliation Act (PL 103-66) extended existing funding for family support and family preservation services. The family support component is designed to decrease social isolation and enhance parental child rearing skills through home visitation, center-based activities, and other supportive services. Family preservation elements are directed toward alleviating family crises that might lead to removal of children from the home (Kaufman & Zigler, 1996).

Although the need continues for legislative reform to address the multiple risk factors associated with child abuse, the initiatives noted above may be used to further develop comprehensive, community-based programs for maltreated children and their families. The 1993 U.S. Advisory Board on Child Abuse and Neglect concluded that successful interventions for maltreated children must have certain characteristics; they must be (1) comprehensive, (2) neighborhood-based, (3) child-centered, and (4) family-focused. Moreover, the board noted the importance of fostering the economic and social development of a community as an element of any child-abuse prevention and intervention effort (U.S. Advisory Board, 1993). We concur with the idea of "neighbors helping neighbors" within a community and endorse the board's conclusions regarding the kind of intervention we must undertake to combat child abuse most effectively. The limited efficacy of treatment services for abusive parents, as well as the economic and psychological costs of abuse, point to prevention as the clear strategy of choice (Cohn & Daro, 1987; Daro, 1993).

SUMMARY

In the relatively short history of child maltreatment as an area of scientific inquiry, we have only begun to understand the complexity of the problem, and its pervasiveness. We also realize that abuse is a multifaceted phenomenon. Where once we defined abuse only as physical battering or the failure to provide the most basic care necessary for survival, we now include in this definition sexual predation and exploitation, emotional persecution, and even more difficult to interpret areas of neglect.

Anyone is a potential child abuser, regardless of social class, present circumstances, or personal history; the typical abuser is not a monster or mentally ill, but troubled and isolated, often as much a victim in the world as the child is. We also know that social and demographic factors play an important part in the physical abuse and neglect of children. In keeping with the knowledge that the abuser is frequently a sufferer as well, we need to redirect our research and policy efforts from the accusatory, investigative mode to a preventive, therapeutic and supportive one. In far too many cases, no services are supplied to a family even after there has been a substantiated report of abuse. In some states, and to an extent on the national level, reforms have been instituted to improve the child welfare and foster care systems. Despite these efforts, the incidence of child abuse in the United States stands at over 1 million substantiated cases a year, with many others remaining unreported. In many states, children continue to be harmed by coercive interventions and lengthy legal proceedings that fail to address their human needs and rights and often deprive them of a permanent home.

Such problems as these, and the problem of child maltreatment itself, cannot be resolved without acknowledging the surrounding social context. Unfortunately children's needs remain at a relatively low priority among the nation's policy makers. We now have a number of promising child-abuse prevention and treatment initiatives designed on the basis of our best scientific evidence. These models form a comprehensive system of child-centered, family-focused, community-based interventions that provide a safety net for children by strengthening their own families and those within their neighborhoods. We have the means needed to make a difference in the numbers of children maltreated each year, yet little change will occur until the protection of children becomes a genuinely important item on the social agenda.

CHAPTER 9

The Changing Face of the American Child

Carmen Arroyo

One of the most dramatic changes in child and family life in the United States over the past three decades concerns the very nature of those children and families. Groups of Americans to whom we typically refer to as "minorities" are well on the way to making up the greatest proportion of the U. S. population. Within the first century of the new millennium, white Americans of non-Hispanic European descent will be fewer in number than Asian Americans, Hispanic Americans, and African Americans combined. Such diversity strengthens and enriches the United States as various groups contribute to its character— U.S. culture is no longer the "melting pot" of old, but a coexistence and blending of many different languages and cultural practices.

In this chapter we will discuss the specific challenges that ethnically diverse, immigrant, homeless, and migrant children present to U.S. educational systems. We will consider how, in a country that has been defined by its ethnic diversity, educational institutions and policies to meet the varying needs of children have evolved over time.

CHANGING DEMOGRAPHICS

Individuals from ethnically diverse and underrepresented groups make up approximately 25 percent of the total population of the United States, with African Americans constituting 13 percent of the total U.S. population and Hispanics about 10 percent (Miller, 1994). However, census projections indicate that U.S. ethnic diversity will continue to increase, resulting in the population of those groups we currently refer to as "minorities" becoming the majority population by as early as 2075 (Miller, 1994). These predictions suggest that by the year 2050, 21 percent of the population will self-identify as Hispanic, 15 percent as African American, 10 percent as Asian American, and 1 percent as Native American (U.S. Bureau of the Census, 1993). In comparison, census figures indicated that Hispanics made up 9 percent of the American population and African Americans 12 percent of the 1990 population (Roberts, 1994).

The projected annual growth rate during the 1990s for Asian Americans is 5 percent; for Hispanics, 3 percent; and for African Americans, 1.3 percent. This contrasts with a 0.6 percent projected annual growth rate for non-Hispanic whites in the 1990s (Exeter, 1993). Furthermore, within the Asian American population, immigration will account for 57 percent of the estimated growth between the years 1990 and 2010. These numbers also reflect a general trend of increasing numbers of immigrants to the United States. In the 1960s, 3.8 million foreigners emigrated to the United States, in the 1970s that number increased to 7 million, and in the 1980s, 10 million foreigners moved to the United States (Tyson, 1994).

The changing demographics of American society as a whole will also bring changes to the school-age populations in this country. In a statistical report concerning trends in school district demographics, Levine (1996) notes that from school year 1986–1987 to school year 1990–1991, the number of the students in the public schools increased by 1 million students. Seventy-nine percent of this growth can be attributed to the addition of 645,000 Hispanics and 140,000 Asian students to the school systems (Levine, 1996). At this time, 30 percent of school-age children are members of ethnically diverse minority groups; projections estimate that this percentage will reach 36 percent by the turn of the century (Hodgkinson, 1993). These statistics are of interest because they indicate that the special needs of children from ethnically diverse backgrounds will require greater attention in the formulation of local and federal educational policies and practices.

Other groups of school-age children requiring special attention include homeless children and children of migrant workers. Due to the difficulty of gathering data on homeless individuals, the estimated number of homeless children nightly ranges from 61,500 to 500,000 (Children's Defense Fund, 1991). Of these homeless children, 1 out of 3 did not attend school while they were homeless.

Population estimates for migrant workers and migrant children are also difficult at which to arrive. Dever (1991) estimates that there are approximately 4.2 million migrant workers in the United States. The number of migrant children under 6 years of age is estimated to be 25 percent of the total migrant population (Siantz, 1991). These migrant families also are often non-English-speaking; their native languages include primarily Spanish, Haitian, and Vietnamese.

Non-English-speaking children are not only found in families of migrant workers. In fact, in the United States 31.8 million people speak a language other than English in the home, and of the children enrolled in urban public schools one-third spoke a foreign language first before they learned English (Headden, 1995). Children who are coming from linguistically isolated households (where no person 14 years or older speaks English only or speaks English very well) and children with limited English proficiency each constitute 4 to 5 percent of the total school-age population (U.S. General Accounting Office, 1993). The educational implications of these trends are significant as states and the federal government debate the best approaches to bilingual education and other programs targeting ethnically diverse students and the distinct need they bring to the American school.

MULTICULTURAL AMERICA AND AMERICAN EDUCATION

Since the period of colonial America, schools have played a key role in facilitating the integration of culturally diverse groups into American life (Vinovskis, 1995). But the relationship between schools and different groups of Americans has varied based on the characteristics of different immigrant groups, and also by changes in American society and economy. Different ethnic groups have had distinct experiences of schooling and their education has been governed by distinct educational policies that have both broadened and constricted their experiences (Fass, 1985; Tyack, 1974; Ueda, 1995).

Historians have noted that America's New England settlers should, in fact, be seen as the first immigrants. Due to their privileged status as the settlers of American society, their experience with schools were very different from those of subsequent immigrants. But colonial America's relations to schools provide an important context for understanding how the schools have approached the challenges presented by the ethnic diversity of the American population (Vinovskis, 1996).

Most children of immigrants to the northern colonies received their education in their households, churches, and local communities. Formal schooling was rare, and educational institutions played a minor role in socializing children (Vinovskis, 1995). One of the earliest attempts to legislate education for children was the 1647 Massachusetts legislation that required communities with more than 100 households to develop and maintain grammar schools; but this legislation was intended to complement the efforts of parents (Vinovskis, 1987). During the eighteenth century, American children typically received five years of schooling.

During this period, compulsory schooling laws were virtually nonexistent; even when enacted, they were only sporadically enforced. Americans believed in the value of education, but formal schooling did not become widespread until early in the nineteenth century. The precise reasons for the expansion of formal schooling in the nineteenth century remain unclear. Historians have speculated that declines in church attendance made necessary the development of large-scale schools that would teach middle-class Protestant values (Jorgenson, 1987; Vinovskis, 1995). If churches could no longer function as one of the primary venues for socializing children, then some other institution had to be created to fill in the gap. The increasing role of educational institutions in American life has also been attributed to dramatic changes, at the turn of the century, in the social composition and economy of America—public schooling was thought to be conducive to a greater uniformity of thinking and of work habits. In the late nineteenth century, there was a great transformation of American communities.

In 1880, less than 30 percent of the U.S. citizenry lived in communities of 2,500 or more individuals. The percentage of Americans living in cities with over a million inhabitants rose steadfastly in the later part of the century (Vinovskis, 1996). This shift in residential patterns, and the economic changes that fueled it, also led to the centralization of education in schools and away from the home. By the late 1800s, the household was no longer the main unit of production, parents were engaged in manufacturing outside of the home, and increasingly specialized agencies were established to take over the tasks that were formerly performed by parents and their neighbors.

Immigrants and Schooling in the Late Nineteenth and Early Twentieth Centuries

Growth of American urban centers and of its manufacturing economy brought about "an immigrant invasion" that, in the minds of many educators, required a "revolution" in American education (Tyack, 1974). The large numbers of first- and second-generation immigrant children who began to enter urban centers and urban schools late in the nineteenth century dramatically transformed the process and goals of American education. Unlike their predecessors, immigrants who arrived in the United Sates between 1880 and 1920 came from southern, central, and eastern Europe. Many were either Jewish or Catholic and most did not speak English. The educational system set as its goal that of "converting a daily arriving city-full of Russians, Turks, Austro-Hungarians, Sicilians, Greeks, and Arabs into good Americans" (Tyack, 1974, p. 230).

This process of Americanization stressed language and mathematics, norms of punctuality and cleanliness, and competence in a common set of standardized performances. The most distinctive feature of this process, however, was its encouragement of immigrant children to assimilate into American culture, to learn styles of thinking and emotional expression that were different from those they had become accustomed to in their native lands or at home (Ueda, 1995). America did not make serious attempts to reevaluate how the schools could teach appreciation of the ethnic diversity offered by immigrants until the period after World War II (Ueda, 1995). Nonetheless, immigrants were viewed as vital to the creation and development of a uniquely American identity. At the turn of the twentieth century, individuals from various ethnic, cultural, and social groups came to America and entered its educational system in hopes that assimilation would allow them to seek economic opportunity and religious and political freedom.

Recent Immigrants

Whereas immigration in the period between 1880 and the 1920s was viewed as a problem requiring management, the recent wave of immigration is viewed as something to be feared. As people begin to believe that immigrants resist assimilation into American culture, pose a threat to the workforce, and drain resources from social welfare and educational programs, attitudes toward immigrants are changing. America has gone from a land that welcomed "the tired, the weak, and huddled masses yearning to breathe free" to a land in which politicians proclaim that "America is for Americans" and Congress and citizens vote for policies that would deny social and educational services to legal and illegal immigrants.

The state of California, which has experienced the greatest immigration-related population growth of any U.S. state, is currently at the forefront of a movement to impose severe restrictions on illegal immigration. Its Proposition 187, which was passed by a wide margin during the 1994 elections, reduces health and education benefits for the children of illegal immigrants. Pete Wilson, California governor at the time of the passage of Proposition 187, also insisted that the federal government should pay back the state for the cost of implementing federal policies that strain the social, educational, and economic resources of the state.

Although the Equal Protection Clause of the Fourteenth Amendment of the U.S. Constitution guarantees all persons born in the United States the same rights held by other citizens, many legislators in California have even suggested that citizenship be denied to the American-born children of illegal immigrants. A federal judge threw out most of the provisions of Proposition 187, ruling that individual states had no authority to act on immigration matters, which the ruling called "unquestionably, a federal power" (Siskind, 1995).

Proposition 187:
State Versus Federal Power

The case of California's Proposition 187, limiting the rights of immigrants to the state, provides a classic illustration of the tension that can arise between state and federal powers over questions of policies affecting children and families. In November 1994, California residents voted Proposition 187 into law. The measure was approved by 58.9 percent of voters and opposed by 41.1 percent. The following day, the constitutionality of Proposition 187 was challenged by four individual defendants in the U.S. District Court governing the Central District of California. By January 1995, Judge Mariana R. Pfaelzer of the district court had issued a preliminary injunction against the proposition, and within a month the state of California had filed a motion asking the district court to abstain from the cases or to dismiss them *on the grounds that they should be adjudicated in state courts.* This motion was subsequently denied by Judge Pfaelzer.

As of this writing, Proposition 187 has been tied up in court since its passage, although its major provisions were thrown out by the court in 1985 on the grounds that "immigration is 'unquestionably, exclusively, a federal power' " (Siskind, 1995). Other states, among which Florida is one of the most prominent, have sought to recoup funds from the federal government for providing social services to immigrant residents. The tension between states and the federal government, both of whom want regulatory jurisdiction over education, health care, and other services and policies for immigrants without having to bear the costs, will continue to fuel debate for years, if not decades.

Attempts to curtail the privileges that were freely granted to immigrants in earlier periods of history have also been considered at the federal level (Siskind, 1995). During the 1996 discussions of the Omnibus Consolidated Appropriations Act of 1997, the House of Representatives passed the Gallegly amendment, which was designed to keep illegal immigrant children out of the public schools. The amendment was omitted from the final immigration bill passed by Congress, but if it had passed it would have been in complete contradiction to the provisions of the Supreme Court decision in *Plyer v. Doe* (1982), in which the Supreme Court held that free public education could not be withheld from undocumented children.

The Personal Responsibility and Work Opportunity Reconciliation Act (PL 104-193), signed into law in 1996 by President Clinton in an effort to reform U.S. welfare policy, has also had a significant negative effect on both undocumented and legal immigrants. The law would prevent legal aliens, including children, from receiving Supplementary Security Income or food stamps. Upon his re-election, President Clinton offered to reconsider these limitations, but as of this writing the debate continues.

Some citizens object to immigrants partly because they believe that the children of immigrants deplete the resources of the local schools by requiring instruction in English and might decrease the overall achievement scores of the school district (American Immigration Law Foundation, 1998). Research, however, shows that like previous generations of immigrants, assimilation is still a goal for many recent immigrants, but only in economic terms and not so much on cultural terms (Baker, 1995). Immigrants want to succeed in American society and many learn English to do so, but culturally they will remain part of their ethnic group.

The cost of helping immigrant or non-English-speaking children succeed within America's educational system is relatively low. In 1996, approximately $188 million of the U.S. Department of Education budget was set aside for bilingual/immigrant education programs. This amount was less than 1 percent of the total dollars appropriated for the U.S. Department of Education.

In its report on the contributions of immigrant children, the American Immigration Law Foundation (1996) cites anecdotal evidence that, in fact, immigrant children excel in school and their achievements raise the standards for other children in the community. The foundation concludes:

> Depending on the local areas, immigrant children either help bolster an otherwise declining population, which could help justify previous capital improvement, or they increase the number of students and may lead to more schools being built. These costs are borne by society in the short-term, while in the long-term society gains significantly by educating these children. It is these long-term benefits that must be kept in mind (p. 74).

THE SCHOOLING OF IMMIGRANT AND NON-ENGLISH-SPEAKING CHILDREN

Immigrant children face many changes in their lives when they enter the United States. Often one of their most pressing needs is to learn English so that they can continue with or begin their education. In the past decade the number of students speaking languages other than English—including Spanish, Vietnamese, Hmong, and Cantonese—has increased by more than 100 percent (Fleischman & Hopstock, 1993).

The U.S. Department of Education estimates that approximately 2.8 million U.S. elementary and secondary school students have limited English proficiency (Christian, 1995). These students have difficulties understanding instruction provided only in English and, therefore, require additional assistance. The federal government helps state and local school districts address the educational needs of limited-English-proficient (LEP) or **English as a Second Language** (ESL) students by providing federal funds that allow schools to develop bilingual education programs. *Bilingual education* is an umbrella term for various types of educational programs that have a long history within the American educational system.

Bilingual Education

The Bilingual Education Act (BEA), enacted in 1968 as Title VII of the Elementary and Secondary Education Act of 1965 (PL 90-247), authorized the use of federal funds for the education of students speaking limited English. The main aim of the BEA was to aid students in their transition from their native language to English (Baker, 1996; August, 1986). Initially there were no attempts to encourage non-English-speaking students to retain their native languages. The 1974 amendments to the act addressed the issue of maintenance of the native language by requiring schools receiving funds to include teaching in a student's native language.

Simultaneously with the enactment of the 1974 BEA amendments, the Supreme Court proclaimed similar sentiments in supporting maintenance programs in a monumental case in the bilingual education movement, *Lau v. Nichols* (1974). The case discussed whether limited-English-proficient students receiving schooling in a language they could not understand were, in fact, being exposed to equal educational opportunities as compared with English-speaking children. The verdict held that public schools had to provide limited-English-proficient students with an education they were able to understand. The decision further outlawed programs in which students were instructed solely in English and resulted in the implementation of "Lau remedies" (Baker, 1996). These remedies provided for the teaching of courses like math and science in the student's native language while she or he learned English-language skills. (These "Lau remedies" were later rescinded by the Reagan administration and do not presently have the force of law.)

With respect to the history of bilingual education, the United States is still making policy and displaying public attitudes corresponding to what Baker (1996) calls a "dismissive" period in bilingual education. Requirements for BEA Title VII funds specify that grants could not be utilized for programs that helped children maintain their native languages. Furthermore, the 1984 and 1988 amendments to the BEA created increases in funding only for programs where students were instructed in English and not in their first languages. By law, every federally funded bilingual education program must include a strong English instruction component. The variety of bilingual education programs that exist differ primarily in the amount and duration of use of English for instruction as well as the length of time students participate in each program (Ramirez, Yuen, & Ramey, 1991). The public debate over bilingual education runs high, and a number of prominent political figures have opposed it (Roman, 1998).

Immersion Strategy Programs

Immersion programs require students to jump right into classes alongside majority-language students; all instruction in an immersion program is provided in English and the native language is used only to clarify English instructions. Children who begin an immersion program in kindergarten are expected to be ready to enter the regular classroom—to be mainstreamed—after first or second grade.

Early-Exit and Late-Exit Transitional Programs

The greatest portion of federal Title VII funds are provided to transitional programs (Baker, 1996). In transition programs students are taught in their native language until they acquire rudimentary English-language skills. In early-exit pro-

The History of Bilingual Education

The history of bilingual education can be divided into four distinct periods characterized by the level of acceptance that policies have had toward the native language of children (Baker, 1996):

THE PERMISSIVE ERA

The permissive period in the history of bilingual education spanned the eighteenth and nineteenth centuries and was characterized by the widespread public acceptance of languages other than English. Many U.S. communities of German immigrants, for instance, were able to establish German-English schools, in which half of the curriculum was taught in German and the other half was taught in English.

THE RESTRICTIVE ERA

Roughly between the 1900s and the 1960s, bilingual education was repressed. This repression was made explicit in the 1919 decree by the Americanization Department of the U.S. Department of Education that all schools must teach their classes in English. The causes for such attitudes and practices are difficult to determine precisely. It is probable, however, this change in public sentiment, and, accordingly, in policy, derived at least partly from a certain level of xenophobia arising from the foreign wars fought during this time, and the rising level of immigration—often at times when the U.S. economy was depressed and employment opportunities were relatively few.

THE OPPORTUNIST ERA

The third period in the history of bilingual education, characterized by a broadening of opportunities available to minority groups, reached its prominence with the civil rights movement of the 1960s and 1970s. During this period bilingual education was restored and legislation was enacted that required schools to provide non-English-speaking children access to educational services. The beginning of this period was marked by the establishment of the Coral Way Elementary School in Dade County, Florida, which was a dual-language (Spanish-English) school instituted by Cuban exiles in 1963. The political support received by the Coral Way school seemed contagious as bilingual legislation began to arise around the same time.

THE DISMISSIVE ERA

The late 1970s to the present have been characterized by what Baker (1996) calls a "dismissive" period in bilingual education. In the past two decades there has been a shift away from programs that encourage children's native languages, and an emphasis among certain conservative groups on formally declaring English the official language of the United States. In 1978, Congress authorized bilingual programs to give instruction in the student's native language only when it was absolutely necessary to help the child achieve competence in English.

grams the child receives instruction in his or her native language for an average of thirty to sixty minutes per day. However, instruction in the native language is phased out over a two-year period. In contrast, in late-exit programs, students receive a minimum of 40 percent of their instruction in the native language and may stay in the program until the sixth grade, regardless of when the student becomes fluent in English (Ramirez & Merino, 1990; Ramirez, Yuen, & Ramey, 1991).

The Effectiveness of Bilingual Education

Many have claimed that students in bilingual programs never catch up with their English-speaking peers (English First, 1994). Most research, however, demonstrates the effectiveness of bilingual education. In the most recent national longitudinal study of bilingual education, Ramirez, Yuen, and Ramey (1991) compared immersion programs with early- and late-exit transitional programs focusing on Spanish-speaking students. Their results indicate that by the end of the third grade there were few differences among the students of the three groups. Research shows that during the early grades, regardless of the type of bilingual program a child is admitted to, classroom activities tend to be teacher-directed and that questions typically involve low-level requests for recall information rather than cognitively demanding requests requiring critical thinking.

Critics of bilingual education point to such research—apparently demonstrations that children in all three types of programs learn English at the same rates—as they argue against the funding and implementation of bilingual education programs. By the sixth grade, however, late-exit transitional students were performing at higher levels in mathematics, English language arts, and English reading than students in the other two types of programs. The authors concluded that instructing minority-language students in their native language does not impede their acquisition of the English language, but rather helps them to reach the achievement levels obtained by their English-speaking peers. Students in immersion programs did not learn English language skills more quickly than their peers, and they might have fallen behind (Ramirez, Yuen, & Ramey, 1991).

Despite these findings, the debate about how best to educate language-minority students will continue, especially because there is still widespread belief that language-minority students are failing to learn. For example, according to Headden (1995),

> bilingual education has emerged as one of the dark spots on the grim tableau of American public education . . . it cannot promise that students will learn English and may actually do some children more harm than good. (p. 44)

There are multiple reasons why language-minority children might be struggling. First, there is a lack of well-trained bilingual teachers. Furthermore, bilingual programs are not consistent across the board. Some students in transition programs receive English lessons three hours a day, five days a week; others receive 30 minutes of instruction a day for only three days a week. Some critics have pointed out that much of what passes for bilingual education in schools teaches neither language very well, and essentially segregates ESL children from their English-proficient peers (Education Week, 1998; Netkin, 1997).

Other Approaches

The primary reason schools are finding it difficult to address the needs of immigrant children is simply that they have been unable to keep up with the demand for services. The immigrant population in many school districts increases at a rate that outpaces the availability of services for language minority students. To help address this problem, in 1988 Congress passed the Emergency Immigration Education Act (EIEA) to provide funds to local school districts experiencing large influxes of immigrants. Monies provided through the EIEA were to be used to develop special educational programs specifically for immigrant children. However, the appropriations for this act have been reduced or held constant at $30 million a year instead of increasing as greater numbers of immigrants and refugees enter the United States. EIEA funds are granted to 529 school districts where 85 percent of language-minority students in the United States are located (Morra, 1994).

Immigrant and limited-English-proficient (LEP) students are also supposed to benefit from supplementary educational services offered through Chapter 1 of the Educational Consolidation and Improvement Act. **Chapter 1** is the largest federal program to provide school districts with funds to serve poor and educationally disadvantaged students. Although many immigrant and LEP students qualify as both economically and educationally disadvantaged, overall only 35 percent of the nation's LEP students currently receive Chapter 1 services (Fix & Zimmerman, 1993). Furthermore, Fix and Zimmerman (1993) note that 12 out of 31 states reported that no Chapter 1 services are provided to their eligible LEP population. The two main barriers to gaining greater access to the LEP population are the mistaken beliefs that bilingual programs and ESL are substitutes for Chapter 1 services and that Chapter 1 services should be delivered only in English. Fix and Zimmerman (1993) recommend that the eligibility requirements for Chapter 1 services be clarified and that services and outcomes for LEP students be monitored to help LEP students gain access to Chapter 1 services.

Ironically, when California voters approved Proposition 227 in 1998, essentially eliminating bilingual education from their state's schools, they may have opened a loophole that will finally put to rest many of the anti-immigrant provisions of Proposition 187: The English-only proposition states, in part, "the public schools of California have a moral obligation and a constitutional duty to provide all of California's children, regardless of their ethnicity or national origins, with the skills necessary to become productive members of our society" (Favish, 1998).

THE SCHOOLING OF AFRICAN AMERICANS

During the nineteenth century, while schools welcomed immigrants from distant shores and promised to provide "a unifying influence of common learning" that would help immigrants become full members of American society, the education of African Americans at worst was ignored and at best took place in segregated schools (Tyack, 1974). Although all citizens, including blacks, believed that education held an "equalizing" and "democratic promise" (Tyack, 1974), throughout the country white and black children attended different schools. In the South, laws specifically prohibited school integration. In northern states, school **segregation** existed *de facto.* Although no laws prohibited integrated northern schools, schools tended to enroll students residing in the immediate neighborhood, and the differing residential patterns for blacks and whites resulted in segregated schools. Across the two educational systems—one white, the other black—the quality of and expenditures in educational resources varied widely. Black students attended schools in broken-down houses and abandoned white schools. Equality of educational opportunity was not a primary concern of most educators until the middle of the twentieth century (Kirp, 1995).

The Brown *Decision*

Unlike the schooling of turn-of-the-century immigrant children, which did not require the development or implementation of any state or federal policy, education for blacks disturbed local and national politics and required a significant amount of federal intervention (Fass, 1988). In 1954, the United States Supreme Court determined, in *Brown v. Board of Education,* that black children, like their immigrant peers, required the education that "is the very foundation of a good citizen" (*Brown v. Board of Education,* 1954).

Brown v. Board of Education centered around the complaint of a black third-grader named Linda Brown, who had to walk one mile, crossing a railroad track, to attend a black elementary school in Topeka, Kansas, even though a white elementary school was only seven blocks from her house. When the white elementary school refused to enroll Linda, Oliver Brown, Linda's father, along with the National Association for the Advancement of Colored People (NAACP), brought an injunction against Topeka's public schools.

In hearings before the U.S. District Court for the District of Kansas, the NAACP argued that segregated schools led black children to believe that they were somehow inferior to whites and that, therefore, the curriculum provided to blacks even in black school could not be equal to that offered to whites. Although the district court agreed that "segregation of white and colored children in public schools has a detrimental effect upon the colored children" and that "A sense of inferiority affects the motivation of a child to learn," it ruled in favor of the Topeka Board of Education.

Brown and the NAACP appealed to the U.S. Supreme Court, where the case was combined with other cases that challenged segregation in South Carolina, Virginia, and Delaware. On May 17, 1954, in a unanimous decision the Supreme Court ruled that:

> Segregation of white and colored children in public schools has a detrimental effect upon the colored children. The impact is greater when it has the sanction of law, for the policy of separating the races is usually interpreted as denoting the inferiority of the Negro group. A sense of inferiority affects the motivation of a child to learn. Segregation with the sanction of law, therefore, has a tendency to [retard] the educational and mental development of Negro children and to deprive them of the benefits they would receive in a racially integrated school system. . . . We conclude that in the field of public education, the doctrine of "separate but equal" has no place. Separate educational facilities are inherently unequal (*Brown v. Board of Education,* 1954).

The Effectiveness of National Desegregation Policies

In principle, the 1954 **desegregation** decision attacked at least two core issues. First, the court decision was based on the assumption that schools should not adversely affect the social and emotional development of children; separate schools were deemed to be detrimental because they led black students to feel a sense of inferiority that lowered their self-esteem and motivation. Second, a system of separate schools was judged to be troublesome because it inherently resulted in the unequal distribution of resources across white and black schools.

Forty-one years after the Brown decision, school systems across the United States continue to struggle with these issues. Questions about how to best help black and other minority students develop positive self-esteem and how to ensure that all children have access to high-quality school buildings, teachers, and other educational resources still dominate current discussions about education. *Brown v. Board of Education* opened the dialogue, but it did not solve the problem. Since this landmark decision, desegregated public schools have had mixed success in fostering effective education for African American and many ethnically diverse students.

In the past 40 years, African Americans have made significant educational progress. Larger numbers of blacks have completed high school, enrolled in college, and obtained degrees from traditionally white universities. These accomplishments, however, are overshadowed by statistics that show a continued gap between black and white achievement. College graduation rates for African Americans doubled between 1965 and 1989, but blacks are only half as likely as whites to finish their college education and receive their degrees (Children's Defense Fund, 1993). Between the 1970s and 1990, African American students made significant progress in math and reading scores. However, after many years of progress, results of the National Assessment of Educational Progress suggest that black and other minority students are beginning to fall farther behind their white peers. In 1969, 17-year-old African Americans scored 54 points below whites on science tests. By 1986 they had narrowed the gap by 45 points, but in 1994 it once again increased to 49 points below that of white students. Similar results were also found in mathematics. The difference between black and white scores was 40 points in 1973, 21 points in 1990, and grew to 27 points in 1994 (Applebome, 1996). In scores for writing, the gap between black and white eighth-graders grew to 27 points in 1994 from 25 points in 1984.

Differences in the educational attainment of black and white students have been attributed to a variety of factors, including continued underfunding of the urban schools, where black and minority students are concentrated; teachers' limited expectations for black students; cultural bias in teaching methods; and ability grouping practices (tracking) that place disproportionate numbers of black children in low-level, unchallenging courses.

Some educators and commentators have argued that the policies that emerged since the *Brown* decision created new problems for school systems throughout America, which have themselves contributed to the continued underachievement among African Americans. For instance, although many school districts moved quickly to undo segregation laws following the *Brown* decision, they still continued to struggle with desegregation that occurred due to differential residential patterns of white and black residents. To rectify this type of desegregation, many school systems instituted the practice of busing children to schools located outside of their own neighborhoods. Under busing plans, some white students were transported to schools located in predominantly black neighborhoods, and some black students were bused to schools located in predominantly white neighborhoods. Many school systems saw busing as the only way to deal with the problems created by the concentration of whites in suburbs and of blacks in the larger urban areas and cities.

Most of the original opposition to busing as a means of desegregating schools came from whites. In recent years, however, many black community leaders have also come to oppose busing and desegregation rules because they feel that the restructuring of schools that occurs under desegregation plans leads to the breakdown of connections between the community and the school. They argue that, prior to desegregation, black students attended schools operated by black teachers and administrators who had high expectations for the children and who served as positive role models for the students (Collins, 1979). These schools also maintained close connections with the children and their families, and thus there were fewer differences between what children knew was expected of them at home and what was expected in school.

Innovative Forms of Desegregation

Many communities in states throughout the nation have begun to bring 20- and 30-year-old busing plans to an end (Lilly, 1996). Citing the failure of busing to bring about significant community integration, the high costs, and the loss of community schools, schools in virtually every part of the country are working on plans in which school busing would be replaced with alternative approaches to desegregation (Aschler, 1996; Weiler, 1997).

Magnet Schools

The concept of magnet schools first surfaced in the late 1960s as an alternative to busing. Although many African American students have benefited from magnet schools, magnet schools were originally intended to specifically attract white parents and their children to public schools and to halt the emerging trend of white flight from majority black school districts. Magnet schools were designed to promote desegregation and to enhance the quality of education for urban children by offering specialized curriculum in arts, sciences, mathematics, or any other academic area. Magnet schools also attempt to introduce innovative curricula and instructional approaches that have been proven to be successful with urban children.

Some magnet schools exhibit successful integration precisely because the staff, volunteer parents, etc. share a common goal in trying an innovation and committing themselves to fostering positive racial relationships. In fact, racial and social diversity is often greater in magnet schools than in many other types of schools (Metz, 1994). Critics of magnet schools, however, point out that magnet schools may no longer be an effective desegregation tool because they are not attracting a sufficient number of white students. Under court-mandated desegregation guidelines, school minority enrollment can not exceed 80 percent or fall below 10 percent.

Afrocentric Curricula and Black-Only Schools

Another recent educational alternative, the most controversial local-level attempt to increase achievement among African Americans, calls for the creation of black-only or African American immersion schools.

Many teachers and school board members argue that traditional educational methods fail African American children, particularly African American boys. They argue for African American schools with more male teachers and an Afrocentric curricula. More than 20 U.S. school districts have begun to implement Afrocentric curricula with positive results (Narine, 1992). For example, the graduates of the Shule Mandela Academy in East Palo Alto, California, who pledge each morning to "think black, act black, speak black, buy black, pray black, love black, and live black," are the only blacks in the local high school's advanced placement classes (Barrientos, 1991).

At the African American Immersion Schools in Milwaukee, students are engaged in an Afrocentric educational experience, meet with a mentor once a week, and attend special classes on Saturdays focusing on such things as values, respect, manners, and how to behave in certain social situations. Because the program is still very young, only anecdotal evidence is available regarding the success of the program. These results suggest that students in these programs are more eager to learn and exhibit increased self-esteem (Narine, 1992).

Critics of Afrocentrism argue that adopting such a curriculum further exacerbates racial tensions, that it does not prepare African Americans for living in the multiracial world, and that it cannot be adopted in settings with various groups of minority students. However, an important lesson can be drawn from schools that embrace Afrocentrism. The dedicated teachers and principals are creating an environment that stresses achievement-oriented learning, and students do learn in this milieu and do raise their performances on standardized tests (Biggs, 1992).

Sister Schools and Event-Based Desegregation

In some communities, the threat of renewed school busing has prompted a new approach to desegregation. Individual schools in mostly white areas are paired with sister schools from areas in which most of the students are members of a minority group. Students at the sister schools are brought together through a variety of events, including pen-pal programs, visits to one another's schools, and shared field trips or cultural events outings. Though such programs might bring children together in ways that forced busing has not, and though they might be less threatening to those who oppose busing, critics argue that such an approach does little, if anything, to achieve more equal educational opportunities like those sought in the original *Brown* case.

THE SCHOOLING OF HOMELESS CHILDREN

Regardless of their ethnic or racial background, homeless children are one of the most difficult groups in society to provide with educational services. They face multiple legal barriers within the school system as well as other logistical barriers, such as lack of transportation. The population of homeless youth is increasing, and it is estimated that 1 out of 3 homeless children does not attend school when homeless (Bassuk, 1988). Therefore, there is concern about homeless children's development and academic achievement.

Homelessness often contributes to developmental delays, emotional problems, poor school attendance, and low academic achievement in school-age children. Multiple studies have reported developmental delays in language development, gross and fine motor coordination, and personal and social development among preschool children living in shelters (Bassuk, 1988). A **developmental delay** is defined as the inability to complete a task that 90 percent of one's age peers are able to master. In a 1988 study, Bassuk and her colleagues assessed the developmental ability of 81 children (5 years old or younger) living in shelters in Massachusetts. They found that 47 percent of the children displayed at least one developmental lag, 33 percent had two or more, and 14 percent failed in all four areas. More than one-third of the children also demonstrated language delays and 34 percent could not complete the personal and social developmental tasks (Bassuk, Rubin, & Lauriat, 1986).

In older homeless children, low academic achievement is prevalent. In a study of homeless youth in New York, Shaffer and Caton (1984) found that 55 percent of the boys and 47 percent of the girls had repeated a grade, 59 percent of the boys and 54 percent of the girls were more than one standard deviation behind other students in their reading achievement test scores, 16 percent of the boys and 10 percent of the girls were functionally illiterate reading at the fourth-grade level, and 71 percent of the boys and 44 percent of the girls had at one time been suspended or expelled from school. Besides repeating grades and not scoring well on achievement tests, 28 percent of homeless children are placed into special or remedial classes (Wood et al., 1990a).

The federal government has attempted to grant educational assistance to homeless children through legislation. One such law is the Runaway and Homeless Youth Act (HR 1801), which was amended and incorporated into the Anti-Drug Abuse Act of 1988 (PL 100-690). The RHYA initially provided short-term shelters, with food and clothing assistance, for homeless youth ages 16 and older. In its amended form, the RHYA created the **Transitional Living Grant Program** for Homeless Youth to help older youth enter into self-sufficient living situations. This program also provides assistance with education and employment training. The RHYA is one of few initiatives focusing on adolescents. Few states have developed programs and services targeting the education of homeless youth after the eighth grade (Zeldin & Bogart, 1990).

The major law addressing the educational needs of homeless children in America is the Stewart B. McKinney Homeless Assistance Act of 1987 (PL 100-77) and its 1990 amendments (PL 101-645). The original McKinney Act provided for grants to ensure access to public education for homeless children through requiring states to review and revise their residency requirements, through the establishment of an office of the Coordinator of Education of Homeless Children and Youth in each state, and through directing the grant monies to programs that successfully address the needs of homeless elementary children. Although noble in its attempt to guarantee access to education for homeless children, it was determined that by the end of 1989 three-fifths of the states were not complying with the law (Children's Defense Fund, 1991) and that none of the granted monies were actually reaching the children (Anderson, 1995).

Legal Barriers to Educating Homeless Children

To understand the implications of the 1990 amendments to the McKinney Act, it is necessary to discuss some of the legal barriers to education for homeless youth and children. Many states prior to 1987 had clauses in their attendance laws specifying that a child would have access to schools in the district where the child's parents reside. Also, many states prohibit the enrollment of students who move into a district without their parents. These requirements are problematic to homeless families because (1) families who move to temporary shelters in other districts are not considered residents of either their previous district or the new one because they have not established permanent residency in the district where they currently are, and (2) homeless families often are split up among two or more residences as children are sent to live with relatives or to other shelters. It follows that another barrier is guardianship requirements. Students must be registered by either parents or official guardians designated by parents or states. Often the relatives with whom homeless children are residing do not qualify as guardians.

A third barrier concerns immunization requirements. Most states mandate that students present immunization records prior to admission to schools. In homeless families, parents might not be aware of immunization requirements, they might not be able to finance immunizations, they might have difficulty contacting physicians, and previously attended schools might be slow in processing school record requests. Lack of availability of records, including not only immunization records but also birth certificates and school records, can also be a barrier to school attendance for homeless children. The logistics involved in obtaining and maintaining records can be extremely daunting for homeless parents. Lastly, transportation has been recognized as a major hindrance to school attendance. Often homeless parents cannot afford to take their children to school, and many students remain away from schools due to delays in receiving city-funded transit passes.

Stewart B. McKinney Homeless Assistance Act
1990 Amendments

The original 1987 McKinney Act highlighted only residency requirements as a barrier to school access for homeless children that needed revision. The 1990 amendments require each state to:

> address problems with respect to the education of homeless children and homeless youths, including problems caused by (I) transportation issues; and (ii) enrollment delays which are caused by (I) immunization requirements; (II) residency requirements; (III) lack of birth certificates, school records, or other documentation; or (IV) guardianship issues. (PL 101-645 Sec. 612 [b] [8] [G])

The amendment further mandates local educational agencies receiving grants to help defray the costs of transportation for homeless students.

Provisions to ensure that the grant funding is actually given to programs that are directly helping the homeless students are also included in the amendments. For example, the following paragraph was inserted into the original 1987 document under Authorized Activities:

> Grants under this section shall be used . . . (2) to provide activities for and services to homeless children and homeless youths that enable such children and youths to enroll in, attend, and achieve success in school. (PL 101-645, Sec. 612 [b] [3] [B])

The amendment more specifically suggests the provision of early childhood programs that are developmentally appropriate as well as the provision of programs for homeless students before and after school where teachers and qualified individuals are available to provide homework assistance and other supervision of educational activities. These guidelines found in the amendments are much more specific and forceful than the vague clauses found in the initial McKinney Act.

Evaluators have noted positive advances in state and local initiatives to help homeless students after the passage of the McKinney Amendments in 1990. Almost all states have revised their laws, regulations, and policies concerning access to schools (Anderson, 1995). Many schools have eased or waived residency and guardianship requirements. Immunization requirements are addressed as many schools arrange for health examinations for students or on-site immunizations prior to enrollment. School staffs have learned to speed up the integration of homeless students by expediting transportation arrangements and access to records. The collaboration of state and local agencies has further hastened the enrollment process. For example, the Texas Office of Assistance to Homeless Children created a database that allows schools to get information on homeless children from a central source (Eddies, 1992).

Program evaluation also suggests that local educational agencies are appropriating their funds to before- and after-school tutorial and homework assistance programs, to initiatives that address the need for school supplies, clothing, and transportation, to awareness raising, to local projects that provide support services to address the special needs of homeless youth, and to alternative school programs. Two alternative schooling programs for which McKinney funds may be utilized are transitional schools and case management approaches. Transitional schools provide short-term intensive and individualized on-site schooling at a shelter or transitional housing facility before children are mainstreamed into the regular school system. Often these schools are run similarly to a one-room schoolhouse, with many children in different grades in the same room. At some regular schools homeless children attend a transitional room before classes begin.

Proponents of separate schools suggest that homeless children need individual attention in a safe setting. However, critics of transitional schools are wary of increases in the stigmatization of homeless children as well as limiting the children's educational opportunities by preventing access to programs such as Chapter 1 and bilingual education programs. These schools also do not follow a prescribed curriculum, and the children remain isolated and experience little educational continuity because their placements are temporary. The second approach to educating homeless children in the public schools is the case management approach, where a case manager works to bring together school staff, counselors, and health and family support services to make sure that children's basic needs are met.

A unique school that houses both a transitional school, First Place, and a case management program, Kids Organized on Learning in School (KOOL-IS), is Seattle's B. F. Day Elementary School, which serves only homeless children. Its uniqueness also stems from its pedagogical approach: homeless students benefit from constant attention to the requirements of their situation. (Quint, 1994) Homeless children are often tired and distracted, thus teachers at the B. F. Day School constantly explain the need to master tasks, encourage their students to ask questions, and engage in much one-on-one teaching and cooperative learning. The school is open early before class and late into the evening. It provides after-school tutoring as well as three meals a day, storage space for personal belongings, clothing, personal hygiene items, and bathing facilities. There is substantial anecdotal evidence of the success of B. F. Day's program, but the expense of maintaining the program is a constant threat to its continued existence (Schwartz, 1995).

The McKinney Homeless Assistance Amendments of 1990 have been influential in improving homeless children's access to education. States are revising their laws and implementing programs to help educate homeless children. However, many issues still need to be addressed. Homeless children still experience difficulty in entering specific educational programs such as Head Start, Chapter 1, and gifted and talented programs. Transportation is still a major barrier to obtaining any educational services. Also there is extreme unevenness between services provided in different districts of the same state. Lastly, states can do more to promote collaboration between state and local agencies.

SUMMARY

In the twenty-first century, white Americans will become a minority group as nonwhite ethnic minority populations swell in numbers. In particular, increases in the number of Hispanic and Asian immigrants—whose children are responsible for close to 80 percent of the recent growth in student numbers—have resulted in changes to the demographic picture of the American child. Over one-third of students in U.S. schools today are nonwhite.

Even so, policies and practices focused on providing culturally appropriate education to these children are slow in changing. Attitudes toward immigrants, and, indeed, among immigrants themselves, have shifted since the days of the nineteenth and early twentieth centuries, when a "melting pot" ethos prevailed. Families and individuals alike still come to the United States seeking educational and economic opportunities, but few these days wish for the cultural assimilation once expected of immigrants. Instead, individual groups strive to retain their cultural identities while still becoming uniquely American.

Such diversity holds the promise of both strength and cultural richness for the United States, but policies and practices related to the provision of educational and other services for immigrants have been, at best, slow to change. Some legislation has overtly created impediments barring immigrants from participation in the offerings of our rich society. Attitudes toward immigration have turned markedly negative as immigration has increased in the last decade. States that have traditionally been witting or unwitting gateways to immigration have led the movement against these newcomers: California residents overwhelmingly passed Proposition 187, which severely restricted public provision of education and medical treatment for illegal immigrants. Other states, most notably Florida, wrangled with the federal government over responsibility for funding immigrant services. In 1996, a key provision of the welfare reform legislation passed under President Clinton proposed barring even legal immigrants or their children from receiving food stamps or Supplemental Security Income.

One of the most sensitive issues related to these demographic changes has to do with the debate over whether children should be educated in their native language or the most commonly spoken language of their new home: English. The debate over bilingual education is decades old. Initially, the most common bilingual education strategy was complete immersion in English-only instruction. A 1974 Supreme Court case, *Lau v. Nichols,* however, successfully challenged the idea that such an education could be equal under the law for the non-native speaker of English. In the wake of this decision, so-called "Lau remedies" permitted children to be instructed in many subjects in their native language. These rules were disallowed by the Reagan administration, however, and many educational systems returned to a more immersion-like program of instruction. In other cases, children were exposed to programs in which minimal initial use of the child's native language is quickly phased out in favor of English-only education.

Evaluations of various forms of bilingual education appear to indicate that, initially, there is little difference in outcome for students in immersion versus transitional programs. By approximately sixth grade, however, students from certain transitional programs are clearly outperforming immersion-program children, achieving levels of expertise comparable to those of their peers who are native speakers of English. Whether to permit bilingual education for ESL students, and the form this education should take, continues to be debated among educators, child advocates, and policy makers.

In the 1954 *Brown v. Board of Education* decision, the U.S. Supreme Court ruled that racially segregated schools implicitly provided inadequate and unequal education to the excluded minority-group children. Almost a half century later, the practical implications of this landmark decision are still being debated and provoke controversy. Busing to forcibly achieve integration, the introduction of magnet schools to encourage integration, even the promotion of black-only schools with Afrocentric curricula as an alternative to desegregation have all been studied and practiced. Again, debate on this issue is likely to continue well into the twenty-first century.

In addition to these issues, concerns over how best to meet the needs of homeless children, who are the fastest growing segment of the U.S. homeless population, and the children of migrant workers, continue to plague advocates and legislatures. These emotionally charged issues are unlikely to be settled soon, or easily, and the implications of decisions reached are certain to be profound and long-lasting.

Making Schools Work

Elizabeth Gilman

Open just about any newspaper today, or tune in virtually any radio or television news program, and the topic of public education in the United States is bound to arise. U.S. public schools currently are the focus of deepening concern and debate among educators, parents, school administrators, and public officials. There is widespread opinion that schools today are in a state of crisis, but even this point is debated. It is easy to imagine that controversy about schooling is a recent phenomenon, but disagreement about virtually every facet of public schooling has a venerable history. The current school "crisis" is really one episode in a sequence of upheavals that extends back as far as the institution of public schooling in America itself.

ARE U.S. SCHOOLS IN TROUBLE?

Facts about public education in the United States form a familiar litany of bad news. Nearly 1 million students a year—the equivalent of more than 5,500 every schoolday—drop out of school before completing the twelfth grade (Children's Defense Fund, 1998g; National Center for Education Statistics, 1994a). In some cities, almost 60 percent of students who start high school drop out before graduation (Kozol, 1991). And rates of school leaving are far from uniform across ethnic groups—the percentage of Hispanic students who dropped out of school in 1993, for instance, was more than twice the percentage of white students who did so (U.S. Department of Education, 1994) (see table 10.1). Income level plays a role as well: High-income black students, for instance, are almost 4 times more likely to complete high school than are low-income black students, a quarter of whom drop out (Children's Defense Fund, 1995).

Even students still officially enrolled in school are not always present and do not always perform at grade level. Approximately 10 percent of fifth- and sixth-graders in Chicago's public schools are absent for all but a handful of days every month, leading one author to call these children "de facto dropouts" (Kozol, 1991). Critics have argued that even those children who do attend school frequently are not being educated properly. On average, over one-third of twelfth-grade students read below a basic proficiency level. Breaking this figure down by ethnicity reveals that figures for ethnic and minority groups are disproportionately low. Almost one-half of black and Native American children,

TABLE 10.1. Percentage of Students Graduating from High School,* by Race

	1973	1995
Blacks	64.1	86.8
Whites	84.0	92.5
Hispanics	52.3	57.2
Total	80.2	86.9

*Or receiving graduate equivalency degree
Source: Children's Defense Fund, 1998g, p. 88.

for instance, are reading below the basic level for their grade (Children's Defense Fund, 1995). High school graduates of all ethnic groups are often poorly prepared either to assume the workload of college courses or to become competent employees. Diane Ravitch, formerly assistant secretary of educational research at the U.S. Department of Education, has brought together data from numerous sources describing the current state of educational achievement. In her recent book, *National Standards in American Education* (1995), she marshals a considerable body of evidence to conclude that the system as a whole is very much in a critical condition.

Negative trends like these translate into calculable losses, in terms of lost wages and taxes, of over $240 billion annually, a figure that would be billions of dollars higher if money spent on social services related to educational deficits, such as crime, welfare, and health care, were factored in. Human losses associated with these figures—loss of opportunity, loss of self-esteem, loss of life satisfaction—are incalculable.

Is There a "School System"?

In the United States today, public education takes place in approximately 85,000 primary and secondary schools in some 15,000 school districts. Although federal oversight for education programs resides with the U.S. Department of Education, U.S. schools are administered almost entirely at the state, city, district, or—as is increasingly the case—even the individual school level. Rather than being part of an essential national structure, schools in the United States resemble a crazy quilt of tiny, self-governed districts characteristic of earlier times. Early in the twentieth century, there were about 150,000 public school districts (Berliner & Biddle, 1995), so today's 15,000 at least shows some consolidation. Yet a student who moves from one state to another, or even one city to another, will find that students in the new school often are performing at a different level and working on vastly different material. This situation led the late Albert Shanker of the American Federation of Teachers to comment that our "nonsystem" makes what children learn a function of where they live.

Indeed, although we speak of "the school system," there is actually no such cohesive network (Mosle, 1996a, 1996c), and any claims, positive or negative, about the educational system as a whole can only be an imprecise generalization. In the lack of continuity and lack of systematic integrity in our educational system, the United States contrasts with most European nations, which typically have a central education ministry charged with developing and enforcing the curriculum, code of regulations, and day-to-day operations of all the schools in that country. Educational standards, teacher training, curriculum, and budgetary matters are all administered by this national body. Such a system obviates many of the difficulties that exist for U.S. schools—fragmentation, variation in curriculum and school quality, continual local debate, and concerns about unequal educational opportunity.

In spite of the decentralization and heterogeneity in U.S. schooling, commentators on education persist in analyzing the workings of American pedagogy as if it were a unitary entity, and many of their conclusions are discouraging. Critics of the way children are taught in the United States describe public education with a litany of alarming statistics: Poor educational performance, high rates of violent crime, a lack of material resources, and disparity among the performance of ethnic groups are among the problems cited. Virtually any discussion of education in the United States has come to include such serious and controversial difficulties.

National Assessment Measures

The federally administered National Assessment of Educational Progress (NAEP) has monitored the country's educational achievement for some 30 years. It regularly tests student competence in four areas: reading, writing, math, and science. The NAEP is considered a valuable measure because its testing and scoring methods have remained consistent over many years. Its scoring focuses on skills, rather than on the factual knowledge students have accumulated (Steinberg, 1996). Thus the NAEP provides data that are reasonably comparable over time, providing evidence of any changes in average academic achievement (Jones, 1996). The results for 9-, 13-, and 17-year-old students are not generally encouraging, although they do show a narrowing of an achievement gap between white children and black and Hispanic children over the past 20 years.

According to the NAEP, achievement levels increased and the degree of disparity among racial groups decreased steadily throughout the 1970s and 1980s. Had progress in these areas continued at 1980s rates, the gap between black and white students would have been eliminated by 1998. Instead, progress began to slow during the 1990s, in some cases leveling off and in other instances backsliding such that student performance was *worse* by the mid 1990s than it had been during the 1980s. Among high school students, math scores now are no higher than they were in the early 1970s. Current reading scores are higher than 1971 scores but do not exceed 1984 scores. Writing ability was first assessed in 1984; no change has been observed since that time. A comparison of pre-1970 Scholastic Achievement Test (SAT) verbal scores and those of today indicates a significant decline in writing ability (Steinberg, Brown, & Dornbusch, 1996). The NAEP concluded that fewer than 10 percent of high school students can read, write, compute, and manage scientific material at the levels today's knowledge-oriented jobs require (National Center for Education Statistics, 1994b).

Much has been made of a reported overall decline in SAT scores since 1970. Some have claimed that this is because since then the SAT has been taken by a broader cross section of the population, including minority and economically disadvantaged students who might not have aspired to college in the past. Yet the decline in scores appears to affect all social groups; in fact, average minority-student scores have been improving relative to 1970s levels. The fairest way to characterize achievement overall in the last two decades might be to consider it rather stagnant—a rise since the 1980s, but little truly heartening change in recent years. The Goals 2000 report issued in 1996 was far from sanguine: after six years of effort on the national goals, performance was described as "virtually static" (The National Educational Goals Panel, 1996).

The Other Side of the Performance Argument

As noted earlier, for every educational pundit who points out what is wrong with America's school system, another is anxious to demonstrate that things are not as bad as they might seem. In spite of calls for educational reform of almost every variety, evidence of what one scholar calls "slow but steady progress" is readily available (Timpane, 1996). Some specialists on education maintain that the achievement picture is not as grim as a brief look at the statistics indicates. Berliner and Biddle (1995), for instance, assert that negative achievement statistics are often inaccurately calculated or are distorted in ways that mask the very real problems of U.S. schools, such as unequal spending for different social groups, the changing student population, the unchecked growth of bureaucratization, and the multiple tasks schools are asked to perform.

The perception of an SAT "crisis," for example, might derive in part from the little-known fact that the scores on the SAT and other commercial tests are recalibrated every seven years to ensure that the "typical" student scores at the fiftieth-percentile level for each subject area assessed. This recalibration virtually washes out achievement gains of the past several years. Were this not done, the tests would likely show that today's students are in fact performing better than the previous generation (Berliner & Biddle, 1995). Whether or not their figures are correct, these scholars compellingly make the point that the unexamined use of statistical data alone is insufficient for an understanding of the complex issue of school performance.

The position that the United States lags behind other industrialized nations in the provision of educational services (National Center for Education Statistics, 1994a) has been refuted in recent years by those who argue that a greater proportion of the population is educated, and educated for more years, in the United States than in most other nations (Grissmer et al., in press; Mianowaney, 1996; Mullis et al., 1994; Timpane, 1996). A recent report from the Organization for Economic Cooperation and Development (1998) reveals another trend that affects the international standing of U.S. schools. This report indicates, for instance, that in the 1950s the United States shared the top position (with Czechoslovakia and Germany) with respect to high school graduation rates: 80 percent of Americans completed high school. Today, the United States is no longer in first place in graduation of high school students, but is currently tied for third place. The change, however, has less to do with changes in U.S. **demographics** than with improvements in other nations: the U.S. still graduates 80 percent of its high school students, but today at least four other nations (the Czech republic, Norway, Canada, and Finland) have higher graduation rates (Bronner, 1998; Organization for Economic Cooperation, 1998).

Clearly, problems do exist that impede the performance of students in the United States. Scholars of education stress, however, that solutions must be targeted at individual school districts and even individual schools, taking into account the problems and strengths unique to each (Bracey, 1991; Mosle, 1996c). Some of the problems discussed most often are largely associated with schools in urban settings in low-income areas, where 40 percent of American children live; the education debate in this country is centered almost entirely upon issues pertaining to these schools (Berliner & Biddle, 1995; Kozol, 1991; Mosle, 1996a, 1996c). Although most citizens might believe that schools are experiencing difficulties, in many communities people believe this of schools nationally but not of their own local schools. Nevertheless, critics argue forcefully, again and again, that the education system is "broken," that it has "failed" our children, and that it is in serious need of reform.

But is this the whole picture? And who should be responsible for assessing—and repairing, if necessary—the infrastructure of the U.S. public school system? What role is played by policy makers at various levels? What role by teachers and parents? Are schools meant to assume the burden of attempting to remedy all social inequities present in the society as a whole? Are they, moreover, intended to fill the gaps created by the lack of a cohesive national social support system for families and children? Finally, what do we know about the nature of child development and the role played by education that can help us find answers to these questions?

From the very beginning, public education has been the focus not only of pedagogical but of political debate. In this sense, little has changed in the 160 years since the first public schools were opened in the United States. Although the trends and themes in public education change, controversy and conflict are constants. Such conflict might occur in part because the schools have been so heavily weighted with social expectations: often, the schools have been seen as a cure-all for all manner of social ills. Disagreements about the nature of schooling in the United States, the quality thereof, and the debates over the means of protecting, preserving and promoting high-quality educational programs for our children sound the same notes decade after decade. Consider the words of this educator:

> There is no need to add to the criticism of our public schools. The critique is extensive and can hardly be improved on. The process of learning and teaching, too, have been exhaustively studied. . . . The question now is what to do (Dennison, in Mosle, 1996c).

Although they were written more than three decades ago, these might be the concluding words of any scholarly essay written on education today. A glimpse at the history of public education in America reveals why we are still embroiled in debate about schools.

A HISTORICAL LOOK AT PUBLIC SCHOOLS

Until the nineteenth century, the nation's schooling was conducted largely in the private domain. Families or communities with the means hired their own teachers or sent their children to private schools; the poor had to rely on charity schools. The public education movement reflected the growing tendency for functions once handled within the family to be given over to the community; in keeping with this trend, education of children moved from the hearth to the community schoolhouse. With the growth of the public welfare movement in the late nineteenth century, public education was encouraged by those who believed that the poor should have opportunities comparable to those of more fortunate families. Charitable groups provided for the welfare of widows and orphans, especially following the Civil War, and this trend, too, was reflected in the assignment of responsibility for the schooling of children to the government (Gatto in Cozic, 1992, 1994; Jacobs & Davies 1994).

As the nineteenth century progressed, the economy became more dependent on industry. At the turn of the century and into the 1920s, waves of immigrants entering the United States gave rise to the demand for a more uniformly educated and English-speaking workforce. The ability to read, write, and perform mathematical calculations, along with the socialization required of employees in this changing world—the ability, for instance, to arrive at work on time, to work cooperatively with fellow employees, and to respond appropriately to authority figures in these settings—were increasingly important. Compulsory public schooling in the United States was first implemented in the state of Massachusetts in 1836, in part through the efforts of the educator Horace Mann.

By 1865, most states had legislated to create public schools. Direct federal influence in the schools was relatively insignificant until the 1950s, when only about 35 percent of students completed high school (Berliner & Biddle, 1995; "Merrow Report," 1996); the federal contribution to the daily operation of state schools was also limited. When the 1954 Supreme Court decision in *Brown v. Board of Education* declared the segregation of schools by race unconstitutional, the states entered an era of federal influence in school affairs. The states lost a large measure of control over the schools when they were ordered to desegregate, and that control has been further eroded by other factors. In 1957, when the Soviet Union successfully launched Sputnik into space, the United States became concerned about its own space and defense programs and about our children's scientific and mathematical literacy. Despite opinion that the federal government should not determine state school curricula, the National Defense Education Act of 1958 was passed to contribute federal dollars to school math and science programs.

A second wave of federal involvement came about through the War on Poverty in the 1960s. To President Lyndon Johnson, education was the high road out of poverty for America's children, as it had been for him. Project Head Start began during this era, in 1965, and it today remains the largest federal program for preschoolers. In 1965, the Elementary and Secondary Education Act was passed to provide federal aid to impoverished schools. Today, as Title I, this legislation provides schools nationally with about $7 billion in federal funds. At the end of the Johnson administration in 1968, the amount of federal support for education was twice what it is today. At that time, about 12 cents of every education dollar was provided by the federal budget; today, federal support for schools amounts to 6 cents per dollar.

The 1970s brought further federal efforts to desegregate the schools through court-ordered busing. In an effort to remedy discrimination against disabled students, Congress passed the Education for all Handicapped Children Act in 1975, which had a direct effect on the makeup of public school classrooms and the funding and programs states were required to provide for students with disabilities, many of whom had previously been excluded altogether from public schools. In 1979, President Carter created the position of federal Secretary of Education. With the Reagan presidency, the United States began viewing improvements in public education as the means of defeating its economic competitors. After the U.S. Department of Education released *A Nation at Risk* (Bell, 1983), documenting the nation's "mediocre educational performance," fears spread that this shortcoming would ultimately lead to the country's economic downfall. States were urged to raise their educational standards and levels of student achievement so that the United States would become more competitive with other nations.

The *Nation at Risk* report gave rise to an avalanche of other reports, commissions, and policy-related activities designed to improve U.S. schools. The educational debates, policy-making sessions, and welter of new initiatives we are experiencing today can be seen as a continuation of the wave of change brought about by this 1983 report. Indeed, Richard W. Riley, Secretary of Education under the Clinton administration, recently observed that "education is the engine that drives our economy" (Applebome, 1997). The schools are still being asked to take responsibility for the state of the economy, if not the state of national security as in the 1950s. Today's call for a major overhaul of public education and for the formulation of national school standards is very much in keeping with the cry of alarm that was sounded in 1983.

The Era After A Nation at Risk

In the years that followed the publication of *A Nation at Risk* (Bell, 1983), the governors of the 50 states took up the challenge of improving their schools; education again became a top issue on the political agenda. State leadership organized political support, appropriated funds, and crafted legislation to assist the schools. Perceiving that federal support for education was unlikely to increase to former levels, the governors assumed the role of formulating educational policies, with a view toward enhancing the future economic growth of their states. Standards for high school graduation, which will be addressed more fully later in the chapter, became a key issue. By 1985, forty-seven states had increased high school requirements, 44 had created new programs for testing students, and 40 had raised standards for teacher preparation (Timpane, 1996; Doyle, Cooper, & Trachtman, 1991). Educational standards and accountability of school administration were the key elements of these efforts, and the National Governors Association became a major force in educational reform. The governors were joined in this enterprise by strong allies in the business community, which began to mount its own initiatives to strengthen the educational system.

In the late 1980s, President Bush and the governors of all 50 states met at a national conference and developed a program of national goals and standards

("A Jeffersonian Compact," 1989) that eventually evolved into the Bush administration's America 2000 program of educational goals. This program, in turn, became the basis for President Clinton's Goals 2000 plan (Mosle, 1996c; Timpane, 1996). The list of goals paints, in broad strokes, a portrait of many of the ills most frequently cited as plaguing schools and school systems in the United States. The Goals 2000 national initiative is based on a perceived lack of school readiness, a high dropout rate, low academic achievement, inadequately trained teachers, and a learning environment sullied by omnipresent criminal activity. It establishes, among other things, very broad goals for school readiness, literacy levels, graduation rates, and freedom from crime in schools.

Critics have attacked the education goals as being unduly vague and overly ambitious, given the brief span of time between their proposal and the year 2000 deadline. The Goals 2000 program also proposes no means for achieving the desired ends, a fact that has drawn both praise and ire (Rose, in Mosle, 1996a; Timpane, 1996). Instead of dictating solutions to the problems it hopes to ameliorate, Goals 2000 places responsibility for solving these problems in the hands of states, towns, and communities. The Educate America Act provides grants to in-

---

 Goals 2000: The National Education Goals

By the year 2000—

- All children in America will start school ready to learn.
- The high school graduation rate will increase to at least 90 percent.
- All students will leave grades 4, 8, and 12 having demonstrated competency over challenging subject matter including English, mathematics, science, foreign languages, civics and government, economics, the arts, history, and geography, and every school in America will ensure that all students learn to use their minds well, so that they may be prepared for responsible citizenship, further learning, and productive employment in our nation's modern economy.
- The nation's teaching force will have access to programs for the continued improvement of their professional skills and the opportunity to acquire the knowledge and skills needed to instruct and prepare all American students for the next century.
- United States students will be first in the world in mathematics and science achievement.
- Every adult American will be literate and possess the knowledge and skills necessary to compete in a global economy and exercise the rights and responsibilities of citizenship.
- Every school in the United States will be free of drugs, violence, and the unauthorized presence of firearms and alcohol, and will offer a disciplined environment conducive to learning.
- Every school will promote partnerships that will increase parental involvement and participation in promoting the social, emotional, and academic growth of children.

Source: The National Educational Goals Panel, 1996.

dividual states as incentives for developing both their own local versions of these goals and for designing and mounting programs aimed at meeting them (National Educational Goals Panel, 1996). Misunderstanding the nature of the program, however, some local groups have refused to accept funding under this plan, fearing that acceptance of these moneys will lead to interference by the U.S. Department of Education directly in the local workings of school districts and state boards of education. Although the Goals 2000 legislation specifically states that "the responsibility for control of education is reserved to the States and the local school systems" (Educate America Act, 1994), local school boards have been fearful that acceptance of Goals 2000 funds would dictate everything from holding schools accountable for specific achievement benchmarks in 0 to 6 education programs to reproductive education services in the schools (National Educational Goals Panel, 1996). In particular, a concern that teachers will be responsible for instituting and meeting specific educational goals for the very young has given rise to vituperative debate around the country.

Belying such concerns, however, Goals 2000 programs across the nation are building federal and state partnerships and galvanizing community awareness of educational needs, parent involvement in the schools, and support for teachers. In Vermont, Goals 2000 incentives have been used to create a set of 20 statewide goals, and has explicitly charged individual communities with arriving at and implementing solutions at the local level. In New Mexico, the program has spurred the growth of a support network with representatives from national educational and scientific foundations, local business and industry, and state and local government officials. In virtually all states, Goals 2000 funding is paying for teacher training, curriculum development, and the development of plans to bring the resources and expertise of business and community leaders to bear on school problems. Deriving potential solutions at the community level puts the solutions in the hands of people who can identify at close range not only the nature and extent of specific problems unique to each school district, but also the strengths of and resources available to each community.

With the activist spirit surrounding Goals 2000 in many states, the business community has been taking an increasingly important role in education issues. Disturbed by what has been perceived as a diminishing level of basic knowledge and skills among young employees, business has been very much involved in the last decade. This involvement culminated in 1996 in a National Education Summit, in which a number of large corporations, along with state governors, launched plans to develop educational standards and to address other school problems such as overcrowding and declining physical condition of school buildings. A number of corporate foundations have contributed substantial grants to support design and implementation of programs to help schools achieve their goals. Whether these goals are best formulated and implemented at the federal, state, or local levels remains a subject for debate.

For each potential problem facing U.S. students today, there is at least one proposed solution. Differences of opinion over the relative efficacy of these solutions, the appropriate level and location of control over their administration, mechanisms for funding them, and the cost-effectiveness thereof lie at the heart of the educational debate. In the sections that follow we will look at some basic issues that have implications for educational policy, as well as at several of the most prominent proposals for improving the educational lot of our children.

THE ROLE OF SCHOOLS

Do public schools work? Should they continue to exist? If so, how should they be changed? To answer these questions, we have to establish some criteria by asking another question first: What do we want schools to do? From its origins, schooling in the United States has always had a social agenda beyond mere instruction in literacy and mathematics; it was intended to act as an agent for socialization into desired values and behavior. In addition, schooling has also had a social justice agenda, the promotion of democratic principles through equal educational opportunity for all (Dumke, 1985).

What do public schools do? Think about this for a moment. If you answered "schools teach children," you would not be wrong. But many other answers are also correct, though many of the functions of education are implied, rather than immediately obvious. In addition to providing instruction on a variety of topics, schools contribute to social unity by exposing children throughout the country to a similar pool of topics and experiences; they prepare young people for participation in the labor force, and, perhaps most importantly, they bring together children from a wide variety of backgrounds to meet and work together for common goals (Shenk, 1996). But this point is also in dispute. For example, Berliner and Biddle (1995) argue that public schools foster competition rather than cooperation toward accomplishing a common goal.

Indeed public competition among students is a frequent and often unacknowledged facet of public education, one that most always operates to the detriment of disadvantaged students who typically are channeled into a lower tier of achievement at an early stage of their educational experience (Berliner & Biddle, 1995). Some scholars argue further that the early inculcation of individualistic, competitive styles of working in schools actually disadvantages future workers by failing to acclimate them to the cooperative environments demanded by most employment settings. Students who drop out of school in part because they feel they cannot compete with their higher-achieving classmates lose the opportunity to succeed, and society loses a portion of its human capital.

Clearly schools do socialize students, but in what ways? Confronted with a changing student body, schools are also charged with the duty to create inclusion for many different kinds of students. (For a discussion of changing student profiles, see chapter 11). Given the inequality of funding, quality of physical facilities, and of level of instruction, it is easy to argue persuasively that some disadvantaged schools are socializing many children to accept a diminished version of themselves and a low level of aspiration. Though articulated educational principles appear to foster the inclusion of all in a quest for equal opportunity, some scholars argue that a hidden agenda of schools might be to perpetuate the existing relations of the economic society—training a majority of students to assume roles as workers while nurturing a privileged few to take places as leaders within the society (Gordon & Bonilla-Bowman, 1996).

Even those who support the current system of public education in the United States, and do not believe that it is fundamentally flawed, debate the appropriate measures for strengthening education. Debate over school reform is as old as formal schooling itself and usually centers around one or more of these issues: overall academic performance, educational equity among ethnic or economic groups, and administrative responsibility for public education. Pushes for reform are seldom single-issue campaigns: The current debate over the education of immigrant children, which can be viewed as a backlash against the civil rights reforms of the 1950s, 1960s, and 1970s (Timpane, 1996), reflects both equality issues and debate over whether the federal or the state governments should take responsibility for the children in question.

In the 1980s and 1990s, however, the single most polarizing issue with relevance for educational policy has been academic performance. Embedded within this performance debate is the issue of inequity in academic outcomes for various social groups, a topic we will discuss below.

Expansion of the School's Role

Even as the argument over academic performance rages, schools are being asked to address several other social issues, some of which are widely held to underlie and influence a child's ability to do well in school. The first of the eight goals in the Goals 2000 plan is that by the year 2000, "All children in America will start school ready to learn." The remaining goals include graduation from high school, competency in basic subject matter, greater achievement in math and science, literacy for all, and schools that are free of drug use and violence (National Educational Goals Panel, 1996). Such goals will not be realized (indeed the society is having difficulty in achieving them) without a deeper social understanding of the factors that influence the poor achievement of public school students, and especially what young children need to emerge from childhood as productive adults.

These needs stem from the well-founded belief that a child's development is determined by the quality of the components of an ecological system consisting of four basic elements: family, health, school, and child care (Bronfenbrenner, 1979; Belsky, 1981; Zigler & Gilman, 1994). When there is a deficit in any of these interdependent areas, the child's readiness for school and ability to succeed in school are jeopardized. This scientific fact is not really in dispute; the issue is whether schools should be the primary provider of these needs in a social context in which they are not met by other institutions. As Bronfenbrenner (1990, p. 27) has noted, the more we know about the conditions that "foster the development of human competence and character, the more we see these same conditions being eroded" in the social environment.

Schools and teachers have become increasingly aware that a wide range of problems now affect their students' performance. A survey of more than a thousand public school teachers revealed that nearly 9 out of 10 beginning teachers believe that many of their young students are too overwhelmed by family and other outside problems to do well in class. Unfortunately, although some 98 percent of the teachers agreed that it is important to work together with parents, 70 percent of those surveyed indicated that many parents seemed to view schools and teachers as "adversaries" (Metropolitan Life Insurance, 1991). Clearly such attitudes do not bode well for children, who need unified support of their parents and their teachers in overcoming the obstacles to good school performance.

Such obstacles have more force in the lives of children when their parents are themselves overwhelmed by the demands of daily life. The major demographic changes America has undergone in the last three or four decades have contributed significantly to the problem. The dramatic increase of mothers in the workplace and the number of single-parent families, headed usually by women, has been paramount among these changes. Today, about 25 percent of all children are raised by a single parent, and this number is increasing. The numbers are increasing far more steeply for black families, in which the majority of children now grow up in single-parent homes (Bronfenbrenner et al., 1996). Moreover, parents are less often present in their homes: in 1995, 77 percent of mothers of school-age children were in the out-of-home labor force (Adams & Poersch, 1997). Not surprisingly, economic strain is also a factor. Between 1973 and 1992, the median annual income for young families with children fell by 34 percent (Children's Defense Fund, 1995). The child poverty rate for young families doubled during the same period, rising to 42 percent (Children's Defense Fund, 1995).

It is unrealistic to expect that children raised with the many daily stresses of poverty will be able to do their best in school (see Greenhouse, 1992). Such stresses grow when families are forced to live in deprived and even dangerous environments that provide few of the supports once present in communities, like stable neighborhoods, supportive institutions like church and community groups, healthy role models, and a network of extended family members.

In many communities, the school is one of the few remaining positive social institutions and, is asked increasingly to assume many roles. Schools that are already overburdened by trying to instruct children who have endured years of deprivation before reaching the classroom door are now also attempting to become full-service community support systems that offer not only academic subjects but also many other services to families. The "full-service" or "community schools" movement has in fact been with us for some 25 years, but it is now coming into its own with the society's growing need for more effective family supports (see Dryfoos, 1994). Much controversy and some resentment on the part of school personnel continues, even as many school systems have resolved to take action to redesign their traditional assumptions and their schools. However, the debate over *whether* the school should take on other roles has become, in many communities, *how* they should carry out new functions, and who should provide funding and governance. Gradually, school districts have recognized the dire need to offer more supports to the families they serve, in order to make possible the exercise of their schools' time-honored function: Education of the child.

The term *education* has now expanded to include fostering many aspects of the child's development, not just the academic. Schools must now respond to a variety of family, child, and community needs, depending upon local requirements. Such schools might offer such services as child care, parenting education, health screening, and literacy classes to parents, while providing nontraditional education in social development, conflict resolution skills, and avoiding substance abuse to their children. In an effort to help teachers and parents become more effective allies in fostering children's growth and well-being, parental involvement (as originally formulated in programs like Head Start) has become a core element in most full-service school programs. Just how parents are to become involved, and the degree to which they should have a voice in establishing school policies, is itself an ongoing subject of debate.

There is increasing sentiment that, for the sake of the students and the school's effectiveness, parents must be welcomed into the school and encouraged to become full and important participants in their children's education. Congress added the goal of increased parental involvement to the list of education goals for 1994; states must now show what they are doing in this regard when they submit plans under the Goals 2000: Educate America Act.

Even though some of the changes discussed above are becoming accepted, there remains the question of whether such changes should be adopted at the federal, state, or local levels. To create more effective schools, should we be working "top-down" from the national Goals 2000 agenda, in which schools follow the dictates of federal, state, or school district guidelines? Or "bottom-up," in a belief that local communities are better equipped to make adjustments within their own schools?

IMPROVING SCHOOLS: SOME CONTRASTING MODELS

The concern over the federal government's role in school administration, as exemplified by reactions to the Goals 2000 program, gives rise to one of the thorniest questions facing all schools today: Who should be responsible for their planning, administration, and oversight? Most school administration takes place at the district level, but individual schools are increasingly decentralized, already making administration, curriculum, staffing, and goals decisions themselves.

Such decision making is often based on the Comer model. The School Development Program, developed by New Haven psychiatrist James Comer, emphasizes the development of "a community of adults working in the best interests of children" (in Abbot, 1995). Goals of the program include not only school improvement, but the strengthening of the entire community, at the center of which, Comer believes, should be the school. Decisions affecting the school are made at the school level, largely by a cooperative team—the School Planning and Management Team—composed of teacher, parent, support staff, community, and administration representatives. This **"school-based management"** enables Comer schools to be flexible in tailoring programs to and responding to the strengths and problems of each individual school. Comer programs have been shown to raise academic performance dramatically. Students at Comer schools in Michigan, for instance, gained an average of 7.5 to 11 percentile points in basic subjects, exceeding the gains achieved by students in non-Comer schools in the same district. Because parent participation is so integral to the program, benefits have also accrued to parents, many of whom returned to school to continue or complete their own education.

Other experiments in public education have altered the form of governance even more dramatically, as in privatization, or allowed public schools to function outside the usual regulations, as in charter schools. A voucher system permits parents to use public money to send their children either to public schools or to private schools in a region, even when they are sectarian schools operated by religious or other groups. **Privatization** involves local school districts being taken over by private firms, in some cases firms that are for-profit educational organizations like the Edison Project, which has reportedly raised $100 million to establish about 25 schools. Such measures often support public schools being kept public, but acknowledge the role of private (and especially parochial) schools as models to emulate, at least in part, in the areas of academic achievement and efficient administration.

Charter schools permit experimentation with new educational models in small, publicly funded schools allowed to operate free of many local and state regulations. The charter school movement has resulted in the passage of laws in many states that allow groups of educators, parents, or entrepreneurs to apply for a state charter to establish schools in which class size is often smaller and various innovative programs can be attempted. If these programs prove successful, the innovations might be implemented on a larger scale in the school system. Twenty-five states now have charter schools, yet the 10 years of the charter movement have resulted in a mere 700 public charter schools nationally (Mosle, 1997). Thus far, the reviews of charter schools have been mixed, making accountability an important issue; however, these schools can provide an opportunity for school districts to study the potential effects of reform measures before they are implemented on a costly, systemwide basis. Similarly, many districts in the nation have instituted site-based management systems whereby individual schools are given enough autonomy to design some new programs tailored to their specific student population. Charter schools have some critics, who claim that such schools, like magnet schools, tend to siphon off the best teachers and students without resulting in systemic improvement. In addition, it is extremely difficult for charter schools to establish, in a short time, the kind of organizational framework they need to operate effectively as they are implementing innovative educational strategies (Weiss, 1997).

Vouchers are intended to permit parents, often inner-city, low-income parents, to send their children to private schools. Initially described as a means to give all parents the "school choice" enjoyed by higher-income families, vouchers have come under fire as a dangerous drain on public school budgets and a potentially disastrous influence on the quality of education for students remaining in the public school system. Critics fear that a plan for universal vouchers might take essential support from public schools only to give it to the most exclusive private schools, sectarian religious schools, and perhaps even schools run by parents. Despite the high profile of voucher plans in the news media, they affect relatively few students. The Milwaukee pilot program, for example, involves only about 1.5 percent of the city's students. The results of voucher programs also have not been dramatic. Low-income vouchers, touted as a means to achieve educational equity for students attending troubled urban schools, have not resulted in clear achievement gains for the students involved, according to Witte (1996). Paul Peterson of Harvard has argued that Witte has underestimated the efficacy of the Milwaukee voucher program (Peterson & Bryan, 1998). Either way, there are serious constitutional issues involved in using public funds to pay sectarian religious schools selected by parents. Considerable controversy has arisen around this issue, and a Wisconsin state judge has found a revision of the Milwaukee voucher program unconstitutional insofar as it included religious schools (Walsh, 1997).

Improvements in the quality and outcomes of school programs associated with decentralization of school administration have led some analysts to call for the abolition of the U.S. Department of Education (Shenk, 1996). This move, proposed by Ronald Reagan during his successful 1980 presidential campaign, is in keeping with political trends that emphasize streamlining the economy and the federal government. In addition, conservative commentators (e.g., Shlaffley, 1995) associate the U.S. Department of Education with undue influence on the education policy process by teachers' unions like the National Education Association and the American Federation of Teachers. The U.S. Department of Education also comes under fire from such groups because Scholastic Aptitude Test (SAT) scores have declined roughly since the time of its inception. As noted earlier, the meaning of changes in the SAT scores over time is subject to more than one interpretation.

Supporters of the U.S. Department of Education argue that this would be the worst possible time to destroy the only federal body with oversight in the area of education (Shenk, 1996). In addition to being an important symbol of the government's commitment to excellence in education, the U.S. Department of Education ensures some degree of uniformity of educational goals and progress from one state to another, disburses program and research funds, and tracks academic progress, condition of school facilities, and nonacademic issues affecting student life and performance, such as drug abuse.

THE DEBATE OVER NATIONAL STANDARDS

Despite apparent advances in the numbers of persons educated, education is not keeping pace with the demands of an increasingly technologically oriented workforce. As early as 1980, a report from the National Commission for Excellence in Education (1983) warned that an unacceptably large proportion of public school students were not being prepared to fill the needs of the nation's workforce, and that the lack of highly skilled workers was compromising the strength and economic security of the United States (Bracey, 1991). Concerns expressed in this and other reports about the lack of emphasis on basic skills training in public schools has led a large group of educators and legislators to push for **national educational standards.**

President Clinton, also citing a potential threat to national security posed by declining skills, announced that increased spending for educational improvement would have top priority in the 1998 federal budget. Developing and promoting "national standards of excellence" are key components in his proposals; in addition, President Clinton plans to commit $105 million to the National Board for Professional Teaching Standards to help it achieve its own goal of certifying 100,000 master teachers by the year 2006 (Hoff, 1997). Despite the strong federal emphasis on standards, there is an effort to preserve the role of the states and local communities in establishing curricula. Under the current federal plan, states would have the option of participating in math and reading assessments developed from, respectively, the Third International Math and Science Study and the reading test of the NAEP. The federal plan is to prepare these tests by 1999 and to offer them to school districts that year.

In the clamor for such standards, the three goals of educational reform—drives toward educational excellence, educational parity, and definition of administrative responsibility—meet (Timpane, 1996). Proponents of national standards (e.g., Ravitch, 1995; Hirsch, 1996) argue that schools in this nation tend to teach too many subjects in too little depth, and to rely too heavily on standardized tests, in spite of the lack of a standardized curriculum. This set of conflicting emphases leads many school districts to advocate "teaching to the test" and to emphasize the teaching of test-taking skills over basic concepts (Mosle, 1996b, 1996c). The late Albert Shanker of the American Federation of Teachers, who was himself a strong proponent of a return to content and standards in American education, decried this state of affairs and observed that there is no such thing as an all-purpose thinking skill. In the view of Shanker and numerous other scholars, imparting a core of knowledge and domain-specific skills to children is essential to their ability to develop a sound foundation for future learning.

For 1997, Congress earmarked $340 million for states participating in the Goals 2000 plan. Under the Goals 2000 legislation, states have some freedom in allocating the federal dollars they receive: Developing standards is only one way they may use this funding for educational improvement. It is extremely difficult to devise such standards, attuned as they must be to each grade level and to the school curricula. Congress has been cautious in insisting on standards at the federal level, aware as it is of the controversy already brewing at the prospect of government interference with local curriculum decision making (Hoff, 1997). Under these circumstances, inconsistent results from Goals 2000 programs among the states are inevitable. Some states have given priority to acquisition of computer equipment and teacher training rather than to the difficult task of developing standards. U.S. Undersecretary of Education Marshall Smith has observed that although many states have put the Goals 2000 money to good use, it has not always been spent "on thoughtful and integrated reform" (Hoff, 1997).

Standards for Teacher Preparation

Along with complaints about schools in general has come widespread criticism of teaching methods and of the ways teachers themselves are being educated. The notion that "anyone" can stand at the head of a classroom and teach is still very much a common idea. The Teach for America program, which places recent college graduates as teachers in public schools, shares this idea and has been condemned by many in teaching circles as " ill-conceived" (Evans, 1997). Effective teaching in today's classrooms is far from easy, particularly in deprived areas where students are highly stressed and ill prepared, classrooms are overcrowded and supplies are low, and all are fearful of attending school because of high crime rates—and in schools with increasing numbers of students from multiple cultures.

Despite the challenges faced by today's teachers, training in the United States for this important profession has been surprisingly neglected over the last few decades. In a recent report by the National Commission on Teaching and America's Future, (1996), a bipartisan panel supported by the Carnegie Corporation of New York and the Rockefeller Foundation, asserts that education reform depends fundamentally on restructuring the teaching profession. After two years of investigation, the commission concluded that, by the standards of other fields and other countries, U.S. teacher training is poorly financed and has a curriculum of uneven quality, resulting in shortages of qualified teachers in specific fields and frequent hiring of unprepared individuals (National Commission on Teaching, 1996).

The same lack of uniformity that produces schools of vastly different quality in different locales also results in teachers with vastly different ability and training. Many states have low requirements for teacher licensing; others require a B.A. or master's degree in the area to be taught, as well as coursework in teaching, learning, and child development and extensive practice teaching (Darling-Hammond, 1997). In some states, teachers must pass a licensing exam, but these exams are criticized for being mere tests of basic knowledge, inadequate to measure the skill needed to instruct students in the challenging and complex material they must learn today (Darling-Hammond, 1986; Shulman, 1986). Disparity is present, too, between schools serving different socioeconomic areas and different racial populations. NAEP reports indicate that schools in low-income neighborhoods and schools serving primarily nonwhite students are less likely to be staffed by teachers with the same level of training as those teaching in predominantly white schools and those serving middle- and upper-income groups (Children's Defense Fund, 1998g).

The problem of insufficient skill does not arise because older teachers are failing to keep up with new material: Roughly 25 percent of newly hired teachers do not have adequate qualifications to teach. More than 12 percent have no formal training in teaching, and 14 percent start their jobs without having met state standards (Darling-Hammond, 1997). In June 1997, it was announced that about 1,200 teachers who failed the state licensing exam in New York City would be retained in their positions because of a teacher shortage. Nationally, over 50,000 teachers without full qualifications have entered classrooms in recent years on substandard or emergency licenses (Feistritzer & Chester, 1996). Such qualification issues are more serious in the poorest schools, where the problem of inadequate teaching is compounded by inadequate resources in other areas. In schools with the highest number of minority students, there is less than a 50 percent chance that a child will have a science or math teacher with a license and a degree in the appropriate field (Oakes, 1990). And trends have not been moving in a positive direction. Between 1987 and 1991, the number of teachers hired with a college major or minor in their fields declined from about 74 percent to 67 percent (Rollefson, 1993).

 Proposals for School Improvement

PLAN: *Extend the school year* from its present 180-day model to one encompassing approximately 240 school days spread over 12 months per year.

PRO: Proponents of this plan (Ballinger, 1990; Cetron & Gayle, 1991; Finn, 1988) argue that the original model, based on an agrarian society in which children were needed at home during growing and harvesting seasons, is outmoded, makes inefficient use of academic materials and buildings, and forces teachers to find other work during the summer months. In some areas where 12-month academic calendars are being tested, student scores have risen at double to triple the rate of those of students on a traditional 9-month plan.

CON: Critics of this plan suggest that, lacking improvements in teacher training and pay, increases in per-pupil expenditures, and uniform national educational standards, more school isn't necessarily better school (McCarthy, 1990).

PLAN: *Establish national teacher certification* as a means of improving the quality of teaching.

PRO: National certification programs would increase the supply of high-quality entrants into the teaching profession (National Board for Professional Teaching Standards, 1992).

CON: Because certification would not guarantee higher salaries, it would not attract better-qualified applicants into teaching; assessments would remove discretion from the hands of local school boards (Raspberry, 1989)

PLAN: *Introduce merit pay programs* to reward and encourage excellence in teaching.

PRO: Pilot programs like Tennessee's Master Teacher initiative have been shown to increase educational attainment (Alexander, 1992).

CON: Critics argue that the program is too expensive and ignores the financial needs of teachers as a whole. Some believe such programs cannot objectively identify appropriate recipients for merit pay awards (Geiger, 1991).

PLAN: School curricula should include **"character education."**

PRO: Shaping behavior toward respect and obedience will lead to improved academic performance.

CON: Critics fear such programs will emphasize unquestioning obedience over reasoning and thoughtful decision making. Questions about who selects the curriculum and whose morals they reflect raise thorny culture bias issues (Herbert & Daniel, 1996).

How do other nations compare? Many other industrialized nations pay their teachers more and provide them with extensive training and ongoing support that allows teachers to work as a team and encourages them to get to know their students. Frequently, teachers in other countries share in school decision making and work in an environment structured to allow teachers to focus on their teaching rather than administrative responsibilities (Darling-Hammond, 1997). In other nations, school staff is composed of more classroom teachers (60 percent to 80 percent) than in the United States, where teachers constitute only about 43 percent of school personnel (Organization for Economic Cooperation, 1998). The National Commission on Teaching and America's Future (1996) has recommended that the United States restructure its schools such that more teachers and administrators are freed from overwhelming bureaucratic detail to focus on the activity of teaching itself.

The Commission on Teaching and America's Future has also urged governors and legislators to establish state professional boards that will oversee teacher training and licensing standards. Further, it asks that states set aside at least 1 percent of their education funding for teacher training based on the standards developed. Local school boards and superintendents are urged to streamline hiring procedures, upgrade qualification levels, and pay more attention to staff development. Universities engaged in training teachers are asked to revise their own curricula to improve the training and skills of both new and practicing teachers. Such efforts, coupled with those of the newly established National Board for Professional Teaching Standards, should encourage a heightened level of competence in the classroom and restore respect to the profession of teaching. Without the timely development of clearer, more stringent, and more uniform standards for both teachers and for students, however, we are likely to be repeating much of the present discussion again in the next decade.

OUTCOME EQUITY

Educational parity, or outcome equity, is one of the primary goals of educational reform. These terms refer to the goal of assuring that all children, regardless of where they live or the relative wealth of their communities, receive equal access to a high-quality public school education. The current huge variations in school quality, per-pupil spending, and student achievement in schools across the country are well documented. Even within individual states, rampant discrepancies exist. The average per-pupil expenditure in New York state, for instance, was $7,794 (U.S. Bureau of the Census, 1993), but within the state individual towns spent as much as $9,586 or as little as $5,034 per pupil (New York State Department of Education, 1994). Not surprisingly, national figures show large differences in expenditures between schools in poverty areas with high minority populations and those located in more affluent areas with predominantly white students (Applebome, 1996).

Clearly, disparities like these have implications for the quality of the education students are receiving, in terms of teacher salaries, qualifications, and training;

class size; classroom furniture and equipment; course offerings; school supplies and books; and even the school's physical facilities (Children's Defense Fund, 1998g; U.S. Department of Education, 1997). Recent findings reveal that poor and minority children are often taught by less qualified teachers (Education Trust, 1996) and that funding inequities virtually doom many poor children to inadequate educations, low-paying jobs, and bleak life prospects (Kozol, 1991).

Although the bare facts about funding inequity are hard to dispute, much argument rages about the proper course to take to remedy the problem. Should money for schools simply be redistributed, Robin Hood style, until each school has an equal amount per student? Will national standards, accompanied by federal dollars to poorer districts, make a large enough difference to narrow the funding and achievement gap? There is no federal entitlement to an "equally funded" education. The U.S. Supreme Court ruled in 1973 that states are not required under the federal Constitution to remedy funding inequities caused by differences in the wealth of school districts. Recently, however, courts in over 40 states have been peppered by lawsuits, brought under their state constitutions' right-to-education clauses, that allege that funding disparities deprive students of equal access to education. Some have argued that permitting such differences in funding levels is tantamount to practicing discrimination against children who live in poor school districts (Hettleman, 1997). Only about half of these suits have been successful. Notably, the funding structure in the state of Illinois was upheld by the Illinois supreme court, despite facts showing that the 1994 per-pupil spending ranged in the state from $2,617 to $14,525 (Hettleman, 1997).

In the state of Connecticut, a suit was brought on grounds of racial segregation. In *Sheff v. O'Neill*, the Connecticut supreme court ruled in 1996 that racial isolation produced by the demographic makeup of the areas served by the Hartford school system violated the state constitution. In an effort to comply with the court's ruling, Connecticut has undertaken measures not only to alleviate racial segregation of the state's schools, but also to address issues of educational parity and improvement in the state as well. These measures include increased state spending on schools, state aid to city schools for after-school and summer programs, increased spending for family resource centers to provide programs like parent education and preschool child care, a school choice program to allow students to attend schools outside their districts, increased numbers of charter schools, and state aid to expand access to preschool programs for 3- and 4-year-olds (Rabinovitz, 1997).

Although Connecticut's response has been promising, it is evident that we cannot rely entirely on lawsuits to remedy the nation's lack of educational equity, nor is it reasonable to expect that districts will voluntarily redistribute their wealth. However, some states and districts have made progress in reducing inequalities, often through restructuring their schools or by instituting measures such as those advocated by the Connecticut *Sheff* panel, like universal preschool education and full-service schools. Georgia and Kentucky are among those states that have established preschool programs for all children in their states, and several other states have planned similar efforts.

Preschool as a Means to Increasing Equity

The importance of high-quality preschool education in preparing a child for school is gaining greater recognition. The Head Start program, in existence since 1965, is predicated on this knowledge, and participation in the program has been shown to offer social and educational advantages to impoverished children. Similarly, evaluations of smaller-scale model programs like the Perry Preschool project and other high-quality interventions for children have revealed lasting program benefits (Schweinhart, Barnes, & Weikart, 1993). A recent Packard Foundation report noted overwhelming evidence that large-scale, as well as smaller-scale, preschool programs result in long-term educational gains, such as better social adjustment, less grade retention, and less likelihood of placement in special education programs (Barnett, 1995). The Carnegie Task Force on Learning in the Primary Grades has also issued a call for universal, high-quality preschool (Carnegie Corporation, 1996).

Because preschool increases **school readiness** and thus helps achieve educational equity, many states have been working to establish their own statewide preschool programs. Two states that offer publicly funded preschool to all low-income 4-year-olds, Washington and Kentucky, have already conducted evaluations of their programs. The Washington evaluation revealed that participating children experience dramatic improvements in language skills and in conceptual and motor abilities. The Kentucky research showed that children in the preschool program surpassed their nonpreschooled peers in social skills, expressive communication, and familiarity with books.

Connecticut has 60 family resource centers providing developmental child care to children ages 3 to 5. Connecticut's research on preschool efficacy found that children who entered kindergarten with some preschool experience received higher scores on a fourth-grade standardized mastery test than their socioeconomic peers who did not participate in preschool (Frahm, 1996). These results are consistent with the opinion of educational experts that high-quality preschool programs are effective in preventing school failure in the early grades (see, e.g., Slavin, Karweit, & Wasik, 1994). Such benefits are enhanced when a child's good preschool experience is not merely one year in length but is made part of an integrated program that extends from age 0 to 5 years.

The strong research findings on the value of high-quality preschools have sparked a movement in several states toward establishment of universal preschool to achieve the goals of educational parity. State officials in Georgia, for example, noted that their educational system was failing and decided as a partial remedy to offer publicly funded preschool to all children, not just impoverished children in the state. These preschools are based on sound early educational models such as that of the Bank Street College of Education and the Montessori system; the programs are funded through the state lottery. Preliminary studies of the efficacy of the Georgia program indicate that it is indeed helping the state's children to succeed in school. Recognizing the clear benefits of such programs, several other states, notably Massachusetts, Ohio, and Connecticut, are evaluating plans to institute publicly funded preschool programs for all resident children.

Given that the promotion of national standards and amelioration of educational inequity have been made priorities in the Clinton administration's Goals 2000 plan, we are likely to see efforts to establish clearer guidelines for student progress in the next decade. The obstacles to formulating standards are daunting, however, and the existence of national standards will not in itself alter student achievement. Seemingly, the course to follow while the standards are being devised is to implement on a wider basis the kinds of schools that have shown clear signs of improving student performance over time, like high-quality preschools. Examples of public schools that offer improvements over traditional schools are discussed in the next section.

SCHOOLS THAT WORK

We know that the problems students have in their lives outside the classroom can affect their school performance. In recognition of this fact, a growing number of educators and scholars have advocated the establishment of "full-service schools" to address the family, health, and social contexts of children, as well as the academic context (Dryfoos, 1994). Such schools vary in their particular components, but they are more like variations on a theme rather than distinct types of reform. Many parents perceive these more individualized approaches to classroom instruction or to administering an entire educational program as better means of achieving the kinds of goals outlined in the Goals 2000 proposal.

For example, a "community schools" project was implemented in four schools by the Children's Aid Society in conjunction with the New York City Board of Education in 1992. These New York City schools offered a variety of programs and services, including before- and after-school programs, Head Start programs, early childhood classes for parents, child care, counseling, on-site health care, adult education, tutoring, and a summer program for community children at the end of the academic year. Not all of the schools offered the same mix of programs, but all were open from 7 A.M. to 10 P.M., six days a week, 12 months a year (Coltoff, 1997). Fully half of the children in these schools were limited-English-proficient, and all were from families with incomes low enough to qualify for the federal school lunch program. Despite these factors, the children's achievement levels improved with each year they participated in the program (Coltoff, 1997). Two other full-service models, the Schools of the 21st Century and the School Development Program (Comer Schools), have been implemented in communities throughout the nation and have enjoyed considerable success in improving the academic performance and social adjustment of their students.

The School of the 21st Century, devised by Yale psychologist Edward Zigler, is based firmly upon principles of child development according to which the child's needs for good health, a supportive family life, and high-quality child care arrangements must be met in order to ensure success in school. In this model, the school buildings house two integrated systems. The first is the traditional, formal school, typically operating from 8 A.M. to 3 P.M., 9 months of the

A School Primer:
Alternative Concepts in Elementary Education

Heterogeneous grouping, or *mixed-ability grouping,* has generated controversy when implemented. A central component is "peer mentoring," in which students help teach each other. In theory, such an approach enhances the self-esteem of the children doing the teaching and improves the basic skills of the "tutees." Some parents, particularly those of high-achieving and gifted students, fear that participation in such classes will slow their children's academic progress, while parents of the lower-achieving children fear that peer tutoring will be substituted for more official teacher time with their children (Educational Leadership, 1991). In some schools, mixed-ability grouping plans are integrated with "inclusion" programs for special education students, so that these children, too, are included in the regular classroom's heterogeneous groups (Gamoran, 1993; Oakes, 1985).

Integrated-day programs originated in British primary schools in the 1960s and 1970s. Based on a philosophy that assumes that different students have different learning styles, the integrated-day approach allows students to work at their own pace and explore topics fully through such assignments as research projects developed by the students themselves. Parents are typically very involved in the school program and are encouraged to volunteer in their children's classrooms and to drop in whenever possible. Test results from schools using both traditional and integrated-day methodologies indicate that students in the latter (many of whom are labeled as being at high risk for school failure) do as well as, if not better than, students from traditional classrooms. The support of parents, careful training of teachers in the integrated-day philosophy and techniques, and commitment of school administrators to the program are critical to its success.

Looping, or multiyear schedules, is the practice of having an entire elementary class (teacher and students) move together into a new school year, instead of forming an entirely new class as children pass from one year in school to the next. The intended and apparent benefits of the practice are many, including reducing children's fears about the new school year, minimizing instructional time lost as children make the transition to a new classroom, encouraging strong relationships with teachers and peers, improving teachers' ability to tailor curricula to student needs, and enhancing student learning. Multiyear programs have been used in Germany for many years and have also been used in rural U.S. schools with small enrollments. Although favored by many communities and educators, looping needs further study to demonstrate and clarify its benefits.

Mainstreaming and **inclusion** both refer to the practice of including special-needs students in regular classrooms. Mainstreaming typically implies the provision of a portion of a special-needs child's educational services in a regular classroom (the remainder being spent in a special education setting), while inclusion implies the full-time placement of a special-needs child in a regular classroom. Teachers in such classrooms often have additional training in how best to integrate special-needs children; such children might also have classroom aides assigned specifically to them to give them extra help during the school day.

Mastery tests are standardized tests on basic topics given at specified intervals during a child's progress through school (e.g., during fourth, sixth, and eighth grade). Individual student performance is assessed, but the emphasis is on the overall educational efficacy of individual schools or school districts. These tests are meant to provide information for educators on how best to improve the curriculum. Supporters believe these tests provide a level of accountability for individual schools and classrooms that results in higher achievement; detractors warn that such testing brings with it a temptation to "teach to the test"—focusing lessons, teaching style, and grading practices to address what is likely to be tested, at the potential expense of other valuable approaches or curriculum areas.

The **whole-language approach** to the teaching of language arts emphasizes the *process* of writing and reading and integrates these throughout the curriculum. Things like correction of spelling errors, take a back seat to encouragement of the creative expression of experiences and ideas; children in whole-language programs are often involved in writing projects from the very beginning of kindergarten.

 ## The Homeschooling Alternative

Over 500,000 children in the United States are "homeschooled"—taught at home by their parents instead of attending a formally structured public or private school. Reasons for choosing this educational option vary, but the most typical homeschooling parents find public schooling to be inconsistent with their religious beliefs, or resist government intrusion in the lives of children and families, or live in areas in which public schools are of poor quality and private school options are limited or prohibitively expensive.

All 50 states now permit homeschooling. Regulations regarding curricula, length of school year, duration of school day, and frequency of progress and achievement evaluations vary widely from state to state (Blau, 1996).

Proponents of **homeschooling** are attracted by its emphasis on individual learning style, the lack of formal constraints on what parents are allowed to teach and the ability to pursue a child-oriented course of study, freedom from a curriculum driven by standardized tests, and what they perceive as a greater opportunity for creativity and achievement. "Progressive homeschoolers," those whose teaching theory is an extension of the philosophy of Jean-Jacques

Rousseau's belief that children are inherently good and will develop naturally if parents shield them from the undue influence of society and formal schooling, tend to select a child-driven approach to study in which children set both the topic and the pace of study (Guterson, 1992).

Critics of homeschooling are concerned with the lack of training required of parents who teach their children at home, the inconsistency among courses of study, the lack of opportunities for the children to socialize in group settings, and the lack of quality controls. In addition, some psychologists argue that parent-child and teacher-student relationships are inherently different, the former being founded on unconditional love and acceptance, and the latter being based on the child's performance at specified tasks. For children to feel that their parents' approval is contingent upon their academic achievement, some argue, is highly stressful. In contrast to homeschooling philosophy, opponents of this practice are more likely to champion Thomas Jefferson than Rousseau, and to cite Jefferson's belief that public schooling, with its emphasis on shared culture and experiences, is the foundation of democracy.

year. The second is a child-care and family support system operating from about 7 A.M. to 6 P.M. year-round, to coordinate with parents' workday. This second system is open to children from age 3 on for parents who need out-of-home care for their preschool children. A highly flexible system, the preschool care is available to parents who need it for full- or for half-day care. It is intended to function like the child-care systems in France and Italy, where children attend preschool at age 3 and receive early education and child-care services at the same time. The early education in the School of the 21st Century is not formal schooling; it is a developmentally appropriate, play-oriented program that fosters optimal development.

A second child-care component serves school-age children 6 to 12 in supervised recreational programs before and after school and during school vacations. The model also incorporates three outreach programs. The first is parent education and family support programming for parents of children 0 to 3; this program, based on the Parents as Teachers Program (PAT), includes home visitation and supportive services for parents and children, such as health screening, parent education, and inoculations for the child. The second part is a family day-care network for children under age 3. In recognition of the need for early child care for some families, and the lack of affordable, good-quality care for these very young children, the 21st Century School organizes existing family day-care homes into a network, using the school as a center for training, monitoring, and supporting day-care workers, thus creating a more uniform and higher-quality system. Finally, the School of the 21st Century provides an information and referral system for community services families might need, such as food stamps and eye testing. A fourth component, a health module that will serve children from birth to age 12, is currently being developed. Schools of the 21st Century are now operating successfully in a growing number of school districts. In some regions, such as Connecticut and Kentucky, they are known as Family Resource Centers. Preliminary results of a program evaluation begun in 1989, indicate that the program is succeeding in meeting parental needs for reliable, high-quality, and convenient child care, as well as for other family supportive services.

The *School Development Program* (SDP), as noted earlier, was developed by New Haven psychiatrist James Comer. This project grew out of a collaboration between the Yale Child Study Center and two public schools in New Haven. Comer schools take into account six developmental pathways deemed essential for successful academic learning: physical, cognitive, psychological, language, social, and ethical (Comer, 1996). A high level of development along all these pathways, Comer asserts, enables a child to achieve to the best of her or his ability. The Comer school is intended to strengthen all of these aspects of the child's development. Based on a belief that the problems facing many schools were due in part to a breakdown in community-school relations, the Comer process seeks to restore the school as an entity interwoven into neighborhood life. Thus it is very much a "social action" model (Carnegie Corporation, 1996).

Today, there are about 700 schools that operate according to the Comer process. The process itself does not prescribe a particular curriculum or type of teaching method; rather, it encourages school personnel to focus on principles of child development, such as children's need to form secure attachments with their teachers. When a school and community have decided to use the SDP process, Yale provides training and professional development support. Three broad principles govern SDP: (1) problem-solving without blame, (2) consensus decision making based on child development principles, and (3) collaborative participation for staff and parents, but with the principal's leadership. The school management team is led by the principal and meets once a week. The team is made up of administrators, teachers, parents, and a mental health specialist, and is responsible for shaping long- and short-term goals for the school.

Other schools that are not full-service schools per se have also succeeded in improving student performance by offering families alternatives to traditional teaching methods. These schools typically offer a breadth of courses and a higher level of instruction than is available in many neighborhood schools. One of these models, Success for All, was designed to restructure elementary schools to enable a greater number of children to succeed in reading, writing, and language arts. This program was devised by a group of education researchers in the Baltimore public schools and at Johns Hopkins University. First piloted in Baltimore in 1987–1988, the program is now used in about 300 schools in 23 states. A related program called Roots and Wings adds similar strategies for teaching mathematics, science, and social studies.

Prevention and early intensive work are featured in the Success for All program. Prekindergarten and kindergarten programs include reading and storytelling units and a focus on letters and the sounds of words. In first grade, students who are still having problems with reading receive individual tutoring. Such attention and intensive learning strategies are continued in grades 2 through 6. Parent involvement is also stressed: Each school has a family support team with a social worker, attendance monitor, and school staff members who work together to engage parents in their children's schooling and to reinforce the school's learning at home. The team also helps parents address concerns like attendance, health and vision problem screening, and behavioral problems. The quality and coordination of the program's various components are monitored by a program facilitator within each school. Evaluative research conducted in nine school districts has shown that the Success for All program consistently increases reading achievement and reduces special education placement. Similarly, evaluation of the Roots and Wings project has shown that it too helps students achieve in math, science, and social studies (Carnegie Corporation, 1996).

Magnet schools, which were originally intended to attract white students to schools in minority communities through the use of specialized curricula, such as a focus on science and mathematics or the arts, have been shown to improve educational performance as well as to achieve a high degree of voluntary racial integration, for which purpose the schools were originally intended. Statistics from the U.S. Department of Education (Steel & Levine, 1994) indicate that 230 magnet schools exist nationwide and are attended by approximately 15 percent of students in communities that have such programs. That the programs invariably have to maintain long waiting lists for students anxious to attend them attests to their popularity with students and their parents. Magnet schools are approximately 10 percent more expensive to run than nonmagnet programs for the same grade levels, giving critics grounds to argue that they take funds away from more traditional programs.

These models are not necessarily mutually exclusive. Some schools subscribe to more than one of these programs. For instance, some schools function as magnet schools and integrate some components of the School of the 21st Century or the Comer Schools. The COZI School is a model that incorporates components of both the Comer School Development plan and the Zigler 21st Century Schools. In both the Comer and the 21st Century models, parental involvement is an essential component in the ongoing life of the school. One of the favorable signs we see in school reforms such as these is the flexibility inherent in the various possible components: Communities are able to devise variations responsive to their particular requirements. One key to all of this—to creating high-quality schools responsive to the needs of students, parents, teachers, and administrators—seems to be assigning individual schools a significant level of autonomy to permit them to be self-managing. This might seem paradoxical when so many responsible, well-informed voices are demanding universal standards, but universal standards are not universal governance. It should be possible to shape a coherent educational system out of many state and local subsystems, if the component districts are permitted to craft their own models in keeping with local needs and performance requirements.

SOLUTIONS FOR THE FUTURE

Compared to other industrialized nations participating in a recent survey, the United States spends a considerable amount of money per pupil on elementary education. The survey, conducted by the Organization for Economic Cooperation and Development in Paris, revealed that the average per-pupil expenditure in the United States was higher than in 22 other industrialized nations, ranking second only to Switzerland (Lawton, 1996). Even though we have noted that per-pupil expenditure is far from consistent within states or even within cities, it is clear that money is not the crux of the matter in attempting to improve our schools. In many instances, more funding can help, but how the money is spent makes the difference. Evidence is beginning to show that money directed carefully, toward reforms like quality preschool education, smaller class size, better teacher development, and expansion of program models with proven success, can reap the benefits of higher achievement for our children (Hettleman, 1997).

Hamburg (1987) has observed that the best school investment strategies include policies tailored to address the needs of the **whole child,** which means that the whole community must be considered within a family/school/community context. To be most effective, schools need to intervene early in the child's life to ensure school readiness. The best early education programs include such components as prenatal and postnatal care, and developmental screening for infants; parent education for mothers and fathers; high-quality child-care arrangements;

and high-quality preschools for 3- and 4-year-olds. High-quality early care and education programs have lasting benefits for children, not only in helping them to succeed in school, but also in helping to prevent delinquency and criminality in later life (Zigler, Taussig, & Black, 1992; Yoshikawa, 1995). Thus, quality early care should be seen by the states as an investment strategy, for the children themselves and for society as a whole.

Although the present might seem to bring new controversy and intractable problems to the field of education, several of these debates and problems are perennial. Among these are the lack of educational equality for those in poverty and for minority groups, two segments of the population that suffer numerous deprivations within society. The particular urgency in the case of education is that education is so central to the economic and social fate of the child in later life. Educational standards have long proven a problem in this country of many cultures and relatively autonomous school districts. Even the lack of uniform preparation for working life and the issue of inadequate academic performance are old complaints—they were the bases for establishing mandatory schooling in the nineteenth century. A disparity in material resources among the schools is also a long-standing difficulty.

Such problems have been exacerbated by the declining levels of support children receive from other institutions in society. Many children do not have safe neighborhoods, continuous healthy contact with their parents, extended families, neighbors they know and can trust, a religious community, or other sources of support. With this decline has come the increase in social and familial factors that endanger children's growth: higher levels of violence, crime rates, poverty, child abuse, and substance abuse. Schools might be one of the few positive forces in these children's lives, if not to protect them fully from the risks posed by the larger society, then at least to provide a firm foundation—to make them stronger and better prepared to cope intellectually and psychologically with these threats to their development.

There are salutary trends on the horizon. Timpane (1996) notes a number of heartening signs. The establishment of higher performance goals for schools is a positive step toward encouraging both schools and students to achieve their best. There has been a growing acceptance of models of learning that take the whole child into account, with attention paid to the child's family life, social and cultural context, physical health, and other factors that influence the ability to learn. Arguments about school choice and multiculturalism are growing less heated; communities are finding a middle ground and increasing access to higher-quality schools for many children and heightening their sensitivity to child and family needs. With a wider recognition that parents must be seen as allies in educating a child, parental involvement has gained a new level of acceptance, and participatory decision making by parents is increasing. School bureaucracies and turf battles might be declining as federal and state decision makers attempt to reconcile their conflicts in order to improve the nation's schools. Moreover, educators and administrators are making efforts to work together with businesses to design programs that will better equip students for the workplace.

Considering the monetary, social, and political support these reforms require, the degree to which known effective strategies to improve schools will be implemented over time will be determined by the will of the community (Timpane, 1996) and by its courage and sense of urgency. As Rudy Crew, the newly appointed chancellor for New York City schools, has noted, we are able to improve single schools in individual communities; the problem is instituting reforms that work on a massive scale (Mosle, 1997). As with any potentially beneficial social policy strategy in the United States, the nation has the financial ability and much of the knowledge to effect the necessary changes; the issue is whether the community will agree that the changes should be made and whether it will create the organizational culture to support the changes. The fiscal argument is in place: For every $1 spent on improving school readiness, we are able to save approximately $6 in the subsequent cost of remediation and correction for the individual whose life would have been blighted by a lack of educational opportunity (Schweinhart, Barnes, & Weikart, 1993). As Timpane (1996) points out, if there is not general agreement and the political intent in this society that all children are able to benefit from and should receive a high-quality education, then reform efforts will not soon achieve their goals. Until the nation as a whole makes high-quality education for all children a priority and takes appropriate, strategic steps to ensure that this goal is realized, we are condemned to repeat many of the themes and debates of the nineteenth-century educational reformers. This time, however, if we fail to improve our schools we jeopardize more than additional generations of young people. This time we also risk the loss of greater and greater portions of the social fabric itself to the crime, violence, and substance abuse that result when increasing segments of the population are undereducated, purposeless, and jobless. The obligation to improve our schools is truly a humane obligation and a compelling social justice concern. But school reform is very much a practical consideration as well: Without more effective education, the entire society will be at risk.

SUMMARY

Public schooling has been available in the United States for well over a century and a half. Throughout that period, educational analysts have disagreed over the most fundamental questions: Is the American system of education working? Who should be responsible for its oversight? How best should American children be provided with effective educational services? How should the outcome of these be evaluated, and what measures should be taken if the system manifests shortcomings? Educational reform sounds like a modern concept, but such efforts have been implemented scores of times during the history of American schooling. Their overall effectiveness, like many other variables, continues to be debated.

One of the most basic questions pertaining to our system of education concerns whether it really is a system at all. With over 15,000 separate school districts and extreme heterogeneity among, and even within, these, American public schooling can scarcely be described as anything as uniform as a system. There are no uniformly enforced national educational goals, and the nature and quality of school administration varies from school to school, often even within the same district. Even so, there is an implicit sense that schools are striving to reach the same ends, though the means by which they try to reach them are as diverse as the schools themselves.

Debate rages about the overall quality of U.S. schools. Rampant criticism of our educational system focuses on high rates of attrition ("dropping out"), declining test scores, poor teacher preparedness, and chronic school violence. Early departure from the educational system is estimated to cost $240 billion annually in terms of loss of productivity, wages, and tax revenues; these costs do not even include social services related to the health, welfare, and justice system costs associated with dropping out of school, nor do they include the incalculable waste of personal opportunities.

But not all critics of American education are so harsh. Many believe that, in spite of evident shortcomings, the American school system is strong and effective. More Americans are educated today, and educated for a greater number of years, than students in most other nations. High school graduation rates are markedly higher than they were at midcentury. Many education experts believe that rhetoric about school failure masks more serious problems, which include unequal educational spending for different social groups, failure to address the unique needs of increasingly ethnically diverse student populations, and the growth of educational bureaucratization.

For every school-related problem identified, advocates, analysts, and policy makers are prepared to suggest a solution: Increasing the length of the school day, strengthening teacher training and status, enforcing national education standards, greater centralization of educational administration, greater decentralization of the same, and decreasing the ratio of administrative personnel to teaching staff have all been suggested. Regardless of the problems identified, one layer of complexity is invariably added in the form of tension over who should be responsible for ensuring educational excellence: Government at the national, state, or local level; schools themselves; teachers; parents; or the private business sector.

In addition, a variety of educational and/or administrative programs, some novel, some old ideas with new names, heavily dot the educational landscape. Magnet schools, charter schools, homeschooling, education vouchers, school-based management, and other programs have all been suggested and tried in many areas of the country. These have brought varying levels of success and various reactions from parents, children's advocates, policy makers, and scholars of educational history. The only thing that seems entirely clear is that these debates will be repeated again and again as new waves of educational reform continue into the future.

CHAPTER 11

Children with Special Educational Needs: A Case Study of Advocacy vs. Policy vs. Research

Sally J. Styfco

Children with disabilities are an extremely diverse group. They range in age from newborns to 21 years, are rich and poor, shy and gregarious, athletic and sedentary, resilient and vulnerable, and every gradation in between. The classifying feature they share—disability—is just as varied. Disabilities include physical handicaps, sensory problems involving sight and/or hearing, speech or language impairments, mental retardation, severe emotional disturbances, and specific learning disabilities. Each of these conditions can range in severity from mild to profound. To further complicate matters, an individual child might be affected by two or more disabilities simultaneously.

If children with disabilities are so heterogeneous, what do they have in common that warrants grouping them together? All have a significant and persistent impediment to learning what, how, and/or where children typically learn. In the school-age population alone, approximately 12 percent of children have disabilities of one type or another that can hinder their achievement in the standard school setting. Wheelchair-bound children, for example, cannot take math classes held on the second floor in schools that do not have elevators, or ramps and students with emotional problems might be so disruptive in the classroom that they (and their classmates) cannot concentrate on the lessons the teacher is trying to present. Children younger than school age might be behind in achieving developmental milestones (grasping objects or speaking, for example) or at risk of experiencing developmental delays—all of which suggest problems with current and future learning.

Yet the majority of children with disabilities are quite capable of learning what they need to learn to lead productive lives when they grow up. But how is that learning best facilitated? Given the diversity of children with special educational needs, a diverse array of teaching methods, curriculum choices, and academic settings would appear to be necessary. Education tailored to each child's unique learning style, strengths, and problems could then be delivered. Today, this is arguably the case. A wide variety of pedagogies have been developed, and placements range from residential settings, special day schools, separate classes in public schools, and part- or full-time inclusion in regular classrooms. These offerings are a far cry from no special services at all, which was the fate of the majority of children with disabilities in the United States as recently as 1975. At that time, 2 million children with disabilities were denied access to the public school system altogether, and another 2.5 million were not receiving educational services appropriate to their needs (Lewit & Baker, 1996).

The change from no to myriad services is the result of the Education for All Handicapped Children Act of 1975 (PL 94-142), now called the Individuals with Disabilities Education Act, or IDEA. The law guarantees a "free, appropriate public education" in the "least restrictive environment" to all children with disabilities. Preschoolers are included, and all states have opted to provide educational and other services to children with disabilities from birth to age 3 as well.

This revolution in the care and education of children with disabilities was moved along not by a sudden influx of knowledge but by a powerful combination of political and social forces. At the time PL 94-142 was passed, there was very little research on how to meet the educational needs of children with disabilities. Advocates had to base their arguments on ideology and on opinions about what should be done. Influential lawmakers and knowledgeable educators were among the advocates, but most of the credit for the legislation goes to a group that had little experience with influencing the legislative process and little clout within the formal educational system—parents of children with disabilities. This unlikely team of players, woefully underarmed with good evidence, nonetheless changed the education of every child with a disability in every school district in America. The story of how these changes came into being and continue to evolve is the focus of this chapter.

We begin with descriptions of the population of children with disabilities. We then recount the historical unfolding of legislation affecting their education. Research on the outcomes to children of a variety of specialized services and settings is reviewed. Against this background, we cover the raging controversy about the appropriate placement for students with disabilities—whether the "least restrictive environment" is different for different children and thus requires a range of options or whether it means nothing short of spending all day in regular classrooms. This controversy is at the heart of another, this one regarding whether social policies should force change in the current special education system or protect its unique administrative and delivery structures. We exit these debates by contemplating the valuable role research can play in settling the arguments and in shaping educational policies that enable all children with disabilities to attain their full potential.

THE SPECIAL-NEEDS POPULATION

People with disabilities constitute the largest minority group in the United States (Herr, 1997). In the school-age population alone, 12 percent of students have disabilities that qualify them for special education. Adding children who are too young to enter school and those between 18 and 21 (college-age) brings the total to over 5.6 million young people with disabilities (National Center for Education Statistics, 1998). It is not surprising, then, that special education is the largest categorical program in public education, estimated to cost between $31 and $35 billion annually (Chambers et al., 1998). The special-needs population and associated costs continue to increase each year, causing many to question both the way children are identified as being in need of special educational services and the way these services are delivered.

Categories of Disability

In general, children are classified as "disabled" because "they have real, persistent, and substantial individual differences and educational needs that regular education has been unable to accommodate" (Terman et al., 1996, p. 5). Beyond this gross classification, learning problems vary so enormously that it is common practice to break them down into smaller groups. Most states follow federal guidelines, which delineate 13 categories of disability that qualify children for special education. Each category is by no means homogeneous; mental retardation, for example, encompasses hundreds of etiologies and IQs ranging from 0 to 70. Nor do the categories dictate what type of services each child receives. (The retarded child with an IQ of 5 has vastly different needs than one with an IQ 60 points higher.) The groupings are used mainly for statistical (census and reporting) purposes and to facilitate identification of children eligible for special services. Once identified, appropriate services are determined on an individual basis. These qualifiers should be kept in mind while reading the following descriptions of the IDEA disability categories, which are presented in general order from least to most prevalent among students 6 to 21 years old.

Orthopedic, Visual, and Hearing Impairments

The stereotypic view of a child with a disability is a child who is crippled, blind, or deaf. In actuality, children with these disabilities constitute only 3 percent of the population of students with disabilities.

Other

The nondescriptive term *other* is often used to group several types of disability that occur infrequently: autism, traumatic brain injury, multiple disabilities, and other health impairments. Together, children with these problems constitute just under 5 percent of those classified as having a disability. The category "other health impairments" was added in revisions to the IDEA fairly recently and is now the fastest growing group. Between 1990 and 1995, this category grew by 89 percent, largely due to the inclusion of some students with attention deficit hyperactivity disorder, or ADHD (U.S. Department of Education, 1996).

ADHD is not specifically covered in the law, so children with this diagnosis are eligible only if they have a co-occurring, listed disability or a significant impairment in school performance.

Severe Emotional Disturbance (SED)

Children with severe emotional disturbance (SED) account for 8 to 9 percent of those eligible for special education. Although the adjective *severe* was dropped from federal law in 1997, it remains in common terminology because these children's problems are indeed severe. Psychiatric symptomology, such as depression or behavior disorders, is typically present. These students have great difficulty forming social relationships, show inappropriate behaviors or feelings in everyday situations, and might develop fears or physical ailments related to their personal or school problems. Outward behaviors often involve aggression, defiance, and lack of control. Teachers are not likely to tolerate such disruptive and dangerous actions, so many children with SED are removed from the regular classroom and taught in separate settings. Not surprisingly, these children are the most difficult to develop instructional programs for (Diamond, 1995), and they generally have the poorest educational outcomes of all children with disabilities (Wagner, 1995).

Attention Deficit Hyperactivity Disorder (ADHD)

Fourth-grader Jimmy hasn't completed a school assignment since he was 6. He loses his homework. He forgets. He doesn't pay attention in class and can't sit still. He blurts out answers without raising his hand and sometimes before the question is finished. On the playground, he intrudes on classmates' games, can't wait his turn for the jungle gym, and talks so much that no one can get a word in edgewise. Life at home is the "Big Struggle" (Hallowell & Ratey, 1994b). Jimmy forgets chores, promises, and where his shoes are. He teases and fights with his siblings from morning until night. His parents have yelled, spanked, ignored, punished, and agonized over their impossible son.

Jimmy's restlessness and disorganization indicate a classic case of attention deficit hyperactivity disorder (ADHD). The defining symptoms are inattention and distractibility, impulsivity, and excess energy or hyperactivity. Some children have attention deficit disorder without the high activity levels that so frustrate parents and teachers. These children are the daydreamers, the ones who are caught off-guard when called on in class and spend more time gazing out the window than at the chalkboard.

The American Psychiatric Association lists ADHD under the category of behavior disorders. The diagnosis is made when symptoms are severe enough to be maladaptive, have lasted at least 6 months, begin before age 7 years, and are present across two or more situations (such as school and home). Despite the fact that ADHD is the most widely studied psychological disorder of childhood, there is no precise test for it. Physicians might employ some measures of attention and impulsivity, but they rely mainly on the child's behavioral history and ratings by teachers and parents.

In the United States, ADHD affects from 3 to 5 percent of the school-age population.* Compared to girls, boys are 3 to 9 times more likely to receive the diagnosis; a plausible explanation is that boys are also more likely to exhibit hyperactivity and aggressive, acting-out behaviors that force exasperated teachers and parents to seek professional help (Gaub & Carlson, 1997). It was once thought that children outgrew their problems with inattention, impulsivity, and hyperactivity. Now studies have indicated that up to two-thirds maintain these impairing symptoms into adulthood (Hallowell & Ratey, 1994b). Hyperactivity might decrease somewhat, but disorganization, not completing tasks, and acting before thinking can create bigger problems for adults than they do for children.

Misunderstood and untreated, ADHD can have serious, lifelong consequences. Children who can't pay attention or remember their homework are destined to do poorly in school. Barkley (1995) estimates that 30 to 50 percent of ADHD students are retained in grade at least once, and up to 35 percent quit school. They often fail in social relationships as well, due to their poor behavior, intrusiveness, and inability to attend to social cues and rules. Underachievement and unpopularity can produce low self-

*The statistics reported here and in the scientific literature vary widely for several reasons: There have been several changes in the diagnostic criteria used by the American Psychiatric Association; ADHD often co-occurs with other psychiatric conditions, so the effects of ADHD in research samples can be confounded with the effects of other disorders; and the sheer number of studies (well over 6,000) makes a variety of findings inevitable.

esteem, low aspirations, and psychiatric problems. On the positive side, individuals with ADHD tend to be highly creative, energetic, resilient, and full of ideas. There are reports that some highly accomplished individuals, including Thomas Edison, Edgar Allen Poe, and Albert Einstein, had ADHD (Hallowell & Ratey, 1994b). Those with the disorder can also be very persistent at times, riveting their attention to tasks they find interesting and going way beyond normal mastery.

The causes of ADHD have still not been pinpointed. Neurological studies suggest a lack of particular neurotransmitters in the frontal lobes of the brain that enable people to regulate attention and emotion and control impulses. There is also evidence that ADHD has a strong hereditary basis. Genes explain only about 50 percent of the chance of having ADHD, however, leaving the environment to explain the other half (Weiss, 1996). Food additives and sugar in the diet, two environmental agents long suspected of making children "hyper," have been ruled out as causes of the disorder.

Treatment of ADHD commonly involves psychotropic drugs, psychotherapy, and behavior modification, often in combination. The most effective class of drugs is stimulants, particularly methylphenidate—better known by the trade name Ritalin. Though it might seem counterintuitive to give stimulants to someone who is already overstimulated, the action of the drugs is to stimulate the neurotransmitters that are lacking in the brain. This helps the individual focus better and stabilizes emotions and moods. Although stimulants have proved safe and nonaddictive in the dosages prescribed, they are not a cure-all for ADHD. Some patients do not respond, or experience undesirable side effects. And pills cannot teach organizational skills or behavior management, nor can they treat the debilitating psychological effects arising from academic and social failure. The efforts of parents, teachers,

psychotherapists, and sometimes a personal coach are still required.

Like LD (for *learning disability*) the label *ADHD* is not without controversy. Critics see it as a bogus diagnosis, yet another way of blaming biology for one's behavior. These cynics argue that all children are inattentive, impulsive, and full of energy and that ADHD is just a fancy excuse for poor grades, laziness, and lack of discipline. They point to statistics showing that the disorder is an American phenomenon. The diagnosis barely exists in Japan, for example, and it occurs 10 times more often in America than in Europe and Britain (Wallis, 1994). Of all the methylphenidate produced in the world each year, 90 percent is taken by U.S. citizens (Livingston, 1997). Some blame American teachers and parents for pressuring doctors to diagnose and medicate children with behavior problems.

The skeptics' arguments are weakened by the scientific literature, which clearly supports the existence of the cluster of symptoms known as ADHD. Studies in biology, neurology, and genetics are moving closer to identifying specific organic causes. To explain why Americans lead the world in ADHD, Hallowell and Ratey (1994a) point out that the country was settled by risk-takers: The immigrants were "restless movers and shakers" who left their homelands in search of adventure and freedom; "Sounds like ADD to me" (p. 230). This gene pool has created a fast-paced lifestyle characterized by fast food, sound bytes, and distractible, hyperactive people. These authors warn, however, that if the disorder is overdiagnosed, it will be dismissed as a fad and lose all meaning.

Although there are many advocacy groups for individuals with ADHD (the largest, Children and Adults with Attention Deficit Disorders, or CHADD, boasts over 30,000 members), they have not been as successful as advocates of children with other disabilities in securing educational rights. ADHD is not specifically covered by the IDEA. Many children with the disorder also have learning disabilities or serious emotional disturbances that qualify them for special education services under the act. Others whose attentional and behavioral problems are so severe that they significantly impair their school performance might qualify under the category "other health impairments." Adults (including college students) are covered under the Americans with Disabilities Act of 1990, which does consider ADHD a disability. The inconsistent treatment of children and adults with ADHD in the nation's laws and in schools around the country underscores the need for continuing work to develop a scientific assessment of the disorder.

Mental Retardation

Mental retardation is defined by an IQ test score below 70 (or on some tests, 75) and "deficits in adaptive behavior," meaning difficulty in adapting to the demands of a given situation or environment. This category comprises about 11 percent of children in special education. The majority (75 to 85 percent) have mild retardation. The others have moderate, severe, or profound levels of retardation that generally (but not always) can be traced to some organic cause. Examples are Down syndrome and prenatal exposure to rubella. Physical and neurological disabilities are more likely to affect these individuals than those in the mild range.

Speech and Language Impairments

Twenty-one percent of children eligible for special education have speech and language disorders. About half of these have speech disorders, generally problems with articulation. Such problems usually can be helped with speech therapy. Language impairments are not so amenable to help. Affected children have difficulty understanding language, discriminating speech, and expressing themselves verbally. Causes range from physical (such as poor hearing) to environmental (such as lack of verbal stimulation in the home). Communication skills can be improved with language therapy, although prognosis differs for each child and each area of verbal, auditory, and written language.

Learning Disability (LD)

LD is by far the largest category of students served in special education, constituting about half of this population. This amounts to 6 percent of all public school students, or more than 2.5 million children (National Center for Education Statistics, 1998). LD is the only classification that federal law specifically defines, but many observers argue that the definition is not specific enough and has allowed too many children into the special education system.

The law defines specific learning disability as a disorder in at least one basic psychological process necessary for understanding or using language or math. Excluded are learning problems associated with mental retardation, emotional disturbance, cultural differences, or poverty. In practice, schools classify LD based on a substantial discrepancy between a child's ability to learn (usually assessed by IQ score) and his or her academic performance (grades and/or achievement scores). Districts define "substantial discrepancy" differently, however, making it possible for a child to meet the medical criteria for a learning disability but not a school's criteria (Silver, 1996).

Part of the reason LD is so difficult to pinpoint is that the majority of specific learning disabilities are mild. Severe LD is easy to spot—the child who can't read a word in the reading primer but has no trouble memorizing a complete story, the one who gets every example wrong on the math test but can multiply two-digit numbers in her or his head, and so on. Mild LD is not so obvious. This explains why LD is not commonly identified until at least the age of 8 or 9 and is most frequently diagnosed among students 12 to 17 years old (Reschly, 1996). By these ages, the child has fallen far enough below grade level to make it impossible to grasp new, harder material, and repeated failure has probably taken its toll on the child's motivation, self-esteem, and relationships with classmates (Lyon, 1996).

The majority of specific learning disabilities are in the area of reading. For example, the child might have difficulty recognizing words or combining syllables into sounds. Early identification and intervention have been shown to be quite successful (Lyon, 1996; Madden et al., 1991) but have not yet found their way into standard practice. Lyon, for one, believes that the incidence of LD (and the cost of special education) could be reduced greatly by screening all children for "deficits in phonological awareness" (the sounds associated with language—for example, with letters or groups of letters) in kindergarten and given help if indicated. As it is now, older children with LD require intensive intervention to achieve just modest improvement. When they have only minimal programming or attend regular classes without special services, they rarely reach the performance level of low-achieving peers without disabilities (Hocutt, 1996). Lyon blames these poor outcomes on the "wait and fail policy," arguing that the longer the disability is not identified, the more the child fails and the harder the problem is to treat.

The rising incidence of LD, which already accounts for the majority of students referred to special education, has become a heated topic in educational circles. Between 1976–1977 (the school year before IDEA was implemented) and 1994–1995, the number of children in most of the other 12 disability categories declined, while those classified with LD increased by more than 300 percent. Lyon (1996) offers several explanations for this dramatic rise. Among those he calls "sound reasons" are better knowledge of LD, heightened awareness of the disability and its harmful effects on academics and personal and social functioning, and an increase in the number of girls being identified as LD.[1] "Un-

---

[1]Boys are overrepresented in all the disability categories (National Center for Education Statistics, 1998; Turnbull et al., 1995). For reading disabilities (the most prevalent type of LD) alone, boys have been identified two to four times more often than girls (Spear-Swerling & Sternberg, 1996). Recent evidence, however, shows the two genders to manifest reading disabilities at equal rates (Lyon, 1996). Spear-Swerling and Sternberg explain that the gender differences in referral for special education might be due to different teacher expectations of boys and girls and the fact that boys are perceived as having more behavior problems. Genetic causes of disabilities might also affect males more than females.

sound reasons" include ambiguous definitions, inadequate preparation of teachers to respond to individual differences in learning needs within the classroom, financial incentives to identify special needs, and the appeal of using the LD label instead of one that is more stigmatizing. The pressure to increase academic standards and test scores has also led to more children falling behind and to increased referrals for special education.

The existence of so many "unsound" explanations has led many to question the reality of LD as a bona fide disability. On the other side of the fence are those who point to the declining social conditions (e.g., poverty, single parenting) that result in greater physical and psychosocial vulnerabilities to learning problems (Hallahan & Kauffman, 1995; Huston, 1991). In the heat of these debates, it is easy to lose sight of the fact that for the children who have them, learning disabilities are a formidable barrier to academic and personal success. The children did not create the problem but were given the label *because* of the problem—their inability to benefit from standard instructional practices (Kauffman, 1995b).

Educational Placements

Less than 30 years ago, school officials could turn away any child they felt would be unable to benefit from public education. Children with disabilities who were denied access to school might receive some training in an institution or private setting, but many simply were not educated. Those who were admitted to public school might be placed in a *special education class*, where they were taught in a separate room but usually in the same building as neighborhood children. In the 1970s, largely in response to the IDEA's mandate for the least restrictive environment, the focus shifted to *mainstreaming*. Mainstreamed students generally spent part of the school day in a special class and the rest (typically the nonacademic portion such as music and recess) with peers who did not have disabilities. The thinking behind mainstreaming was to promote acceptance of individual differences by encouraging social contact among children with and without disabilities.

In the 1980s the trend shifted to the *Regular Education Initiative* (REI), a plan to transform regular classrooms to meet all children's individual needs regardless of disability status. This ideal was soon overtaken by the *inclusion* movement. Inclusion involves educating students with disabilities in regular classrooms for most, if not all, of the school day. They might still spend some time in a **resource room** (generally a part-time special education class) or they might receive special instruction in the integrated class. This movement is now intensifying to become *full inclusion,* or the practice of educating all students full-time in regular classes. As with all of these educational shifts, the full-inclusion bandwagon is moving with alarming speed—so swiftly that the authors of at least one textbook for special education teachers have chosen to concentrate exclusively on fully inclusive practices on the premise that new teachers will not encounter anything else (Turnbull et al., 1995).

Although the IDEA does encourage full inclusion, the law clearly requires that a range of settings be available. What is "least restrictive" for one child can be more or less restrictive for another. An autistic child, for example, might need a classroom with very few children and no distractions in order to benefit from the lessons, but this setting would be far too restrictive for a child with mild mental retardation. Today, only a small percentage of special education students are in totally segregated settings. About 1.4 percent are taught at home or in residential facilities, including hospitals; just under 4 percent attend separate schools. The rest attend integrated schools: 23.5 percent in separate classes, 36 percent in resource rooms, and 35 percent in regular classes (Hocutt, 1996). There is a great deal of overlap in these settings, with many children in regular classes spending at least some time in resource rooms, and many in resource and special classes spending part of their day in regular classes.

THE LEGISLATIVE HISTORY OF SPECIAL EDUCATION

The story of how children with disabilities gained rights to a "free, appropriate public education" is a story that relates more to United States history than it does to the professions of education or developmental psychology. The story begins with the civil rights movement that gained momentum in the early 1960s. In 1954, the Supreme Court had ruled in *Brown v. Board of Education* that the practice of maintaining separate schools for blacks was a violation of equal rights under the U.S. Constitution. Within a decade, activists were trying to remediate the harm caused to minorities by centuries of segregation and unequal access to education, employment, and the political process. Special education was later identified with this movement. The overrepresentation of minorities in special education was viewed by many as another form of discrimination, segregation, and denial of equal opportunity.

Parent Advocacy

About the same time, another movement was slowly gathering steam—this one devoted to improving the care and education of children with mental retardation. Earlier in this century, having a retarded child was typically a source of shame and embarrassment. Families were likely to hide the fact from neighbors by secluding the children at home or placing them in institutions. In the 1950s, however, some famous parents began to "come out of the closet." Writer and Nobel Prize winner Pearl S. Buck confessed that she had a retarded daughter and shared the torment she experienced when she made the decision to institutionalize her child (Trent, 1994). Later, the high-profile Kennedy family let out their secret about Rosemary, their retarded daughter. By the time John F. Kennedy became president of the United States, having a retarded child was becoming less of a stigma. Parents had a new sense of freedom, association, and courage to advocate for their retarded children.

The first issue demanding their attention was the residential institution. By the late 1960s, an exposé of institutions was opened that rapidly led to efforts to close them. Books and the popular media showed the nation, in graphic detail, retarded individuals living in sordid conditions—naked in windowless rooms, with trash and human excrement strewn about. The places that loving parents had chosen to give their children a safe, nurturing environment were dens of negligence and abuse. To force change, they needed to organize.

Many local parent groups already existed. Most functioned as social support groups, but some had been able to influence local school officials to start special education classes. (Note that at this time, parents were demanding separate classes to meet their children's needs and to avoid the ridicule and rejection they might experience in regular classrooms.) On the national level, in 1950 some middle-and upper-class parents and professionals founded a small group called the National Association for Retarded Children, or NARC. (The group is now called The Arc.) As early as 1953, NARC had drafted a position statement entitled "The Education Bill of Rights for the Retarded Child," detailing the right of every retarded child to a program of education and training suited to his or her individual needs (Zigler, Hodapp, & Edison, 1990). NARC was soon to become one of the most powerful human services lobbies of the times, and parents "as 'angry lobbyists' became a powerful source of change" (Trent, 1994, p. 241).

"Scientific" Theories

The field of mental retardation was not a very sophisticated discipline prior to the 1960s. But despite the lack of sound empirical and theoretical foundations, some scholars were able to sway colleagues, policy makers, and the public to a new way of thinking about educating retarded children.

At roughly the time when the deplorable living conditions in institutions was being exposed, Wolf Wolfensberger brought the notion of "normalization" to American shores. **Normalization** was an idea begun in Sweden, where scientists were arguing that people with mental retardation had a right to a normal lifestyle—getting up at a regular time, going to work or school, enjoying recreation with family and friends. Wolfensberger (1972) stretched this idea to the normalization of services as well. He argued that not just institutions but sheltered workshops and special classes called attention to the "devalued" qualities of retarded individuals, which only reinforced these qualities (Trent, 1994). He believed that if we treated retarded people with more dignity and respect, they would lead more dignified, respectable lives.

Another tack was introduced by Lloyd Dunn (1968). Writing during the height of the civil rights movement, Dunn questioned the motives behind placing children in special education classes (Semmel, Gerber, & MacMillan, 1995). He argued that these classes had become a dumping ground for "undesirables," especially blacks who were being overidentified and forced into this poor excuse for an education. He gave credence to his views by drawing on science. He "proved," through a "selective" literature review (only those studies that supported his position) that labeling and special class placement had deleterious effects on minority children (Hallahan & Kauffman, 1995).

With this "scientific" backing, a realization that institutions were bad places, a growing army of parent advocates, and a nation determined to end racial discrimination, the elements were in place for a radical reform of education for children with disabilities. All the movement needed was some friends in the right places (Turnbull & Turnbull, 1996). President Kennedy had left a legacy of improving services for retarded individuals. His (and Rosemary's) sister Eunice Kennedy Shriver had a prominent position on the President's Panel on Mental Retardation; her husband, Sargent Shriver, was a powerful figure in national politics. NARC had become a savvy and well-organized lobby. What is now called the Council for Exceptional Children, a professional group of special educators with some parent members, was working hard on the cause. The time was ripe for Congress to act to ensure the educational rights of children with disabilities.

Early Lawsuits and Laws

The courts were the first to prod Congress to move. In the 1971 case of *Pennsylvania Association for Retarded Children (PARC) v. Commonwealth of Pennsylvania*, a parent group was successful in overturning a state law that allowed public schools to deny access to retarded children. The court ruled that not only did the state have to provide them with an education until the age of 21, but the education had to be appropriate to each child's individual capacity to learn (Martin, Martin, & Terman, 1996). The next year, suit was filed against the District of Columbia on behalf of children with retardation or behavioral disabilities. In this case, *Mills v. Board of Education* (1972), the school board argued that it did not have enough money to serve the more than 12,000 children with disabilities in the district. The court ruled that this practice violated the equal protection clause of the Fourteenth Amendment because it allowed "the burden of insufficient funding to fall more heavily on children with disabilities than on other children" (Martin, Martin, & Terman, 1996, p. 28). These landmark cases, and a spate of appeals and state court rulings, firmly established the constitutional right of children with disabilities to a free, appropriate education. These various rulings were soon codified in federal laws.

The Rehabilitation Act of 1973 was the first major effort to end discrimination against people with disabilities, just as earlier laws had made it illegal to discriminate against citizens on the basis of race. The act applied to all recipients of federal funds. Public schools at the time received very little federal money, but they did get some and therefore had to comply with the law. Later, the Americans with Disabilities Act of 1990 (ADA) expanded the rights of handicapped individuals by barring discrimination in employment, public accommodations, transportation, and telecommunications. This law does not specifically apply to education, but it gives parents many legal remedies for fighting discrimination. For this reason, many suits filed against schools for alleged violations of the rights of children with disabilities are filed under the ADA (Martin, Martin, & Terman, 1996). This law also protects the rights of older students attending private colleges.

THE INDIVIDUALS WITH DISABILITIES EDUCATION ACT (IDEA)

Although most of the successful battles for a public education were waged by parents of children with mental retardation, children with all types of disabilities shared in their success. The deciding victory came in 1975 with the passage of PL 94-142, the Education for All Handicapped Children Act. An ardent supporter of the bill and the one who shepherded it through Congress was Senator Lowell Weicker, the father of a child with Down syndrome. Signed by President Gerald Ford, the act took effect during the 1977–1978 school year. It was renamed the IDEA (PL 101-476) in 1990.

As explained in the previous section, the educational rights of children with disabilities had been interpreted by the courts in the context of the Constitution. PL 94-142 did not establish any new rights but served as "a comprehensive scheme set up by Congress to aid the states in complying with their Constitutional obligations to provide public education for children with disabilities" (Martin, Martin, & Terman, 1996, p. 30). Critical elements of the scheme include identification, evaluation, and determination of eligibility; an individualized education program for each eligible child; education in the least restrictive environment; parent participation; and due process (the rights of parents throughout this process and procedures for appeals).

Identification

Referrals of children thought to be in need of special services may be made by parents and pediatricians but, at least for the school-age population, they are generally made by teachers. The basis for the referral can be anything that suggests that the child's educational needs are not being met in the classroom: Examples are academic failure, behavior problems, poor social relationships, and lagging motor skills. Nationally, 3 to 5 percent of the school-age population is referred each year; 92 percent of these children are tested, and 74 percent of those tested ultimately receive special education services (Hocutt, 1996).

Eligibility Determination

Referred children are tested by a team that might include regular and special education teachers; speech, language, and physical therapists; school psychologists; and physicians. Not all of these specialists are required for each child, of course, but testing must cover all areas related to the educational problem. IQ and achievement tests, personality assessments, and physical exams are examples of the measures that might be used. Parents must consent to testing, but they do not have to accept the results. They are free to obtain an independent evaluation, which the school must consider in conjunction with its own. Children must be reevaluated every three years, or sooner at parental request. If the evaluation uncovers a learning problem that meets the diagnostic criteria used by the school (often the disability categories of the IDEA) and it is determined

Gifted and Talented Children

The average range for intelligence encompasses IQ scores between two standard deviations below and above the mean of 100. Individuals with IQs below 70 are considered retarded; those with IQs above 130 are generally called gifted. Having an exceptionally high IQ does not guarantee a successful career in school or in the professions. As with any child, gifted children must have academic stimulation, guidance, and nurturance to realize their inherent potential. Because their potential to make significant contributions to society is high, education for gifted children is a common topic in discussions of school reform and raising academic standards.

Unlike children with disabilities, gifted students have no guarantee of a "free, appropriate education." Where there are laws mandating that such students be identified, specialized education services do not necessarily follow. In Connecticut, for example, school districts must identify the top 5 percent of their student populations as gifted, but whether or not programs for these students are provided depends on local choice and finances. Where gifted programs exist, referrals are commonly made on the basis of standard achievement test scores, grades, and/or teacher recommendations. Just as cultural bias in any of these sources can lead to the overrepresentation of minorities in some disability categories, it can lead to their underrepresentation in the gifted grouping.

There is much debate about what constitutes an appropriate education for gifted children. One approach is to accelerate them through coursework and perhaps grades so they will be able to work on scholastics commensurate with their abilities. Another practice is to enrich the content and depth of the curriculum and concentrate on the development of critical thinking and problem-solving skills. Many private schools and camps turn handy profits providing such activities. Some public schools offer them in talented and gifted classes—typically pull-out programs that meet a few times a week. In the majority of schools, regular classroom teachers are responsible for keeping their bright students challenged.

Defenders of the more intensive of these methods argue that gifted children need specialized services as much or more than children with disabilities. They argue that regular class teachers have neither the time nor training to nurture the development of high intelligence. In one study, for example, 84 percent of gifted children in regular classes were found to receive the same instruction and curricula in core academic subjects as the rest of the class (Westberg et al., 1993). Thus it is not surprising that a common memory gifted adults have of their school years is boredom. Boredom and frustration explain why psychologists testing children for behavioral problems often find not some learning or socioemotional disability but superior intelligence (Tammi, 1991). These children easily become underachievers and have conflicts with teachers and parents who know they can do better. Although research has shown that gifted individuals are not more prone to mental illness than people with average intelligence, many report having low self-esteem and poor social relations in childhood as a result of their being "different." When they are grouped with intellectual peers, they might fit in better socially and achieve at a higher level.

On the other side of the controversy are those who feel that labeling and providing special programs for "gifted" students are elitist and counter to the premise of free public schooling—to provide equal opportunities for all. They believe that bright children do not need special services because they are bright and can do well no matter what. This is one reason gifted and talented programs are among the first to go when school districts have financial problems. During budget hearings these programs enlist few supporters (mainly parents and some teachers) and many detractors (especially parents who feel slighted because their children were not included). Joining the critics are some civil rights activists, who have argued before the federal Civil Rights Commission that gifted, honors, and advanced classes are discriminatory against *those who attend them.* Their reasoning is that students (particularly Asian Americans) who are labeled "whiz kids" and put in separate classes are deprived of exposure to "other aspects of education" and mainstream social interactions (Will, 1997).

What will become of education for the gifted and talented in the future? It seems unlikely that mandates for special-

ized education will be forthcoming. The movement lacks a strong, organized advocacy group, and the public is growing tired of more bureaucratic (and unfunded) mandates. Public education dollars are limited, and the mandated expenditures for special education for children with disabilities are consuming a growing share. On the brighter side, efforts to improve America's schools revolve around setting high academic standards for all children. The Regular Education Initiative, the Schoolwide Enrichment model (Renzulli & Purcell, 1995), and the recent "detracking" movement (Lynn & Wheelock, 1997) are examples of efforts to raise expectations for all students. When all students, not just "the best and brightest," are given quality educational opportunities, the brightest can be expected to benefit along with everyone else. Schools have a long way to go to achieve these ideals, so arguments about how best to educate gifted students will surely continue for some time.

that an appropriate education requires special services, the child is admitted to the special education system (Reschly, 1996). There is nothing to prevent schools from serving children with disabilities that are not listed (ADHD, for example) or who have other exceptional academic needs, but the majority do not.

Individualized Education Program (IEP)

A key plank of the IDEA is that children must receive education appropriate to their needs. The law requires that an **Individualized Education Program** (IEP) be developed for each child that describes her or his educational needs and goals, and what and where services will be provided to carry out the plan. The courts have ruled that the goals need not be restricted to academics. Social, behavioral, and mental health outcomes are appropriate when problems in these areas interfere with learning. Planning and placement team (PPT) meetings of staff and parents must be held every year to develop a new IEP.

Least Restrictive Environment

Each child in special education must receive services in the **least restrictive environment.** Where the child will be educated is determined in the PPT meeting and written into the IEP. Generally, staff first attempt to work within the regular classroom, modifying the program and providing educational supports to meet the child's needs. These changes are sometimes carried out by the classroom teacher, in consultation with special education teachers, or the special educator might come to the class to work with the child. If the child is still not benefiting, placement outside the classroom for at least part of the school day might be tried, or the child might be sent to a specialized school.

Placement decisions are a common source of contention between school boards and parents, accounting for 70 percent of due process cases (Rostetter, 1994). Some of these cases arise when parents want their child in a regular class and the school does not agree; more typically, parents demand a private school placement while administrators believe an appropriate education can be provided in the public district. Private settings are expensive, but the law prohibits schools from considering cost when determining what services a child requires. The only exception is when more than one appropriate program is available. Schools may then weigh costs in deciding among the alternatives (Martin, Martin, & Terman, 1996).

Parent Participation

The IDEA gives parents the right to be involved in their child's education to a degree envied by parents of children without disabilities. Parents must consent to evaluation once their child has been referred. They must be given the opportunity to participate in the design of the IEP. They must agree to the placement decision; if they do not, the child must "stay put" until a hearing is held. If parents need transportation or an interpreter to participate in any of these meetings, schools must provide them.

The strength of the parent involvement provisions of the IDEA can be traced to the strength of the parent advocacy that fueled passage of the law. The parent activists of the 1970s were fighting for their children's right to an education, a right to which children without disabilities had long been entitled. This was a noble and empowering cause that could not be pursued as effectively by anyone else. Aware of their critical role, they were determined to make it permanent. They succeeded, for the IDEA acknowledges parents as the primary agents in their child's development and accords them a respected partnership in decisions regarding every aspect of their child's education (Pizzo, 1995).

Due Process

Due process is a legal term that spells out the procedures that must be followed to protect individual rights and liberties. Due process under the IDEA involves the specific avenues available to parents in ensuring that schools carry out their legal obligations to the child. If parents are not given timely notice of an IEP meeting, for example, or do not agree to its content, they may pursue specific legal remedies. When services or placements are in dispute, parents may appeal before an impartial hearing officer. If they are still not satisfied, they may bring civil action against the school district in court.

Part H

Thus far, our discussion has focused on Part B of the IDEA, the part that applies to children between the ages of 3 and 21. Amendments passed in 1986 added Part H, which pertains to children with disabilities from birth until their third birthday. The disability must meet one of two criteria: (1) there must be a developmental delay in cognitive, physical, communication, social or emotional, or adaptive skills, or (2) there must be a diagnosis of a physical or mental condition that is likely to result in such a delay. States may use a third criterion and choose to serve children who are at risk of experiencing developmental delays without early intervention (Martin, Martin, & Terman, 1996). Risks are commonly determined by the presence of medical problems or environmental conditions such as poverty.

Like the IDEA itself, the adoption of Part H was propelled by parents who wanted helping services for their children and support in their roles of raising a child with a disability (Pizzo, 1995). Also like the original law, Part H is not mandatory. (States are obligated to ensure the constitutional rights of school-age children with disabilities, but they do not have to follow the procedures for doing so outlined in the IDEA. Nonetheless, all states do. All have also chosen to implement Part H.)

There are few other similarities between Part B and the Handicapped Infants and Toddlers Program, as Part H is formally titled. The federal government helps states with some of the costs incurred in providing educational services under the IDEA. Part H, however, provides very minimal resources to help states plan and develop services, not deliver them. Whereas Part B applies to education and public school systems, Part H applies to comprehensive services and multiple service providers. Each child referred with a suspected disability is given a comprehensive assessment of functioning and needs by professionals from several disciplines (for example, pediatricians, early childhood educators, developmental psychologists). An **Individualized Family Service Plan** (IFSP) is then written that details the needs and strengths of both the child and family and the services to be provided. Parents are involved in developing the IFSP, which is updated at least every six months. A case manager is appointed for each family to oversee the implementation of the plan and to coordinate the services of the professionals and agencies involved.

Though constitutional rights were behind the passage of the original IDEA, Part H is based more on the desire of members of Congress (particularly Senator Weicker) to spread the benefits of early intervention. Their goals were to enhance the development of young children with disabilities, reduce future educational costs, minimize institutionalization, and enhance the abilities of the family to meet the child's special needs (Gallagher, 1989). But why would states choose to comply with this largely unfunded massive overhaul of their human services? The answer,

The Progression of Laws Affecting Children with Disabilities

- **1996 Elementary and Secondary Education Act (ESEA), Title VI.** Established a Bureau for the Education of the Handicapped in the U.S. Office of Education. Also provided grants to states to develop and expand educational programs for children with disabilities.
- **1970 Education of the Handicapped Act.** Included in the ESEA. Codified many existing federal programs and funds targeted for education of children with disabilities into a comprehensive law.
- **1973 Rehabilitation Act, Section 504.** All recipients of federal funds (including schools and businesses with federal contracts) cannot discriminate in providing services or benefits to people with disabilities.
- **1975 Education for All Handicapped Children Act (PL 94-142).** All children with disabilities are entitled to a free, appropriate education in the least restrictive environment. Parental involvement and due process protections are established.
- **1986 Handicapped Infants and Toddlers Program (Part H of the Education for All Handicapped Children Act Amendments of 1986 (PL 99-457).** Encourages the development of comprehensive, multidisciplinary preventive and remedial services to very young children with or at risk of disabilities and their families.
- **1990 Individuals with Disabilities Education Act (IDEA).** PL 101-476 replaces PL 94-142. The main change is the new name.
- **1990 Americans with Disabilities Act.** Guarantees civil rights for people with disabilities by barring discrimination in employment, public accommodations, transportation, and telecommunications.
- **1996 Welfare reform changes eligibility for the Supplemental Security Income (SSI) program of the Social Security Administration.** This program provides cash benefits to over 6 million low-income persons with disabilities, including almost 1 million children. Stricter eligibility criteria, particularly for mental disorders, removed over 95,000 children from SSI rolls in the first year alone.
- **1997 Individuals with Disabilities Education Act Amendments of 1997 (PL 105-17).** The current version of the 1975 law governing the educational rights of children with disabilities.

Sources: "Appendix," 1996; Martin, Martin, & Terman, 1996; Pear, 1997; Weisz & Tomkins, 1996.

of course, is parent advocates—and a growing enchantment with the success of early, comprehensive service programs such as Head Start (see chapter 4).

OUTCOMES OF SPECIAL EDUCATION

Despite the huge number of children receiving special education, there is relatively little research demonstrating the results of the services in terms of child outcomes. Part of the reason is logistical. Special education services are tailored to the needs of each child, so researchers cannot compare groups who receive different treatments because all the members in all the groups receive different treatments. And the law will not allow evaluators to withhold services to form a control group. Another reason for the lack of empirical attention is that Congress has rejected the notion that services must be provided only if there are expected benefits (Herr, 1997). If services must be given regardless of outcome, there is no compelling reason to spend much time studying outcomes.

Keeping in mind the problems invading special education research, there is enough of it to draw some definite conclusions. First, no single intervention has been found to be uniformly successful for all students with disabilities (Terman et al., 1996). (The same can surely be said for teaching methods for nondisabled children.) Second, the contents of the intervention are more important than placement in benefiting children with disabilities (Hocutt, 1996). Third, research simply does not support the value of inclusion over special education (Siegal, 1996) or vice versa. Although one can easily find individual studies to contradict these conclusions, they are based on reviews of the entire literature presented in scholarly volumes (e.g., Kauffman & Hallahan, 1995a; *Special Education for Students with Disabilities*, 1996). The variation in findings that has led many scientists to call for more and better research will become apparent now as we discuss some of the evidence regarding placements and long-term outcomes.

Effects of Placement

The effects of special education and where it is delivered can be expected to vary with type and severity of disability. Results can also vary depending on whether one is looking at academic, social, or other outcomes. The goal for some children with severe disabilities, for example, is to be able to live in the community rather than an institution. One finding that is rather clear is that students without disabilities generally do not suffer academically by having children with disabilities in their classroom, and they might in fact benefit from the greater resources and better student–teacher ratio resulting from inclusion (Hocutt, 1996). However, when full inclusion brings into the classroom numbers of children with disabilities without additional support for teachers, Baines, Baines, and Masterson (1994) report, children without disabilities are "the big loser" (p. 62). These students must endure "constant, daily disruptions and lack of attention to their needs," and often the "instructional level to the entire class [is] lowered because of the special needs students." Teacher burnout is not uncommon.

There is some evidence that students with physical and sensory impairments might fare slightly better academically in regular classrooms (Hocutt, 1996; Wagner & Blackorby, 1996). As reported in Hocutt's (1996) review, children with severe mental retardation have more social interaction in integrated settings. Students with mild retardation, however, might or might not succeed as well academically and socially. Classroom and teacher characteristics appear to make the difference. Age might too, as some studies show that preschoolers with disabilities advance more in social skills in heterogeneous groups (Odom, McConnell, & McEvoy, 1992b), which theoretically at least can enhance cognitive, language, and motor development (Odom, McConnell, & McEvoy, 1992a).

Children with learning disabilities or SED generally do not fare as well in regular classes (Hocutt, 1996; Kauffman, 1995b). Both are likely to frustrate teachers by their low achievement and often poor peer relationships that lead to conflict in the classroom. Children with SED might present aggressive, disruptive, defiant, and/or dangerous behavior that teachers simply will not tolerate (Hocutt, 1996). Because these children are usually unable to adjust to the demands of the regular classroom, it is understandable that they are more successful in an environment designed to help them control their behavior. For both SED children and those with learning disabilities, social and academic failures can be reduced in separate settings, improving the children's self-image and ultimately effort to learn. Dramatic improvements, however, are not to be expected. Children with LD, in particular, are likely to have only modest gains from fairly intensive intervention (Terman et al., 1996), but without this help they only fall farther behind.

Whether a particular student fares better in an inclusive or a separate class has a lot to do with the particular modifications he or she needs. Some special educational services (speech therapists or reading specialists, for example) are easily brought to the regular classroom. Others, such as pervasive behavior management or crisis intervention, are not. By the same token, standard classroom practices can be more or less difficult to adapt to the needs of children with disabilities. As a group, these children need instruction that is more focused, consistent, and individually paced (Terman et al., 1996), and they need a lot more structure and individual attention. Regular classroom methods (independent study; whole-group instruction with the same content and pace) conflict with these needs. In fact, teachers with the most effective instructional and classroom management styles have been found to be most likely to resist the placement of special-needs children in their classes (Hocutt, 1996).

What makes the difference between success and failure in the regular classroom? The reviewers and books cited above are unanimous in concluding that successful inclusion requires significant resources, including extensive use of specialists and aides, smaller classes, and ongoing support and training for regular classroom teachers. Without these supports, and the personnel to implement them, children with disabilities might not have their educational needs met. This is why, to be effective, full inclusion will cost at least as much as, if not more than, out-of-class alternatives (Hocutt, 1996; Pilch, 1997; Terman et al., 1996).

Long-Term Outcomes

Concern about the cost of special education services and reports that recipients were not doing very well during the school years and beyond led Congress to take a hard look at long-term outcomes. They directed the U.S. Department of Education to commission a study of special education students after they left school. The National Longitudinal Transition Study of Special Education Programs (NLTS) was launched in 1987. The results reported here are taken from Wagner and Blackorby (1996).

The NLTS included over 8,000 students who had been served in special education in more than 300 school districts throughout the country. As would be expected, the results varied with type and degree of disability as well as classroom placements in high school. Students with physical or sensory disabilities had better employment rates if they attended regular academic classes. Regular classes, however, only helped those who succeeded in them—circular reasoning that offers no insights as to why (Wagner & Blackorby, 1996). Students with mild disabilities or SED were more successfully employed if they had attended vocational, regular education classes. Employment and wages increased in time for those who had taken a concentration in vocational education as opposed to survey courses.

Postsecondary education rates were not high. Among students with disabilities who graduated from high school, only 37 percent had some type of further education, compared with 78 percent of graduates in the general population. Only 4 percent went on to a four-year college. Getting through high school, however, was much less likely for special education students: 30 percent dropped out of high school, and 8 percent dropped out before they even got to high school. The most significant prediction of dropping out was course failure. Among those with SED, three-fourths failed a course and almost half dropped out (Wagner, 1995). Students with LD also had high dropout rates and poor outcomes for employment and further education.

What this complex array of findings tells us is, "What schools do can make a difference in what students later achieve" (Wagner & Blackorby, 1996, p. 118). Wagner and Blackorby (1996) believe that the current emphasis on more advanced courses and higher academic standards in high schools allows for less time for vocational education, the type of training that the NLTS found to be more beneficial to many students with disabilities. They argue that schools must do more to enable students with disabilities to succeed in school, because no class—academic or vocational, regular or special—can help a child who has left the system.

Certainly the clearest finding from the placement and long-term outcome research is that special education services cannot erase disabilities. Children with learning problems, by definition, do not learn as easily as those without disabilities. No program can change this fact. Programs can, however, help them overcome some obstacles to learning and be successful in school and eventually in work.

THE PLACEMENT CONTROVERSY

Today there is a strong movement to eliminate special education classes and serve all students in regular classrooms. Full inclusionists insist that separate classes are ineffective and demeaning. The defense argues that all the needs of all children with disabilities could never be met in regular education and calls for keeping a choice of placements. Surprisingly, both sides use the same principles to defend their positions: Inclusion is (or is not) practical, research supports their claims, it is morally wrong to segregate children or morally wrong not to, and their constitutional rights to equal educational opportunities are violated or protected in general education (Morse, Paul, & Rosselli-Kostoryz, 1997).

Pro and Con

Complaints against special education classes are necessarily generalizations. There are hundreds of thousands of these classes in schools across the nation, so no description could possibly apply to all of them. A common accusation is that special classes are a dumping ground for problem children whom teachers don't want in their classrooms. Critics argue that curricula in special education are generally poor and that academic standards are low. They point out that students almost always pass to the next grade and end up with diplomas they did not earn. Some believe that special education teachers are not well trained and see the high turnover in this field as evidence that they are inexperienced and not very dedicated. Finally, they appeal to the civil rights arguments that spurred passage of the IDEA. Just as it was wrong to segregate students by race, it is wrong to segregate them because of disability. The injustice is compounded because racial minorities are disproportionately identified as disabled. The association with race gives the inclusionists a degree of emotional appeal and moral superiority that has grabbed the attention of policy makers (Kauffman, 1995b).

Proponents of special education say that it can only be good for children to have highly trained teachers, smaller classes, and individual lesson plans (Morse, 1995). They point out that children are referred to special education in the first place because they did not succeed in the regular class. They believe that regular education is not equipped to accommodate individual differences in learning style or speed and cannot provide the social skills training or behavior modification that are often required. On their side are research findings that self-esteem is lower for disabled students in regular classes (Hocutt, 1996). Although they might be stigmatized by their separate placement, they are more stigmatized by their low achievement or poor behavior, which stand out in heterogeneous settings (Kauffman, 1995b). Regular education teachers often acknowledge that they do not have the training to meet special needs in their classrooms and need extensive resources and support to do so (Terman et al., 1996).

Those in favor of special classes also use the moral argument that it is wrong to deny children special educational treatment if they need it. Although they acknowledge that minorities are overrepresented in special education, they believe that this can be partly explained by the harmful effects of poverty. More minorities might be identified with "discretionary disabilities" like SED or LD, but more are also diagnosed with demonstrable problems like deafness and orthopedic impairments that are defined more objectively (Wagner, 1995).

It is important to note that parents of children with disabilities stand in numbers on both sides of the fence. Many want their children in separate settings, and many lawsuits have been filed against school boards that insist on regular class or school placement. Yet the full-inclusion movement is spearheaded by a group of parents with different leanings. They comprise The Association of Persons with Severe Handicaps, or TASH, a small group of advocates for children with severe intellectual disabilities. They are well organized and active, and have had considerable success in influencing school policies promoting full inclusion (Fuchs & Fuchs, 1995). Their power should not be underestimated. Recall that the massive reform of schools embodied by the IDEA was itself brought about by the parents of retarded children.

What is sometimes lost in the argument over where special education occurs is its content. Special education is an experience, not a place. Inclusion is a means, not an end (Siegel, 1996). Some children can be expected to thrive in the more challenging atmosphere of the regular class; others will experience failure and social isolation (Terman et al., 1996). Inclusion is an unacceptable option if the child will fail (Lieberman, 1988). Successful education should be the ultimate goal, regardless of placement.

Labeling

Even those who have no particular complaints against separate classes still worry about the deleterious effects of labeling. When a child is labeled "disabled," there is an unavoidable stigma that can hurt the child's self-esteem and call attention to the child's imperfect qualities. Common sense tells us that people often respond to labels (be they *nerd* or *genius*) by living up to them. Common sense, however, can be more common than sensible.

Labels can be harmful, but they can also be helpful. Hobbs (1974) advises that labels should never be used unless the benefits outweigh the potential harm. If the benefits are helpful services, they can be more valuable than the label is stigmatizing. Some hypothetical examples make this position clear. Intensive care units in hospitals exist for patients labeled "seriously ill." If the label and placement were taken away as discriminatory, it is unlikely that the patients would be served as well in the general ward (Diamond, 1995). By the same token, handicapped parking permits clearly identify people as handicapped and give them special places to park. Without these obvious symbols, it is wishful thinking to believe that the spaces in front of public buildings will be left open and only people with disabilities will use them (Kauffman, 1995b).

As in these examples, the use of labels and special placements in education can be condoned when they are more helpful than detrimental. A child labeled "disabled" has the door opened to a host of individualized services, parent involvement in education, and due process rights. Without identification and labeling, that door is locked and the child flounders in the regular class. This was the fear of an association of parents of children with learning disabilities, admittedly a relatively nonstigmatizing label. They argued for the preservation of the LD label and special education status because they believe the intensity of services their children need is not readily available in regular classrooms to unidentified students (Fuchs & Fuchs, 1995). Others have pointed out that the use of labels to segregate and discriminate against blacks in the days before civil rights is not the same as using them for children with disabilities. Race is educationally irrelevant, whereas disabilities are extremely important for educational programming (Kauffman & Hallahan, 1995b; Smelter, Rasch, & Yudewitz, 1994).

Hallahan and Kauffman (1995) argue that an extreme concern with labels represents an unwillingness to confront what the labels represent. They point out that associations for blind individuals have railed against the politically correct label "visually impaired" because they believe the word *blind* better conveys their needs. They have been joined by organizations for the deaf (not "hearing impaired") to protect their labels *and* separate educational settings. Without special classes, blind and deaf children would not identify with the culture of blind and deaf people and would not benefit from the interaction and support of their group (Fuchs & Fuchs, 1995). The opposite stance was taken by NARC, which in 1991 changed its name to The Arc. *The Arc* is a name, not an acronym. As explained on the group's Web site, the word *retarded* was removed "because of increased sensitivities from self-advocates, young parents, and others who object to the title." Several years ago there was an unrelated movement to replace the label *retarded* with *exceptional.* The effort backfired when financial contributions plummeted because donors were more willing to support retarded children than exceptional ones.

The debate over the value of labels has raged for decades and will undoubtedly continue in the years ahead. Federal law does require that children with disabilities be identified but does not mandate the use of labels. The 13 disability categories in the IDEA are optional. Massachusetts, for example, groups all children with disabilities into one category (Lewit & Baker, 1996). But that one category and one label entitle children to the full gamut of special educational services.

LEGISLATIVE CONTROVERSIES

When the latest revision of the IDEA was being formed, the debates in Congress were the most heated in recent memory. The main battleground was on administrative aspects of the IDEA, particularly on ways to reform special education finance and establish accountability mechanisms. School officials, government agents, and parents lined up en masse to make their views known. So heated was the discussion that the 104th Congress failed to reach agreement, leaving reauthorization of the IDEA until the next year. The bill (PL 105-17) was finally passed in 1997, but continuing debates have meant that regulations that help schools implement the law have not yet been issued at this writing in late 1998.

The guiding principle of the original law was the best interests of children with disabilities. As often happens in the policy-making process, however, the original purpose blurs as lawmakers attend to nitty-gritty details and listen to witnesses with different agendas. Children's needs thus garnered little attention during the recent hearings. Some discussion was devoted to defining the "least restrictive environment" as the regular classroom but, as discussed earlier, the range of placements was maintained. Congress did concede to inclusionists the requirement that the IEP contain an explanation if the child will not fully participate in general education. To stem the size and growth of the learning disability category in particular, the U.S. Department of Education recommended that the IDEA categories be dropped and replaced by a definition like that used in the Americans with Disabilities Act. With this change, only children with physical or mental impairments that substantially limit learning would be eligible for special education (Lewit & Baker, 1996). This proposal will undoubtedly be visited again in future hearings.

The only other matter discussed that directly related to children was whether they could be expelled from school for behavioral transgressions. Congress allowed expulsions for weapons, drugs, and serious violations of school rules not arising from a child's disability. School boards, however, might still have to provide educational services to students with disabilities who have been suspended from school for more than a few days.

Most of the debates centered on the cost of special education. The federal government actually pays a very small part of the bill. When the IDEA was first passed, funds were authorized to increase each year until 1982, when they were to cover 40 percent of average per-pupil expenditures (Parrish & Chambers, 1996). President Ford was reluctant to sign the bill because of its anticipated costs (Martin, Martin, & Terman, 1996). He should not have worried, because the federal share never reached authorized levels. Today it amounts to about 7 percent of the cost (Chambers et al., 1998), or $575 per student in 1998–1999. The rest is paid from state and local taxes. Because it costs more than twice as much (and in some cases many times more) to provide special as opposed to regular education, and because these costs are rising sharply, many worry that they are siphoning funds from regular education students.

Much discussion was devoted to changing federal funding formulas. Currently the government pays by the actual number of children served, limited to 12 percent of each state's school population. States must serve all children with disabilities, however, and some officials argued that the cap imposes an undue burden on states that have larger special-needs populations. On the other side were those who felt that the current system encourages schools to overidentify disabilities in order to receive higher subsidies. The U.S. Department of Education proposed a census-based approach to funding that would give states grants based on their total school enrollment instead of the actual numbers served. Proponents of this change argued that it would encourage states to serve more children outside of the special education system by providing more support to regular classrooms. Opponents were adamant that without specific funds targeted for specific children, the monies would not be used for their intended purpose. Their fears had been confirmed in New York State, which combined regular and special education funds back in the 1960s. The separation had to be reinstated when lawmakers noticed a precipitous drop in the number of children receiving special services (Martin, Martin, & Terman, 1996). In the end, Congress maintained existing funding methods but promised to move toward census-based funding when federal allocations reach a set amount.

The cost controversy also swirled around the issue of least restrictive environment. In many states, schools are reimbursed at higher rates to cover the expense of placing children in separate schools. This practice can obviously encourage placements in restrictive settings. Although O'Reilly (1995) found little evidence that schools were actually sending children off-campus to shift the financial burden to the state, the incentive to do so clearly exists (Parrish, 1994). On the other hand, special school tuition is very expensive and schools might overlook this option if they get no extra help to pay for it. Congress left this battle to the states, guiding them only by reemphasizing their duty to choose the least restrictive setting where a child's educational needs can be met.

Another cost consideration involves the expense of complying with the many provisions of the IDEA. According to Parrish and Chambers (1996), only 62 cents of every special education dollar go to instruction; 13 cents go to student assessments, and 11 cents are spent on administration. (The remainder is spent on related services and transportation.) The high costs of assessment are of particular concern. The average price of determining whether a child qualifies for special education is $1,648. For students with mild disabilities in resource room programs, further assessments consume 22 cents of every dollar. Numbers like these support Rostetter's (1994) contention that all of the legal and regulatory processes surrounding the IDEA have hindered the development of special education services because professionals are so absorbed in paperwork that they have little time to devote to the content and quality of their programs. He places part of the blame on administrators who "overinterpret" the law and go far beyond its requirements regarding eligibility and classification. They often do so out of fear of litigation if they overlook any due process rights. Congress has no authority over such attitudes, but it did help districts with due process costs by modifying the requirement that schools reimburse legal expenses to parents who bring their lawyers to IEP meetings and mediation.

One area that lawmakers had really hoped to strengthen is accountability in the special education system. The Government Performance and Results Act requires that all federally funded programs improve their performance and accountability. This mandate has proven difficult to apply to special education because the IDEA is administered at different levels that have different performance requirements. The federal government is interested in whether due process requirements are met. Schools prove that they are accountable in this sense by keeping detailed records of referral, assessment, and programming steps taken for each child and by collecting the related documents signed by parents or guardians. Accountability at the state level focuses on fiscal management—whether the funds targeted for special education are being used for special education. None of these agents encourages accountability in terms of educational outcomes (Terman et al., 1996).

Although every child's IEP details her or his educational goals, there has never been a workable requirement that progress be demonstrated toward achieving them. The 1997 IDEA takes a small step in this direction by requiring that the goals be "measurable." Terman et al. (1996) warn that this might not be such a good rule because it could lead to purposefully low goals being written into IEPs. Another weakness is that, although standardized tests are encouraged as measures, they may be given under modified conditions or substituted with other tests. Neither alternate must have demonstrated validity ("Legislative Action Moves Forward," 1997), however, so the results might not be meaningful.

This halfhearted attempt to establish accountability pales in comparison to the accountability demands being placed on the nation's public schools. Nonetheless, now that the NLTS has documented the poor outcomes of special education students in and out of school, the pressure for accountability will be increasingly felt in special education (Duchnowski & Kutash, 1997). It will be interesting to observe how the interests of lawmakers, school administrators, taxpayers, and parent advocates come to bear on the development of ways to hold schools responsible for the wise use of special education funds.

THE ROLE OF RESEARCH

Is special education a costly villain that labels children with unkind names, separates them from their friends, and denies them the opportunity to learn very much (Hallahan & Kauffman, 1995)? Or is it an effective system that ensures access to education, invites parents to be active participants, and provides appropriate, individualized services to children with disabilities? The answers to these questions are, of course, a matter of opinion. Opinions might hinge on the answers to more specific questions like which services are most effective for children with different types of disability and where these services are best delivered. These are empirical questions that are the province of applied research.

It has been over 20 years since schools began providing special education services under the IDEA, but there is little scientific evidence to support or negate the value of these practices. Much of the research is so old or poorly conducted that it sheds little light on issues of current importance (Hallahan & Kauffman, 1995). And much is presented in position papers and policy reports rather than in peer-reviewed scientific journals (Siegel, 1996).

The dearth of research causes problems that go beyond the obvious lack of guidance to improve services. A telling example is in the area of learning disabilities. The diagnostic criteria for LD are still ill-defined and have poor reliability and validity. This permits wide discrepancies in prevalence rates. Thus, children are twice as likely to be identified as LD in California as in Georgia (Lewit & Baker, 1996). When identification is so arbitrary, there is potential for abuse. There is also a mother lode of ammunition for those who question the reality of the diagnosis itself.

 Learning Disabilities: Overuse, Abuse, or Excuse?

Learning disabilities are a huge branch of special education. Children with LD constitute half of the special-needs population. Up to 80 percent of these students have reading disabilities (Lyon, 1996). Before the IDEA was enacted in 1975, LD was a tiny category and reading disabilities were almost unheard of. Children who had difficulty with learning were called "slow," and those who were slow to grasp reading were simply called poor readers. Today these students get a lot of special help and a lot of special privileges. They might be given a reduced course load and extra time to take exams and standardized tests. And because the rate of declassification is low, special treatment extends into college and sometimes into the workplace. Shalit (1997) describes instances of college students receiving extensive tutoring, personal note-takers, waivers of academic requirements, and options to take written tests orally and have exam questions explained to them. One law student sued the administrators of the New York bar exam for refusing to allow her unlimited time for the test, access to food and drink, and other accommodations. She won her suit and most likely access to a "life-long buffet of perks" under the Americans with Disabilities Act when she becomes a lawyer who can't read very well (p. 18).

The right to such perks is suspected as one reason the number of identified LD students has soared. Everyone would like to have special treatment and a competitive edge in school and work. Who would not welcome extra time to take the Scholastic Aptitude Test, Advanced Placement exams, or medical boards? (Shalit reports that untimed SATs give students an average 100-point increase in scores.) Many collegians would love to skip math or foreign language requirements. Every parent of a grade-schooler wants their child to have extra help and attention. Many parents, particularly in the middle class, seek the LD label to soothe their own disappointment when they realize that their little genius isn't getting straight A's by second grade.

What can be done to stem the growth of the ill-defined, impossible-to-measure category of LD? In addition to developing better definitions and measures, some practical suggestions deserve consideration. To weed out "impostors," Boston University president Jon Westling tightened documentation standards by requiring students to submit evaluations prepared by a physician or licensed psychologist within the last three years. He also refused to waive academic requirements (Shalit, 1997). (These policies were upheld in a court challenge, although students who appealed did receive monetary awards.) Zuriff (1996–1997) advises college professors to invoke their own First Amendment rights and resist intrusions into their classroom teaching for accommodations that are unreasonable or significantly alter their program's academic mission.

Reschly (1996), Spear-Swerling and Sternberg (1996), and others argue that educators should end their preoccupation with the learning-disabled or nondisabled dichotomy and view reading abilities as a continuum ranging from difficulty to facility in skill acquisition. Appropriate interventions could thus be offered to any child who appears to be stumbling anywhere along the road to reading. The large majority of reading disabilities, and consequently LD, will be nipped in the bud and never require costly extended services or extra time on the SATs. Spear-Swerling and Sternberg (1996) warn, however, that "as long as children need to be labeled to receive intensive educational services, and as long as the 'LD' label is the most appealing one available, the LD field will be popular" (p. 47).

The huge number of children and dollars involved in special education beg for some scientific attention to outcomes as well. Not only is there little evidence to convince taxpayers that special education "works," but the lack of theoretically sound and empirically tested objectives has allowed the system to be judged by impossible goals. For instance, critics are quick to cite low declassification rates as proof that special education has failed. Although it is true that only 4 percent of students return to regular education each year (U.S. Department of Education, 1996), it might be unreasonable to expect more. It is absurd to hope that deaf children will hear after a year or two of special services, that children with psychiatric disorders will be cured by a teacher, or that LD students will be taught not to have problems with learning. Instead of asking how many children no longer have disabilities after special education, a more appropriate question is whether they learned more than they would have without special attention. This question cannot be framed, nor can answers be forthcoming, without a lot of good scientific work.

Part of the reason for the lack of empirical attention to special education is historical. The IDEA was shaped by groups of "angry parents" and sympathetic public officials (Trent, 1994). Their actions were based on civil rights, and they carried them out in the courts and in the halls of Congress. Scientists were not invited into the process, although interpreting the U.S. Constitution was not their province anyway. As the battle for public education gained publicity and popularity, many scientists joined as followers. Their endorsements gave the movement a degree of scientific credibility that it did not really deserve.

A telling illustration is the thrust toward normalization and deinstitutionalization discussed earlier. Professionals lined up behind these slogans, although they had no evidence at all that these practices were of any benefit. Their enthusiasm drowned out their few colleagues who were saying that research was needed to determine if these changes would do more good than harm and that institutions should remain in place until the findings were in (Zigler, 1978). So institutions have all but disappeared, but there is no proof that successors like group homes are any better and some that they are just as bad or worse (Zigler, Hodapp, & Edison, 1990). We do know that deinstitutionalization of mentally ill individuals has had far-reaching, deleterious effects (Fuchs & Fuchs, 1995).

How did special education policies and practice drift so far from their foundations in knowledge (Paul & Rosselli-Kostoryz, 1997)? For one thing, best practices have been determined by slogans and the loudest voices rather than by sound developmental principles; secondly, the current focus is on input, on where and what services are delivered, rather than output (MacMillan, Semmel, & Gerber, 1995). Developmental science is well equipped to evaluate outcomes but has not done a very good job of it. For strong data to replace strong opinions, researchers will have to assume a much larger role than they ever had in the field of special education.

The stakes are high. Special education can be completely replaced by full inclusion if its worth cannot be proven and fierce antagonists have their way. By then it will be too late to prove that special education is or is not of value or that full inclusion is or is not the better alternative.

Research needs are clear and immediate. Scientists must identify appropriate and meaningful social and academic outcomes to children and methods to evaluate them (Siegel, 1996). They must work on definitional issues and test competing theories about best placements. Learning from past mistakes with deinstitutionalization, they should use their authority to advise against widespread implementation of full inclusion to the exclusion of other options. They should constantly remind policy makers and the public that inclusion is not a proven treatment but can be justified as an experiment in need of careful study to establish its value, to discern problems, and to develop ways to improve it. For academics to jump on this bandwagon before full inclusion has had such empirical scrutiny "is an invitation to eventual ridicule" (Kauffman, 1995a, p. 205). Finally, even if civil rights remain a theme in the special education arena, developmentalists have over the years learned a lot about applying research to other areas of children's rights, such as child custody and the use of children as witnesses (Siegel, 1996). They should be able to extend this expertise to the educational rights of children with disabilities.

This careful scientific attention will do much more than add to the knowledge bank of effective educational practices for children with special needs. It will focus the spotlight on the best interests of the child and away from the competing ideologies of those on either side of the inclusion fence. By standing as child advocates rather than program advocates (MacMillan, Semmel, & Gerber, 1995), scientists can become much-needed role models for what is really at stake here—enabling all children with disabilities to fulfill their potential and contribute all they can to society.

SUMMARY

Children with disabilities are an extremely diverse population. Whether they have physical or sensory impairments, mental retardation, speech or language problems, severe emotional disturbances, or specific learning disabilities, all have persistent educational needs that are not well met in standard classroom environments. Less than 25 years ago, many children with disabilities were excluded from public schools altogether or did not receive education suited to their needs. In 1975, Congress passed PL 94-142, now called the IDEA. The law gave children with disabilities access to schooling, gave their parents a role in their education, assured appropriate individualized services in the least restrictive setting, and protected these rights by establishing due process procedures. Beyond these amazing achievements, the IDEA had an enduring impact on the humane treatment of individuals with disabilities. It "fostered and reinforced a positive climate of belief and set of attitudes concerning the handicapped" (Singer & Butler, 1987, p. 151).

The IDEA resulted from successful advocacy by parents of children with disabilities. The law represents democratic principles at their best—government of, by, and for the people, all of whom are treated equally. Over time, however, this wonderful idea has become bogged down in administrative details and troubled by burgeoning populations and costs. Concerns have been raised that the practice of labeling children as having disabilities results in stigma, low academic expectations, and the overidentification of minorities. Debates over the meaning of education in the "least restrictive environment" have become especially heated. Full inclusionists argue that all children with disabilities have a right to spend the entire school day in the regular class. Those who would preserve the current range of placement options counter that resource rooms, special classes, and separate schools *are* the least restrictive settings for children who cannot receive appropriate instruction in regular classes. Yet another debate arises from the recent emphasis on accountability in education. There are few data to show how well special education works, provoking many to wonder whether it is worth the money.

Developmental scientists have an important role to play in settling these debates and guiding the future evolution of education for children with disabilities. Their job is to generate the best data they can and to share it with those who need it to make informed decisions.

Epilogue: From Consciousness to Consensus

Throughout this volume we have tried to emphasize that virtually every topic in the field of child development and social policy can be viewed from at least two, and usually many more, perspectives. In the past two or three decades, however, one point of view has prevailed with respect to children and families. In newspapers, on television, and in other media, at professional conferences, in legislative hearings at all levels of government, the word is out: Children and families are in crisis. Headlines trumpet that the family is breaking down, that marriage is defunct, that America's children are morally, spiritually, and educationally bankrupt. Much of what is said and written has an apocalyptic flavor—the decay of family life is "unique and unprecedented" (Popenoe, 1996, p. 194)—but most of the stories that follow these headlines are bolstered by statistics: Over 3,000 children an hour are neglected or abused (Children's Defense Fund, 1997d). Illicit drug use is on the rise (Hall, 1998). Children are the poorest Americans (National Center for Children in Poverty, 1998).

The tone of current writing about the state of children and childhood today is largely negative. Titles of academic and popular books about childhood, too, are likely to emphasize the problems children face, as they are characterized as "vulnerable" (Weissbourd, 1996), "a generation in crisis" (Hamburg, 1992), or "at risk" (American Bar Association, 1993), and their policy concerns as "futile" (Steiner, 1981). Among all of this alarm, one view of the present state of the American family is especially prevalent—and especially fallacious. This is the view that the problems facing children and families at the start of the twenty-first century represent a significant decline in status *relative to some earlier, mythic golden age*. The present day is continually compared, implicitly if not always overtly, to this temporal Shangri-la. The problem is not new, of course. Much as pundits and politicians in the 1980s and 1990s longed for the supposed stability and integrity of the 1950s, so, too, did the rapid social changes of the 1950s inspire nostalgia for the allegedly simple, stable, and more innocent days of the 1920s and 1930s—a time, ironically, viewed contemporaneously as an age of revolutionary sexual freedom and social change (Gillis, 1996).

We stand with those who challenge idealized notions of perfect families, images in part created, not merely captured, by 1960s television sitcoms like "The Donna Reed Show" and "Leave it to Beaver" (Coontz 1993, 1997; Skolnick, 1991). Gillis (1996), for instance, views the origins of these concepts as being both recent and politically driven, a reaction to a time of demographic statistics that, taken out of context, appear frightening and hopeless. The United States is a young nation, and viewing important topics in light of our history is still a relatively novel approach. When we hear or read of child and family issues in the popular presses today, what we most often get is a snapshot of "children now" or "today's children." Rarely do popular journalists or even academicians reach back more than a half century in their efforts to make sense of the issues that define children's lives. We believe, however, that for the student of social policy and child development, a thoughtful analysis of the state of children requires not merely a developmental perspective, but a historical one as well.

CHILDHOOD'S HISTORY: THE LONG VIEW

Earlier in this volume we discussed the insights that, taking a long view of the history of childhood, can be brought to bear on our understanding of child maltreatment. Child development experts have long wrestled with the history of childhood. A small but notable group of psychologists—insightful, but too sel-

---

Milestones in the Culture of American Childhood

1946	Dr. Spock first publishes *Baby and Child Care*.
1976	First Gymboree opened.
1938	March of Dimes Birth Defects Foundation begun.
1937	Political cartoonist Theodor Geisel ("Dr. Seuss") publishes his first children's book, *And to Think That I Saw It on Mulberry Street*.
1964	First patented infant safety seat designed to protect and not merely restrain infants traveling in cars is marketed.
1938	Rhode Island becomes first state to require syphilis screening of all pregnant women.
1942	Penicillin successfully purified from molds.
1947	Children's aspirin first marketed.
1943	First list of Recommended Dietary Allowances of nutrients and calories published.
1939	Commercial television makes its debut at the World's Fair; sets won't be available to the public until 1946.
1972	Introduction of the videocassette recorder (VCR).
1969	"Sesame Street" premiers.
1938	View-Master toys are introduced; during World War II they are used as training aides for the U.S. Armed Forces.
1952	Mr. Potato Head first marketed.
1959	Barbie makes her debut; Ken will follow in 1961.

1953	James Watson, Francis Crick, and Rosalind Franklin describe the structure of DNA.
1963	Maurice Sendak publishes *Where the Wild Things Are*.
1976	Drs. Marshall Klaus and John Kennell publish *Maternal-Infant Bonding*; though the theory of a critical period at birth for bonding is later modified, the book revolutionizes hospital labor, delivery, and maternity care practices.
1963	Betty Friedan's feminist classic, *The Feminine Mystique*, is published, leading to changes in attitudes about women's roles, workplace participation, and family demographics.
1961	Procter & Gamble first mass-markets Pampers disposable diapers.
1935	The Social Security Act is passed, providing assistance to poor, elderly, and widowed Americans.
1970	The use of lead-based paints in dwellings is banned.
1956	Mary White and Marion Thompson found La Leche League to encourage breast-feeding by offering education and support to nursing mothers.
1960	Oral contraceptives approved for use in the United States.

Source: "Fifty Ideas That Changed the American Baby," *American Baby*, May 1988.

dom heeded—have emphasized the need to view children and families from a historical, as well as a developmental, perspective (e.g., Ariès, 1962; Cahan et al., 1993; Elder, Model & Parke, 1993; Kessen, 1965, 1979; Vinovskis, 1985). We cannot truly understand children or childhood, these workers argue, until we understand their history. In this chapter, as we seek to make predictions about the near futures of the children we study today, we must begin by looking backward, and thus we began this epilogue with a brief overview of the history of childhood.

How Are Today's Children Doing?

We hope that you have supplemented your reading of this volume, either formally or more casually, by taking note of children's issues featured in the media as you have read these chapters. Perhaps a story about health care legislation caught your ear as you listened to the news on the radio. Perhaps friends or family members have described to you their difficulty in finding high-quality, affordable day care. Maybe you are more likely to read a news item in the paper about welfare reform than you would have been before using this book. If so, you are now in a better position to evaluate current and future topics having to do with child and family policy. Most of all, we hope, you now have a better sense of perspective with respect to the status of children today. Children and families have a number of urgent needs that are being addressed with greater or lesser effectiveness, but in no case will a sense of hysteria or hyperbole serve you—or them—as you evaluate their condition and the resources necessary to better that condition.

If you look back over the historical material presented in chapter 1 and other chapters, it should become immediately apparent that, in many important respects, children in America today are infinitely better off than their counterparts of 200, 100, or even 50 years ago. No longer are children the legally disposable property of their families; no longer are children's murders at the hands of their parents taken in stride by our society. Infant mortality rates today are vast improvements over those of even a few decades ago. More American children than ever before in our history have access to educational services; more American children than ever before complete high school. Poverty rates overall are lower today than they were even 50 years ago (Danziger & Danziger, 1993; Minow & Weissbourd, 1993).

This does not mean, however, that we can be entirely sanguine about the status of our children. The rate of births to teen mothers are only about half of what they were in the 1950s, but teens who became pregnant then were more likely to be married and to have the support of immediate and extended family. Furthermore, attenuated educational attainment as a result of early pregnancy was not widely held to be as detrimental in the society of the 1950s as it is today, although in both cases early pregnancy limited a girl's options. In this case, as in others, it is difficult to say who is at more of a disadvantage, today's pregnant teen or her forerunner in the 1950s (Coontz, 1997). Today concern is more likely to focus on the fact that nearly one-third of all pregnancies in the United States occur outside of marriage than on the age of the mother per se (Popenoe, 1996).

Analyses that compare the status of children today with those of another era miss almost as many points as they make. If any level of infant mortality is unacceptable, if poverty levels are *still* too high, even if low compared with those of a century or a decade or a week ago, what do we gain from making comparisons of this sort? Social historian Stephanie Coontz (1997) suggests that an historical understanding of these issues provides a sense of perspective on what is a true crisis and what is a perennial issue. It is often said, for instance, that teen pregnancy is epidemic in the United States, but a look backward at demographic data reveals that, in fact, adolescent childbearing is endemic to our society and probably always will be. This understanding informs our policy options. We might, for instance, recommend taking a less crisis-oriented stand on adolescent sexuality, contraceptive use, pregnancy, and child rearing, and "normalize" services targeting this group and their children, making them more widely available. We might, on the other hand, accept the perennial nature of the phenomenon in this country, but compare our adolescent pregnancy rates with those of other Western nations (which tend to be far lower than ours), and strive to identify and emulate the conditions that more successfully promote delayed childbearing in other countries, or, indeed, in segments of our own country.

Is a Sense of Crisis Justified?

We believe the sense of crisis related to children's issues today is driven by many phenomena. One might well be the age in which we are living. As we embark on a new century, a sense of millenialism informs human behavior (Gould, 1997). We are driven to take stock of our human situation and to expect patterns to emerge in our lives, especially those that reflect superlatives and shortcomings. The journey of the baby-boom generation into parenthood and grandparenthood also has an impact on the prominence and urgency with which child and family issues are discussed and deliberated, and adds to our perception of these issues the filter of nostalgia for a time perceived as less complex and more orderly.

The wealth of information available to us on the needs of children and on a variety of perspectives on the best way to meet these needs is almost overwhelming today, and this, too, fuels this sense of urgency. In particular, the disjunction between what we know about child development—recent research on brain development being a case in point—and what we as a nation actually *do* for children and families is all too apparent today. Parents are better informed about child development by virtue of their access to hundreds of parenting periodicals and literally thousands of books on child development and child rearing, not to mention an almost oppressively large body of resources available on the Internet. Children's issues are routinely featured on television as well now, both in programs devoted exclusively to child development and in prime-time news digest programs. As a result, we are better informed consumers of child care, health care, and educational services. We are also more demanding consumers of child-care legislation, though this does not imply that there is always a consensus on *what* we demand.

Political changes, as well, have lent a sense of exigency to examinations of child and family concerns. Conservatives and liberals alike are concerned for the welfare of children, but changing political trends change the focus and spin of the dialogue; during the ascendancy of a conservative zeitgeist, social phenomena at odds with expressed values might be demonized and portrayed as being historically anomalous instead of merely passing, and not unprecedented, trends.

We are currently living in an era in which much attention is being paid to children and family issues. It remains to be seen whether the media and government continue to pay so much attention, and whether topics with practical applications to child and family life continue to be acceptable foci of scholarly pursuits. Making progress in the ways in which our society *thinks* about children will require nothing short of the kind of general consciousness raising that led to the civil rights movement and the women's movement (see Stolley, 1993), as well as strategies aimed at addressing specific problems.

ISSUES SHAPING THE FUTURE

We have tried in this volume to present basic issues that define the social and political landscape of the study of child development and social policy. By the time you read this, the legislative measures described herein will be old news, and new forces will be shaping life for children and families. The basic *principles* discussed here, however, can help you to determine whether the needs of children are being addressed by the actions of adults, and to decide what more *should* be done, and what more *might* be done—keeping in mind that these are seldom the same.

Further, for the foreseeable future, the major *issues* described here will in all likelihood continue to inform and lie at the core of children's policy. Day care, health care, mental health, public health issues (e.g., substance abuse and community violence), workplace issues, and children's rights and parents' rights will continue to be researched, discussed, and debated as long as there are children and families.

Even if the topics themselves remain constant, few issues in child development and child policy reflect a static consensus of either expert or popular opinion. The attendant policy issues, too—the extent to which government should be involved in finding and supporting solutions to problems in these areas, for example—will also reflect ideological shifts. Even if a question appears to be fundamental, the answer will vary with the political tides, the nation's economic strength, or the current focus of research. Throughout your life, try to be aware of these pendulum swings. Ask yourself: Has this position always prevailed? What was believed about this issue 20 years ago? What has changed to bring about a difference of opinion, and what changes might swing the pendulum back in the opposite direction? What constants exist, either in the nature of the child, or in our treatment of children, to solidify and advance our understanding of this issue?

Ironically, even though the questions about child development often change, many of the answers not only remain the same, but reflect a certain consensus among experts of most political and ideological persuasions (Hamburg, 1992; Kamerman & Kahn, 1995; Leach, 1994; Popenoe, 1996; Schorr, 1988; Weissbourd, 1996). Though we might disagree on the nature and extent of supports provided to families, virtually all experts on children and families can agree on a few basics:

- Children benefit from being in a loving, dependable nuclear family, in which at least one—and preferably two—parents are physically and emotionally available to the child.
- A supportive community, beginning with the extended family, promotes optimal parenting and healthy child development.
- Support and intervention in the early years are critical, but should not be discontinued as children grow into preschool, middle childhood, or adolescence.
- The availability of a broad spectrum of future options—both educational and occupational—along with adequate preparation to take advantage of these, promotes optimal outcomes for children.
- Interventions and supports that focus on families as a whole are more effective than those that treat children in isolation.
- An investment in children is an investment in the future strength of our nation.

The basics of what we know about child and family development will continue to be the foundation of what we ought to do for children and families, and social policies—whether intended to benefit children, parents, or the economy—will continue to have an impact on both individual families and the strength of the nation as a whole. It is now up to you, the student—whether you influence the lives of children as a parent, an educator, an employer, a community member, a voter, or even a policy maker yourself—to remember this and to practice the principles learned here.

Glossary

applied research   Research conducted in an effort to solve a problem or to provide information that can be put to some specific use.

attachment   The loving and enduring bond between the infant and the caregiver. Mary Ainsworth identified three types of attachments: secure, anxious, and avoidant.

attrition   The loss of participants from the pool of evaluation study subjects over time.

baseline data   A set of data gathered at the beginning of a study, or prior to an intervention, that allows one to compare to subsequent data and examine changes over time.

blended family   A family created by the remarriage of a parent with children following divorce.

block grants   Federal funds awarded to the states, who have responsibility for their allocation and administration.

boarder babies   Infants hospitalized beyond a period of medical necessity following birth solely because their parents are unable or unwilling to provide care for them.

busing   Provision of transportation for schoolchildren to schools outside their communities in order to achieve racial desegregation.

Chapter 1   The largest federal program providing school districts with funds to serve poor and educationally disadvantaged students.

character education   A curriculum designed to instill integrity and deference toward authority, with the eventual goal of improved academic performance.

charter schools   Small public schools endorsed and funded by public school districts but operated by private individuals or groups of individuals.

child allowance   Government funds, disbursed annually to parents in some nations on a per-child basis, intended to subsidize parental leaves, child care, or educational costs.

Child Care and Development Block Grant   A 1997 block grant that provides some subsidy monies for child care for low-income families. States are required to match the funding, and the subsidies are available to families with incomes below 85 percent of the state median income, though individual states might set levels lower than this.

Child Health Insurance Program (CHIP)   A recent federal initiative that provides funding to make health insurance available to previously uninsured children.

child welfare era   The period in the United States from 1870 to 1920, considered a renaissance for children with the passage of legislation that restricted child labor and established reform schools, orphanages, and child study institutes.

cluster analysis   A statistical method that defines patterns across a set of variables, allowing variables with similar outcomes to be grouped together.

comparison group (also: **control group**) Group of subjects in a study or experiment who receive no intervention or treatment, to be compared with treatment subjects in order to determine the effectiveness of an intervention.

congenital abnormalities Abnormalities present at birth.

cost-effectiveness A program is said to be cost-effective when it saves more money per participant than it costs to mount the program.

critical period A specific developmental period during which environmental influences can play a crucial role in how an individual's genetic potential is expressed; a time in the developmental process when the organism is especially sensitive to a particular influence.

demographics Information and statistics that describe the makeup and balance of a population.

desegregation Reduction or elimination of the segregation of minority groups.

developmental delay Inability to complete a task that the majority of one's peers are able to master at a specific age or stage.

developmental screenings Assessment of a child's health, developmental skills, or capacities (e.g., hearing or vision) intended to identify problems that can impede healthy development, educational progress, etc.

developmental sequences More or less orderly and universal phases that developmental psychologists have identified in the growth and development of children.

developmentally appropriate Said of a service, curriculum, intervention, or activity that supports a child's developmental level.

due process A legal term for the procedures that must be followed to protect individual rights and liberties.

early intervention The initiation of medical and developmental screenings, services, and assistance early in life, which has been empirically demonstrated in many cases to reduce or attenuate negative health, psychosocial, and educational development.

ecological approach An approach to child development according to which all spheres of the child's environment (e.g., home, school, community), and those who interact with the child within those spheres, are important influences on the child.

education voucher Allocation of public education funds to families who wish to send their children to schools other than the public schools—often private or religious schools.

educational parity A condition in which students from heterogeneous racial, ethnic, or economic backgrounds receive educational services that are of equal or comparable quality.

English as a Second Language (ESL) A program in which non-English-proficient students spend most of their school day in full-English classrooms but also receive supplemental instruction in English.

environmental deprivation Suboptimal conditions in which children lack the social and cognitive stimulation deemed necessary for their healthy development.

epidemiology The study of the cause of a disease or disorder, its distribution (geographic, ecological, and ethnic), its method of spread, and measures for control and prevention.

estimation phase The second stage of policy development, during which the full scope of the problem is evaluated.

etiology The cause of a disease or disorder.

evaluation phase The fifth stage of policy development, during which the effectiveness of a program or plan is assessed following its implementation.

family allowance See *child allowance*.

family preservation   A movement or trend in which courts attempt to allow children to remain with their biological parents and to provide social supports to these families, as opposed to foster care placement.

family support programs   Programs in which basic services and educational opportunities are provided to parents in order to help them help themselves and their children, with the long-term goal of enhancing parenting skills and parent and child educational, health, and psychosocial outcomes.

flex time   An employer-sponsored service, intended to enhance family life and to help parents meet the needs of their children, in which employees are given a high level of flexibility in scheduling their arrival and departure times and their days off.

homeschooling   An alternative to public education in which children are taught at home by parents.

home visitation   Provision of early intervention or remedial services to a child or family by a health or education professional or paraprofessional in the child's own home; often coupled with parent support and education.

immersion programs   Educational programs in which limited-English-proficient students spend all day in full-English classes where their native language is used only to clarify English instructions.

implementation stage   The fourth stage of policy development, in which proposed solutions to policy problems are set into motion.

incidence   The frequency with which an event, disorder, or problem occurs during a given period of time.

inclusion   The practice of including special-needs students in regular classrooms, often accompanied by an educational aide to assist the classroom teacher.

Individualized Education Program (IEP)   An individualized plan for a child with a disability, required by law, describing the educational program that will be implemented to meet the child's educational needs and goals.

Individualized Family Service Plan (IFSP)   An education plan developed for a young child who is suspected to have a disability. An IFSP includes a comprehensive assessment by a team of professionals and a written plan developed in conjunction with parents that details the needs and strengths of the child and family and the services to be provided.

initiation phase   The first stage of policy development, during which a problem is identified.

integrated day program   An alternative to traditional public schooling, first developed in Britain, wherein students work at their own pace and design much of their own curriculum.

kinship care   An informal arrangement in which a nonparent relative cares for a foster child as an alternative to foster care placement.

least restrictive environment   Placement of special-needs children in the most inclusive setting appropriate to meet their needs; an outgrowth of the Individuals with Disabilities Act.

licensed care   Child-care settings certified as having met or exceeded minimal health, safety, and quality criteria set by the state.

lobbying   Seeking to influence legislators in favor of a special interest.

longitudinal research   Investigative methods used to observe the same individuals repeatedly over time, often over many years.

looping   The practice of keeping the same students and teacher together as a class as they pass through two or more grades in school.

low birthweight   For a human newborn, weight at birth less than or equal to 5 1/2 pounds (2,500 grams).

magnet schools   Public schools that feature a specialized curriculum, such as arts or sciences or a particular vocational field.

mainstreaming   See *inclusion.*

matched comparisons   Pairing participants and control-group members for statistical comparison on the basis of pertinent demographic characteristics.

means-tested   Said of a service or program available only to families and children living below certain income levels.

meta-analysis   A statistical synthesis of effects across multiple studies.

migrant families   Families who move from region to region following available work.

national educational standards   Uniformity throughout the country with regard to educational goals and performance.

neonatal period   The first month following birth.

NICU   Newborn intensive care unit.

normalization   Providing as normal a lifestyle as possible for individuals with special needs. See *inclusion* and *least restrictive environment.*

outcome evaluation   Evaluation in which the assessed variables have to do with the short- or long-term effectiveness of a particular policy or program.

paid infant care leave   Time off following the birth of a child, with at least partial income replacement and a guarantee of continued employment.

perinatal period   The period encompassing the last month of pregnancy and first month after birth.

plasticity   Amenability to a certain amount of change (in health or psychosocial functioning) through intervention.

poverty level   An index, used by the federal government to define poverty, calculated at three times the current "economy food budget."

predictive validity   A measure or process is said to have predictive validity if it is significantly related to outcome variables in the expected direction.

prematurity   The birth of a baby prior to 37 weeks gestation, regardless of birthweight.

primary prevention   Interventions aimed at preventing problems from developing in the future.

privatization   The act of reducing the role of government or increasing the role of the private sector in an activity or field, such as education.

process evaluation   A type of evaluation intended to assess the nature and efficacy of service delivery as it occurs, and to identify any unexpected positive or negative side effects arising from the program. See also *outcome evaluation.*

program evaluation   An assessment of a program's effectiveness at achieving its stated goals.

random assignment   Assignment of subjects to either the experimental or the control group of a study by methods ensuring that every subject has an equal chance of being placed in either of the groups.

resiliency   Experiencing a positive outcome in a given situation in spite of having suffered through stressful or traumatic events.

resource room   An area of a school used exclusively for special education.

school readiness   Possessing skills and cognitive and emotional characteristics that enable children to learn from and interact appropriately with teachers and peers.

school-based management   A model for decentralizing school administration such that teams comprised of a principal, teachers, and other staff, often in conjunction with parents, have significant decision-making power.

segregation Separating individuals or groups on the basis of some variable, such as race or gender.

selection bias A condition under which certain individuals are more likely to be selected or to volunteer for participation in research (or to be assigned to a study group). Contrast with *random assignment.*

sensitive period Similar to *critical period,* except a sensitive period is broader and less time-constrained.

sequelae Abnormalities following a disease, condition, or experience.

sleeper effect A delayed outcome of an intervention or other experience, one not discernible immediately after the intervention.

snowball effect A mechanism through which one experience, such as participation in an early intervention, increases the likelihood of other successful experiences in school and other social contexts, increasing self-esteem, motivation, sociability, and physical and mental health.

social competence A measure of a child's everyday effectiveness in dealing with the environment and, later, responsibilities of school and life.

socioeconomic status (SES) An index of social class that includes assessments of educational level, occupation, and income level.

solution stage The third stage of policy development, during which possible courses of action (including taking none) are outlined.

suntan effect A positive outcome that appears to fade out over time after the intervention is stopped.

teratogenic agent A substance or agent that interferes with fetal development and can produce abnormalities; it can be a disease agent, an environmental toxin, or other.

transition programs Bilingual programs in which students are taught in their native language until they acquire rudimentary English-language skills.

two-generation program Intervention designed to work with both the parent and the child simultaneously.

whole-child approach A program approach that encourages development not only of the child but also of the family or even of a broad portion of a child's social and/or physical environment.

whole-language approach An approach to teaching language arts that stresses the broader processes related to reading and writing, as opposed to learning individual letters and sounds.

References

AARONSON, S., & HARTMANN, H. (1996). Reform, not rhetoric: A critique of welfare policy and charting of new directions. *American Journal of Orthopsychiatry, 66,* 583–599.

ABBOT, R. (1995). *Schooling that works.* Hartford: Connecticut Public Television.

ABELSON, W. D. (1974). Head Start graduates in school: Studies in New Haven, Connecticut. In S. Ryan (Ed.), *A report on longitudinal evaluations of preschool programs: Vol. 1. Longitudinal evaluations.* Washington, DC: U.S. Department of Health, Education, and Welfare.

ABER, J. L., & CICCHETTI, D. (1984). The socio-emotional development of maltreated children: An empirical and theoretical analysis. In H. Fitzgerald, B. Lester, & M. Yogman (Eds.), *Theory and research in behavioral pediatrics* (Vol. 2, pp. 147–205). New York: Plenum.

ABER, J. L., III., & ZIGLER, E. (1981). Developmental considerations in the definition of child maltreatment. In R. Rizley & D. Cicchetti (Eds.), *Developmental perspectives on child maltreatment* (pp. 1–29). San Francisco: Jossey-Bass.

ADAMO, A. (1980, April). *Sweden and the International Year of the Child.* Stockholm: Swedish Institute.

ADAMS, G. C., & POERSCH, N. O. (1997) . *Key facts about child care and early education: A briefing book.* Washington, DC: Children's Defense Fund.

ADAMS, P. F., & BENSON, V. (1990). *Current estimates from the National Health Interview Survey, 1989.* Vital and Health Statistics, Series 10, No. 176. (DHHS Pub. No [PHS] 90-1504. Hyattsville, MD: National Center for Health Statistics.

ADLER, J. (1997, Spring/Summer). It's a wise father who knows . . . . *Newsweek,* p. 73.

ADMINISTRATION FOR CHILDREN AND FAMILIES. (1996). *Fact sheet: Family preservation and family support services.* Advisory Committee on Immunization Practices (1998). Recommended childhood immunization schedule. Washington, DC: American Academy of Pediatrics and the American Academy of Family Physicians. Retrieved from the World Wide Web: http://www.act.dhhs.gov/ACFPrograms/FamilyPreservation/fampres.txt.

AGENCY FOR TOXIC SUBSTANCES AND DISEASE REGISTRY. (1988, July). The nature and extent of lead poisoning in children in the U.S. A report to Congress. Atlanta, GA: Public Health Service.

AINSWORTH, M. D. S., BLEHAR, M. C., WATERS, E., & WALL, S. (1978). *Patterns of attachment.* Hillsdale, NJ: Erlbaum.

ALBELDA, R., FOLBRE, N., & CENTER FOR POPULAR ECONOMICS. (1996). *The war on the poor: A defense manual.* New York: New Press.

ALLAN, L. (1978). Child abuse: A critical review of the research and the theory. In H. Martin (Ed.), *Violence and the family* (pp. 43–80). New York: Wiley.

ALLEN, L., & GROBMAN, S. (1996). Multiculturalism and social policy. In E. Zigler, S. L. Kagan, & N. W. Hall (Eds.), *Children, families and government: Preparing for the 21st century* (pp. 355–377). New York: Cambridge University Press.

AMERICAN ACADEMY OF CHILD AND ADOLESCENT PSYCHIATRY. (1988). *Policy statement: Corporal punishment in schools.* Washington, DC: Author.

AMERICAN ACADEMY OF PEDIATRICS. (1990). *Children first: A legislative proposal.* Washington, DC: Author.

AMERICAN ACADEMY OF PEDIATRICS. (1991). *Policy statement: Corporal punishment in schools* (RE9207). Washington, DC: Author.

AMERICAN ACADEMY OF PEDIATRICS. (1997a, December 1). AAP releases new breastfeeding recommendations [Press release]. Washington, DC.

AMERICAN ACADEMY OF PEDIATRICS. (1997b, June 2). Breastfed infants less likely to develop diarrhea or ear infections [Press release]. Washington, DC.

AMERICAN ACADEMY OF PEDIATRICS. (1998a, January 5). Breastfeeding improves cognitive and academic outcomes into adolescence [Press release]. Washington, DC.

AMERICAN ACADEMY OF PEDIATRICS. (1998b, March 24). New mother's breastfeeding promotion and protection act [Press release]. Washington, DC.

AMERICAN BAR ASSOCIATION. (1993). *America's children at risk: A national agenda for legal action. A report of the American Bar Association Presidential Working Group on the Unmet Legal Needs of Children and Their Families.* Washington, DC: Author.

AMERICAN HUMANE ASSOCIATION. (1993). *Evaluation of the Pennsylvania approach to risk assessment: An executive summary of the results for project objectives 1, 2, and 4.* Unpublished manuscript, Boston, MA.

AMERICAN IMMIGRATION LAW FOUNDATION ASSOCIATION. (1998). Immigration policy reports. http//www.ailf.org/projects/polrep/htm.

AMERICAN PSYCHOLOGICAL ASSOCIATION, COMMISSION ON VIOLENCE AND YOUTH. (1993). *Psychology's response.* Washington, DC: Author.

ANDERSON, J. E. (1956). Child development: An historical perspective. *Child Development, 27,* 181–196.

ANDERSON, L. M. (1995). *An evaluation of state and local efforts to serve the educational needs of homeless children and youth.* Washington, DC: Policy Studies Associates. (ERIC Document Reproduction Service No. ED 385 667.)

ANDERSON, R., AMBROSINO, R., VALENTINE, D., & LAUDERDALE, M. (1983). Child deaths attributed to abuse and neglect: An empirical study. *Children and Youth Services Review, 5,* 75–89.

ANDERSON, S. (1977). *Early identification and primary prevention of potential parent-child interactional problems.* Unpublished doctoral dissertation, University of Colorado.

ANDREWS, E. (1992, September 30). Broadcasters, to satisfy law, define cartoons as education. *New York Times,* pp. A1, A15.

ANDREWS, W. (1995). *Lobbyist's checklist. Lobbying and government relations activities: The whats, whys and hows.* Unpublished seminar material. Butera & Andrews, Washington, DC.

ANNIE E. CASEY FOUNDATION. (1998). 1998 Kids Count database online. Available on the World Wide Web: http://www.aecf.org.

APPENDIX: SELECTED FEDERAL PROGRAMS SERVING CHILDREN WITH DISABILITIES. (1996). *Future of Children, 6,* 162–173.

APPLEBOME, P. (1996, December 27). After years of gains, minority students start falling behind. *New York Times,* p. A1.

APPLEBOME, P. (1997, March 16). Better schools, uncertain returns. *New York Times,* p. 5.

APPLEWHITE, A. (1997). *Cutting loose.* New York: HarperCollins.

ARIÈS, P. (1962). *Centuries of childhood: A social history of family life.* New York: Knopf.

ARONSON, S. (1993). *0–3 Conference.* Presentation on Pennsylvania's ECELS Program, Washington DC., Biennial Training Institute.

ARTIST V. JOHNSON, 917 F.2d 980 (7th Cir. 1990).

ASCHLER, C. (1996). *The changing face of racial isolation and desegregation in urban schools.* ERIC Digest, retrieved from the World Wide Web: http://eric-web.tc.columbia.edu/digests/dig91.html.

ASNES, R. S., & MONES, R. L. (1982). Infantile colic: A review. *Journal of Developmental and Behavioral Pediatrics, 4,* 57–62.

AUGUST, D. L. (1986). Bilingual education act, Title II of the education amendments of 1984. *Washington Report* (Washington, DC: Washington Liaison Office and the Committee on Child Development and Social Policy of the Society for Research in Child Development), *1,* 5.

AZER, M., & CAPRARO, B. (1997). *Data on child care licensing.* Boston: Wheelock College, Center for Career Development in Early Care and Education.

BADEN, R. K., GENSER, A., LEVINE, J. A., & SELIGSON, M. (1982). *School-age child care: An action manual.* Dover, MA: Auburn House.

BAINES, L., BAINES, C., & MASTERSON, C. (1994, September). Mainstreaming: One school's reality. *Phi Delta Kappan,* pp. 39–64.

BAKAN, D. (1971). *Slaughter of the innocents: A study of the battered child phenomenon.* San Francisco: Jossey-Bass.

BAKER, C. (1996). *Foundations of bilingual education and bilingualism.* Philadelphia: Multilingual Matters.

BAKER V. OWEN, 96 S.Ct. 210 (1975).

BALANCED BUDGET ACT OF 1997. (1997). PL 105-33, August 1.

BANE, M. J., & ELWOOD, D. T. (1996). *Welfare realities: From rhetoric to reform.* Cambridge, MA: Harvard University Press.

BARKLEY, R. A. (1995). *Taking charge of ADHD: The complete, authoritative guide for parents.* New York: Guilford Press.

BARNARD, K. E. (1993). Sharpening the focus in early intervention. *Child, Youth and Family Services Quarterly, 16,* 8–11.

BARNETT, D., MANLY, J. T., & CICCHETTI, D. (1993). Defining child maltreatment: The interface between policy and research. In D. Cicchetti & S. L. Toth (Eds.), *Child abuse, child development, and social policy* (pp. 7–73). Norwood, NJ: Ablex.

BARNETT, W. S. (1993). Benefit-cost analysis of preschool education: Findings from a 25-year follow-up. *American Journal of Orthopsychiatry, 63,* 500–508.

BARNETT, W. S. (1995). Long-term effects of early childhood programs on cognitive and school outcomes. *Future of Children, 5,* 21–44.

BARNETT, W. S., & ESCOBAR, C. M. (1990). Economic costs and benefits of early intervention. In S. J. Meisels & J. Shonkoff (Eds.), *Handbook of early childhood intervention* (pp. 560–582). New York: Cambridge University Press.

BARRIENTOS, M. (1991, March 4). In Camden, afrocentrism is bringing academic gains. *Philadelphia Inquirer,* p. B1.

BARTON, M., & WILLIAMS, M. (1993). Infant day care. In C. H. Zeanah (Ed.), *Handbook of infant mental health* (pp. 445–461). New York: Guilford Press.

BASSUK, E. L., RUBIN, L., & LAURIAT, A. (1986). Characteristics of sheltered homeless families. *American Journal of Public Health, 76,* 1097–1101.

BECK, J. (1996). Family preservation can be fatal to a child. Retrieved from the World Wide Web: http://www.tribnet.com/~tnt/news/31018.htm.

BEER, V., & BLOOMER, A. C. (1986). Levels of evaluation. *Educational Evaluation and Policy Analysis, 8,* 335–345.

BEGLEY, S. (1996, February 19). Your child's brain. *Newsweek,* pp. 34–39.

BEGLEY, S. (1997, Spring/Summer). How to build a baby's brain. In *Your Child from Birth to Three* [Special edition]. *Newsweek,* pp. 28–31.

BELLINGER, D., LEVITON, A., WATERNAUX, C., NEDDLEMAN, H., & RABINOWITZ, M. (1987). Longitudinal analyses of prenatal and postnatal lead exposure and early cognitive development. *New England Journal of Medicine, 326,* 1037–1043.

BELSKY, J. (1980). Child maltreatment: An ecological integration. *American Psychologist, 35,* 320–335.

BELSKY, J. (1981). Early human experience: A family perspective. *Developmental Psychology, 17,* 3–23.

BELSKY, J. (1986). Infant day care: A cause for concern? *Zero to Three, 6,* 1–9.

BELSKY, J. (1987). Risks remain. *Zero to Three, 7,* 22–24.

BELSKY, J., & ROVINE, M. J. (1988). Nonmaternal care in the first year of life and the security of infant-parent attachment. *Child Development, 59,* 157–167.

BELSKY, J., SPANIER, G. B., & ROVINE, M. (1983). Stability and change across the transition to parenthood. *Journal of Marriage and the Family, 45,* 567–577.

BENDER, W. N. (1994). Joint custody: The option of choice. *Journal of Divorce and Remarriage, 21,* 115–131.

BERLINER, D. C., & BIDDLE, B. J. (1995). *The manufactured crisis: Myths, fraud, and the attack on America's public schools.* Reading, MA: Addison-Wesley.

BERREUTA-CLEMENT, J. R., SCHWEINHART, L. J., BARNETT, W. S., EPSTEIN, A. S., & WEIKART, D. P. (1984). *Changed lives.* Ypsilanti: MI: High/Scope.

BESHAROV, D. (1988a, August 4). The child abuse numbers game. *Wall Street Journal,* A-12.

BESHAROV, D. (1988b). The need to narrow the grounds for state intervention. In D. Besharov (Ed.), *Protecting children from abuse and neglect: Policy and practice* (pp. 47–90). Springfield, IL: Charles C. Thomas.

BESHAROV, D. J. (Ed.). (1995). *When drug addicts have children.* Washington, DC: Child Welfare League of America & the American Enterprise Institute.

BESHAROV, D. J. (1996, Winter). The children of crack: A status report. *Public Welfare,* pp. 32–37.

BIGGS, S. A. (1992, January–April). The plight of black males in American schools: Separation may not be the answer. *Negro Educational Review, 43,* 11–16.

BLAIR, D., KEEGAN, J., NEWMAN, B., & PEABODY, V. (Eds.). (1995). *The FMLA guide: Practical solutions to administration and management* (Alexander Consulting Group Series on Employee Benefits). New York: Richard D. Irwin.

BLAU, M. (1996, September). Home schooling. *Child,* 18–22.

BLOCH, M. (1992, August/September). Tobacco control advocacy: Winning the war on tobacco. *Zero to Three,* 4–5.

BLOM, G. E., KEITH, J. G., & TOMBER, I. (1984). Child and family advocacy: Addressing the rights and responsibilities of child, family and society. In R. P. Boger, G. E. Blom, & L. E. Lezotte (Eds.), *Child nurturance (Vol. 4, pp.157–174). Child nurturing in the 1980s.* New York: Plenum.

BLOOM, B. S. (1964). *Stability and change in human characteristics.* New York: Wiley.

BOSWELL, J. (1988). *The kindness of strangers: The abandonment of children in western Europe from late antiquity to the Renaissance.* New York: Pantheon Books.

BRACEY, G. (1991, May 5). The greatly exaggerated death of our schools. *Washington Post,* p. K01.

BRANDWEIN, R. A. (1995, December 22). New York's child welfare caseload threatens more tragedies. *New York Times,* p. A38.

BRAUER, D., & McCORMICK, J. (1998, April 8). The boys behind the ambush. *Newsweek,* pp. 20–28.

BREAKEY, G., & PRATT, B. (1991, April). Healthy growth for Hawaii's "Healthy Start": Toward a systematic statewide approach to the prevention of child abuse and neglect. *Zero to Three,* 16–22.

BREDEKAMP, S. (Ed.). (1987a). *Accreditation criteria and procedures.* Washington, DC: National Association for the Education of Young Children.

BREDEKAMP, S. (Ed.). (1987b). *Developmentally appropriate practices in early childhood programs serving children from birth through age 8.* Washington, DC: National Association for the Education of Young Children.

BREMNER, R. H. (1971a). *Children and youth in America: A documentary history. (Vol 2: 1600–1865).* Cambridge, MA: Harvard University Press.

BREMNER, R. H. (Ed.). (1971b). *Children and youth in America: A documentary history. (Vol 2: 1866–1932).* Cambridge, MA: Harvard University Press.

BRETHERTON, I. (1987). New perspectives on attachment relations: Security, communication, and internal working models. In J. D. Osofsky (Ed.), *Handbook of infant development* (pp. 1061–1100). New York: Wiley.

BREWER, G. D. (1983). The policy process as a perspective for understanding. In E. Zigler, S. L. Kagan, & E. Klugman (Eds.), *Children, families and government.* New York: Cambridge University Press.

BRICKER, D., & VELTMAN, M. (1995). Early intervention programs: Child-focused approaches. In S. J. Meisels & J. Shonkoff (Eds.), *Handbook of early childhood intervention.* New York: Cambridge University Press.

BRONFENBRENNER, U. (1975). Is early intervention effective? In M. Guttentag & E. Struening (Eds.), *Handbook of evaluation research* (Vol. 2, pp. 519–603). Beverly Hills: Sage.

BRONFENBRENNER, U. (1979). *The ecology of human development: Experiments by nature and design.* Cambridge, MA: Harvard University Press.

BRONFENBRENNER, U. (1988). Strengthening family systems. In E. Zigler & M. Frank, (Eds.), *The parental leave crisis: Toward a national policy.* New Haven, CT: Yale University Press.

BRONFENBRENNER, U. (1990). Discovering what families do. In D. Blankenhorn, S. Bayme, & J. B. Elshtain (Eds.), *Rebuilding the nest: A new commitment to the American family* (pp. 27-38). Milwaukee: Family Service America.

BRONFENBRENNER, U., MCCLELLAND, P., WETHINGTON, E., MOEN, P., & CECI, S. (1996). *The state of Americans: This generation and the next.* New York: Free Press.

BRONNER, E. (1998, November 23). Long a leader, U.S. now lags in high school graduation rate. *New York Times,* pp. A1, A22.

BROWN V. BOARD OF EDUCATION (1954). 347 U.S. 483.

BROWN, J. H., D'EMIDIO-CASTON, M., & POLLARD, J. A. (1997). Students and substances: Social power in drug education. *Educational Evaluation and Policy Analysis, 19,* 65–82.

BROZEK, J., & SCHURCH, B. (Eds.). (1984). *Malnutrition and behavior: Critical assessment of key issues.* Lausanne, Switzerland: Nestle Foundation.

BRUERD, B. (1990). Smokeless tobacco use among Native American school children. *Public Health Reports, 105,* 196–201.

BURCHINAL, M. R., ROBERTS, J. E, NABORS, L. A., & BRYANT, D. M. (1996). Quality of center child care and infant cognitive and language development. *Child Development, 67,* 606–620.

BUREAU OF NATIONAL AFFAIRS. (1988, May 16). Flex-time opportunities on the rise. *BNA's Employee Relations Weekly,* 819.

BUTTS, M. (1993, November). Daycare laws: An essential guide. *Parenting, pp. 46–47.*

CAFFEY, J. (1946). Multiple fractures in the long bones of infants suffering from chronic subdural hematoma. *American Journal of Roentgenology, 56,* 163–173.

CAHAN, E., MECHLING, J., SUTTON-SMITH, B., & WHITE, S. H. (1993). The elusive historical child: Ways of knowing the child of history and psychology. In G. H. Elder, J. Modell, & R. D. Parke (Eds.), *Children in time and place* (pp. 173–191). New York: Cambridge University Press.

CAHN, R., & CAHN, W. (1972). *No time for school, no time for play: The story of child labor in America.* New York: Julian Messner.

CALDWELL, B. M. (1987). Professional child care. In B. Caldwell (Ed.), *Group care for young children: A supplement to parental care* (p. 214). Lexington, MA: Toronto.

CAMPBELL, F. A., HELMS, R., SPARLING, J. J., & RAMEY, C. T. (IN PRESS). Early childhood programs and success in school: The Abecedarian study. In W. S. Barnett & S. S. Boocock (Eds.), *Early care and education: Lasting effects for children in poverty.* Albany: State University of New York Press.

CAMPBELL, F. A., & RAMEY, C. T. (1994). Effects of early intervention on intellectual and academic achievement: A follow-up study of children from low-income families. *Child Development, 65,* 684–698.

CARNEGIE CORPORATION. (1994). *Starting points: Meeting the needs of our youngest children.* New York: Author.

CARNEGIE CORPORATION. (1996). *Years of promise: A comprehensive learning strategy for America's children* (Report of the Task Force on Learning in the Primary Grades). New York: Author.

CARROLL, N. (1993, April 1). Child care licensing not a must to moms. *USA Today,* p. 80.

CASPER, L. (1997). *Who's minding our preschoolers?* Current population reports household economic studies, P70-62. Washington, DC: U.S. Census Bureau.

CATHOLIC INSTITUTE FOR INTERNATIONAL RELATIONS. (1993). *Baby milk: Destruction of a world resource.* London: Author.

CECI, S., & BRUCK, M. (in press) The suggestibility of the child witness: A historical review and synthesis. *Psychological Bulletin.*

CECI, S. J., LEICHTMAN, M. D., PUTNICK, M. E., & NIGHTINGALE, N. N. (1993). The suggestibility of children's recollections. In D. Cicchetti & S. Toth (Eds.), *Child abuse, child development and social policy* (pp. 117–138). Norwood, NJ: Ablex.

CENTER ON HUNGER AND POVERTY. (1998). *State investments in work participation: Meeting the promise of welfare-to-work.* Medford, MA: Author.

CENTERS FOR DISEASE CONTROL AND PREVENTION. (1990a). Homicide among young black males: United States, 1978–1987. *Morbidity and Mortality Weekly Report, 39,* 869–873.

CENTERS FOR DISEASE CONTROL AND PREVENTION. (1990b). *Morbidity and Mortality Weekly Report, 38* (54).

CENTERS FOR DISEASE CONTROL AND PREVENTION. (1998). *Preliminary CDC 1997 data on SIDS.* Atlanta, GA: Author.

CHAMBERS, J. G., PARRISH, T., LIEBERMAN, J., & WOLMAN, J. (1998). What are we spending on special education in the U.S.? *CSEF Brief No. 8* (Chapter 11). Palo Alto, CA: Center for Special Education Finance.

CHASE-LANSDALE, P. L., & OWEN, M. T. (1987). Maternal employment in a family context: Effects of infant-mother and infant-father attachments. *Child Development, 58,* 1505–1512.

CHILD CARE ACTION CAMPAIGN. (1989). *Child care: The bottom line.* New York: Author.

CHILD WELFARE LEAGUE OF AMERICA. (1984). *Standards for day care.* New York: Author.

CHILD WELFARE LEAGUE OF AMERICA. (1993). *Charting a new course: Children's legislative agenda 1993.* Washington, DC: Author.

CHILDHOOD SPANKING AND INCREASED ANTISOCIAL BEHAVIOR. (1998, February). *American Family Physician,* 84-89.

CHILDHOOD VACCINATION RATES IN THE UNITED STATES REACH RECORD LEVELS IN 1993. (1995, February). *Parenting,* p. 21.

CHILDREN'S BUREAU. (1942). *Standards for the day care of children of working mothers.* Children's Bureau Publication No. 284. Washington, DC: Author.

CHILDREN'S DEFENSE FUND. (1990). *Children 1990: A report card, briefing book, and action primer.* Washington, DC: Author.

CHILDREN'S DEFENSE FUND. (1991). *Homeless families: Failed policies and young victims.* Washington, DC: Author.

CHILDREN'S DEFENSE FUND. (1992a). *Child care under the Family Support Act: Early lessons from the states.* Washington, DC: Author.

CHILDREN'S DEFENSE FUND. (1992b). *An opinion maker's guide to children in election year 1992.* Washington, DC: Author.

CHILDREN'S DEFENSE FUND. (1994a, August). *CDF Reports, 15.*

CHILDREN'S DEFENSE FUND. (1994b). *The state of America's children: Yearbook 1994.* Washington, DC: Author.

CHILDREN'S DEFENSE FUND. (1995). *The state of America's children: Yearbook 1995.* Washington, DC: Author.

CHILDREN'S DEFENSE FUND. (1997a, November 20). Adoption and Safe Families Act (H.R. 867) protects children's safety and promotes permanent homes for children [Press release]. Washington, DC.

CHILDREN'S DEFENSE FUND. (1997b, October 24). Federal and state government: Partners in child care [Press release]. Washington, DC: Author.

CHILDREN'S DEFENSE FUND. (1997c). FY 1998 budget proposal. *CDF Reports, 18,* 1–2.

CHILDREN'S DEFENSE FUND. (1997d). *The state of America's children: Yearbook 1997.* Washington, DC: Author.

CHILDREN'S DEFENSE FUND. (1998a). Child care and after-school programs curb teen smoking and promote a healthy future for children. Available on the World Wide Web: http://www.childrensdefense.org/cc_smoking.html.

CHILDREN'S DEFENSE FUND. (1998b). *Child care challenges.* Washington, DC: Author.

CHILDREN'S DEFENSE FUND. (1998c, March). *Facts about child care in America.* Washington, DC: Author.

CHILDREN'S DEFENSE FUND. (1998d, March 14). Key facts about uninsured children [Fact sheet]. Washington, DC: Author.

CHILDREN'S DEFENSE FUND. (1998e, May 4). Key findings: The high price of poverty for children of the South [Press release]. Washington, DC.

CHILDREN'S DEFENSE FUND. (1998f, May). Locked doors: States struggling to meet child care needs of low-income working families [Press release]. Washington, DC: Author.

CHILDREN'S DEFENSE FUND. (1998g, May 27). New studies look at status of former welfare recipients. [Press release]. Washington, DC.

CHILDREN'S DEFENSE FUND. (1998h, May 4). One in three poor children in America lives in the South. [Press release]. Washington, DC.

CHILDREN'S DEFENSE FUND. (1998i, May 29). Parents face higher tuition costs for quality child care than for public college [Press release]. Washington, DC: Author.

CHILDREN'S DEFENSE FUND. (1998j). *Poverty matters.* Washington, DC: Author.

CHILDREN'S DEFENSE FUND. (1998k). *The state of America's children: Yearbook 1998.* Washington, DC: Author.

CHILDREN'S DEFENSE FUND. (1998l, May 27). Welfare in the states: CDF, new studies look at status of former welfare recipients. [Press release]. Washington, DC.

CHILDREN'S DEFENSE FUND. (1999). *Yearbook of children.* Author: Washington, DC.

CHILDREN'S RIGHTS COUNCIL OF MARYLAND. (1998). Joint custody: Questions and answers (U.S.). Retrieved from the World Wide Web at the Shared Parenting Information Group home page: *http://www.*sharedparenting.com.

CHIRA, S. (1993, August 15). Family leave is law: Will things change? *New York Times,* p. E3.

CHRISTIAN, D. (1995). Two-way bilingual education: Students learning through two languages. Report published by the National Center for Research on Cultural Diversity and second language learning, NY, NY.

CHUGANI, H. (1993). Positron emission tomography scanning in newborns. *Clinics in Perinatology, 20,* 398.

CHUGANI, H., PHELPS, M. E., & MAZZIOTTA, J. C. (1987). Positron emission tomography study of human brain functional development. *Annals of Neurology, 22,* 495.

CICCHETTI, D., & CARLSON, V. (1993). *Child maltreatment.* New York: Cambridge University Press.

CICCHETTI, D., & LYNCH, M. (1993). Toward an ecological/transactional model of community violence and child maltreatment: Consequences for children's development. *Psychiatry, 56,* 96–118.

CICCHETTI, D., & RIZLEY, R. (1991). Developmental perspectives on the etiology, intergenerational transmission and sequelae of child maltreatment. *New Directions for Child Maltreatment, 11,* 32–59.

CICIRELLI, V. G. (1966). *The impact of Head Start: An evaluation of the effects of Head Start on children's cognitive and affective development* (Vol. 1). Athens: Ohio University & Westinghouse Learning Corporation.

CIGLER, A. J., & LOOMIS, B. A. (1995). *Interest group politics* (4th ed.). Washington, DC: Congressional Quarterly.

CITY NEEDS MORE CHILD CARE SLOTS. (1998, April 14). *New York Times,* p. A1.

CLARKE-STEWART, A., THOMPSON, W., & LEPORE, S. (1989, May). *Manipulating children's interpretations through interrogation.* Paper presented at biennial meeting of the Society for Research in Child Development, Kansas City.

CLARKE-STEWART, K. A. (1987). Predicting child development from day care forms and features: The Chicago study. In. D. A. Phillips (Ed.), *Quality in child care: What does the research tell us?* (pp. 21–42). Washington, DC: National Association for the Education of Young Children.

CLARKE-STEWART, K. A. (1989). Infant day care: Maligned or malignant? *American Psychologist, 44,* 266–273.

CLOUD, J. (1999). What can the schools do? *Time, 153,* May 19, 62–63.

CLYMER, A. (1993, October 17). Many health plans: One political goal. *New York Times,* p. 22.

COHEN, D. L. (1993a, September 8). Elementary principals' group publishes standards for school-based child care. *Education Week, p. 3.*

COHEN, D. L. (1993b, March 3). First national study of after-school care cites progress, pitfalls. *Education Week, p. 2, 4.*

COHN, A., & DARO, D. (1987). Is treatment too late? What ten years of evaluative research tells us. *Child Abuse and Neglect, 11,* 432–433.

COLEMAN COMMISSION ON PERMANENCY PLANNING. (1985). *The Coleman commission report on permanency planning.* Lansing: Children's Charter of the Courts of Michigan.

COLLINS, T. W. (1979). From courtrooms to classrooms: Managing school desegregation in a deep south high school. In R. Rist (Ed.), *Desegregated schools: Appraisals of an American experiment* (pp. 89–114). New York: Academic Press.

COLTOFF, P. (1997, January 24). "Full service" schools broaden definition of educational reform. *Christian Science Monitor,* p. 19.

CONE, T. E. (1983). Historical trends: Evolving pediatric concepts of variation and deviation up to 1920. In M. D. Levine, W. B. Carey, A. C. Crocker, & R. T. Gross (Eds.), *Developmental-behavioral pediatrics* (pp. 3–14). Philadelphia: Saunders.

CONGRESSIONAL QUARTERLY. (1988). *Congressional Quarterly A–Z.* Washington, DC: Author.

CONGRESSIONAL QUARTERLY ONLINE. (1995). Lobbying regulations. Retrieved from the World Wide Web at http://www.cq.com.

CONSORTIUM FOR LONGITUDINAL STUDIES. (1983). *As the twig is bent.* Hillsdale, NJ: Erlbaum.

COOLSON, P., SELIGSON, M., & GARBARINO, J. (1985). *When school's out and nobody's home.* Chicago: National Committee for the Prevention of Child Abuse.

COONTZ, S. (1993). *The way we never were: American families and the nostalgia trap.* New York: Basic Books.

COONTZ, S. (1997). *The way we really are: Coming to terms with America's changing families.* New York: Basic Books.

CORDES, H. (1997, May). Is the FMLA working? *Parenting,* p. 45.

CORSARO, W. A. (1980). Friendship in the nursery school: Social organization in a peer environment. In S. R. Asher & J. M. Gottman, (Eds.). *The development of children's friendships.* New York: Cambridge University Press.

COST, QUALITY, AND OUTCOMES STUDY TEAM. (1995). *Cost, quality, and child outcomes in child care centers, public report.* Denver: University of Colorado, Economics Department.

COSTIN, L., & RAPP, C. A. (1984). *Child welfare policies and practice.* New York: McGraw-Hill.

COTTLE, T. J. (1975, November 22). Review of Naomi F. Chase, "A child is being beaten". (New York: Holt, Rinehart & Winston, 1975). *New Republic,* pp. 28–30.

COZIC, C. P. (1992). *Education in America: Opposing viewpoints.* San Diego: Greenhaven Press.

CRAIG, C. (1995, January 5). Removing barriers to adoption. A crucial step toward reshaping troubled foster care. *Knight-Ridder/Tribune News Service.*

CRAVENS, H. (1987). Recent controversy in human development: An historical view. *Human Development, 30,* 325–335.

CRITTENDEN, P., & BONVILLIAN, J. (1984). The relationship between maternal risk status and maternal sensitivity. *American Journal of Orthopsychiatry, 54* (2), 250–262.

CRNIC, K. A., GREENBERG, M. T., RAGOZIN, A., ROBINSON, N., & BASHAM, R. (1983). Effects of stress on social support on mothers of premature and full-term infants. *Child Development, 54,* 209–217.

CROCKENBERG, S. (1981). Infant irritability, mother responsiveness and social support influences on the security of infant-mother attachment. *Child Development, 52,* 857–865.

CROCKENBERG, S., LYONS-RUTH, K., & DICKSTEIN, S. (1993). The family context of infant mental health: II. Infant development in multiple family relationships. In C. H. Zeanah (Ed.), *Handbook of infant mental health* (pp. 38–55). New York: Guilford Press.

CRUMBLEY, J. & LITTLE, R. L. (Eds.). (1997). *Relatives raising children: An overview of kinship care.* Washington, DC: Child Welfare League of America.

CUMMINGS, E. M., & BEAGLES-ROSS, J. (1983). Towards a model of infant daycare: Studies of factors influencing responding to separation in daycare. In R. C. Ainslie (Ed.), *Quality of variations in daycare* (pp. 159–182). New York: Praeger.

DANIEL, J. H., & HYDE, J. N. (1975). Working with high-risk families. *Children Today, 4,* 23–25.

DANZIGER, S. K., & DANZIGER, S. (1993). Child poverty and public policy: Toward a comprehensive antipoverty agenda. *Children and Youth Services Review, 24,* 57–84.

DANZIGER, S. K., & DANZIGER, S. (1995). Will welfare recipients find work when welfare ends? In I. Sawhill (Ed.), *Welfare reform: An analysis of the issues* (pp. 41–44). Washington, DC: Urban Institute.

DARLING-HAMMOND, L. (1986). Teaching knowledge: How do we test it? *American Educator,* pp. 18–21.

DARLING-HAMMOND, L. (1997). What matters most: A competent teacher for every child. *Phi Deltan Kappan.* Retrieved from the World Wide Web: http://www.kiva.net/~pdkint/kappan/kappan.htm.

DARLINGTON, R. B., ROYCE, J. M., SNIPPER, A. S., MURRAY, H. W., & LAZAR, I. (1980). Preschool programs and later competence of children from low-income families. *Science, 208,* 202–204.

DARO, D. (1988). *Confronting child abuse.* New York: Free Press.

DARO, D. (1993). Reducing child abuse rates through support programs for new parents. *Child, Youth and Family Services Quarterly, 16,* 3–5.

DARWIN, C. (1877). A biographical sketch of an infant. *Mind, 2,* 258.

DAVIDSON, C. E. (1994). Dependent children and their families: A historical survey of United States policies. In F. H. Jacobs & M. W. Davies (Eds.), *More than kissing babies? Current child and family policy in the United States* (pp. 65–90). Westport, CT: Auburn House.

DAWSON, D. A. (1991). *Family structure and children's health: United States, 1988* (Vital and Health Statistics, Series 10, No. 178. National Center for Health Statistics, DHHS Publication No. [PHS] 91–1506). Washington, DC: U.S. Government Printing Office.

DEBORD, K. B. (1997). *Focus on kids: The effects of divorce on children* (Human Environmental publication GH6600). Columbia: University of Missouri Extension Service.

DELEY, W. W. (1988). Physical punishment of children: Sweden and the U.S.A. *Journal of Comparative Family Studies, 19,* 419–431.

DEPARLE, J. (1996a, December 8). Mugged by reality. *New York Times Magazine,* pp. 64–67, 99–100.

DEPARLE, J. (1996b, October 20). Slamming the door. *New York Times Magazine,* pp. 52–57 et seq.

DIAMOND, S. C. (1995). Special education and the great god, inclusion. In J. M. Kauffman & D. P. Hallahan (Eds.), *Illusion of full inclusion* (pp. 247–254). Austin, TX: Pro-Ed.

DIAMOND, A. (1999). Where were the parents? *Time, 153,* May 19, 49–53.

DINA, R. P. (1995, December 19). System with no cash can't halt child abuse. *New York Newsday,* p. A33.

DODSON, L., JOSHI, P., & MCDONALD, D. (1998). *Welfare in transition: Consequences for women, families and communities.* Retrieved from the World Wide Web: http://www.radcliffe.edu/pubpol/contents.html.

DODSON, L., & RAYMAN, P. (1998). Welfare in transition. Cambridge, MA: Radcliffe Public Policy Institute.

DONOVAN, B., & MOORE, T. H. (1994). House incumbents raise money at record rate for 1994. *Congressional Quarterly Weekly Report, 52,* 417–419.

DONOVAN, B., THOMAS, J. S., & VERNON, I. J. (1993). Senate PAC funds. *Congressional Quarterly Weekly Report, 51,* 727.

DOWNS, S. W., & SHERRADEN, M. W. (1983). The orphan asylum in the nineteenth century. *Social Service Review, 57,* 272–290.

DOYLE, D. P., COOPER, B. S., & TRACHTMAN, T. W. (1991). *Taking charge: State action on school reform in the 1980s.* Indianapolis: Hudson Institute.

DRAZEN, S., & HAUST, M. (1994). *Increasing children's readiness for school by a parental education program.* Binghamton, NY: Community Resource Center.

DRUG STRATEGIES. (1998). *Safe schools, safe students: A guide to violence prevention strategies.* Washington, DC: Author.

DRYFOOS, J. G. (1994). *Full-service schools: A revolution in health and social services for children, youth, and families.* San Francisco: Jossey-Bass.

DUBANOSKI, R. (1981). Child maltreatment in European- and Hawaiian-Americans. *International Journal of Child Abuse and Neglect, 5,* 457–465.

DUCHNOWSKI, A. J., & KUTASH, K. (1997). Future research in special education: A systems perspective. In J. L. Paul, M. Churton, H. Rosselli-Kostoryz, W. C. Morse, K. Marfo, C. Lavely, & D. Thomas (Eds.), *Foundations of special education* (pp. 236–246). Pacific Grove, CA: Brooks/Cole.

DUGGER, C. W. (1993, September 8). Troubled children flood ill-prepared care system. *New York Times,* pp. 1A, B7–8.

DUMAS, L. (1994, January). Banding together to create care. *Working Mother,* pp. 38–39.

DUMKE, G. (1985). Epilogue. In *Education on trial: Strategies for the future.* San Francisco: Institute for Contemporary Studies.

DUNN, L. M. (1968). Special education for the mentally retarded: Is much of it justifiable? *Exceptional Children, 35,* 5–22.

DURRANT, J. E. (1996). The Swedish ban on corporal punishment: Its history and effects. In *Family violence against children: A challenge for society* (pp. 19–25). Berlin, NY: Walter de Gruyter.

DWYER, M. (1990). Characteristics of eighth grade students who initiate self care in elementary and junior high school. *Pediatrics, 86,* pp. 1122–1126.

EBERLE, P., & EBERLE, S. (1993). *The abuse of innocence: The McMartin Preschool trial.* New York: Prometheus Books.

EDDIES, E. A. (1992). Children and homelessness: Early childhood and elementary education. In J. H. Stronge (Ed.), *Educating homeless children and adolescents: Evaluating policy and practice* (pp. 99–114). Newbury Park, CA: Sage.

EDUCATION WEEK. (1998). *Bilingual education.* Retrieved from the World Wide Web: http://www.edweek.org/context/topics/biling.htm.

EGBUONO, L., & STARFIELD, B. (1982). Child health and social status. *Pediatrics, 69,* 550–557.

EHRENHAFT, P. M. (1987). *Health technology case study 38: Neonatal intensive care for low-birthweight infants: Costs and effectiveness.* Washington, DC: Office of Technology Assessment.

ELDER, G. H., MODELL, J., & PARKE, R. D. (1993). *Children in time and place: Developmental and historical insights.* New York: Cambridge University Press.

ELKIND, D. (1981). *The hurried child: Growing up too fast too soon.* Reading, MA: Addison-Wesley.

ELLWOOD, D. (1988). *Poor support.* New York: Basic Books.

EMENS, E. F., HALL, N. W., ROSS, C. J., & ZIGLER, E. (1996). Preventing juvenile delinquency: An ecological, developmental approach. In E. Zigler, S. L. Kagan, & N. W. Hall (Eds.), *Children, families and government: Preparing for the 21st century.* New York: Cambridge University Press.

ENCYCLOPAEDIA BRITANNICA. (1890). 9th ed., vol. 13.

EXECUTIVE OFFICE OF THE PRESIDENT. (1998). *FY 1999 drug budget program highlights.* Washington, DC: Office of National Drug Control and Policy.

EXETER, T. G. (1993). The declining majority. *American Demographics, 15,* 1.

FALCO, M. (1992). *The making of a drug-free America.* New York: Times Books.

FAMILIES AND WORK INSTITUTE. (1994). *The study of children in family child care and relative care.* New York: Author.

FAMILIES AND WORK INSTITUTE. (1995). *Women: The new providers.* New York: Author.

FAMILIES AND WORK INSTITUTE. (1997a). *The changing workforce: Highlights from the national study.* New York: Author.

FAMILIES AND WORK INSTITUTE. (1997b). *The 1997 national study of the changing workforce.* New York: Author.

FAMILIES AND WORK INSTITUTE. (1998a). More about us. Retrieved from the World Wide Web: http://familiesandworkinst.org/about.html.

FAMILIES AND WORK INSTITUTE. (1998b). *1998 business work-life study: A sourcebook.* New York: Author.

FAMILIES AND WORK INSTITUTE. (1998c). *The 1997 national study of the changing workforce.* New York: Author.

FARBER, E., ALEJANDRO-WRIGHT, M., & MUENCHOW, S. (1988). Managing work and family: Hopes and realities. In E. Zigler & M. Frank (Eds.), *The parental leave crisis: Toward a national policy.* New Haven, CT: Yale University Press.

FARRINGTON, D. P., LOEBER, R., ELLIOTT, D. S., HAWKINS, J. D., KANDEL, D. B., KLEIN, M. W., MCCORD, J., ROWE, D. C., & TREMBLAY, R. E. (1990). Advancing knowledge about the onset of delinquency and crime. In B. B. Lahey & A. E. Kazdin (Eds.), *Advances in clinical child psychology* (Vol. 13, pp. 283–342). New York: Plenum.

FAVISH, A. J. (1998, January 9). Bilingual ban could override Proposition 187. *Los Angeles Times,* p. A1.

FEDERAL INTERAGENCY DAY CARE REQUIREMENTS (FIDCR). (1968). U.S. Department of Health, Education and Welfare: U.S. Department of Economic Opportunity: U.S. Department of Labor. Pursuant to Sec. 522 (d) of the Economic Opportunity Act. Washington, DC: U.S. Government Printing Office.

FEDERAL INTERAGENCY DAY CARE REQUIREMENTS. (1972). Revisions prepared by the Office of Child Development, U.S. Department of Health, Education, and Welfare.

FEDERAL INTERAGENCY DAY CARE REQUIREMENTS. (1980, March 19). *Federal Register,* Part V, *45* (55), 17870, 17885.

FEISTRITZER, E., & CHESTER, D. T. (1996). *Alternative teacher certification: A state-by-state analysis.* Washington, DC: National Center for Education information.

FESHBACH, N. D. (1980). Corporal punishment in the schools: some paradoxes, some facts, some possible directions. In G. Gerbner, C. J. Ross, & E. Zigler (Eds.), *Child abuse: An agenda for action* (pp. 204–224). New York: Oxford University Press.

FINGERHUT, L. A., & KLEINMAN, J. C. (1990). International and interstate comparisons of homicide among young males. *Journal of the American Medical Association, 263,* 3292–3295.

FINKELHOR, D. (1984). *Child sexual abuse: New theories and research.* New York: Free Press.

FINKELHOR, D. (1990). Is child abuse overreported? *Public Welfare, 69,* 23–29.

FINKELHOR, D. (1993). The main problem is underreporting, not overreporting. In R. Gelles & D. Loseke (Eds.), *Current controversies in family violence* (pp. 273–287). Newbury Park, CA: Sage.

FINKELHOR, D., HOTALING, G. T., LEWIS, I. A., & SMITH, C. (1990). Sexual abuse in a national survey of adult men and women: Prevalence, characteristics, and risk factors. *Child Abuse and Neglect, 14,* 19–28.

FISCHER, J. L. (1989). *Family day care: Factors influencing the quality of caregiving practices.* Unpublished manuscript, University of California.

FIX, M., & ZIMMERMAN, W. (1993). *Educating immigrant children: Chapter 1 in the changing city* (Urban Institute Report 93–3). Washington, DC: Urban Institute. (ERIC Document Reproduction Service No. ED 377 282).

FONG, V. (1996, March 3). Family preservation programs still better than foster care (Press release). University Park: Pennsylvania State University.

FOOD RESEARCH AND ACTION CENTER. (1998a). *Federal food programs: Fact sheet.* Washington, DC: Author.

FOOD RESEARCH AND ACTION CENTER. (1998b). *Food stamp program frequently asked questions.* Washington, DC: Author.

FOOD RESEARCH AND ACTION CENTER. (1998c). *Hunger in the U.S.* Washington, DC: Author.

FOOD RESEARCH AND ACTION CENTER. (1998d). *National school lunch program: Fact sheet.* Washington, DC: Author.

FOOD RESEARCH AND ACTION CENTER. (1998e). *School breakfast program: Fact sheet.* Washington, DC: Author.

FOOD RESEARCH AND ACTION CENTER. (1998f). *Special supplemental nutrition program for women, infants and children: Fact sheet.* Washington, DC: Author.

FOR HEAD START, TWO STEPS BACK. (1992, June 30). *New York Times,* p. A22.

FORBES, S. (1995). Real care for the kids: Adoption and foster care laws need to be reformed. *Forbes, 156,* 24.

FORDHAM INSTITUTE FOR INNOVATION IN SOCIAL POLICY. (1995). *Index of social health: Monitoring the well-being of the nation.* Tarrytown, NY: Author.

FRAHM, R. A. (1996, February 24). Preschool benefits outlined. *Hartford Courant,* p. B–4.

FRANK, M., & ZIGLER, E. F. (1996). Family leave: A developmental perspective. In E. F. Zigler, S. L. Kagan, & N. W. Hall (Eds.), *Children, families and government: Preparing for the 21st century* (pp. 117–133). New York: Cambridge University Press.

FRANK PORTER GRAHAM CHILD DEVELOPMENT CENTER. (1998). *The Carolina Abecedarian Project: Overview, design, findings.* Retrieved from the World Wide Web: http://www.fpg.unc.edu/overview/abc/abcfind.htm.

FREDE, E. C. (1995). The role of program quality in producing early childhood program benefits. *Future of Children, 5,* 74–93.

FRONTLINE. (1996, January 30). So you want to buy a president. *Frontline.* PBS.

FUCHS, D., & FUCHS, L. S. (1995). Inclusive schools movement and the radicalization of special education reform. In J. M. Kauffman & D. P. Hallahan (Eds.), *Illusion of full inclusion* (pp. 213–242). Austin, TX: Pro-Ed.

GALAMBOS, N. L., & GARBARINO, J. (1985). Adjustment of supervised children in a rural setting. *Journal of Genetic Psychology, 146,* 227–231.

GALLAGHER, J. J. (1989). A new policy initiative: Infants and toddlers with handicapping conditions. *American Psychologist, 44,* 387–391.

GAMBLE, T. J., & ZIGLER, E. (1986). Effects of infant day care: Another look at the evidence. *American Journal of Orthopsychiatry, 56,* 26–42.

GARBARINO, J. (1976). A preliminary study of some ecological correlates of child abuse: The impact of socioeconomic stress on the mother. *Child Development, 47,* 178–185.

GARBARINO, J. (1977). The human ecology of child maltreatment: A conceptual model for research. *Journal of Marriage and the Family, 39,* 721–735.

GARBARINO, J. (1998, March 30). Moral development and violent boys. *All Things Considered.* National Public Radio.

GARBARINO, J., DUBROW, N., KOSTELNY, K., & PARDO, C. (1992). *Children in danger: Coping with the consequences of community violence.* San Francisco: Jossey-Bass.

GARDNER, M. (1994, January). Big ideas from small companies. *Working Mother,* pp. 33–40.

GARMEZY, N. (1985). Stress resistant children: The search for protective factors. In J. E. Stevenson (Ed.), *Recent research on developmental psychopathology* (pp. 213–233). Oxford, England: Pergamon.

GARRISON, F. H. (1965). Abt-Garrison history of pediatrics. In I. A. Abt (Ed.), *Pediatrics* (Vol. 1). Philadelphia: Saunders.

GARWOOD, S. G., PHILLIPS, D., HARTMAN, A., & ZIGLER, E. (1989). As the pendulum swings: Federal agency programs for children. *American Psychologist, 44,* 434–440.

GELLES, R. J. (1973). Child abuse as psychopathology: A sociological critique and reformulation. *American Journal of Orthopsychiatry, 43,* 611–621.

GELLES, R. J. (1989). Child abuse and violence in single parent families: A test of the parent-abuse and economic deprivation hypotheses. *American Journal of Orthopsychiatry, 59,* 492–501.

GELLES, R. J (1996). *The book of David: How preserving families can cost children's lives.* New York: Basic Books.

GELLES, R. J., & CORNELL, C. P. (1985). *Intimate violence in families. Family studies text services* (Vol. 2). Beverly Hills: Sage.

GELLES, R. J., & STRAUS, M. A. (1988). *Intimate violence: The causes and consequences of abuse in the American family.* New York: Simon & Schuster.

GERBNER, G. (1980). Children and power on television: The other side of the picture. In G. Gerbner, C. J. Ross, & E. Zigler (Eds.), Child abuse: An agenda for action (pp. 239–248). New York: Oxford University Press.

GIBBS, N. (1993). Up in arms: A train massacre intensifies the demand for gun control and for guns. *Time.* Retrieved from America Online on the World Wide Web: http://www.time.com/magazine/archive.

GIL, D. (1970). *Violence against children: Physical child abuse in the United States.* Cambridge, MA: Harvard University Press.

GILLIS, J. R (1996). *A world of their own making: Myth, ritual, and the quest for family values.* New York: Basic Books.

GILMAN, E., & ZIGLER, E. (1996). Not just any care: Shaping a coherent child care policy. In E. Zigler, S. L. Kagan, & N. W. Hall (Eds.), *Children, families and government: Preparing for the 21st century* (pp. 94–116). New York: Cambridge University Press.

GILMAN, J. L. (1998). Parenting during divorce. Retrieved from the World Wide Web at http://www.parent/net.articles/archives/pndiv1.html.

GIOVANNONI, J., & BILLINGSLEY, A. (1970). Child neglect among the poor: A study of parental adequacy in families of three ethnic groups. *Child Welfare, 49,* 196–204.

GLAZER, S. (1993). Adoption: Do current policies punish kids awaiting adoption? *CQ Researcher, 3,* 1035–1052.

GLEICK, E. (1995, May 3). A Congressional proposal to eliminate nutrition programs raises an outcry. *Time,* 74.

GOELMAN, H., & PENCE, A. (1987). Effects of child care, family and individual characteristics on children's language development: The Victoria Day Care Research Project. In D. A. Phillips (Ed.), *Quality in child care: What does research tell us?* (pp. 89–104). Washington, DC: National Association for the Education of Young Children.

GOELMAN, H., SHAPIRO, E., & PENCE, A. (1990). Family environment and family day care. *Family Relations, 39,* 14–19.

GOLDMAN, L. (1998). Ignorance about environmental toxins threatens children's health. http://www.islandnet.com.

GOLDSTEIN, J., SOLNIT, A. J., GOLDSTEIN, S., & FREUD, A. (1996). *The best interests of the child: The least detrimental alternative.* New York: Free Press.

GOODMAN, G., BATTERMAN-FAUNCE, J., & KENNEY, R. (1993). Optimizing children's testimony: Research and social policy issues concerning allegations of child sexual abuse. In D. Cicchetti &

S. Toth (Eds.), *Advances in applied developmental psychology: Vol. 8. Child abuse, child development, and social policy* (pp. 139–166). Norwood, NJ: Ablex.

GOODMAN, G., TAUB, E., JONES, D., ENGLEND, P., PORT, L., RUD, L., & PRADO, L. (1992). *Testifying in criminal court: Emotional effects on child sexual abuse victims. With commentaries by J. Myers and G. Melton* (Monograph SRCD. Monograph for the Society for Research in Child Development, 57, 5, Serial No. 229).

GOODWIN, S. (1990, December). Child health services in England and Wales: An overview. *Pediatrics, 86* (6, pt. 2, Suppl.).

GORDON, E., & BONILLA-BOWMAN, C. (1994). Equity and social justice in educational achievement. In R. Berne & L. O. Pincus (Eds.), *Outcome equity in education* (pp. 24–44). Thousand Oaks, CA: Corwin Press.

GORE, S. (1980). Stress buffering functions of social supports: An appraisal and clarification of research models. In B. S. Dohrenwend & B. P. Dohrenwend (Eds.), *Stressful life events: Their nature and effects.* New York: Wiley.

GORMAN, B. K., & HAYNIE, D. L. (1998). *Rural women face greater risk of poverty.* Unpublished manuscript, Department of Sociology, University of Pennsylvania, University Park.

GOULD, S. J. (1997). *Questioning the millennium: A rationalist's guide to a precisely arbitrary countdown.* New York: Harmony Books.

GRABER, D. A. (1989). *Mass media and American politics.* Washington, DC: Congressional Quarterly.

GRAVES, B. J. (1998, January). *The Texas Parents as Teachers Program and the reduction of aggression in boys from single-parent homes.* Paper presented to the Texas Youth Commission, Austin.

GREENHOUSE, L. (1992, June 7). The coming crisis of the American work force. *New York Times,* p. 14.

GREIDER, W. (1992). *Who will tell the people? The betrayal of American democracy.* New York: Simon & Schuster.

GRISSMER, D., KIRKY, S. N., BERENDS, M., & WILLIAMSON, S. (in press). *Student achievement and the changing American family* (Rand Report MR-488-LE/P & R). Santa Monica, CA: Rand Corporation.

GUTERSON, D. (1992). *Family matters: Why homeschooling makes sense.* New York: Harcourt Brace Jovanovich.

HALE, B. A., SEITZ, V., & ZIGLER, E. (1990). Health services and Head Start: A forgotten formula. *Journal of Applied Developmental Psychology, 11,* 447–458.

HALL, N. W. (1991). Pediatrics and child development: A parallel history. In F. S. Kessel, M. H. Bornstein, & A. J. Sameroff (Eds.), *Contemporary constructions of the child* (pp. 209–224). Hillsdale, NJ: Erlbaum.

HALL, N. W. (1992, June/July). The painful truth (about infant pain). *Parenting,* 102–107.

HALL, N. W. (1998, January). What you need to know now to keep your child off drugs later. *Parents,* pp. 123–126.

HALL, N. W., & ZIGLER, E. (1993). *Substance abuse prevention: A review relevant to preschool interventions: Theory, practice, and programs.* Unpublished manuscript, Yale University Bush Center in Child Development and Social Policy, New Haven, CT.

HALL, N. W., & ZIGLER, E. (1997). Drug abuse prevention efforts for young children: A review and critique of existing programs. *American Journal of Orthopsychiatry, 67,* 134–143.

HALL, N. W., & ZIGLER, E. (1997). Drug abuse prevention efforts in early childhood. *American Journal of Orthopsychiatry, 67*(1), 134–143.

HALLAHAN, D. P., & KAUFFMAN, J. M. (1995). Toward a culture of disability. In J. M. Kauffman & D. P. Hallahan (Eds.), *Illusion of full inclusion* (pp. 59–74). Austin, TX: Pro-Ed.

HALLOWELL, E. M., & RATEY, J. J. (1994a). *Answers to distraction.* New York: Bantam Books.

HALLOWELL, E. M., & RATEY, J. J. (1994b). *Driven to distraction: Recognizing and coping with attention deficit disorder from childhood through adulthood.* New York: Simon & Schuster.

HAMBURG, D. (1987). *Fundamental building blocks of early life.* New York: Carnegie Corporation.

HAMBURG, D. (1992). *Today's children: Creating a future for a generation in crisis.* New York: Times Books.

HANWAY, J. (1785). *A sentimental history of chimney sweepers.* London.

HARVEY, B. (1990, December). Child health in 1990: The United States compared to Canada, England and Wales, France, the Netherlands, and Norway [Presidential address delivered April 30,

1990, at the spring meeting of the American Academy of Pediatrics]. *Pediatrics, 86* (6, pt. 2, Suppl.).

HARWOOD, R. (1985). Summary: Work, parenting, and stress in the early postpartum months. In *Infant care leave project: Summaries of research components*. Unpublished manuscript, Bush Center in Child Development and Social Policy, Yale University, New Haven, CT.

HASS, N. (1995, September 10). Margaret Kelly Michaels wants her innocence back. *New York Times Magazine*, sec. 6, pp. 37–41.

HAUSER, R. M., BROWN, B. V. , & PROSSER, W. R. (Eds.). (1998). *Indicators of children's well-being.* New York: Russell Sage.

HAUSER-CRAM, P. (1995). Designing meaningful evaluations of early intervention services. In S. J. Meisels & J. Shonkoff (Eds.), *Handbook of early childhood intervention.* New York: Cambridge University Press.

HAWKINS, D. J., & WEISS, J. G. (1983). *The social development model: An integrated approach to delinquency prevention.* Seattle: University of Law and Justice.

HAWKINS, J. D., & CATALANO, R. F. (1992). *Communities that care: Action for drug abuse prevention.* San Francisco: Jossey-Bass.

HAWKINS, J. D., CATALANO, R. F., & MILLER, J. Y. (1992). Risk and protective factors for alcohol and other drug problems in adolescence and early adulthood: Implications for substance abuse prevention. *Psychological Bulletin, 112,* 64–105.

HEADDEN, S. (1995, September 25). Tongue-tied in the schools: Bilingual education began as a good idea. Now it needs fixing. *U. S. News & World Report*, p. 44.

HEGER, R., & SCANNAPIECO, M. (Eds). (1998). *Kinship foster care: Policy, practice, and research.* New York: Oxford University Press.

HELFER, M. E., & KEMPE, R. S. (1997). *The battered child.* Chicago: University of Chicago Press.

HELFER, R., & KEMPE, E. (Eds.). (1968). *The battered child.* Chicago: University of Chicago Press.

HERNANDEZ, D. (1995, Winter). Changing demographics: Past and future demands for early childhood programs. *Future of Children, 5,* 145–160.

HERR, S. S. (1997). Perspectives: Reauthorization of the Individuals With Disabilities Education Act. *Mental Retardation, 35,* 131–137.

HETHERINGTON, M., HAGAN, M. S., & ANDERSON, E. R. (1989). Marital transitions: A child's perspective. *American Psychologist, 44,* 303–312.

HETTLEMAN, K. R. (1997, March 10). State's rights, school wrongs. *Nation*, pp. 23–24.

HIGGINBOTHAM, A. L. (1993). *America's children at risk: A national agenda for legal action.* New York: American Bar Association.

HIROKAZU, Y. (1995). Long-term effects of early childhood programs on social outcomes and delinquency. *Future of Children, 5,* 45–62.

HIRSCH, E. D., JR. (1996). *The schools we need and why we don't have them.* New York: Doubleday.

HITE, S. (1994). *The Hite report on the family: Growing up under patriarchy.* New York: Grove Press.

HOBBS, N. (1974). *Futures of children.* Nashville, TN: Vanderbilt University.

HOCHSCHILD, A. R. (1997a, April 20). There's no place like work. *New York Times Magazine*, pp. 51–55.

HOCHSCHILD, A. R. (1997b). *The time bind: When work becomes home and home becomes work.* New York: Metropolitan Books.

HOCUTT, A. M. (1996). Effectiveness of special education: Is placement the critical factor? *Future of Children, 6* (1), 40–53.

HODGKINSON, H. (1993, April). American education: The good, the bad, and the task. *Phi-Delta Kappan,* 619–623.

HOFF, D. J. (1997, January 22). Goals 2000 loses its way on standards. *Education Week*, p. 1.

HOFFERTH, S. L. (1989, July). What is the demand for and supply of child care in the United States? *Young Children*, pp. 28–33.

HOFFERTH, S. L., BRAYFIELD, A., DEITCH, S., & HOLCOMB, P. (1991). National child care survey, 1990. Washington, DC: Urban Institute.

HOFFERTH, S. L., & PHILLIPS, D. A. (1987). Child care in the United States: 1970–1995. *Journal of Marriage and the Family, 49,* 559–571.

HOFFMAN-PLOTKIN, D., & TWENTYMAN, C. T. (1984). A multimodal assessment of behavioral and cognitive deficits in abused and neglected preschoolers. *Child Development, 55,* 794–802.

HOLCOMB, B., CARTWRIGHT, C., DREISBACH, S., & HUTTER, S. (1998, July/August). Child care: How does your state rate? *Working Mother*, pp. 22–38.

HOPPER, P., & ZIGLER, E. (1988). The medical and social science basis for a national infant care leave policy. *American Journal of Orthopsychiatry, 58*, 324–338.

HORGAN, C. (1993). *Substance abuse: The nation's number one health problem. Key indicators for policy.* Princeton, NJ: Robert Wood Johnson Foundation.

HORN, W. (1996, Summer). Assessing the effects of the "devolution revolution" on children and families: A policy point of view. *Child Poverty News and Views*, pp. 1–2.

HORNBLOWER, M. (1995, December 11). Fixing the system: Los Angeles County creates a model plan to get help into troubled homes. *Time*, p. 146.

HORNER, T. M., & GUYER, M. J. (1993). Infant placement and custody. In C. H. Zeanah (Ed.), *Handbook of infant mental health* (pp. 462–479). New York: Guilford Press.

HOWARD, J. (1990). Substance abuse. Proceedings of the National Health/Education Consortium conference, Crossing the Boundaries Between Health and Education. Washington, DC, May 29–30. Washington, DC: National Health/Education Consortium.

HOWELL, J. (1993). Selected state legislation: A guide for effective state laws to protect children. Office of Juvenile Justice and Delinquency Prevention. Office of Justice Programs, U.S. Department of Justice. National Center for Missing and Exploited Children, Washington, DC.

HOWES, C. (1983). Caregiver behavior in center and family day care. *Journal of Applied Developmental Psychology, 1*, 99–107.

HOWES, C. (1990). Can age of entry into child care predict adjustment in kindergarten? *Developmental Psychology, 26*, 292–303.

HOWES, C., KEELING, K., & SALE, J. (1988). *The home visitor: Improving quality in family day care homes.* Unpublished manuscript, University of California–Los Angeles.

HOWES, C., & RUBENSTEIN, J. (1985). Determinants of toddlers' experience in day care: Age of entry and quality of setting. *Child Care Quarterly, 14*, 140–151.

HOWES, D., & OLENICK, M. (1986). Family and child care influences on toddlers' compliance. *Child Development, 57*, 202–216.

HUMAN SERVICES REAUTHORIZATION ACT. (1990). P.K. 101–501. Infant day care [Special issue]. *Early Childhood Research Quarterly, 3.*

HUNGER STILL SEVERE PROBLEM IN PROSPEROUS U.S. (1998). *Nation's Health, 28*, 11.

HUNT, J. McV. (1961). *Intelligence and experience.* New York: Ronald Press.

HUNTER, R. S., & KILSTROM, N. (1979). Breaking the cycle in abusive families. *American Journal of Psychiatry, 136*, 1320–1322.

HUSTON, A. C. (1991a). Antecedents, consequences and possible solutions for poverty among children. In A. C. Huston (Ed.), *Children in poverty.* New York: Cambridge University Press.

HUSTON, A. C. (Ed.). (1991b). *Children in poverty.* New York: Cambridge University Press.

IMIG, D. (1995). Advocacy by proxy: The children's lobby in American Politics. *Journal of Children and Poverty, 2*, 21–29.

INGRAHAM V. WRIGHT, 430 S.Ct. 651 (1977).

INSTITUTE OF AEROBIC RESEARCH. (1987). *Get fit.* Dallas: Author.

INSTITUTE OF MEDICINE. (1990). *Nutrition during pregnancy.* Washington, DC: National Academy Press.

JACOBS, F. H., & DAVIES, M. W. (1994). *More than kissing babies? Current child and family policy in the United States.* Westport, CT: Auburn House.

JACOBS, J. (1994, December 6). A mother who abuses drugs has rights, but her baby has none. *Knight-Ridder/Tribune News Service.*

JENCKS, C. (1992). *Rethinking social policy: Race, poverty and the underclass.* Cambridge, MA: Harvard University Press.

JOHNSON, D., & BRECKENRIDGE, J. N. (1982). The Houston Parent-Child Development Center and the primary prevention of behavior problems in young children. *American Journal of Community Psychology, 10*, 305–316.

JOHNSON, K. (1993, December). *Health care reform under the proposed Clinton plan.* Address given at Biennial Training Institute of Zero to Three.

JOIN TOGETHER. (1994). Tools for social change. *Strategies, 3* (1), 4.

JONES, L. (1996, October). A history of the National Assessment of Educational Progress and some questions about its future. *Educational Researcher*, pp. 15–22.

JUNEWITZ, W. J. (1983). A protective posture toward emotional abuse and neglect. *Child Welfare, 62*, 243–252.

KAGAN, S. L. (in press). Human development: Research and social policy. *Encyclopedia of education*, NY: Macmillan.

KAGAN, S. L., KLUGMAN, E., & ZIGLER, E. (1983). Creating social policies for children and families: An overview. In E. Zigler, S. L. Kagan, & E. Klugman (Eds.), *Children, families and government* (pp. 3–9). New York: Cambridge University Press.

KAGAN, S. L., & PRITCHARD, E. (1996). Linking services for children and families: Past legacy, future possibilities. In E. Zigler, S. L. Kagan, & N. W. Hall (Eds.), *Children, families and government* (pp. 378–393). New York: Cambridge University Press.

KAITIN, K. K. (1994). Congressional responses to families in the workplace: The Family and Medical Leave Act of 1987–1988. In F. H. Jacobs & M. W. Davies (Eds.), *More than kissing babies? Current child and family policy in the United States* (pp. 91–120). Westport, CT: Auburn House.

KAMERMAN, S. (1996). Child and family policies: An international review. In E. Zigler, S. L. Kagan, & N. W. Hall (Eds.), *Children families and government* (pp. 31–50). New York: Cambridge University Press.

KAMERMAN, S., & KAHN, A. J. (1995). *Starting right: How America neglects its youngest children and what we can do about it.* New York: Oxford University Press.

KAMERMAN, S., KAHN, A. J., & KINGSTON, P. (1983). *Maternity policies and working women.* New York: Columbia University Press.

KANTROWITZ, B. (1992, January 27). A head start does not last. *Newsweek*, p. 44.

KAUFMAN, J. (1991). Depressive disorders in maltreated children. *Journal of the American Academy of Child and Adolescent Psychiatry, 30*, 257–265.

KAUFMAN, J., & CICCHETTI, D. (1989). The effects of maltreatment on school-aged children's socioemotional development: Assessments in a day camp setting. *Developmental Psychology 15*, 516–524.

KAUFMAN, J., & ZIGLER, E. (1989). The intergenerational transmission of child abuse. In D. Cicchetti & V. Carlson (Eds.), *Child maltreatment: Theory and research on the causes and consequences of child abuse and neglect* (pp. 129–150). New York: Cambridge University Press.

KAUFMAN, J., & ZIGLER, E. (1996). Child abuse and social policy. In E. Zigler, S. L. Kagan, & N. W. Hall (Eds.), *Children, families and government.* New York: Cambridge University Press.

KAUFFMAN, J. M. (1995a). How we might achieve the radical reform of special education. In J. M. Kauffman & D. P. Hallahan (Eds.), *Illusion of full inclusion* (pp. 193–212). Austin, TX: Pro-Ed.

KAUFFMAN, J. M. (1995b). The regular education initiative as Reagan-Bush educational policy: A trickle-down theory of education of the hard-to-teach. In J. M. Kauffman & D. P. Hallahan (Eds.), *Illusion of full inclusion* (pp. 125–156). Austin, TX: Pro-Ed.

KAUFFMAN, J. M., & HALLAHAN, D. P. (Eds.). (1995a). *Illusion of full inclusion: A comprehensive critique of a current special education bandwagon.* Austin, TX: Pro-Ed.

KAUFFMAN, J. M., & HALLAHAN, D. P. (1995b). Toward a comprehensive delivery system for special education. In J. M. Kauffman & D. P. Hallahan (Eds.), *Illusion of full inclusion* (pp. 157–192). Austin, TX: Pro-Ed.

KAZIN, A. (1957). The Freudian revolution analyzed. In B. Nelson (Ed.), *Freud and the 20th century* (pp. 59–74). Cleveland: World.

KEMPE, C., SILVERMAN, F., STEELE, B., DROEGMUELLER, W., & SILVER, H. (1962). The battered child syndrome. *Journal of the American Medical Association, 181*, 17–24.

KESSEN, W. (1965). *The child.* New York: Wiley.

KESSEN, W. (1979). The American child and other cultural inventions. *American Psychologist, 34*, 815–820.

KEYSERLING, M. D. (1972). *Windows on day care.* New York: National Council of Jewish Women.

KILBORN, P. T. (1996, November 30). Shrinking safety net cradles hearts and hopes of children. *New York Times*, pp. A1, A8.

KIMBEL, G. (1989). Psychology from the standpoint of a generalist. *American Psychologist, 44*, 491–499.

KINDERGARTEN STUDENT FACES GUN CHARGES. (1998, May 11). *New York Times*, A13.

KIRP, D. L. (1995). Changing conceptions of educational equity. In D. Ravitch & M. A. Vinovskis (Eds.), *Learning from the past: What history teaches us about school reform*. Baltimore: Johns Hopkins University Press.

KLAUS, J. H., & KENNEL, M. (1976). *Maternal-infant bonding*. St. Louis: Mosby.

KLEIN, M., & STERN, L. (1971). Low birth weight and the battered child syndrome. *American Journal of Diseases of Children, 122,* 15–18.

KLERMAN, L. V. (1991). The health of poor children: Problems and programs. In A. C. Huston (Ed.), *Children in poverty*. New York: Cambridge University Press.

KLERMAN, L. V. (1996). Child health: What public policies can improve it? In E. Zigler, S. L. Kagan, & N. W. Hall (Eds.), *Children, families and government* (pp. 188–206). New York: Cambridge University Press.

KNITZER, J. (1996). Children's mental health: Changing paradigms and policies. In E. Zigler, S. L. Kagan, & N. W. Hall (Eds.), *Children, families and government* (pp. 207–232). New York: Cambridge University Press.

KOLB, B. (1989). Brain development, plasticity, and behavior. *American Psychologist, 44,* 1203–1212.

KOOP, C. E., & LUNDBERG, G. D. (1992). Violence in America: A public health emergency. *Journal of the American Medical Association, 267,* 3075.

KOPP, B. (1983). Risk factors in development. In M. M. Haith & J. Campos (Eds.), *Handbook of child psychology: Vol. 44. Infancy and developmental psychobiology* (4th ed., pp. 1081–1188). New York: Wiley.

KOZOL, J. (1991). *Savage inequalities: Children in America's schools*. New York: Crown.

KYLE, J. E. (Ed.). (1987). *Children, families and cities: Programs that work at the local level*. Washington, DC: National League of Cities.

LAKSHMANAN, I. A. R. (1995, October 2). Doubts arise on "fast track" adoptions. *Boston Globe*, p. A1.

LAMB, M. E. (1981). The development of father-infant relationships. In M. E. Lamb (Ed.), *The role of the father in child development* (2nd ed.). New York: Wiley.

LAMB, M. E., STERNBERG, K. J., & PRODROMIDIS, M. (1992). Nonmaternal care and the security of infant-mother attachment: A reanalysis of the data. *Infant Behavior and Development, 15,* 71–83.

LAMBERT, R. D. (1981). Ethnic/racial relations in the United States in comparative perspective. *Annals of the American Academy of Political and Social Science, 454,* 189–206.

LANG, S. S. (1994, August). Low-income boys found to be most hurt financially by parents' divorce. *Family Economics*, pp. 44–49.

LANTIER, G. (1998, September). Youth policy in hyper-drive? *Youth Today*, p. 26.

LANTING, O. I., FIDLER, V., HUISMAN, M., TOUWEN, B. G. L., & BOERSMA, E. M. (1994). Neurological differences between 9 year old children fed breast-milk or formula-milk as babies. *Lancet, 344,* 1519.

LAWTON, M. (1996, December 11). U.S. is big spender in global study. *Education Week*, p. 3.

LEACH, P. (1993). *Children first*. New York: Vintage Books.

LEACH, P. (1994). *Children first*. New York: Vintage Books, 2/e.

LECCA, P. J., & WATTS, T. D. (1993). Preschoolers and substance abuse: Strategies for prevention and intervention. New York: Haworth Press.

LEE, R. W. (1956). The elements of Roman law. London: Sweet and Maxwell. *American Journal of the Disabled Child, 122,* 15–18.

LEE, V. D., BROOKS–GUNN, J., SCHNUR, E., & LIAW, F. R. (1990). Are Head Start effects sustained: A longitudinal follow-up comparison of disadvantaged children attending Head Start, no preschool, and other preschool programs. *Child Development, 61,* 495–507.

LEGISLATIVE ACTION MOVES FORWARD ON EDUCATIONAL TESTING ISSUES. (1997, July/August). *Psychological Science Agenda*, p. 12.

LERNER, B. (1998, April 21). Sometimes spanking can't be beat. *Wall Street Journal*, p. A22.

LeSHAWN V. DIXON, 762 F.Supp.959 (D.D.C. 1991).

LEVINE, C. (Ed.). (1988). *Programs to strengthen families*. Chicago: Family Resource Coalition.

LEVINE, R. E. (1996). *Trends in school district demographics, 1986–87 to 1990–91*. Washington, DC: American Institute for Research in the Behavioral Sciences.

LEVITAN , S., & CONWAY, E. (1990). *Families in flux: New approaches to meeting workforce challenges for child, elder, and health care in the 1990's*. Washington, DC: Bureau of National Affairs.

LEWIS, D. O., SHANOK, S. S., PINCUS, J. H., & GLASER, G. H. (1989). Toward a theory of the genesis of violence: A follow-up theory of delinquents. *Journal of American Academy of Child and Adolescent Psychiatry, 28,* 431–436.

LEWIT, E. M., & BAKER, L. S. (1996). Child indicators: Children in special education. *Future of Children, 6* (1), 139–151.

LIEBERMAN, A. F. (1993). *The emotional life of the toddler.* New York: Free Press.

LIEBERMAN, A. F. (1994). *The emotional life of the toddler.* New York: Free Press.

LIEBERMAN, L. M. (1988). *Preserving special education . . . for those who need it.* Newtonville, MA: Glo Worm.

LILLY, D. (1996, November 12). Seattle ending school busing. *Seattle Times,* p. A1.

LINDESMITH CENTER. (1998, June 9). Drug policy experts criticize anti-drug advertising campaign [Press release], New York City.

LINDSEY, L. B. (1988, July 5). Better child care, cheaper. *Wall Street Journal,* pp. A–1, A–12.

LITTEL, J. H., & SCHUERMAN, J. R. (1995). A synthesis of research on family preservation and reunification programs. Chicago: Westat. Retrieved from the World Wide Web: http://aspe.os.dhhs .gov/hsp/cyp/fplitrev.htm.

LIVINGSTON, K. (1997). Ritalin: Miracle drug or cop-out? *Public Interest, 127,* 3–18.

LONG, L., & LONG, T. (1982). *Latchkey children: The child's view of self-care.* Baltimore: Loyola College. (ERIC Document Reproduction Services No. ED 211 299)

LOUIS HARRIS ASSOCIATES. (1989). *The Philip Morris, Inc. Family Survey II: Child care.* New York: Author.

LOWE, B. A. (1993, November 30). Testimony before the U.S. Senate Finance Committee Subcommittee on Health Care for Families and the Uninsured.

LYNN, L., & WHEELOCK, A. (1997). Making detracking work. *Harvard Educational Letter, 13* (1).

LYON, G. R. (1996). Learning disabilities. *Future of Children, 6* (1), 54–76.

MACCOBY, E. E., KAHN, A. J., & EVERETT, B. A. (1983). The role of psychological research in the formation of policies affecting children. *American Psychologist, 38,* 80–84.

MACCOBY, E. E., & MNOOKIN, R. H. (1992). *Dividing the child: Social and legal dilemmas of custody.* London: Harvard University Press.

MACMILLAN, D. L., SEMMEL, M. I., & GERBER, M. M. (1995). The social context: Then and now. In J. M. Kauffman & D. P. Hallahan (Eds.), *Illusion of full inclusion* (pp. 19–38). Austin, TX: Pro-Ed.

MADDUX, J. E. (1993). Social science, social policy, and scientific research. *American Psychologist, 48,* 689–691.

MANCIAUX, M., JESTIN, D., FRITZ, M., & BERTRAND, D. (1990). Child health care policy and delivery in France. *Pediatrics,* special supplement, *121,* 18-22.

MANN, C., & GUYER, J. (1997). *Overview of the new child health block grant.* Washington, DC: Center on Budget and Policy Priorities.

MARCH OF DIMES. (1994). *Health care reform: Will it improve the health of mothers and babies? Analysis of six legislative proposals.* Washington, DC: Author.

MARKUS, A. (1997, Summer). Revisiting EPDST. *Health Policy and Child Health,* pp. 24–27.

MARTIN, E. W., MARTIN, R., & TERMAN, D. L. (1996). The legislative and litigation history of special education. *Future of Children, 6* (1), 25–39.

MARTINEZ, P. E., & RICHTERS, J. E. (1993). The NIMH Community Violence Project: II. Children's distress symptoms associated with violence exposure. *Psychiatry, 56,* 22–35.

MATAS, L., AREND, R. A., & SROUFE, L. A. (1978). Continuity of adaptation in the second year: The relationship between quality of attachment and later competence. *Child Development, 49,* 547–556.

MATHIEU, S. (1995). *The status of Parents as Teachers program in Texas: 1995.* Unpublished manuscript, University of Texas at Austin.

MAURER, A., & WALLERSTEIN, J. S. (1987). The influence of corporal punishment on crime. Retrieved from the World Wide Web at http://silcon.com/~ptare/maurer1.htm.

MCCARTHY, C. (1990, October 27). The school year needs to be better, not longer. *Washington Post,* A-6.

MCCARTNEY, K. (1984). The effect of quality of day care environment upon children's language development. *Developmental Psychology, 20,* 244–260.

MCCURDY, K., & DARO, D. (1992). *Current trends in child abuse reporting and fatalities: The results of the 1992 Annual Fifth State Survey Z.* Chicago: National Center on Child Abuse Prevention Research.

McDonald, T. P., Allen, R. I., Westerfelt, A., & Piliavin, I. (1997). *Assessing the long term effects of foster care: A research synthesis*. Washington, DC: Child Welfare League of America.

McKey, R., Condelli, L., Ganson, H., et al. (1985). *The impact of Head Start on children, families, and communities: Final report of the Head Start Evaluation, Synthesis, and Utilization Project*. Washington, DC: USDHHS.

McLanahan, S. S., Astone, N. M., & Marks, N. F. (1991). The role of mother-only families in reinforcing poverty. In A. Huston (Ed.), *Children in poverty* (pp. 51–78). New York: Cambridge University Press.

McLear, S., Callaghe, M., Hentry, D., & Waller, J. (1994). Psychiatric disorders in sexually abused children. *Journal of the American Academy of Child and Adolescent Psychiatry, 33*, 313–319.

Mead, L. (1996). Welfare reform and children. In E. Zigler, S. L. Kagan, & N. W. Hall (Eds.), *Children, families and government* (pp. 51–76). New York: Cambridge University Press.

Medrich, E., Ruizen, J., Rubin, V., & Buckley, S. (1982). *The serious business of growing up: A study of children's lives outside of school*. Berkeley: University of California Press.

Meisels, S. J., & Shonkoff, J. (1995). Preface. In S. J. Meisels & J. Shonkoff (Eds.), *Handbook of early childhood intervention*. New York: Cambridge University Press.

Melton, G. B., & Thompson, R. A. (1987). Legislative approaches to psychological maltreatment: A social policy analysis. In M. R. Brassard, R. Germain , & S. N. Hart (Eds.), *Psychological maltreatment of children and youth* (pp. 203–216). New York: Pergamon.

Merrow Report: In schools we trust. (1996). *Learning Matters*. South Carolina ETV.

Metropolitan Life Insurance. (1991). *The American teacher survey*. New York: Author.

Metz, M. H. (1994). Desegregation as necessity and challenge. *Journal of Negro Education, 63* (1), 64–76.

Mianowaney, J. (1996, July 27). [Untitled report on education as a campaign issue]. AOL News Column, retrieved from the World Wide Web: URL not available.

Miller, E. (1994). *Context of trends: Reshaping of America*. Brooklyn: EPM Communications.

Mills, K. (1998). *Something better for my children: The history and people of Head Start*. New York: Dutton.

Minow, M., & Weissbourd, R. (1993, Winter). Social movements for children. *Dædalus, 122* (11), 1–30.

Miringoff, M. L. (1995). Toward a national standard of social health: The need for progress in social indicators. *American Journal of Orthopsychiatry, 65*, 462–467.

Miringoff, M. L., Miringoff, M. L., & Opdycke, S. (1996). Monitoring the nation's social performance: The Index of Social Health. In E. Zigler, S. L. Kagan, & N. W. Hall (Eds.), *Children, families and government*. New York: Cambridge University Press.

Morra, L. G. (1994). *Immigrant education: Federal funding has not kept pace with student increases*. Washington, DC: U.S. General Accounting Office. (ERIC Document Reproduction Service No. ED 371 061).

Morse, W. C. (1995). Comments from a biased viewpoint. In J. M. Kauffman & D. P. Hallahan (Eds.), *Illusion of full inclusion* (pp. 105–120). Austin, TX: Pro-Ed.

Morse, W. C., Paul, J. L, & Rosselli-Kostoryz, H. (1997). The role of basic knowledge and the future of special education. In J. L. Paul, M. Churton, H. Rosselli-Kostoryz, W. C. Morse, K. Marfo, C. Lavely, & D. Thomas (Eds.), *Foundations of special education* (pp. 11–22). Pacific Grove, CA: Brooks/Cole.

Moskowitz, M. & Townsend, C. (1995, October). 100 best companies for working mothers. *Working Mother*, pp. 18–99.

Mosle, S. (1996a, October 27). The answer is national standards. *New York Times Magazine*, pp. 44–68.

Mosle, S. (1996b, September 8). Scores count. *New York Times Magazine*, pp. 41–45.

Mosle, S. (1996c, June 17). What we talk about when we talk about education. *New Republic*, pp. 27–36.

Mosle, S. (1997, August 31). The stealth chancellor. *New York Times Magazine*, pp. 30–61.

Muenchow, S. (1996). The media and child and family policy. In E. Zigler, S. L. Kagan, & N. W. Hall (Eds.), *Children, families and government*. New York: Cambridge University Press.

Mullis, I. V. S., Dossey, J. A., Campbell, J. R. , Gentile, C. A., O'Sullivan, C., & Latham, A. S. (1994). *NAEP 1992 trends in academic progress*. Washington, DC: U.S. Government Printing Office.

Murray, D. M., & Perry, C. L. (1985). The prevention of adolescent drug abuse: Implications of etiological, developmental, behavioral, and environmental models. In C. L. Jones & R. J. Battjes (Eds.), *Etiology of drug abuse: Implications for prevention* (NIDA Monograph 56). Washington, DC: U.S. Government Printing Office.

Musto, D. (1983). Drug policy: The American evolution. In E. Zigler, S. L. Kagan, & N. W. Hall (Eds.), *Children, families and government* (pp. 371–391). New York: Cambridge University Press.

Narine, M. (1992). *Single-sex, single race public schools: A solution to the problems plaguing the black community?* (ERIC Document Reproduction Service No. ED 348 423).

National Center for Children in Poverty. (1990). *Five million children: A statistical profile of our poorest young citizens.* New York: Columbia University School of Public Health.

National Center for Children in Poverty. (1995). Welfare reform seen from a child's perspective. *Child Poverty News and Issues, 5,* 1–2.

National Center for Children in Poverty. (1997). Wake up America: Columbia University study shatters stereotypes of young child poverty. Retrieved from the World Wide Web: http://cpmcnet.columbia.edu/edpt/nccp.

National Center for Children in Poverty. (1998, July). *Early childhood poverty research briefs.* NY: Author.

National Center for Clinical Infant Programs. (1988). *Infants, families and child care: Toward a research agenda.* Washington, DC: Author.

National Center for Education Statistics. (1993). *The condition of education, 1993.* Washington, DC: Author.

National Center for Education Statistics. (1994a). *Dropout rates in the United States: 1993.* Washington, DC: U.S. Government Printing Office.

National Center for Education Statistics. (1994b). *Report in brief: National Assessment of Educational Progress (NAEP) 1992 trends in academic progress.* Washington, DC: U.S Department of Education.

National Center for Education Statistics. (1998). *The condition of education 1998* (NCES Publication No. 98-013). Washington, DC: U.S. Government Printing Office.

National Center for Health Statistics. (1993, August 31). Advance Report of Final Mortality Statistics, 1991. *Monthly Vital Statistics Report, 42* (2, Suppl.).

National Child Care Staffing Study. (1998). *National Child Care Staffing Study, 1988–1997: Worthy work, unlivable wages.* Washington, DC: Author.

National Clearinghouse on Child Abuse and Neglect Information. (1998). *What is child maltreatment? Fact sheet.* Washington, DC: Author.

National Coalition to Abolish Corporal Punishment in Schools. (1991). *Corporal punishment fact sheet.* Columbus, OH: Author.

National Commission on Children. (1991). *Beyond rhetoric: A new American agenda for children and families.* Washington, DC: U.S. Government Printing Office.

National Commission on Excellence in Education. (1983). A nation at risk: The imperative for educational reform. Washington DC: U.S. Government Printing Office.

National Commission on Teaching and America's Future. (1996). What matters most: Teaching for America's future. Washington, DC: Author.

National Commission for the Prevention of Infant Mortality. (1992). *Troubling trends persist: Shortchanging America's next generation.* Washington, DC: U.S. Government Printing Office.

National Council for Early Childhood Professional Recognition. (1990). *Improving childcare through the Child Development Associate Program.* Washington, DC: Author.

National Council of Jewish Women. (1993). *The experience of childbearing women in the workplace: The impact of family-friendly policies and practices.* Washington, DC: Author.

National Education Goals Panel. (1996). *Goals report: Building a nation of learners.* Washington, DC: Author.

National Institute of Child Health and Development. (1997). Infant child care and attachment security: Results of the NICHD Study of Early Child Care. *Child Development, 68,* 860–879.

National Institute of Child Health and Human Development. (1998). *NICHD Study of Early Child Care, Executive Summary.* NIH Pub. No. 98-4318. Washington, DC: National Institutes of Health.

National Law Center on Homelessness and Poverty. (1997). *"Back to school" is not for everybody.* Washington, DC: Author.

NATIONAL ORGANIZATION FOR WOMEN. (1998). *Washington state chapter, position paper on joint custody.* Seattle: Author.

NATIONAL PUBLIC RADIO. (1998, August 14). Effects of an unstable home environment during the prenatal period. *Morning Edition.*

NATIONAL RESEARCH COUNCIL. (1993). *Understanding child abuse and neglect.* Washington, DC: National Academy Press.

NETKIN, H. (1997, July 24). English not taught here. *Wall Street Journal,* p. A12.

NEW, C., & DAVID, M. (1984). *For the children's sake.* New York: Penguin.

NEW YORK STATE DEPARTMENT OF EDUCATION. (1994). *New York, the state of learning: Statewide profile of the educational system.* Albany: Author.

NEWBERGER, C., REID, R., DANIEL, J., HYDE, J., & KOTELCHUCK, M. (1977). Pediatric social illness: Towards an etiological classification. *Pediatrics, 60,* 178–185.

NEWMAN, L., & BUKA, S. (1991, January 8). *Preventing risks of learning impairment: A report for the Education Committee of the States,* Washington, DC: GPO.

NIXON, R. M. (1971, December 10). *Congressional Record,* S21129.

NOBLE, B. F. (1993, April 18). Worthy child care pay scales. *New York Times,* p. F25.

NOBLE, B. F. (1994, January 9). A guide to lower health care costs. *New York Times,* p. F25.

NUDD, M. E. (1989). Parents as Teachers project. *Prevention in Human Services, 6,* 67–70.

OAKES, J. (1985). *Keeping track: How schools structure inequality.* New Haven, CT: Yale University Press.

OAKES, J. (1990). *Multiplying inequalities: The effects of race, social class and tracking on opportunities to learn mathematics and science.* Santa Monica, CA: Rand Corporation.

ODOM, S. L., MCCONNELL, S. R., & MCEVOY, M. A. (1992a). Peer-related social competence and its significance for young children with disabilities. In S. Odom, S. McConnell, & M. McEvoy (Eds.), *Social competence of young children with disabilities: Issues and strategies for intervention* (pp. 3–35). Baltimore: Paul H. Brookes.

ODOM, S. L., MCCONNELL, S. R., & MCEVOY, M. A. (Eds.). (1992b). *Social competence of young children with disabilities: Issues and strategies for intervention.* Baltimore: Paul H. Brookes.

OFFICE FOR SUBSTANCE ABUSE PREVENTION. (1992, March/April). New study shows that children bond with Old Joe. *Prevention Pipeline,* p. 5.

OHIO STATE UNIVERSITY. (1998). *Divorce still often means money trouble for moms.* Columbus: Ohio State University Extension Service.

OLDS, D. (1992). Home visitation for pregnant women and parents of young children. *American Journal of Diseases in Children, 146,* 704–708.

OLDS, D. L. (1997). The Prenatal/Early Infancy Project: Fifteen years later. In G. W. Albee & T. P. Gullotta (Eds.), *Primary prevention works: Issues in children's and families' lives* (Vol. 6, pp. 41–67). Thousand Oaks, CA: Sage.

OLDS, D. L., & HENDERSON, C. R., JR. (1989). The prevention of maltreatment. In D. Cicchetti & V. Carlson (Eds.), *Child maltreatment: Theory and research on the causes and consequences of child abuse and neglect* (pp. 722–763). New York: Cambridge University Press.

OLSEN, D., & ZIGLER, E. (1989). An assessment of the all-day kindergarten movement. *Early Childhood Research Quarterly, 4,* 167–186.

ONTARIO MINISTRY OF COMMUNITY AND SOCIAL SERVICES. (1991). *Factors related to quality in child care: A review of the literature.* Toronto: Author.

O'REILLY, F. E. (1995). *State special education funding formulas and the use of separate placements for students with disabilities: Exploring linkages* (CSEF Policy Paper No. 7). Palo Alto, CA: Center for Special Education Finance.

ORGANIZATION FOR ECONOMIC COOPERATION AND DEVELOPMENT. (1998). *Education indicators at a glance.* Paris: Author.

OSOFSKY, J. D., & FENICHEL, E. (Eds.). (1994). *Caring for infants and toddlers in violent environments: Hurt, healing, and hope.* Arlington, VA: Zero to Three/National Center for Clinical Infant Programs.

OSTER, R. M. (1979). Children in a promised land. *Scandinavian Review, 67,* 6–15.

OWEN, M. T., & MULVIHILL, B. A. (1994). Benefits of a parent education and support program in the first three years. *Family Relations, 43,* 206–212.

PACKARD, V. (1972). *A nation of strangers.* New York: Simon & Schuster.

PAKIZEGI, B. (1985). Maladaptive parent-infant relationships. *Journal of Applied Developmental Psychology, 6,* 199–246.

PAKROO, P. H. (1997). Shifting fronts in the war on drugs. Retrieved from the World Wide Web at Nolo press release archive: www.nolo.com.

PARENTS AS TEACHERS. (1998). Program summary. Retrieved from the World Wide Web: http://www.patnc.org.

PARKE, R., & COLLMER, C. (1975). Child abuse: An interdisciplinary analysis. In M. Hetherington (Ed.), *Review of child development research* (Vol. 5). Chicago: University of Chicago Press.

PARRISH, T. B. (1994). *Fiscal issues in special education: Removing incentives for restrictive placements* (CSEF Policy Paper No. 4). Palo Alto, CA: Center for Special Education Finance.

PARRISH, T. B., & CHAMBERS, J. G. (1996). Financing special education. *Future of Children, 6* (1), 121–138.

PARROT, S. (1998, January 27). *Expanding the DCTC without making it refundable: Who will it help?* Washington, DC: Center on Budget and Policy Priorities.

PAUL, J. L., & ROSSELLI-KOSTROYZ, H. (1997). The future of special education. In J. L. Paul, M. Churton, H. Rosselli-Kostroyz, W. C. Morse, K. Marfo, C. Lavely, & D. Thomas. (Eds.), *Foundations of special education* (pp. 229–235). Pacific Grove, CA: Brooks/Cole.

PAVETTI, L. (1995). Who is affected by time limits? In I. Sawhill (Ed.), *Welfare reform: An analysis of the issues* (pp. 31–34). Washington, DC: Urban Institute.

PEAR, R. (1997, August 15). After a review, 95,000 children will lose cash disability benefits. *New York Times,* pp. A1, A28.

PELCOVITZ, D., KAPLAN, S., GOLDENBERG, B., MANDEL, F., LEHANE, J., & GAURRERA, J. (1994). Posttraumatic stress disorder in physically abused adolescents. *Journal of American Academy of Child and Adolescent Psychiatry, 33,* 305–312.

PETERS, S., WYATT, G., & FINKELHOR, D. (1986). Prevalence. In D. Finkelhor (Ed.), *A sourcebook on child sexual abuse.* Beverly Hills: Sage.

PFANNENSTIEL, J., LAMBSON, T., & YARNELL, V. (1991). *Second wave study of the Parents as Teachers program.* Overland, KS: Research & Training Associates.

PFANNENSTIEL, J., & SELTZER, D. (1985). *Evaluation report: New Parents as Teachers project.* Overland, KS: Research & Training Associates.

PHILLIPS, D., & HOWES, C. (1987). Indicators of quality in child care: Review of the research. In D. Phillips (Ed.), *Quality in child care: What does the research tell us?* Washington, DC: National Association for the Education of Young Children.

PHILLIPS, D., MCCARTNEY, K., SCARR, S., & HOWES, C. (1987). Selective review of infant care: A cause for concern. *Zero to Three, 6,* 18–24.

PHILLIPS, D., & ZIGLER, E. (1987). The checkered history of federal child care regulation. In E. Z. Rothkopf (Ed.), *Review of research in education* (Vol. 14, pp. 3–14). Washington, DC: American Educational Research Association.

PILCH, M. (1997, May). Personal communication from Pupil Personnel Director, Connecticut Regional School District #16.

PILIPONIS, C. (1996). The failure of family preservation and P. L. 96-272. Retrieved from the World Wide Web: http://worldaccess.com/~clg46/celeste.htm.

PIOTRKOWSKI, C. S. (1996). Welfare reform and access to family-support benefits in the workplace. *American Journal of Orthopsychiatry, 66,* 539–547.

PIZZO, P. (1983). Slouching toward Bethlehem: American federal policy perspectives on children and their families. In E. Zigler, S. L. Kagan, & E. Klugman (Eds.), *Children, families and government* (pp. 48–67). New York: Cambridge University Press.

PIZZO, P. (1995). Parent advocacy: A resource for intervention. In S. J. Meisels & J. P. Shonkoff (Eds.), *Handbook of early childhood intervention* (pp. 668–678). New York: Cambridge University Press.

PLAYGROUND SAFETY AT ISSUE. (1994a, May 26). Reuter News Service.

PLESS, I. B. (1990). Child health in Canada. *Pediatrics, 86* (6, pt. 2, Suppl.), 1027–1032.

PLYER V. DOE. (1982). 457 U.S. 2020.

POPENOE, D. (1996). *Life without father.* New York: Free Press.

PRESCOTT, J. W. (1979). Deprivation of physical affection as a primary process in the development of physical violence: A comparative and cross-cultural perspective. In D. Gil (Ed.), *Child abuse and violence* (pp. 66–137). New York: AMS Press.

PROVENCE, S., & NAYLOR, A. (1983). *Working with disadvantaged parents and their children: Scientific and practice issues.* New Haven, CT: Yale University Press.

PUBLIC BROADCASTING SYSTEM (1997a). Innocence lost: The plea. Other well-known cases. http://www.pbs.org/wgbh/pages/frontline/shows/innocence/other.html.

PUBLIC BROADCASTING SYSTEM (1997a). Innocence lost: The plea. Summary. http://www.pbs.org/wgbh/pges/frontline/shows/innocence/summary/html.

PUBLIC LAW 103-227. (1994). Education America Act.

PUBLIC LAW 104-235. (1996). Child Abuse Prevention and Treatment Act.

QUINT, S. (1994). *Schooling homeless children: A working model for America's public schools.* New York: Teachers College Press.

RABINOVITZ, J. (1997, January 23). Report urges school choice in Connecticut. *New York Times,* p. B1.

RADBILL, S. (1974). A history of child abuse and infanticide. In R. Helfer & C. H. Kempe (Eds.), *The battered child* (2nd ed.). Chicago: University of Chicago Press.

RAMEY, C. T. (1994). The Abecedarian Project. In R. R. Steinberg (Ed.), *The encyclopedia of intelligence* (Vol. 1, pp. 1–3). New York: Macmillan.

RAMEY, C. T., & CAMPBELL, F. A. (1992). Poverty, early childhood education, and academic competence: The Abecedarian experiment. In A. Huston (Ed.), *Children in poverty* (pp. 190–221). New York: Cambridge University Press.

RAMEY, C. T., CAMPBELL, F. A., & BLAIR, C. (in press). Enhancing the life-course for high-risk children: Results from the Abecedarian Project. In J. Crane (Ed.), *Social programs that really work.* New York: Sage.

RAMIREZ, J. D., & MERINO, B. J. (1990). Classroom talk in English immersion, early-exit and late-exit transitional bilingual education programs. In R. Jacobson & C. Faltis (Eds.), *Language distribution issues in bilingual schooling.* Cleveland: Multilingual Matters.

RAMIREZ, J. D., YUEN, S. D., & RAMEY, D. R. (1991). *Final report: Longitudinal study of structured English immersion strategy, early-exit and late-exit programs for language-minority children* (Report submitted to the U. S. Department of Education). San Mateo, CA: Aguirre International.

RAUCH, R. (August 1989). Children as capital. *Atlantic Monthly,* 43-47.

RAVITCH, D. (1995). *National standards in American education: A citizen's guide.* Washington, DC: Brookings Institution.

REID, J. B. (1983). *Final report: Child abuse: Developmental factors and treatment* (Grant No. 7ROl MH 37938, NIMH 4, U.S. Ph.S.). Washington, DC, White paper for National Institutes of Mental Health.

REITMAN, A., FOLLMAN, J., & LADD, E. (1972). *Corporal punishment in the public schools: The use of force in controlling behavior.* New York: American Civil Liberties Union.

RENZULLI, J. S., & PURCELL, J. H. (1995). A schoolwide enrichment model. *Education Digest, 61* (4), 14–17.

REPLOGLE, E. (1994). Community: What two programs show us about the right focus for Head Start. *Children Today, 23,* 32–36.

RESCHLY, D. J. (1996). Identification and assessment of students with disabilities. *Future of Children, 6* (1), 40–53.

RESCORLA, I. A., PROVENCE, S., & NAYLOR, A. (1982). The Yale Child Welfare Research Program: Description and results. In E. F. Zigler & E. W. Gordon (Eds.), *Day care: Scientific and social policy issues* (pp. 183–199). Boston: Auburn.

REYNOLDS, A. (1997, April). *Long-term effects of the Chicago Child-Parent Center Program through age 15.* Paper presented at the biennial meeting of the Society for Research in Child Development, Washington, DC.

REYNOLDS, R. J. (in press). *Success in early intervention: The Chicago Parent Centers and youth through age 15.* Lincoln: University of Nebraska Press.

RICHTERS, J. E., & MARTINEZ, P. E. (1993a). The NIMH Community Violence Project: I. Children as victims of and witnesses to violence. *Psychiatry, 56,* 7–21.

RICHTERS, J. E., & MARTINEZ, P. E. (1993b). Violent communities, family choices, and children's chances: An algorithm for improving the odds. *Development and Psychopathology, 5*, 609–627.

ROBERTS, S. (1994). Hispanic population outnumbers blacks in four major cities as demographics shift. *New York Times*, p. 1.

RODMAN, H., PRATTO, D., & NELSON, R. (1985). Child care arrangements and children's functioning: A comparison of self-care and adult-care children. *Developmental Psychology, 21*, 413–418.

ROGERS, J. A. (1979). Child abuse in humans: A clinician's view. In M. Reite & N. G. Caine (Eds.), *Child abuse : The nonhuman primate data.* New York: Alan R. Liss.

ROSS, C. J. (1983) Advocacy movements in the century of the child. In E. F. Zigler, S. L. Kagan, & E. Klugman (Eds.), *Children, families and government: Perspectives on American social policy* (pp. 165–176). Cambridge: Cambridge University Press.

ROSTETTER, D. (1994). Flexibility and accountability: Critical elements in ensuring an entitlement. In R. Berne & L. O. Picus (Eds.), *Outcome equity in education* (pp. 122–143). Thousand Oaks, CA: Corwin Press.

RUBIN, Z. (1980). *Children's friendships.* Cambridge, MA: Harvard University Press.

RUOPP, R., TRAVERS, J., GLANTZ, F., & COELEN, C. (1979). *Children at the center.* Cambridge, MA: Abt Associates.

RUSSO, E. (1991, December). Stress and lack of support are driving foster parents away. *Lincoln Journal Star*, p. 1A.

RYAN, K. (1995, July 1). Foster care in trouble. *America*, pp. 15–18.

SALTZER, E. M. (1979). *To combat violence in the child's world.* Stockholm: Swedish Institute.

SAMHSA. (1998). *National household survey on drug abuse.* Washington, DC: Author.

SAMUELS, D. (1996, March). Presidential shrimp: Bob Dole caters the political hors d'oeuvres. *Harpers*, pp. 45–52.

SCARR, S., EISENBERG, M., & DEATER-DECKARD, K. (1994). Measurement of quality in child care centers. *Early Childhood Research Quarterly, 9*, 131–151.

SCARR, S., PHILLIPS, D., & MCCARTNEY, K. (1990). Facts, fantasies and the future of child care in the United States. *Psychological Science, 1*, 26–35.

SCHACHERE, K. (1990). Attachment between working mothers and their infants: The influence of family processes. *American Journal of Orthopsychiatry, 60*, 19–34.

SCHROEDER, S. (1993). *Access to health care: Key indicators for policy.* Princeton, NJ: Robert Wood Johnson Foundation.

SCHUERMAN, J., & ROSSI, P. (1998). *Family preservation and family support.* Chicago: University of Chicago, Chapin Hall Center for Children.

SCHWARTZ, W. (1995). *School programs and practices for homeless students.* Washington, DC: Office of Educational Research and Improvement. (ERIC Document Reproduction Service No. ED 383 783).

SCHWEINHART, L. J., BARNES, H. V., & WEIKART, D. P. (1993). Significant benefits: The High/Scope Perry Preschool Study through age 27. *Monographs of the High/Scope Educational Research Foundation* (No. 10).

SCOTT, M. M. (1993). Recent changes in family structure in the United States: A developmental-systems perspective. *Journal of Applied Developmental Psychology, 14*, 213–230.

SEDLAK, A. J. (1991a). *Study findings: Study of national incidence and prevalence of child abuse and neglect.* Washington, DC: USDHHS.

SEDLAK, A. J. (1991b). *Supplementary analyses of data on the national incidence of child abuse and neglect.* Rockville, MD: Westat.

SEDLAK, A. J. (N.D.). *Relation between type and severity of maltreatment, recognition of maltreated children, and CPS awareness of recognized children.* Rockville, MD: Westat.

SEITZ, V. (1985). Effects of family support intervention: A ten-year follow-up. *Child Development, 56*, 376–391.

SEITZ, V., & APFEL, N. H . (1994). Parent-focused intervention: Diffusion effects on siblings. *Child Development, 65* (2), 677–683.

SEITZ, V., & PROVENCE, S. (1995). Caregiver-focused models of early intervention. In S. J. Meisels & J. Shonkoff (Eds.), Handbook of early childhood intervention. New York: Cambridge University Press.

SEITZ, V., ROSENBAUM, L. K., & APFEL, N. H. (1985). Effects of family support intervention: A ten-year follow-up. *Child Development, 56,* 376–391.

SELECT COMMITTEE ON CHILDREN, YOUTH AND FAMILIES. (1984). *Families and child care: Improving the options.* Washington, DC: U.S. Government Printing Office.

SELIGSON, M., & COLTIN, L. (1991). Approaches to school-age child care. *ERIC Digest,* EDO-PS-91-7.

SELIGSON, M., FERSH, E., MARSHALL, N. L., MARX, F., & BADEN, R. K. (1990, June). School-age child care: The challenge facing families. *Journal of Contemporary Human Services,* pp. 324–331.

SELIGSON, M., & FINK, D. B. (1989). *No time to waste: An action agenda for school-age child care.* Wellesley, MA: School-Age Child Care Project.

SELMAN, R. L. (1981). The child as a friendship philosopher. In S. R. Asher & J. M Gottman (Eds.), *The development of children's friendships.* Cambridge, UK: Cambridge University Press.

SEMMEL, M. I., GERBER, M. M., & MACMILLAN, D. L. (1995). A legacy of policy analysis research in special education. In J. M. Kauffman & D. P. Hallahan (Eds.), *Illusion of full inclusion* (pp. 39–58). Austin, TX: Pro-Ed.

SHAFFER, D., & CATON, C. L. (1984). *Runaway and homeless youth in New York City: A report to the Ittleson Foundation.* New York: Division of Child Psychiatry, New York State Psychiatric Institute, and Columbia University College of Physicians and Surgeons.

SHALIT, R. (1997, August 25). Defining disability down. *New Republic,* pp. 16–22.

SHARP, G. B., & CARTER, M. A. (1992). *Use of restraint devices to prevent collision injuries and deaths among welfare-supported children.* (Public Health Reports, 107). National Institute of Health, Washington, DC: GPO.

SHEEHAN, S. (1993, January 11). A lost childhood. *New Yorker,* pp. 54–66.

SHELLENBARGER, S. (1993a, December/January). Big business, big impact. *Parenting,* pp. 117–118.

SHELLENBARGER, S. (1993b, August). Taking care of family business: Family and Medical Leave Act. *Parenting,* p. 27.

SHENK, J. W. (1996). Saving education: The public schools' last hurrah? *Current, 384,* 3–8.

SHOKRAII, N. H., & FAGAN, P. F. (1998, July). After 33 years and $30 billion, time to find out if Head Start produces results. *Heritage Foundation Backgrounder,* pp. 1–2.

SHONKOFF, J. F. (1993). Blending science and advocacy: Foundations for a rational policy for early childhood intervention. *Child, Youth and Family Services Quarterly, 16,* 11–13.

SHORE, M. F. (1993). Social policy: The wheels of change. *American Journal of Orthopsychiatry, 633,* 498.

SHULMAN, L. (1987, January). Knowledge and teaching: Foundations of the new reform. *Harvard Educational Review,* pp. 1–22.

SIA, C. (1992). The medical home: Pediatric practice and child advocacy in the 1990s [Abraham Jacobi Award address, April 4, 1992]. *Pediatrics, 90,* 419–423.

SIANTZ, M. DE LEON. (1991). *The migrant head start program* [Social Policy Report]. Ann Arbor, MI: Society for Research in Child Development.

SIDEL, V. (1997). Annotation: The public health impact of hunger. *American Journal of Public Health, 87,* 1921–1923.

SIEGEL, B. (1996). Is the emperor wearing clothes? Social policy and the empirical support for full inclusion of children with disabilities in the preschool and early elementary grades. *SRCD Social Policy Report, 10* (2).

SILVER, L. B. (1996). Developmental learning disorders. In M. Lewis (Ed.), *Child and adolescent psychiatry: A comprehensive textbook* (2nd ed., pp. 520–526). Baltimore: Williams & Wilkins.

SILVERSTEIN, L. (1991). Transforming the debate about child care and maternal employment. *American Psychologist, 46,* 1025–1032.

SKOLNICK, A. (1991). *Embattled paradise: The American family in an age of uncertainty.* New York: Basic Books.

SLAVIN, R. E. (1998, January). Can education reduce social inequity? *Educational Leadership,* pp. 6–10.

SMELTER, R. W., RASCH, B. W., & YUDEWITZ, G. J. (1994, September). Thinking of inclusion for all special needs students? Think again. *Phi Delta Kappan,* pp. 35–38.

SMITH, S. (1991). Two-generation program models: A new intervention strategy. *Social Policy Report, 5,* 1–15.

SMOLOWE, J. (1995, December 11). Making the tough calls: Beset by budget cuts and burnout, case-workers weigh whether to save the family—or the child. *Time*, p. 146.

SOLNIT, A. (1980). Too much reporting; too little service: Roots and prevention of child abuse. In G. Gerbner, C. Ross, & E. Zigler (Eds.), *Child abuse : An agenda for action* (pp. 135–146). New York: Oxford University Press.

SOTO-MALDONADO, E. (1996, March 9). To be 18 years old and homeless (New York governor George Pataki should continue funding for young adult foster care). *New York Times*, p. 19.

SPEAR-SWERLING, L., & STERNBERG, R. J. (1996). *Off track: When poor readers become "learning disabled."* Boulder, CO: Westview Press.

SPECIAL EDUCATION FOR STUDENTS WITH DISABILITIES. (1996). *Future of Children, 6* (1). Special issue.

SPINETTA, J. J., & RIGLER, D. (1972). The child abusing parent: A psychological review. *Psychological Bulletin, 77,* 296–304.

ST. PIERRE, R., LAYZER, J., GOODSON, B., & BERNSTEIN, L. (1997, June). *National impact evaluation of the Comprehensive Child Development Program: Final report.* Cambridge, MA: Abt Associates.

STEINBERG, L. (1986). Latchkey children and susceptibility to peer pressure: An ecological analysis. *Developmental Psychology, 22,* 433–439.

STEINBERG, L. (1996). *Beyond the classroom: Why school reform has failed and what parents need to do.* New York: Simon & Schuster.

STEINER, G. (1981). *The futility of family policy.* Washington, DC: Brookings Institution.

STENDLER, C. B. (1950). Sixty years of child training practices. *Journal of Pediatrics, 36,* 122–134.

STERN, D. N. (1977). *The first relationship: Infant and mother.* Cambridge, MA: Harvard University Press.

STERN, D. N. (1985). The interpersonal world of the infant. NY: Basic Books.

STERN, E. S. (1948). The Medea complex: The mother's homicidal wishes to her child. *Journal of Mental Sciences, 94,* 324–325.

STIPEK, D., & McCROSKEY, J. (1989). Investing in children. Government and workplace policies for children. *American Psychologist, 44,* 416–423.

STITH, S. M. & DAVIS, A. J. (1984). Employed mothers and family day care: A comparative analysis of infant care. *Child Development, 55,* 1340–1348.

STOLLEY, R. B. (1993, October). An American tragedy: The childcare challenge. *Parenting,* pp. 92–93.

STRAUS, M. A., GELLES, R. J., & STEINMETZ, S. (1980). *Behind closed doors: Violence in the American family.* Garden City, NY: Anchor/Doubleday.

SUGARMAN, J. (1988). *A proposal to create the Children's Trust Fund.* Olympia, WA: Department of Social and Health Services.

SURGEON GENERAL ELDERS URGES DOCTORS, HOSPITALS TO PUSH BREAST-FEEDING. (1994, August 29). *Jet,* p. 28.

TAMMI, L. A. (1991, March/April). Programs for the gifted are not "elitist." *Education Week,* pp. 8–9.

TAYLOR, L. (1997, August 6). Home-visit program seeks to prevent child abuse. *Detroit Free Press,* p. 8A.

TERMAN, D. L., LARNER, M. B., STEVENSON, C. S., & BEHRMAN, R. E. (1996). Special education for students with disabilities: Analysis and recommendations. *Future of Children, 6* (1), 4–24.

THOMPSON, R. A. (1993). Developmental research and legal policy: Toward a two-way street. In D. Cicchetti & S. Toth (Eds.), *Child abuse, child development, and social policy: Advances in applied developmental psychology* (Vol. 8, pp. 75–115). Norwood, NJ: Ablex.

TIMPANE, P. M. (1996). The uncertain progress of educational reform, 1983–1994. In E. F. Zigler, S. L. Kagan, & N. W. Hall (Eds.), *Children, families and government: Preparing for the twenty-first century* (pp. 77–93). New York: Cambridge University Press.

TRENT, J. W., JR. (1994). *Inventing the feeble mind: A history of mental retardation in the United States.* Berkeley: University of California Press.

TURNBULL, A. P., TURNBULL, H. R., SHANK, M., & LEAL, D. (1995). *Exceptional lives: Special education in today's schools.* Englewood Cliffs, NJ: Prentice Hall.

TURNBULL, H. R., & TURNBULL, A. P. (1996). The synchrony of stakeholders: Lessons from the disabilities rights movement. In S. Kagan & N. Cohen (Eds.), *Reinventing early care and education: A vision for a quality system* (pp. 290–305). San Francisco: Jossey-Bass.

TYACK, D. B. (1974). *The one best system: A history of American urban education.* Cambridge, MA: Harvard University Press.

TYSON, A. S. (1994, July 7). Ethnic, economic divisions of U.S. growing. *Christian Science Monitor,* p. 3.

UEDA, R. (1995). The construction of ethnic diversity and national identity in the public schools. In D. Ravitch & M. Vinovsks (Eds.), *Historical perspectives on the current education reforms.* Baltimore: Johns Hopkins University Press.

ULLMAN, F., BRUEN, B., & HOLAHAN, J. (1997). *The State Children's Health Insurance Program: A look at the numbers.* Washington, DC: Urban Institute.

UNIVERSITY OF ALABAMA. (1998). Corporal punishment. Retrieved from the World Wide Web at the Children in a Changing Society website: http://www.uab.edu/educ/corp.htm.

U.S. ADVISORY BOARD ON CHILD ABUSE AND NEGLECT. (1990a). *Child abuse and neglect: Critical first steps in response to a national emergency.* Washington, DC: U.S. Government Printing Office.

U.S. ADVISORY BOARD ON CHILD ABUSE AND NEGLECT. (1993). *Neighbors helping neighbors: A new national strategy for the protection of children* (U.S. Advisory Board on Child Abuse and Neglect. Fourth Report. DHHS (Stock No. 017-092-00106-1). Washington, DC: U.S. Government Printing Office.

U.S. BUREAU OF THE CENSUS. (1974). *Social indicators 1973.* Washington, DC: U.S. Government Printing Office.

U.S. BUREAU OF THE CENSUS. (1977a). *Social indicators II.* Washington, DC: U.S. Government Printing Office.

U.S. BUREAU OF THE CENSUS. (1977b). *Money income and poverty status in the U.S.* Series R-42. Washington, DC: U.S. Government Printing Office.

U.S. BUREAU OF THE CENSUS. (1977c). *Population projections of the United States, by age, sex, race, and Hispanic origin: 1993–2050.* Report No. 25-1104. Washington DC: U.S. Government Printing Office.

U.S. BUREAU OF THE CENSUS. (1981). *Social indicators III.* Washington, DC: U.S. Government Printing Office.

U.S. BUREAU OF THE CENSUS. (1997). *Fertility of American women: June 1995 update.* Current Population Survey P20-499. Washington, DC: Author.

U.S. BUREAU OF LABOR STATISTICS. (1997). *1996 median annual earnings of full-time workers in the U.S.* Washington, DC: U.S. Government Printing Office.

U.S. CHILDREN'S BUREAU. (1913). *Handbook of Federal statistics of children: Part I. Washington, DC: 1913.* (Vassar College Library, Special Collections, the Papers of Julia Lathrop.)

U.S. CONFERENCE OF MAYORS. (1994). *A status report on hunger and homelessness in America's cities: 1994.* Washington, DC: Author.

U.S. DEPARTMENT OF EDUCATION. (1989). *What works: Schools without drugs.* Washington, DC: Author.

U.S. DEPARTMENT OF EDUCATION, NATIONAL CENTER FOR EDUCATION STATISTICS. (1994). *Dropout rates in the United States: 1993.* Washington, DC: U.S. Government Printing Office.

U.S. DEPARTMENT OF EDUCATION. (1996). *Eighteenth Annual report to Congress on the implementation of the Individuals with Disabilities Education Act.* Washington, DC: Author.

U.S. DEPARTMENT OF EDUCATION. (1997). *Report on the condition of education.* Washington, DC: U.S. Government Printing Office.

U.S. DEPARTMENT OF HEALTH, EDUCATION, AND WELFARE. (1976). *Child health in America.* Rockville, MD: Author.

U.S. DEPARTMENT OF HEALTH AND HUMAN SERVICES. (1987). *The Children's Bureau at 75. 1912–1987: The commitment continues.* Washington, DC: Author.

U.S. DEPARTMENT OF HEALTH AND HUMAN SERVICES. (1992). *Child health '92.* Washington, DC: U.S. Government Printing Office.

U.S. DEPARTMENT OF HEALTH AND HUMAN SERVICES. (1993). *Vital statistics of the United States, 1991: Vol. 1. Natality.* Washington, DC: U.S. Government Printing Office.

U.S. DEPARTMENT OF HEALTH AND HUMAN SERVICES. (1996). *Family preservation and family support services.* Washington, DC: U.S. Government Printing Office.

U.S. DEPARTMENT OF HEALTH AND HUMAN SERVICES. (1997a). *Length of stay of children exiting foster care.* Washington, DC: U.S. Government Printing Office.

U.S. DEPARTMENT OF HEALTH AND HUMAN SERVICES. (1997b). *National study of protective, preventive, and reunification services delivered to children and their families: Final report.* Washington, DC: U.S. Government Printing Office.

U.S. DEPARTMENT OF HEALTH AND HUMAN SERVICES. (1998a). *Child maltreatment 1996: Reports from the states to the National Child Abuse and Neglect Data System.* Washington, DC: U.S. Government Printing Office.

U.S. DEPARTMENT OF HEALTH AND HUMAN SERVICES, ADMINISTRATION FOR CHILDREN AND FAMILIES. (1998b). *Welfare caseloads by state, May.* Washington, DC: U.S. Government Printing Office.

U.S. DEPARTMENT OF HOUSING AND URBAN DEVELOPMENT. (1990). *Comprehensive and workable plan for the abatement of lead-based paint in privately owned housing: Report to Congress.* Washington, DC: Author.

U.S. DEPARTMENT OF HOUSING AND URBAN DEVELOPMENT. (1994). *Priority: Home! The federal plan to break the cycle of homelessness.* Washington, DC: U.S. Government Printing Office.

U.S. DEPARTMENT OF LABOR, BUREAU OF LABOR STATISTICS. (1992). *Current population survey, March.* Washington, DC: U. S. Department of Labor.

U.S. DEPARTMENT OF LABOR, BUREAU OF LABOR STATISTICS. (1994, April). *Bulletin 2452.* Washington, DC: US. Government Printing Office.

U.S. GENERAL ACCOUNTING OFFICE. (1992, June 12). *HRD 92-124: Job training partnership act: Actions needed to improve participant support services.* Washington, DC: U.S. Government Printing Office.

U.S. GENERAL ACCOUNTING OFFICE. (1993, August). *School age demographics: Recent trends pose new educational challenges* (Briefing report to Congressional requesters). Washington, DC.

U.S. GENERAL ACCOUNTING OFFICE. (1997, March). *Drug control: Observations on elements of the Federal drug control strategy* (Report to Congressional requesters, GGD-97-42). Washington, DC.

VAN BIEMA, D. (1993, October 3). Health care: Out in the cold? *Time,* 56–59.

VAN BIEMA, D. (1995, December 11). Abandoned to her fate. *Time,* p. 146.

VANDELL, D. L., & CORASANITI, M. S. (1988). The relationship between third graders' after-school care and social, academic, and emotional functioning. *Child Development, 59,* 868–875.

VAUGHN, B. E., GOVE, F. L., & EGELAND, B. (1980). The relationship between out-of-home care and the quality of infant-mother attachment in an economically disadvantaged population. *Child Development, 51,* 1203–1214.

VINOVSKIS, M. (1985). Young fathers and their children. Some historical and policy perspectives. In A. B. Elster & M. E. Lamb (Eds.), *Adolescent fatherhood* (pp. 171–192). Hillsboro, NJ: Erlbaum.

VINOVSKIS, M. A. (1995). *Education, society, and economic opportunity: A historical perspective on persistent issues.* New Haven, CT: Yale University Press.

WAGNER, M. M. (1995). Outcomes for youths with serious emotional disturbance in secondary school and early adulthood. *Future of Children, 5* (2), 90–112.

WAGNER, M. M., & BLACKORBY, J. (1996). Transition from high school to work or college: How special education students fare. *Future of Children, 6* (1), 103–120.

WALLERSTEIN, J. S., & BLAKESLEE, S. (1996). Second chances: Men, women and children a decade after divorce. New York: Houghton Mifflin.

WALLERSTEIN, J. S., & KELLY, J. B. (1996). *Surviving the breakup: How children and parents cope with divorce.* New York: Basic Books.

WALSH, M. (1997). Judge overturns expanded Wisconsin voucher plan. *Education Week,* p. 24.

WARD, J. (1915). *The house on Henry Street.* New York: Holt, Rinehart & Winston.

A WARM CHAIN FOR BREASTFEEDING: ENCOURAGING WOMEN TO BREASTFEED. (1994). *Lancet, 344,* 1259.

WARREN, A., HULSE-TROTTER, K., & TUBBS, E. (1991). Inducing resistance to suggestion. *Law and Human Behavior, 15,* 273–285.

WEILER, J. (1997). Recent changes in school desegregation. *ERIC Digest.* Retrieved from the World Wide Web: http://eric- web.tc.columbia.edu/digests/dig133.html.

WEININGER, O. (1998). In the remote chance winking at your rebellious brat fails, try spanking. *Alberta Report, 25,* 2.

WEINREB, L., & BUCKNER, J. C. (1993). Homeless families: Program responses and public policies. *American Journal of Orthopsychiatry, 63,* 400–409.

WEISS, B., DODGE, K. A., BATES, J. E., & PETIT, G. S. (1992). Some consequences of early harsh discipline: Child aggression and a maladaptive social information processing style. *Child Development, 63,* 1321–1335.

WEISS, C. H., & JACOBS, F. (Eds.). (1988). Evaluating family programs; NY: Aldine de Gruyter.

WEISSBOURD, R. (1996). *The vulnerable child: What really hurts America's children and what we can do about it.* Reading, MA: Addison-Wesley.

WELLESLEY COLLEGE CENTER FOR RESEARCH ON WOMEN. (1996). *Fact sheet on school-age children.* Wellesley, MA: Author.

WELLS, W. M. (1997). Serving families who are hard to reach, maintain, and help through a universal access home visiting program. *Zero to Three, 17* (4), 22–26.

WERTSCH, J. V., & YOUNISS, J. (1987). Contextualizing the investigator: The case of developmental psychology. *Human Development, 30,* 18–31.

WEST, MRS. MAX [SIC]. (1914). *Infant care.* Washington, DC: U.S. Government Printing Office.

WESTBERG, K. L., ARCHAMBAULT, F. X., JR., DOBYNS, S. M., & SLAVIN, T. J. (1993). *An observational study of instructional and curricular practices used with gifted and talented students in regular classrooms: Executive summary* (Research Monograph No. 93104). Storrs, CT: University of Connecticut, National Resource Center on the Gifted & Talented.

WHITE, S. H. (1979). Children in perspective. *American Psychologist, 34,* 812–814.

WHITEBOOK, M., HOWES, C., & PHILLIPS, D. (1989). *Who cares? Child care teachers and the quality of care in America: Final report, National Child Care Staffing Study.* Oakland, CA: Child Care Employee Project.

WHITE HOUSE. (1995, July 25). House Republicans cut $36 billion from current education and training investments [Press release]. Washington, DC.

WHITE HOUSE DOMESTIC POLICY COUNCIL. (1993). *The President's health security plan: The Clinton blueprint.* New York: New York Times Books.

WIDNER, J. (1993, August). Colorado helps babies by helping mothers breastfeed. *Food & Nutrition,* p. 22.

WIDOM, C. S. (1989). Child abuse, neglect, and violent criminal behavior. *Criminology, 27,* 251–271.

WILBURN, D., & MCMORRIS, M. (1994, May). The working mother trail. *Working Mother,* pp. 50–51.

WILCOX, B. L., & KUNKEL, D. (1996). Taking television seriously: Children and television policy. In E. Zigler, S. L. Kagan, & N. W. Hall (Eds.), *Children, families and government: Preparing for the 21st century.* New York: Cambridge University Press.

WILL, G. (1997, September 14). New victim class is populated by successful people. *Waterbury Republican-American,* p. 3A.

WILLER, B. (Ed.). (1991). *The demand and supply of child care in 1990: Joint findings from the National Child Care Survey 1990 and a profile of child care settings.* Washington, DC: National Association for the Education of Young Children.

WILLER, B., HOFFERTH, S. L., KISKER, E. E., DIVINE-HAWKINS, P., FARQUHAR, E., & GLANTZ, F. B. (1991). *The demand and supply of child care in 1990.* Washington, DC: National Association for the Education of Young Children.

WIRPSA, L. (1994, June 3). Breast-fed infants are more likely to survive, thrive. *National Catholic Reporter,* p. 13.

WITHORN, A. (1996). "Why do they hate me so much?" A history of welfare and its abandonment in the United States. *American Journal of Orthopsychiatry, 66,* 496–509.

WITTE, J. (1996). *Reply to Greene, Peterson and Du: "The effectiveness of school choice in Milwaukee: A secondary analysis of data from the program's evaluation": Executive summary.* Madison, WI: Robert LaFollette Institute of Public Affairs.

WOLFE, D. A. (1993). Child abuse intervention research: Implications for policy. In D. Cicchetti & S. L. Toth (Eds.), *Child abuse, child development, and social policy* (pp. 369–397). Norwood, NJ: Ablex.

WOLFENSBERGER, W. (1972). *The principle of normalization in human services.* Toronto: National Institute on Mental Retardation.

WOOD, D. L., HAYWARD, R. A., COREY, C. R., FREEDMAN, H. E., & SHAPIRO, M. F. (1990). Access to medical care for children and adolescents in the United States. *Pediatrics, 86,* 666–673.

WOOD, D. L., VALDEZ, R. B., HAYASHI, T., & SHEN, A. (1990, December). Health of homeless children and housed poor children. *Pediatrics, 86,* 858–866.

WOODS, M. B. (1972). The unsupervised child of the working mother. *Developmental Psychology, 6,* 14–25.

WORSNOP, R. L. (1994, June 10). Gun control: The issues. *CQ Researcher, 4,* 507–511.

WULCZYN, F. H., HARDEN, A. W., & GEORGE, R. M. (1997). *Foster care dynamics 1983–1994: An update from the Multistate Foster Care Data Archive.* Chicago: University of Chicago, Chapin Hall Center for Children.

YETTER, M. V. (1991, March 22). Small firms: Big solutions. *Human Resource Executive,* pp. 25–26.

YIP, R., BINKIN, N. J., FLESHOOD, L., & TROWBRIDGE, F. L. (1987). Declining prevalence of anemia among low-income children in the United States. *Journal of the American Medical Association, 258,* 1619-1623.

YOSHIKAWA, H. (1994). Prevention as cumulative protection: Effects of early family support and education on chronic delinquency and its risks. *Psychological Bulletin, 115,* 28–54.

YOSHIKAWA, H. (1995). Long-term effects of early childhood education programs on social outcomes and delinquency. *Future of Children, 5* (3), 51–75.

YOUNG, K. T., MARSLAND, K. W., & ZIGLER, E. (1997). The regulatory status of center-based infant and toddler child care. *American Journal of Orthopsychiatry, 67,* 535–544.

ZELDIN, S., & BOGART, J. (1990). *Education and community support for homeless children and youth: Profiles of fifteen innovative and promising approaches.* Washington, DC: Policy Studies Associates. (ERIC Document Reproduction Service No. ED 322 249).

ZERO TO THREE. (1992). *Heart Start: The emotional foundations of learning.* Arlington, VA: Author.

ZIEGERT, K. A. (1983, November). The Swedish prohibition of corporal punishment: A preliminary report. *Journal of Marriage and the Family, 45,* 917–926.

ZIGLER, E. (1978). National crisis in mental retardation research. *American Journal of Mental Deficiency, 83,* 1–8.

ZIGLER, E. (1980). Controlling child abuse: Do we have the knowledge and/or the will? In G. Gerbner, C. Ross, & E. Zigler (Eds.), *Child abuse: An agenda for action* (pp. 293–304). New York: Oxford University Press.

ZIGLER, E. (1987). *A solution to the nation's child care crisis: The School of the Twenty-First Century.* Paper delivered at the tenth anniversary of the Bush Center for Child Development and Social Policy, New Haven, CT.

ZIGLER, E. (1989). Addressing the nation's child care crisis: The School of the 21st Century. *American Journal of Orthopsychiatry, 59,* 484–491.

ZIGLER, E. (1992, June 27). Head Start falls behind. *New York Times,* p. A23

ZIGLER, E. (1993, July 24). Head Start: The whole story. *New York Times,* p. A45.

ZIGLER, E. (1995). Foreword. In S. J. Meisels & J. Shonkoff (Eds.), *Handbook of early childhood intervention.* New York: Cambridge University Press.

ZIGLER, E. (1998). A place of value for applied and policy studies. *Child Development, 69,* 532–542.

ZIGLER, E., & BERMAN, W. (1983). Discerning the future of early childhood intervention. *American Psychologist, 38,* 894–906.

ZIGLER, E., & FINN, M. (1981, May). From problem to solution: Changing public policy as it affects children and families. *Young Children,* pp. 31–59.

ZIGLER, E. F., & FINN-STEVENSON, M. (1989). Child care in America: From problem to solution. *Educational Policy, 3,* 313–329.

ZIGLER, E., & FINN-STEVENSON, M. (1993). *Children in a changing world.* Pacific Grove, CA: Brooks/Cole.

ZIGLER, E., & GILMAN, E. (1993). Day care in America: What is needed? *Pediatrics, 91,* 175–178.

ZIGLER, E., & GILMAN, E. (1994). What's a school to do? Meeting educational and family needs. In R. Berne & L. O. Pincus, *Outcome equity in education* (pp. 71–86). Thousand Oaks, CA: Corwin Press.

ZIGLER, E., & HALL, N. W. (1984). *Child abuse: Using multidisciplinary research to improve measurement and control.* (Contract no. 1287-4464), Washington, DC: National Academy of Sciences.

ZIGLER, E., & HALL, N. W. (1988). Day care and its effects on children: An overview for pediatric health professions. *Journal of Developmental and Behavioral Pediatrics, 9,* 38–45.

ZIGLER, E., & HALL, N. W. (1989). Physical child abuse in America: Past, present, and future. In D. Cicchetti & V. Carlson (Eds.), *Child maltreatment: Theory and research on the causes and consequences of child abuse and neglect* (pp. 38–75). New York: Cambridge University Press.

ZIGLER, E., & HALL, N. W. (1994). Seeing the child in child care: Day care, individual differences, and social policy. In W. B. Carey & S. C. McDevitt (Eds.), *Prevention and early intervention: Individual* differences as risk factors for the mental health of children: a festschrift for Stella Chess and Alexander Thomas. New York: Bruner/Mazel.

ZIGLER, E., HODAPP, R. M., & EDISON, M. R. (1990). From theory to practice in the care and education of mentally retarded individuals. *American Journal on Mental Retardation, 95,* 1–12.

ZIGLER, E., HOPPER, P., & HALL, N. W. (1993). Infant mental health and social policy. In C. H. Zeanah (Ed.), *Handbook of infant mental health* (pp. 480–492). New York: Guilford Press.

ZIGLER, E., KAGAN, S. L., & HALL, N. W. (1996). *Children, families and government: Preparing for the 21st century.* New York: Cambridge University Press.

ZIGLER, E., & LANG, M. E. (1991). *Child care choices: Balancing the needs of children, families and society.* New York: Free Press.

ZIGLER, E., & MUENCHOW, S. (1985). A room of their own: A proposal to renovate the Children's Bureau. *American Psychologist, 40,* 953–959.

ZIGLER, E., & MUENCHOW, S. (1992). *Head Start: The inside story of America's most successful educational experiment.* New York: Basic Books.

ZIGLER, E., & STYFCO, S. (1993). *Head Start and beyond: A national plan for extended childhood intervention.* New Haven, CT: Yale University Press.

ZIGLER, E., & STYFCO, S. (1996). Head Start and early childhood intervention: The changing course of social science and social policy. In E. F. Zigler, S. L. Kagan, & N. W. Hall (Eds.), *Children, families and government: Preparing for the 21st century* (pp. 132–155). New York: Cambridge University Press.

ZIGLER, E., TAUSSIG, C., & BLACK, K. (1992). Early childhood intervention: A promising preventative for juvenile delinquency. *American Psychologist, 47,* 997–1006.

ZIGLER, E., & VALENTINE, J. (Eds.). (1979). *Project Head Start: A legacy of the War on Poverty.* New York: Free Press.

ZILL, N., & SCHOENBORN, C. A. (1990). *Health of our nation's children: Developmental, learning, and emotional problems, United States, 1988* (Advance Data, No. 190). Hyattsville, MD: National Center for Health Statistics.

ZILL, N., SIGAL, H., & BRIM, O. G. (1983). Development of childhood social indicators. In E. Zigler, S. L. Kagan, & E. Klugman (Eds.), *Children, families and government.* New York: Cambridge University Press.

ZINSSER, C. (1989, July). Special survey results: Your message to the president on child care. *Working Mother,* p. 36.

ZUCKERMAN, B. (1991). Drug exposed infants: Understanding the medical risk. *Future of Children, 1,* 26–35.

ZURIFF, G. E. (1996–1997). Learning disabilities in the academy: A professor's guide. *Academic Questions, 10* (1), 53–65.

Author Index

326   *Author Index*

Subject Index